Deinstitutionalizing Art of the Nomadic Museum

Deinstitutionalizing Art of the Nomadic Museum explores the possibility of the "nomadic museum" to facilitate social and political resistance through engagement with critical art practices and imagery. Grounded in a decade-long art therapy project in a contemporary art museum setting, this book offers a theoretically rich conceptualization of this experience.

The text establishes an institutional critique of both the dominant psychopathology discourse and the instrumentalizations of art practices. Innovative in its approach, the results are analyzed in the framework of subjects such as hegemony-subalternity, subjectivity, resistance, the nomadic, critical art practices, narratives and minor language, deinstitutionalization, anti-psychiatries as well as institutional therapy. With a special focus on Latin America, international artists' writings and works are intersected with the thoughts of curators and museum decision makers. The inevitable connection of the arts with social and political fields is highlighted, enabling the exploration of the intersections of art, critical analysis, social science, psychoanalysis, and political philosophy.

This text will be of great interest to graduate and postgraduate students, academics, researchers, libraries and museums curators in the fields of art therapy, psychoanalysis, contemporary art, social & cultural anthropology, and political philosophy.

Eva Marxen is Assistant Professor of Art Therapy at the School of the Art Institute of Chicago, US.

Explorations in Mental Health

Deinstitutionalizing Art of the Nomadic Museum
Practicing and Theorizing Critical Art Therapy with Adolescents
Eva Marxen

Frantz Fanon's Psychotherapeutic Approaches to Clinical Work
Practicing Internationally with Marginalized Communities
Edited by Lou Turner and Helen A. Neville

Perspectives on Intercultural Psychotherapy
An Igbo Group Analyst's Search for his Social Identity
Okeke Azu-Okeke

Africana Peoples in China
Psychoanalytic Perspectives on Migration Experiences, Identity, and Precarious Employment
C. Jama Adams

Evil Eye, Jinn Possession, and Mental Health Issues
An Islamic Perspective
G. Hussein Rassool

Narratives of Loneliness
Multidisciplinary Perspectives from the 21st Century
Edited by Olivia Sagan and Eric D. Miller

For more information about this series, please visit www.routledge.com/Explorations-in-Mental-Health/book-series/EXMH

Deinstitutionalizing Art of the Nomadic Museum

Practicing and Theorizing Critical Art Therapy with Adolescents

Eva Marxen

Routledge
Taylor & Francis Group
NEW YORK AND LONDON

First published 2020
by Routledge
52 Vanderbilt Avenue, New York, NY 10017

and by Routledge
2 Park Square, Milton Park, Abingdon, Oxon, OX14 4RN

Routledge is an imprint of the Taylor & Francis Group, an informa business

Library of Congress Cataloging-in-Publication Data
A catalog record for this title has been requested

ISBN: 978-0-815-36126-8 (hbk)
ISBN: 978-1-351-11666-4 (ebk)

Typeset in Baskerville
by codeMantra

Contents

Acknowledgements

I am grateful to the MACBA museum politics between 1999 and 2010. Particularly, I want to thank Jorge Ribalta, director of Public Programs at the time, for launching, implementing, co-conceiving, and supporting the MACBA devices as explained in Chapter 2. At the same time, I want to extend special thanks to his follower Marta García as well as Yolanda Nicolás for her immense support during the mentioned time period and beyond. My gratitude goes also to the collaborative educational institutions. Most importantly, I am indebted to all the adolescent participants of the art (therapy) devices, their engagement, insights, humor, and institutional critiques. Altogether, they have helped me to think the de-institutional.

Regarding the process of this book, I am indebted to Argentinean medical anthropologist and PhD fellow Analía Abt (Universidad Nacional de Quilmes) who has reviewed Chapter 3.

Furthermore, I acknowledge the funding from SAIC Earl and Brenda Shapiro Center in Chicago. Special recognition goes to Allie McCormick (MAATC SAIC) and Emily Hoyler (Liberal Arts, SAIC) for their thorough copyedits as well as their critiques, and at the same time encouraging comments on the manuscript. The same credit belongs to Jacqueline Chaidez (MAATC 2020 SAIC) for translating some of my former research memos from Spanish into English and her help for literature research. Additionally, I am incredibly thankful to all the artists who have given me permission to include their images.

Finally, I would like to extend my gratitude to Routledge and the publishing house's support, encouragement, and flexibility from the beginning to the completion of this book. A big thanks to all, as this process has become a highly rewarding one.

1 Introduction

Art and the Political Exercise of Thinking

This book is based on a decade-long experience carried out in a museum of contemporary art. Precisely, from 2002 to 2013, the Museum of Contemporary Art Barcelona (MACBA) brought together professionals from the fields of psychoanalysis, art therapy, and anthropology with the aim of generating innovative formulations that are adapted to the use of artistic productions.

During this period and leaning on the museum's policies and activities, I was able to conceive art in political and social terms that go beyond bourgeois, romantic, and expressionist conceptions. Benjamin's and Brecht's ideas regarding the secularization and proletarianization of the arts, as well as their techniques of shock and the distancing effect (*Verfremdung*), informed this redefinition (see Marxen, 2019, 2018, 2012, 2011, 2009a, 2009b; Brecht, 2014; Benjamin, 1998, 1968).

The aim of the museum was not only to set up exhibitions but also to provide different types of services for a variety of groups and subjects, thus creating new forms of socialization between the museum and the city. In the words of the former director of MACBA's Public Programs, the intention was "to restore forms of subjective appropriation of artistic methods in processes outside the mainstream and outside the museum" going "beyond the idea of visibility whose paradigm is the exhibition" (Ribalta, 2004, p. 9). This necessarily involved removing art from its supposed traditional elitist pedestal and taking it to groups within the community that would not ordinarily visit a contemporary art museum. These intentions go clearly along with the core ideas of art therapy, and that is the reason why MACBA brought together professionals with corresponding inquiries.

Concretely, the author's project was based on the use of art therapy with a psychoanalytic slant and an anthropological understanding. It took place at education centers with teenagers with challenging behaviors and who had previously been labeled "at risk of social exclusion."

The aim of the book is to give visibility to this project and theoretically adapt the results arising from these applications. In this sense, the inevitable connection of the arts with the social and political fields is highlighted and so are the possible intersections of art, critical analysis, social science, and political philosophy.

The work took place with the support and sponsorship of the museum, and the purpose was to explore the possibility of the "nomadic museum" to facilitate a work of subjectivities of resistance by the use of imagery with groups that are politically positioned on the social margins. The capacities for "minor" narratives are analyzed and in how far they can refract the dominant discourse and deinstitutionalize institutionalized lives.

The interconnection of the arts with social, political, therapeutic, and research inquiries has been described as "de- and re-territorialization" (Carnevale, 2013), "de-definition" (García Canclini, 2014), and "re-definition" (Marxen, 2009b). In the face of a new fashion—a steady increase in the inclusion of art in different disciplines—a critical view seems necessary to distinguish those artistic practices which can challenge the hegemonic discourse from those that reify it, using the arts for social control.

In the context of art's transdisciplinarity, Holmes (2006, p. 421) had suggested the term "artistic device," drawing on Foucault's descriptions of the device—or dispositif. The dispositif, according to Foucault (2001), is "a thoroughly heterogeneous ensemble consisting of discourses, institutions, architectural forms, regulatory decisions, laws, administrative measures, scientific statements, philosophical and moral propositions" (Holmes, 2006, p. 413). Given this multiplicity of purpose and elements, the dispositif establishes nets of and by these elements. It always has strategic and concrete functions and is situated at the crossroads of power and knowledge. It is a form of relationality (Agamben, 2014).

At the same time, the artistic dispositif is based on Guattari's *agencement collectif d'énonciation*—an articulation of collective speech. It encompasses artistic inquiries which refrain from overcoding realities and is able "to produce new figures, forms, constellations—in short, original material and cultural configurations that are inseparable from collective statements" (Holmes, 2006, p. 421). Additionally, according to Deleuze (1995) and Guattari (1995, 1989), these artistic "assemblages" should result "from the flow of desire,"

> a kind of delirium in relation to others, to language, to images and to things. It is this drifting and at least partially delirious flow of productive energies that alone can articulate a collective statement: which is the whole interest and passion of the artistic device.
>
> (Marxen, 2018; Holmes, 2006, p. 412)

Yet, in the face of a steady instrumentalization of the arts, many artistic institutions, such as museums, universities, art schools, often function like normalizing dispositifs, following the rules and imperatives of the finance economy. Bourdieu and Haacke (1995) have very well explained how mainly corporate foundations abuse the arts in order to accumulate symbolic capital, "good press," in order to hide less popular capitalist methods behind.

In order to defy dominant discourses of capitalist exploitation, social control, and oppression, counterdispositifs must be constructed that openly contest the abuse of the arts by far-right politicians and are at least critical with corporate sponsoring.

The *artistic dispositif* responds in its "multiplicity of purpose... in accordance with a strategy dictated by a need, by a structural imperative." Nowadays, it seems to reflect people's "urgent need for an articulation of aesthetics and thinking—about the need for an intellectualized art, or for what might be called 'cognitive creativity,' in the particular kinds of societies that we inhabit" (Holmes, 2006, pp. 413–414).

A response to this need can be found in multi- and transdisciplinary encounters with the arts. These emerge, in the main, from artistic inquiry transgressing its supposed limits, addressing the complexities of human life. Today, many artists are less interested in constructing tangible objects than in participating in *cultural ecologies*, "a collaborative production of desires" or a "display of *experimental* communities" (Laddaga, 2006, pp. 9, 13, 15, my translation from Spanish). From these practices, a new definition of art has emerged: "a mobile laboratory and experimental theatre for the investigation and instigation of social and cultural change" (Holmes, 2006, p. 2).

These phenomena are explored in *Estética de la emergencia* (Laddaga, 2006), *The Art of Emergency,* and expanded upon through *Estética de la inminencia*, *The Aesthetics of Imminence* (subtitle of García Canclini's 2010 book, my literal translation, in opposition to the official English translation 2014).

The "cultural ecologies" described by Laddaga (ibid., pp. 29–30) interrupt "the common course of actions in the world," which means they disrupt the hegemonic discourse. For social sciences and other disciplines, like philosophy, art offers "epistemological experiences," due to its "epistemological resiliency" (García Canclini, 2014, p. 157; Buck-Morss, 2011, p. 227): "Art processes are epistemological places where art and society, aesthetics and sociology, rethink their ways of making and knowing" (García Canclini, 2014, p. 162). Focusing mainly on the encounters between contemporary art and anthropology, García Canclini (2014) points out the "ethnographic turn" and "transdisciplinary turn" in contemporary art (bridging art, anthropology, and sociology). For Brian Holmes:

> One of the strong possibilities of art today is to combine theoretical, sociological or scientific research with a feel for the ways that aesthetic form can influence collective process, so as to de-normalize the investigation and open up both critical and constructive paths. Projects carried out in this way have complex referential content, but they also depend on a highly self-reflexive and deeply playful exercise of the basic human capacities: perception, affect, thought, expression and relation.
>
> (2006, p. 411)

Critical analysis of artistic practices is necessary, especially since they are ever-expanding. This analysis should distinguish between those which operate with required critical rigor from those which simply follow banal fashion, exempt from critical reflection.

These options may seem of limited significance, but can, in fact, lead to repeated and or worsening control and oppression (Marxen, 2018, 2013; Sajnani, Marxen, & Zarate, 2017). The result is "the cultural experience on a similar footing to processes of consumption" and "a progressive trivialisation and impoverishment of experience, in which the critical, emancipatory dimension of cultural experience is eliminated" (Ribalta, 2010, p. 230).

As already mentioned, the purpose of this book is to describe and explain the art therapeutic device in the museum context. The experience and its results are analyzed and conceptualized in the framework of subjects such as hegemony-subalternity, subjectivity, resistance, the nomadic, critical art practices, narratives and minor language, deinstitutionalization, anti-psychiatry as well as institutional therapy.

In this vein, theories, sources, and authors from social science (mainly anthropology), political philosophy, political science, and psychoanalysis are employed. They are intersected with artists' writings and works, art and museum critique as well as the thoughts of curators and museum decision makers. The relation of the mentioned disciplines with the arts is crucial just because of the capacity of the arts to offer epistemological experiences and to influence collective processes (García Canclini and Holmes above). Already Antonio Gramsci and Ernesto de Martino as well as later Chantal Mouffe have all stressed the importance of the artist to subvert hegemony. Particularly, critical art should foster dissent and "agonistic confrontation… [challenging] the dominant consensus by making visible what it tends to obscure and obliterate" (Mouffe, 2012, p. 271).

Following Oscar Masotta, the theoretical dimension is considered "a specific mode of emancipatory political intervention" (MACBA, 2018 exhibition text, of his retrospective show with its so excellently chosen title *Theory as Action*). Opposing the sole focus on "practice" in many socially engaged art circles and in art therapy, I insist with Masotta on "the political condition of the exercise of thinking" (Longoni, 2017, p. 22; translated by myself from Spanish).

An interesting question is the place of institutions or the institutional within the inquiry of the political exercise of thinking.

The term "institution" has been diversely conceived in different languages and cultures.

> While in English, the word 'institution' conveys forms of social organisation that are close to state institutions, or similarly formal organisations, in French the term 'institution' refers to any form of social formation, as well as to that which is 'instituted' and therefore to the act of 'instituting'.
> (Caló, 2019, pp. 129–130)

Differentiating institution from establishment, the former has been understood as a dispositif of thoughts, a "metabolization of daily life events" in a certain frame, determined in place and time. Institution in this sense is inseparable from collective life. It also depends on the interactions with its own multiplicity. In the context of institutional therapy, the institution in the first place has to critically treat and analyze itself. It should facilitate the symbolization of experience through the relational network of institutional or community therapy. A collaboration is instituted and dedicated to both the individual and the collective. Through the dialogues with different interlocutors, in steady connection among themselves, the client/patient can find a model to coordinate the fragments of their psychological life, an organization of their thoughts, and empowerment through the active participation in daily life tasks within the institution. The task of institutional therapy goes clearly beyond psychiatry and embraces the psychological, the social, and the political.

Theoretically and practically, institutional therapy is based both on Freud and Marx, an articulation between the two, treating the psychological alienation with the first and social as well as political alienation with the second. Yet, the institutional and instituting therapists did not consider themselves neither Marxists nor Freudians (Hochmann, 2015; Tosquelles, 2014, 2001; Oury, Guattari, & Tosquelles, 1985).

This understanding of institutional also applies beyond clinical work, especially in the context of contemporary precarization of collective life. We should focus on

> the institutional processes that led to this, such as forms of work, the ways in which cities are designed, the types of collective practices and spaces that are available, etc., and therefore with the effects on our mental health; as well as with the resulting consequences for the types of social relations we establish among ourselves and the world we inhabit. It is to be concerned with care.
>
> (Caló, 2019, p. 130)

This care should include spaces of "listening and talking, of the creation of polyphonic and plurisemiotic possibilities beyond speech expression, of aesthetic modes of exchange, of management and organisation as empowerment, and on transversality between the representational and the subjective" (Caló, 2019, p. 131).

"Institution" as conceived in English has been for many good reasons the target of protest, such as expressed by various authors of different anti-psychiatry movements.

How to achieve the institution as a continuous construction of practice of collectivity requires an ongoing exercise of redefinitions, critical thinking, the political exercise of thinking.

If this is not happening, any so supposedly progressive practice easily becomes institutionalized in a way that converts its own progressiveness into reactionaryness or "institutional sclerosis" (Tosquelles, 2001, p. 19). Institution then is to be defined according to Basaglia and the Italian and Brazilian deinstitutionalization movements as that what resists change (García, 2010, p. 14). Throughout this book, diverse artists, thinkers, and practitioner-thinkers articulate their rage against this form of institution, institutionalized art, and institutionalized forms of therapy. At the same time, we propose ways to deinstitutionalize them.

The book is composed of the following chapters: Chapter 2 is the detailed explanation of Marxen's art therapeutic device and its application within the institutional logics of the MACBA museum of the relevant time period.

In Chapter 3, concepts of hegemony, counter-hegemony, and subalternity are outlined in the sense of Gramsci and as further developed by de Martino and Mouffe. The terms are analyzed in the context of (mental) health and psychopathology, following authors of medical anthropology. In the same chapter, the (neo) Gramscian ideas are related to art, artists, and artistic practices.

Going beyond the concrete MACBA experience, Chapter 4 explores the possibilities of the museum as an institution and in how far it can allow a specific social relation between the arts and the subject, an experience of subjectivity. Breaking the fiction of art's autonomy, protected traditionally by the museums' walls, it is also a question of amplifying the experience of subjectivity out of the actual building. The "nomadic" museum facilitates this experience of resistance within and beyond its walls, probing society and its institutions with its poetic needles beyond a mere quantitative discourse of "accessibility."

Chapter 5 starts with the description and potentialities of "critical art," defining it mainly as able to challenge the hegemonic discourse of society. Different ways of critical and relational art practices are outlined with a special attention in favor of those practices that offer a space of alternative narratives. A link is drawn to contemporary elaborations about the thresholds and intersections of anthropology and contemporary art, particularly regarding shared inquiries about detotalizing proposals in opposition to dominant narratives. Afterwards, the limitations of alternative narratives in form of cooperate co-options, neutralizations, and instrumentalizations are conveyed with a special focus on the art museum. Finally, thoughts and strategy of resistance are explored.

The last chapter summarizes deinstitutionalizing practices as well as anti-psychiatry-approaches as developed by psychiatrists, psychoanalysts, and scholars such as Basaglia (Italy); Tosquelles, Oury, Guattari, Fanon; Deligny; Mannoni; Foucault (France); Laing, Cooper (Great Britain); Goffman, Szasz (USA); the Socialist Patients' Collective (Germany); da Silveira (Brazil), and Masotta (Argentina). In spite of various differences in their approaches, they all were joined by a common profound critique and rejection of conventional or traditional psychiatry.

Retrieving the anti-psychiatries should form part of the endeavor to transform society. At the same time, we should analyze the resistance of society to reclaim this knowledge and detect the agendas behind hegemonic psychiatry and psychology that have either already successfully erased it from the map or are working profitably to diminish it. Hegemony feels very much likely threatened by ways of knowing and doing that are bound to different traditions and theories strongly rooted in left-wing thoughts that have reinscribed mental trouble within community and the collective. At the same time, its followers did not stop to question and to subvert moral habits and established so-called scientific knowledge. In this sense, they never paused to insist in the function of the discipline and punish mode of a society that reduces community to competition and struggle for life (Montejo Alonso, 2013).

Within this panorama, it is of special interest that artists have taken the role to retrieve these powerful, unruly knowledges. Dora García with her series *Mad Marginal*, Ana Longoni and Cloe Masotta curating Oscar Masotta, Maurizio Lazzarato together with Angela Melitopoulos actualizing the thoughts of Tosquelles, are sophisticated examples.

Coming back to the museum of contemporary art, Álvarez de Toledo (2009) stressed its role in the context of MACBA's work on anti-pedagogue Fernand Deligny. The museum as an institution questions itself "about its institutional practices, its political responsibility, its objective of inquiry in an epoch when art is self-indulging in the denial of its history and its anthropological meaning" (p. 5).

In our times, when the mental has been *totally commodified, individualized, fragmented, decontextualized, and dehistoricized, we more than appreciate the artists and institutions that revive subaltern eruditions. Once located around the '68 revolutions and rebellions, they are nowadays once again needed to oppose neoliberal oppressions and injustice. In conjunction with the arts, these works can show us different ways of being in the world and of living together beyond commodification and exchange rate paced agendas.*

References

Agamben, G. (2014). *¿Qué es un dispositivo?* [What is a dispositif?] Buenos Aires, Argentina: Adriana Hidalgo Editora.

Álvarez de Toledo, S. (2009). Introducción [Introduction]. In S. Álvarez de Toledo (Ed.), *Fernand Deligny. Permitir, trazar, ver* [To allow, to trace, to see] (pp. 5–13). Barcelona, Spain: MACBA.

Benjamin, W. (1998). *Understanding Brecht.* London, UK: Verso.

Benjamin, W. (1968). The work of art in the age of mechanical reproduction. In H. Arendt (Ed.), *Illuminations: Essays and reflections* (pp. 217–251). New York, NY: Schocken Books.

Bourdieu, P., & Haacke, H. (1995). *Free exchange.* Cambridge, UK: Polity Press.

Brecht, B. (2014). *Brecht on theatre.* London, UK: Bloomsbury Academic.

Buck-Morss, S. (2011). Visual studies and global imagination. In C. Bottici, & B. Challand (Eds.), *The politics of imagination* (pp. 214–233). Abingdon, UK: Birbeck Law Press.

Caló, S. (2019). Can an institution be militant? In Prospections (Ed.), *Metabolic rifts. A reader* (pp. 115–131). Lisbon, Portugal and Berlin, Germany: Atlas Projectos.

Carnevale, G. (2013). Pensar/decir/intervenir [Thinking/saying/intervening]. *Concreta* 01. Retrieved from: http://www.editorialconcreta.org/Pensar-decir-intervenir [Accessed 21 October 2019].

Deleuze, G. (1995). *Difference and repetition.* New York, NY: Columbia University Press.

Foucault, M. (2001). *Dits et écrits* [Sayings and writings]. Vol. II. Paris, France: Gallimard.

García, D. (2010). *Mad Marginal Cahier #1. From Basaglia to Brazil.* Berlin, Germany: Sternberg Press; Trieste, Italy: Fondazione Galleria Civica di Trento and Mousse Publishing.

García Canclini, N. (2014). *Art beyond itself. Anthropology for a society without a story line.* Durham, NC: Duke University Press.

García Canclini, N. (2010). *La sociedad sin relato. Antropología y estética de la inminencia.* Buenos Aires, Argentina: Katz [English version: (2014). *Art beyond itself. Anthropology for a society without a story line.* Durham, NC: Duke University Press].

Guattari, F. (1995). *Chaosmosis: An Ethico-aesthetic paradigm.* Bloomington, IN: Indiana University Press.

Guattari, F. (1989). *Cartographies schizoanalytiques.* Paris, France: Galilée [English version: (2012). *Schizoanalytic cartographies.* London, UK: Bloomsbury].

Hochmann, J. (2015). *Les antipsychiatres. Une histoire* [The anti-psychiatrists. A history]. Paris, France: Odile Jacob.

Holmes, B. (2006). The artistic device, or, the articulation of collective speech. *Ephemera*, 6(4), 411–432.

Laddaga, R. (2006). *Estética de la emergencia* [Aesthetics of emergence]. Buenos Aires, Argentina: Adriana Hidalgo Editora.

Longoni, A. (Ed.). (2017). *Oscar Masotta. Revolucion en el arte* [Oscar Masotta. Revolution in the art]. Buenos Aires, Argentina: Mansalva.

Marxen, E. (2019). Transforming traditions: Walter Benjamin, art, and art therapy. In R. Hougham, S. Pitruzzella, & H. Wengrower (Eds.), *Traditions in transition: New articulations in the arts therapies* (pp. 251–271). London, UK: Ecarte (European Consortium of the Arts Therapies).

Marxen, E. (2018). Artistic practices and the artistic dispositif – A critical review. *Antípoda. Journal of Anthropology and Archeology*, 33, 37–60.

Marxen, E. (2013). Arte, experiencia y terapia [Art, experience, and therapy]. *La Vanguardia Cultura/s.* Cultural Supplement of La Vanguardia, Barcelona, 594, 2–3.

Marxen, E. (2012). 'La comunidad silenciosa'. Migraciones filipinas y capital social en el Raval (Barcelona) ['The silent community'. Filipino migrations and social capital at Raval (Barcelona)]. PhD thesis. On-line publication: Tarragona, Spain: University Rovira i Virgili. http://www.tdx.cat/bitstream/handle/10803/96667/TESIS.pdf?sequence=1 [Accessed 20 October 2019].

Marxen, E. (2011). *Diálogos entre arte y terapia. Del 'arte psicótico' al desarrollo de la arteterapia y sus aplicaciones* [Dialogues between art and therapy. From 'psychotic art' to the development of art therapy and its applications]. Barcelona, Spain: Gedisa.

Marxen, E. (2009a). La etnografía desde el arte. Definiciones, bases teóricas y nuevos escenarios [Ethnography from art. Definitions, theoretical bases and new sceneries]. *Alteridades* [Alterities], 19(37), 7–22.

Marxen, E. (2009b). Therapeutic thinking in contemporary art. Psychotherapy in the arts. *The Arts in Psychotherapy*, 36, 140–147. doi: 10.1016/j.aip.2008.10.004.

Montejo Alonso, F.J. (2013). En un lugar de la Mancha… Francesc Tosquelles y Max Hodnan, creadores de las primeras comunidades terapéuticas durante la guerra civil española [A place in La Mancha … Francesc Tosquelles and Max Hodnan, creators of the first therapeutic communities during the Spanish Civil War]. *XIV Congreso Virtual de Psiquiatria.com. Interpsiquis 2013* [XIV Virtual Congress of Psiquiatria.com. Interpsiquis 2013]. Retrieved from: https://psiquiatria.com/bibliopsiquis/en-un-lugar-de-la-mancha-francesc-tosquelles-y-max-hodann-creadores-de-las-primeras-comunidades-terapeuticas-durante-la-guerra-civil-espanola [Accessed 21 October 2019].

Mouffe, C. (2012). Alfredo Jaar: The artist as organic intellectual. In A. Jaar (Ed.), *The way it is. An aesthetics of resistance* (pp. 264–281). Berlin, Germany: Realismus-Studio of NGBK, New Society for Visual Arts.

Oury, J., Guattari, F., & Tosquelles, F. (1985). *Pratique de l'Institutionnel et Politique* [Practice of the institutional and political]. Vigneux, France: Matrice Editions.

Ribalta, J. (2010). Experiments in a new institutionality. In M.J. Borja-Villel, K. Cabañas, & J. Ribalta (Eds.), *Relational objects. MACBA collection 2002–2007* (pp. 225–265). Barcelona, Spain: MACBA.

Ribalta, J. (2004). Mediation and construction of publics. The MACBA experience. Retrieved from: http://republicart.net/disc/institution/ribalta01 en.htm [Accessed 29 September 2019].

Sajnani, N., Marxen, E., & Zarate, R. (2017). Critical perspectives in the arts therapies: Response/ability across a continuum of practice. *The Arts in Psychotherapy*, 54, 28–37. doi:10.1016/j.aip.2017.01.007.

Tosquelles, F. (2014). *L'enseignement de la folie* [Teaching of madness]. Paris, France: Dunod.

Tosquelles, F. (2001). Préface [Preface]. In J. Oury (Ed.), *Psychiatrie et psychothérapie institutionnelle* [Psychiatry and institutional psychotherapy] (pp. 11–20). Lecques, France: Les éditions du Champ social.

2 Beyond the Walls

Art Therapy Applied to Adolescents with Challenging Behaviors and the Museum

Introduction and Context of the Art Therapy Practice

In 2003, after the seminar *Image, Look, Appearance. Consequences of Lacanian Theory*, which was carried out by Lacanian psychoanalyst Enric Berenguer at the Museum of Contemporary Art of Barcelona (MACBA), Jorge Ribalta, by then the director of the Department of Public Programs of the same museum, together with Eva Marxen, who had participated in Berenguer's seminar, began to conceive of art therapy workshops for the museum. They were to be directed to teenagers in the Raval neighborhood of Barcelona who had previously been classified as "at social risk." The point of connection between the three professionals—Berenguer, Ribalta and Marxen—had been a refusal to exhibit the artistic productions created by mentally ill or other subjects in situations of social vulnerability or in context of institutionalization. Rather, they aspired, in agreement with Ribalta (2004, p. 9), to go "beyond the regime of visibility, whose paradigm is the exhibition" and to "restore forms of subjective appropriation of artistic methods in processes on the margins and outside the museum." These reflections were part of the policies of the MACBA during the direction of Manuel Borja-Villel (1999–2007), which, apart from the programming of exhibitions of highly political content, had the intention of bringing art to groups whose priorities do not necessarily include visits to contemporary art museums. Of course, in order to achieve this objective, the Public Programs Department would need to play a key function and, as a result, was endowed with a decent budget to achieve these goals.

At the same time, another motivation to initiate practices of "subjective appropriation of artistic methods on the margins and outside the museum" was the rearticulation of the relationship between the museum and its urban environment (Ribalta, 2010, 2004, p. 9), precisely with the Raval neighborhood. This space, which includes the area of what was previously called *Barrio Chino*,[1] was traditionally considered—under monarchical, parliamentary, nationalist, leftist, fascist, and democratic governments—a problem area and even a place of misfortune, misery, drug addiction, delinquency, prostitution, poverty, dirt, and disease, among other attributes and adversities (McDonough, 2005). To face the supposed miseries associated with the Raval or the old Barrio Chino, the City Council of Barcelona had designed various urban plans for this territory, located in the center of Barcelona, that would support the creation of a "presentable" vision of the area. In doing so, different mayors aimed at satisfying tourism and encouraging national and international investments of banks, real estate, and other institutions. Among the reforms carried out, the construction of emblematic squares (e.g., the Plaza dels Àngels, the square of the MACBA museum) and the big avenue "Rambla del Raval" excelled, as did the location of culture and science centers: the Center for Contemporary Culture of Barcelona (CCCB), the MACBA, the Center of Decorative Arts (FAD), the International Center for Information and Documentation of Barcelona (CIDOB), the Center for Cultural Studies and Resources (CERC), the Film Center La Filmoteca, and the buildings of the Ramon Llull University and the University of Barcelona (Subirats & Rius, 2006; Delgado, 2005). The purpose of this massive introduction of various institutions of culture and science was to change the social life of the neighborhood with a demand for a new public: the users of these institutions. At the same time, efforts have been made to displace the old and newly unwanted inhabitants, partly in an illegal way (Fernández González, 2014; Delgado, 2005, 2002; Marginyà and Maza, 2001; Smith, 2000; as well as the films Work in progress by Guerín, 2001, *Playing with* children by Jordà, 2003, and the artwork by Banal and Canudas, *Hospital 106, 4t 1a*, 2005, about one particular apartment affected by gentrification; Figure 2.1a–c).

On the other hand, the medieval name of "Raval" had been recovered to erase the myths of "Chinatown," a direct but imperfect translation of this same area's former colloquial name, and the misfortunes that have been associated with it. In this scenario, the MACBA, without a doubt, was part of the "museumification" of Barcelona's southern district Ciutat Vella (Delgado, 2005, pp. 61–62, translated by myself from Spanish), as well as "the big capital investments in museums" occurring in many cities around the world. It has been an essential part of the gentrification and remodeling of historic or abandoned centers, something that has also been called "Guggenheim effect," referring to the Guggenheim museum in Bilbao and the respective changes in this city made in favor of tourism (Rosler, 2013; Smith, 2009, pp. 141, 143; Laddaga, 2006). Like Maza, McDonogh, & Pujadas have described in their article (2002, p. 122, translated by myself from Spanish), the MACBA in Barcelona is an "immaculate" white color, which contrasts with the buildings and the adjoining streets. It is not in vain that the young people of the neighborhood call this square, not Plaza del MACBA or dels Àngels (the square's official name in Catalan), but the "the white square." This can be interpreted in such a way that young people are very aware of the contrast of this museum with the rest of the neighborhood or, at least, with what the neighborhood was. However, as Delgado (2005, p. 13) points out, "the planned city is opposed to the city practiced," because people have used this plaza in their own way: the skaters dominate it while circulating passers-by seem oblivious to the museum and young people who use the façade as a mirror for their techno

Figure 2.1 (a) Publication *Hospital 106, 4t 1a. El lloc i el temps* [Hospital 106, 4t 1a. The place and the time]. Isabel Banal-Jordi Canudas. Barcelona, 2005. (b) Publication *Hospital 106, 4t 1a. El lloc i el temps* [Hospital 106, 4t 1a. The place and the time]. Isabel Banal-Jordi Canudas. Barcelona, 2005. (c) Project *Hospital 106, 4t 1a*. Isabel Banal-Jordi Canudas. Poster digital print, 50 × 70 cm. Barcelona, 2002. A project that directs the look on the urbanistic and social transformations that happened in the Raval neighborhood Barcelona, 1995–2002.

dance choreographies. Uninterruptedly, the guards watch the square and, above all, the entrance to the museum (Marxen, 2012).

Obviously, the social problems of a neighborhood cannot be resolved through the construction of a museum. It is an illusion to believe that degraded city districts could be regenerated merely by urbanistic reforms (González Virós, 2005). Instead of (or beside) elite art and architecture projects, different social and political interventions, guided by a major sensitivity towards different collectives, are paramount.

However, it is necessary to thoroughly examine the MACBA museum and the policies and activities that it has carried out. In this sense, we must differentiate the museum as a building that was part of urban planning strategies and the museum as an institution, since the museum staff had not intervened in the urban planning. The museum's director from 1999 to 2007, Manuel Borja, worked with his team in favor of considering art in a social and political redefinition. He acceded to the position after the MACBA had been inaugurated and committed in public to focus on relations with the communities affected by gentrification. In the same vein, seminars and workshops were organized with subsequent publications of a highly critical vision of gentrification processes, locally and globally (i.e. Smith, 2009; Smith, Metropolitan Observatory, Rolnik, Ross, & Davis, 2009). It is surprising that despite everything that has been published and said about the Raval and the MACBA, almost no one has taken the trouble to inquire about what was happening *inside* the museum. It is as if the anthropological or sociological vision of researchers had been hindered by the museum walls. In one of his conferences, Smith (2009) spoke precisely of the responsibility of professionals of gentrifying museums, including the artists hired by them, to develop a critical public discourse on the processes which led to the museum's existence and to further use its platform to establish a critical discourse on gentrification, including affected displaced neighbors. Another reference within his discourse is the artist Krzysztof Wodiczko and his artworks such as *Homeless Projection* (1986) and *Homeless Vehicles* (1988–1989) by which Wodiczko undertook an effective criticism in public space against the effects of gentrification processes in New York, "one of the cities which concentrates the greatest wealth in the world while housing about one hundred thousand homeless people" (Smith, 2009, p. 146, translated by myself from Spanish). In the same city, ambiguities of museums between the desire to promote a critical discussion on gentrification and to be part of it as "potential agents (…), if they are not *de facto*" (Smith, 2009, p. 147), were evident in the *Real Estate Show* by Hans Haacke, first commissioned and later censored by the Guggenheim Museum in New York. The artist documented the degradation of real estate for speculative purposes in the same city and showed how some members of the museum's board were involved in the same speculation (Haacke, 1975).

Often, curators and artists who work in and with museums feel a political and social alliance with the populations affected by urban gentrification, rather than with the patrons of museums, who are frequently allies and accomplices of capitalist hegemony. Although such efforts will not always be successful, art in conjunction with political resistance remains an effective tool to highlight and combat social injustice, instead of "being mere, neutral witnesses who twist their hands and contemplate the scene from haughtiness, far from the harshness of a political change that, in all probability, inspires more antipathy to them than anything else" (Smith, 2009, pp. 147–148).

Within the institutional logics of the museum, the MACBA financed, from 2004 to 2011, art therapy practices parallel to the project of the Lacanian psychoanalyst Montse Rodríguez with adults diagnosed as "psychotic," clients of the day centers of Mental Health of Barcelona and the periphery. Rodríguez (2015) has called her method a Lacanian psychoanalysis applied to the museum.

Practical Operation and Institutional Contexts of the Art Therapy Workshops

During the eight years of uninterrupted operation the following groups have been continuously carried out

- Two groups in the Public High School Miquel Tarradell located in the same Raval neighborhood, in first and second of ESO (Escolarización Secundaria Obligatoria, Mandated Secondary Education), including youth from 12 to 14 years of age.
- One or two groups in the UEC (Unidad de Escolarización Compartida, Shared Schooling Unit) managed by the Casal dels Infants del Raval (Casal of the Raval Children), now Casal dels Infants per a l'Acció Social als Barris (Casal of the Children for Social Action in the Neighborhoods). The UEC includes young people officially expelled from public secondary school, usually because of their challenging behavior that supposedly cannot be contained in regular classrooms. Once there, they work in smaller groups with an adapted curriculum, particularly training in crafts like wood, cooking, electricity workshops. Although it is an official resource of the Department of Education of the Generalitat (the local government), professionals—social educators—usually have to work in more precarious conditions than the teachers in the regular schools. In addition, young people are separated from normal schooling, which implies certain segregation, stigmatization, and a loss of positive reference.
- During one school year, a group of underage Romanys was also taken in, which, according to Juvenile Justice, had to attend a "re-socialization" program that was also managed by the Casal dels Infants in the Raval that year. It was not possible to continue the work in this context because the resocialization program itself was modified. It was moved to the periphery of Barcelona where it is managed by another entity.
- During another school year, a group was set up in a "leisure" center (*Lleure* in Catalan) frequented by young people from families that were

quite "unstructured and at risk." This was also managed by the Casal dels Infants. This context proved difficult from the organization's point of view as the participants arrived at the art workshop after a busy day: They had started classes at their high school around eight or nine in the morning and finished at five in the evening. Afterwards, in the center, it was mandatory to attend the reinforcement classes. Then finally, at 6:45 pm we could start the group, when, in fact, the young people only wanted to listen to music or to chat with their friends. After finishing their activities in the center, some still had to pick up younger siblings; that is to say, after a 12-hour day family responsibilities still awaited them, all this at the young ages of 12–14. These circumstances made it practically impossible to concentrate and compromise the obligation to attend the art therapy workshop. In no way do I mean that this context is inadequate for workshops or groups of art therapy, but it is important to thoroughly reflect on the schedules, the space, and the composition of possible groups.

With all groups, it was about working with maximum continuity. After having worked the first year, three times a week in the Special Schooling Unit and in a block at the high school, in accordance and in close collaboration with the professionals of the centers, we were able to find the most suitable formulas for users and centers: All groups then met with a frequency of one session per week and a duration of 60 minutes in the school, in congruence with the duration of all other classes, and 45 minutes in the UEC. In this institution, a shorter duration has been chosen due to problems, at least in the beginning, of prolonged concentration with the participants and also because there was more room to be flexible with the schedules.

The art therapy practices described here are distinguished from other specific artistic interventions in their continuity and regularity. In this sense, we worked weekly during the entire school year at the high school. Obviously, it is necessary to allow some time at the beginning of the course (September) for teachers to compose together; that is why, the groups began in October, after a month of organizational meetings. For the same purpose, at the school unit UEC it has concluded to start in January, after the seasonal holidays, for the following reason: As it has already been stated, the adolescents arriving there have been expelled from public high schools, a procedure carried out throughout the operation of a school year. As such, it has been decided to wait for the first months until a certain number of participants have arrived.

Of course, after January, expelled students continued to arrive at the UEC. As it has been necessary to work with closed groups in order to guarantee a certain degree of stability, we were unable to admit new participants once the group started. Instead, it was decided to reserve a part of the budget in order to initiate a second group, with the same characteristics, later on during the school year if necessary.

In the resocialization program of the Romanys minors, the group worked under the same premise: meeting once a week during the whole course.

However, it was impossible to keep the group closed given the fluctuation of the participants: some fulfilled the legal ruling before others, some did not comply, and there were permanent readmissions, as well as new additions.

Composition of the Groups

Regarding the composition of the groups, it is foundationally essential to work with very small groups. The fact that the group is small forms part of the process.

In this sense, they should be as small as can be negotiated with the institution. The absolute maximum, in my opinion, is four participants per group at the UEC and six at high school. We must bear in mind that one of the most important aspects of working with children who present the so-called disrupt behavior is the potential space and the ability to hold it in Winnicott's sense (1971). This is impossible to guarantee in larger groups.

For the British psychoanalyst and pediatrist, the potential space is located between the internal and external world. It is the space where the child can develop its play as well as adolescents and adults can experiment their creativity. For Winnicott (id.), play is crucial for bringing the personal, psychological world together with outer reality. The potential space should offer the possibility to pass from the interior to the exterior world. In short, it makes symbolization possible. Art therapy is especially suitable for achieving potential spaces because, as opposed to verbal therapies, it is based in a creative method. For the potential space, a safe and welcoming setting must be constructed. Children that do not feel safe, difficultly start to develop their play. The task of the therapist consists in creating a setting of therapeutic *holding*. It is determined by safety, security, continuity, confidentiality, empathy as well as certain boundaries like stable schedule, frequency, duration, and space. This information is transmitted in words and also the therapist's attitude: They respect and welcome the participants' creation without submitting them under academic judgments. In art therapy, another advantage lies in the tangible safe storage of the artworks. Thus, the art therapist literally contains or holds them, which is a symbolic form of the empathic holding too. Furthermore, they show that they value and appreciate the artworks (see also the ideas of Melanie Klein's play technique, 1955/1975, and her ideas on the importance of every client having their own box of toys and art materials that will not be mixed with others).

In any case, the therapeutic holding is a continuous work in process. It has to be developed during the entire process of therapy and to be renewed in every session. The preparation and training of the professional is crucial in this process.

Generally, the UECs are frequented by adolescents who have experienced very little holding in their lives, coming from very dysfunctional and socially disadvantaged families. In most cases, they have also experienced social exclusion and uprootedness. From their behaviors, it can be deduced that their relationship with one another has been altered (Bröcher, 1999). The art therapy groups must be able to provide the emotional holding absent in the adolescents' previous life phases. The holding capacity of the art therapist is constantly challenged because the teens demand a lot of adult attention, as if to stop them; in other words, they want to be noticed, even if it is through quarrels. This is actually a sign of their health, they are able to call attention for their personal and social unease (Winnicott, 1984; Figure 2.2).

Now, if these behaviors multiply, the containment on the part of the adult is impossible and the group dynamics usually end in provocations on the part of the teens and exhaustion on the part of the teacher, that is to say in an uncontainable chaos that no longer serves any of the users. On the contrary, they end up repeating the same chaotic dynamics they often come from, and the dynamics become quite counterproductive. For this reason, it should be kept in mind that in this institutional context, there are almost always children who would benefit from an individual therapeutic art process. In my experience, this is difficult to negotiate on an institutional level, because generally in their schedules, they contemplate exclusively group activities. In short, the ideal is mini-groups of three teens.

To compose the groups, tutors or social educators should reflect on which children could benefit from the art therapy practice, talk to them, and explain the process. The educational professionals—that is, the social educators in the UEC or the teachers, tutors, and coordinators at the high school—should be able to adequately communicate the details of the program to coworkers and students. In order to do so, they must understand its basic functioning, its objectives, its underlying philosophy. To this end, it is essential to coordinate and meet with the professionals of the centers. In an ideal case, an explanatory meeting would be organized for all the staff of the institution. At the same time, it would be convenient to provide them with additional written information that can circulate through the center.

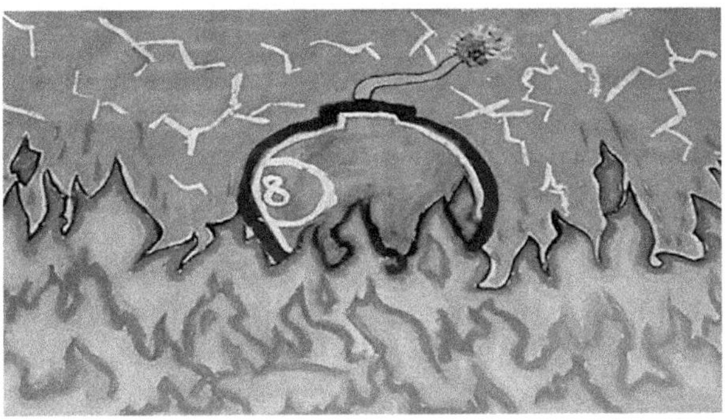

Figure 2.2 Art therapy practice, special school unit, UEC, Barcelona, 2004.

If the institution had not been familiarized with art therapy previously, Bion's (1995) reflections about how the "new idea" reaches the establishment are relevant: Said new idea can be absurdly received as if it were a messianic arrival that knows how to solve all—or many—problems of the institution or its clients, but, often, it can be rejected, since the new idea has a disruptive force, causing anguish and anxiety by endangering the old known and conventional operations. They are unsettled "through moments of disorganization, pain, and frustration" (Grinberg, Sor, & Tabak de Bianchedi, 1991, p. 34, translated by myself from Spanish). According to Bion's model of containment (1995), the new idea needs to be held in the container, in this context, the institution where it is presented. Its proper function would be the representation of the new idea, "limiting in part its disruptive power and at the same time making it accessible to the members of the group" (Grinberg et al., 1991, p. 35). In Bion's terms, its function would be alpha, of *rêverie*, that is, knowing how to detoxify and digest the new idea to properly return it to its members. However, the reactions frequently correspond more to Bion's beta function, or the fierce expulsion of the new idea due to lack of adequate elaboration. This in turn leads to defensive reactions and catastrophic change for the receiver of the new idea. In turn, the reception of the new idea by the receiver is complicated, it is rejected and criticized, something that can happen in an excessive way (Pichón Rivière in Zito Lema, 1990). In this sense, the importance of language and the communicability of the new idea to promote it in a successful manner is highlighted. Of course goodwill is required from both the sender and the receiver. The change provoked by the new idea should not lead to disaster, but to transformation, to growth, and should be the starting point of an evolution (Grinberg et al., 1991). Even so, the bearer of the idea must have both a capacity to insist and to resist strange reactions when introducing their "new idea" (see Marxen, 2011).

Successful communication is even more important if we take into account that groups are carried out inside the schools, which is why we depend on collaboration throughout the process. The environment is decisive since we need to negotiate at least a minimum of infrastructure to develop the activity such as a closed space, a location outside the views of professionals and other students outside the group, a consistent schedule, as well as the safe storage both of the artworks and art materials. Without the guarantee of these requirements, the practice cannot be successfully developed: the privacy of the process on one hand and on the other an adequate evaluation of the works made by the participants through secure storage.

It is worth keeping in mind that we have two different professional cultures: that of the education professions and that of creative therapists. Already in several places (Payne, 1996; Lefley & Pederson, 1986; Frost, 1985; according to Wengrower, 2001) the existence and importance of professional cultures have been explained: People define themselves to a lesser or greater degree with their profession, wherein practitioners share ideas, motivations, convictions, concerns, readings, jargon, forms of expression and communication.

As Wengrower (ibid) explains, professional culture manifests itself especially clearly in international congresses where practitioners of a profession from different countries and continents exchange experiences and knowledge as professional culture is often posed on top of national culture.

When two different professional cultures meet, each experiences it as an encounter with the "other" (Wengrower, ibid), especially in regard to the ideologies and underlying formations of the professions. In the case of the insertion of a therapeutic activity based in psychoanalytic thinking, into the educational field, we have observed such an encounter: Notions such as process, development, results, and advances are different. The educational aspect is usually guided by tangible and measurable results in numerical notes. The activities are timetabled and more preset. The method is directive, that is to say, concrete tasks are given and then checked. Meanwhile, in a psychoanalytic dynamic, one usually works in a non-directive manner, without giving specific themes or guidelines but leaving the choice of subject(s) to the participants. There are no scripts or simplified recipes. The work is oriented toward introspection. In psychoanalytic art therapy, it is about creating the necessary conditions for a subjective work with the capacity of symbolization. The results are subjective and never generalizable or quantifiable; in no way is it a question of establishing success criteria in advance.

In art therapy, more attention is paid to the process compared to the tangible results in the form of artworks. The development of the process is different in each person, since each person has their unique trajectory that can never be identical to that of others; as such, diversity of styles is allowed and each one is left their own time and rhythm. This way of working confronts the therapeutic professional with uncertainty, even with the anguish, which they must know how to endure, the result of training that includes their own psychoanalytic treatment and the permanent extension of their own epistemological base (see the differences between the principles of school education and creative therapies: Wengrower, ibid, and regarding uncertainty in psychoanalytic therapy Fiorini, 2010).

In this sense, when performing art therapy in educational centers, the supposed need on the part of educators or teachers to measure results can manifest by confusing it with art classes, with an overvaluation of the tangible results that can manifest in ideas to expose the works or to decorate the center with them. They might also ask for a program with topics, tasks, or "success" criteria annotated by dates. A frequent argument against the application of non-directive dynamics is that the youth, accustomed to working in a directive way in schools, may get confused. Yet, it forms part of the process of learning and knowing how to discriminate between different dynamics.

Sometimes teachers or social educators may feel somewhat jealous of the relationship established between specific participants and the therapist. The participants might idealize the more intense and unshared therapeutic relationship or experience a split between a "bad" teacher and a "good," idealized therapist. Especially in the UEC, because of the precarious conditions in which they work, educators sometimes feel envy towards the therapist, considering their preferable work situation and particularly their schedules, in comparison with theirs (in congruence with Wengrower, ibid).

In fact, due to the same precariousness in the UEC, there is a lot of fluctuation amongst the staff. The wear and tear of daily life at such institutions is considerable and most seek another professional environment after nothing more than a school year. Regarding the communicability of the new idea, this also means having to repeat the explanation of the "new idea" every year with each new coordinator. How then to approach this meeting of cultures without it becoming a disagreement that hinders the work of all, or, in case it is a drag, duplicates the tasks of the art therapist? It should also be taken into account that in this meeting, the therapist is in the minority, or perhaps the only one, considered as "outsider." It is critical to highlight that such a misunderstanding harms, more than anything, those who should benefit from the activity: the children.

There are no simplified recipes or magic solution in this matter. Molloy (1997) warns of excessive rigidity in the therapist's position and stubborn adherence to their "philosophy," which can cause isolation and hostility towards their team. Referring to different professional cultures, Wengrower (2001) speaks of an "intercultural dialogue." The reflections of Marie Rose Moro (2002, 1998); Moro, de La Noë, and Mouchenik (2004) about the professional's attitude in transcultural psychiatry can contribute: They advocate for a decentralization of one's own values and beliefs in order to be open to "another" and to avoid ethnocentric positions, in this context too focused on the profession itself. Decentralization should be accompanied by a certain critical analysis of one's professional convictions and ideologies. Even so, it is always a difficult balance to maintain, with adequate negotiations, a communicative capacity on the one hand and not renouncing the minimum essential framework to be able to successfully perform the work on the other hand. In this case, at the very least, the professionals of the centers must understand why the artworks should not be exposed, the need for a space without interference, and the safe storage of the materials including, above all, the artworks. On a practical level regarding performance evaluation, individual evaluation interviews with participants have been shown to be adequate, as opposed to numerical notes as the schools might typically demand—something absurd in a therapeutic task.

Wengrower (2001) proposes that therapists participate in team meetings to achieve greater inclusion. Furthermore, the school calendar with its field trips, holiday parties, class trips should not interrupt the therapeutic continuity. Hence, it is recommended that the therapist keeps abreast of these dates. It is also recommended that groups finish before the last weeks of the course, which are usually reserved for the aforementioned class trips, exams, parties, and extracurricular activities.

Especially in the UEC, continuity can be threatened by expulsions: Children who repeatedly behave "badly" are often expelled for a day up to a month. Still, one can try to negotiate that the expulsion be suspended for participation in the art therapy group.

What helps the external therapist a lot is to work with external financing to fund programming since it grants a certain independence; in my case, my funding came entirely from the museum so I did not have to accept all the impositions from the educational institutions. Besides the financial, the museum supported my work significantly by organizing common meetings with educators, myself, and the public program director with his staff. The latter always backed the essential requests for the group works.

In the bibliography on creative therapies in schools, importance has been given to the non-stigmatization of the students chosen for the therapeutic groups. It is advisable to match the start and end of the group with those of the school day or recesses so as not to remove the participating students from the others (i.e. Case & Dalley, 1999). However, in many cases, I have observed that, on the part of the children, participation is considered a privilege, with non-participants frequently insisting on being included in the group (Marxen, 2011).

Reference has already been made to the composition of the groups; namely, that they should be small and closed. Regarding the selection of the students, we need the collaboration of the center's professionals, who can share information about the profiles of the young people and reflect on who can take advantage of the resource. In some preliminary meetings, the groups are composed jointly with such staff. As it concerns minors, written permission from the parents or legal guardian is additionally required. The need for negotiation mentioned above is broadened by the provision of certain information about the participants that educational professionals may sometimes want to retain.

Regarding the profiles of the participants, it is necessary to repeat that we have worked in institutions frequented by young people labeled as being at risk of social exclusion. Now, what almost all the participants, both in high school and the special unit, have had in common is that they come from very unstructured families in social and economic situations that range from worrying to extreme. Their fathers and mothers are overwhelmed by economic survival and, for this reason, have not been able to provide adequate emotional containment. In the UEC, they were often single-parent families, mostly mothers stressed because they had minimum income to take care of their children, maintain a house, and contact their children's schools. Some worked cleaning buildings during the night shifts because of its slightly higher wages, compared to day work. As a result, however, many were unable to control their children's school attendance in the morning. In the UEC, we work with children—almost exclusively boys—expelled from public high schools. However, at the social level, this formal procedure reflects their greater expulsion from society. Teachers argue that they reach this extreme by not being able to deal with disruptive, often aggressive behaviors, in combination with school absenteeism, in the classroom. However, in the UEC, adolescents meet their peers, between 14 and 16 years of age, with similar trajectories and sometimes arrive at a competition of challenging rules and disruptiveness. Some have been derivatives by Juvenile Justice.

In high school, there are also children with challenging behavior, although to a lesser degree. While in the UEC there used to be a balance between native and immigrant families with a slightly higher percentage in favor of the former, in the mentioned secondary school, 90% were of foreign origin, among them some with serious problems of school adaptation and linguistic order. Some, instead of manifesting disruptive behaviors were very introverted, almost never relating to others through verbal language.

With some exceptions, in this context, it is not because of psychiatric problems but rather these young peoples' complicated behaviors and difficulty keeping them in the classroom that has led their teachers or educators to refer them to mental health services. It is noteworthy that almost none of the participants attended mental health service. They and their parents have shown an important resistance against psychology and psychiatry. It is, in my opinion, a phenomenon that lies in the culture of social exclusion, where people feel twice excluded: first by their social situation and second by associating themselves as users of a mental health center and therefore mentally ill or "crazy." To this is added the fear that in psychological or psychiatric treatments family secrets will be revealed, such as abuse, for example. Yet to me, it seems as if this rejection mainly lies in the functioning of mental health centers and their professionals, who very often lack the "experience near" with respect to the mentioned youth in the sense of Kohut (1984, 1977) and Geertz (1974). Both authors have stressed in their respective disciplines, psychoanalysis (Kohut) and anthropology (Geertz), the importance of an empathic observation which aims at being able to imaging the other's point of view. According to my observations over 20 years in the mental health field, many professionals do not recognize the different knowledge that children have about society and, frequently, consider them exclusively "carriers of faults" (lack of knowledge, lack of skills, lack of insight) or—as is the case with a charitable or paternalistic/maternalistic attitude—mere victims. The children, in turn, challenge the knowledge of professionals, which they perceive as very alien to their own (already explained in Sajnani, Marxen, & Zarate, 2017; Marxen, 2016, 2011). Now, the knowledge of the young people includes resisting psychiatric institutionalization. As a consequence, art therapy groups are the only spaces of psychological introspection that children are willing to attend. This is an aspect that radically differentiates the participants of the program described here compared to those working with Montse Rodríguez. She worked with adults diagnosed as psychotic and totally institutionalized by Psychiatry at large.

All together there is a high degree of rejection and resistance presented by the adolescents against any activity with the prefix "psych" or the name "therapy."

For these reasons, in collaboration with their educators, the name "art workshop" has been given preference. The activity starts from a psychoanalytic orientation and an anthropological understanding of problematic behaviors. In my opinion, it is necessary to continue thinking about a better denomination for the activity. To call it in this way means to develop a work of holding—of which the adolescents often lack—through art, without reaching a psychotherapeutic level. This would require deepening into psychological aspects, mainly related to transference and countertransference that would be treated on a verbal level (see for the difference: Schaverien, 2000). Moreover, much more information about the children would be needed compared to what is normally provided or collected by the educators.

As for the setting, that is, the spaces and infrastructures, it is advisable to have spaces that exclude interference with people who do not participate in the art therapy workshop and that allow work without too much distraction. It would be ideal to have a running sink in the room to allow access to water. Otherwise, I recommend using two buckets, one for clean water and one for dirty water, respectively, as commuting to the bathroom would mean interrupting the group, with children entering and exiting whenever they require the use of water, which can be quite frequent depending on the medium being used.

If it is a group with participants with high levels of aggressiveness, it is also helpful to have an educator nearby in the center who can intervene and apply limits in cases that are difficult to control. It should be a professional the teens are accustomed to and whose authority they respect in extreme situations. In very extreme cases when a child can no longer be controlled in the space, the educator should take the teen out of the room, to work with them on the course of the conflict in an individual classroom; it would be under extremely unique circumstances that it would be appropriate for such a participant to be left alone. The reason I insist that this should be done only in exceptional cases is because the children have been previously expelled, e.g., from the high schools. Thus, they eventually repeat traumatic episodes of their previous lives. This assumption has been confirmed when observing the reactions of the participants after an intervention that ends with the expulsion from the group, even if it is temporary: They frequently oppose with all their strengths leaving the classroom.

On the other hand, it is not recommended to include educators in the actual group. This is because, typically, such persons possess previous connotations about the teens beyond art therapy that would influence group dynamics too much; by extension, the educator would no longer be a sufficiently neutral person for the art group.

The infrastructure of the space also covers the storage of materials and works. Spatially, it is convenient to organize these aspects very well. In art therapy, it is always important to securely store materials and works (see above in the context of therapeutic holding). In the UEC, not keeping the importance of material and work storage in mind can make the work fail.

Again it is worth reflecting on the social and family background of the adolescents and their shortcomings. For the group to be a positive (and constructive) experience, it is essential to achieve a safe and secure environment, which is achieved by setting boundaries regarding aggressions against furniture, materials, colleagues, mates, and other professionals. Yet, an excess of boundaries inhibits the creative potential. In this sense, it should be noted that institutions usually impose more rules than those mentioned above and that these do not always make sense for artistic production.

Another essential aspect is to ensure that the artistic creations produced by the participants are respected and valued, stored in a safe place, inaccessible to anyone outside the group. Often, this means a new experience for the adolescents, whose work is frequently despised or even destroyed at home, in other words not appreciated at all. In this sense, during the eight years that I have worked in the UEC, no participant has ever wanted to take their folder or a single piece of work to their home. On the other hand, sometimes they request to see work after they have finished the group, even one or two years later, if they are still in the institution.

The same can be said of materials: They should also be kept in a safe place, to prevent people outside the group from intentionally or unintentionally removing them; a negative experience with which the children are likely and sadly already familiar with.

Regarding the selection of materials, the ideas of Linesch (1988), working in similar adolescent context, are relevant. I could confirm a great deal of her observations in the work with the UEC (Marxen, 2011).

In short, she classifies techniques and materials according to the control they offer and has elaborated a scale of controllability (id). In this sense, the technique that provides the most control is collage, because it is a slow process, controlled and controllable because it consists of different steps. Participants hardly "get lost" in these steps. Another advantage of collage lies in the fact of working with pre-existing images, which reduces the fear of having to make "aesthetically correct" images, something that is often associated with graphic material, as charcoals, pencils, etc., as these are materials associated with the art academy.

At the other end of the scale are clay and plasticine, since they are materials that, in themselves, do not have any structure; rather, the participants must create it. For this reason, it is convenient to introduce them at the end of the process, when the participants are already familiar with the activity, the group, the professional, and the rest of the materials.

Painting is located in the middle of the scale. It does not have an existing structure either, but with the help of brushes, it is easier to manipulate than clay.

The adequate selection of materials in this context also includes dosage in the sense of the quantity of materials available. An over-stimulation should be avoided, given that these young people are very deprived at a social, material, economic, and affective level. It would be an illusion to think that a very wide and abundant offering of materials would serve as compensation for other deprivations, or that art making itself is therapeutic for children. More likely, they would respond with a state of confusion, aggression, or even boycott the activity. It is the art therapist's job to offer the materials in "digestible" doses and to choose them in such a way that they contribute to the potential space in which the participants experience control of their aggression through the process of symbolizing in a holding environment—in short, in a crisis management space (Marxen, 2011; Dannecker, 1999; Domma, 1999).

Particularly at the aforementioned high school in Barcelona, most of the participants are from immigrant families. Regarding the advantages of art therapy within the context of immigration, detailed information has already been offered elsewhere, in congruence with the international bibliography (see Marxen, 2011, 2005, 2004a, 2004b). They can be summarized as follows:

- Art therapy reduces the importance of the verbal and offers an alternative form of expression. If the participant (still) does not master the language or languages of the destination, this alternative can provide some relief in a prolonged stress experience.
- The client can use their symbolism and choose their rhythm without having to adapt them to the professional and the dominant culture of the target society. This is an advantage of art therapy that is hardly achievable by verbal treatment.
- Through art-therapy work, a safe focus can be established to explore cultures, both one's own and that of others in the case of group work. An advantage lies in operating with an indirect, symbolic expression that respects the defenses of people and thus provides more security.
- Because of the ability of the art to link alleged opposites and also to condense different times in one work (see Fiorini, 2010; Gadamer, 1997), it serves to create bridges and links into personality aspects dissociated into parts acculturated according to the destination society and parts that feel lost from the cultures of origin. In this way, art can be a support to maintain cultural identities.
- Especially for adults and adolescents, artistic expression can have regressive effects: with participants perhaps remembering the last time when they painted or played. For people who did not continue with art, it could have been at primary or middle school. This way the multiple migratory loss can emerge. It may include the grieving for family, friends, languages, landscapes, and the habits of the country of origin. Additionally, participants may grieve the loss of social status and even the experience of loss of physical integrity due to a risky emigration or permanent social and political exclusion in the place of destination (see for the multiple grief of migration: Achotegui, 2000). Once again, these losses can be elaborated indirectly through art therapy, which can reduce anxiety and better respect people's defense mechanisms.

We then have in the groups behavioral problem as well as precedents of very dysfunctional families, whether immigrant or native, with many social and economic deficiencies. This means for any professional who works in these areas, it is important to know in depth the social and political circumstances;

how they have occurred, how they are reified, and what consequences they have, primarily for participants but also for professionals. It should interest not only the individual but also the social practice as well as its reproduction processes and consequently, its potential for transformation. Giddens states (1979, p. 65): "Activities or practices are brought into being in the context of overlapping and connected sets of rules, given coherence by their involvement in the constitution of social systems in the movement of time."

The art therapist—like other professionals—must study the sociological and anthropological contexts of the field in which they navigate. In this case, this includes the sociology of exclusion, deviation, and labeling that analyze how labels are constructed in permanent interaction and almost always in dichotomies ("correct-deviated," "healthy-ill"), being the actors in positions of social and political power who establish said hierarchies (see especially Becker, 1963/1997, for a summary Bergalli, 1980, also Foucault, 2006, 1975).

The therapist must also research youth cultures (e.g. Reguillo, 2012; Fize, 2007; Feixa, 2006; Feixa, Porzio, & Recio, 2006), including critical studies of the applicability of the "psy-practices" in juvenile cultures of deprivation (Loewenthal, 2015; Winnicott, 1984; Aichhorn, 1965), as well as basic aspects of the developmental psychology of adolescence (Aberastury & Knobel, 2001; Hartmann, Quaglia, & Kuffer, 2000; Blos, 1979), while also submitting this knowledge to a contemporary critical analysis.

Working in the field of immigration requires the professional to go through the personal work of decentering, i.e. analyze and question their own values, beliefs and prejudices and how they influence their interaction with the other (see Moro, 2002, 1998; Moro et al., 2004). Likewise, it is about avoiding "archaeologizing" the other and making them a prisoner of their supposed traditions and customs; the decision of the individual to adhere to or reject these is always considered more decisive (Fernando, 2010; Delgado, 2002, 1998; Rechtman, 1997).

In addition, when working with groups, even small ones, the group is not to be ignored as an entity. Critically, the group structure includes multiple transferential directions: between the different members, between the group as an entity and the art therapist, and between each member with the therapist (Foulkes, 2018; Case & Dalley, 2014; Bion, 1991). In short, the professional must know about group theories, the psychological mechanisms that are in question in adolescence, the critical analysis of the psychological theories of this vital phase, as well as the social and political context of social exclusion and migration, the art therapy applications with deprived adolescents, including a critical review of the existing literature (i.e. Camilleri, 2007; Sudres, 2005; Hampe, Ritschl, & Waser, 1999; Riley, 1999; Kramer, 1998, 1993, 1958; Linesch, 1988;) and, in addition, of its institutional situation: the educative centers (see Wengrower above).

Only with this solid epistemological foundation can the knowledge of the art therapist develop within the hermeneutic circle described by Heidegger (1927/1986) and Gadamer (1960/1990). They understood prejudices as a form of foreknowledge that constantly has to be revised. Then, it is contrasted, verified and constantly expanded until achieving a new knowledge that once again becomes foreknowledge that is corroborated again. All this happens in a circular, interminable movement. Being aware of this dynamic, the professional can handle the uncertainty generated by the non-directive way of working (see also Fiorini, 2010).

Group Dynamics

Without meaning to generalize the groups, and even less about the participants, I have observed that groups and their dynamics are developed in different steps, which can be called (1) start, (2) "fire test," (3) catharsis, and (4) dissolution. Instead of presenting the case of a specific group or participant, I will illustrate this group development, interspersing theoretical aspects and practical examples of different groups throughout.

Start of the group

I recommend to start the groups with collage technique because it is a slow, structured, and safe process, composed of different steps. This makes it controlled and controllable. First, the recycled material, that is the magazines, newspapers, brochures, photos, etc., has to be looked over. Then, a decision has to be made regarding what images will be worked with. Afterwards, these images will need to be cut out in order to compose a new image from the existing ones—in fact, this is the most significant step of the collage. As a last step, the images are fixed to a surface—often paper—with glue. In the end, more elements can be added, using pencils, markers, crayons, etcetera (Marxen, 2011; Hyland Moon, 2010; Linesch, 1988).

In this way, the assimilation of the concept of process begins, since the collage invites a gradual reorganization of the images taken from the real world (Aragon, 2001). It also offers the possibility of recomposing narratives, resignifying inner material by recomposing tangible ("outer") materials that allow a "symbolic layering of inner experience, images, emotions, thoughts, and ideas" (Hyland Moon, 2010, pp. 18–19, referring to Malchiodi, 2002). Simultaneously, collage allows us to combine supposedly "distant" materials, i.e. from different contexts or previous life phases, with the present and can draw links between present attitudes and their origins. These outcomes can themselves be worked upon and shaped in order to pave the way for new perspectives and outlooks.

In this context, it is also worth considering some reflections of contemporary art theory about collage. Didi-Huberman (2018) has dedicated almost an entire book to the "epic distancing" effect elaborated by Bertolt Brecht both in his Epic Theater (1963/2014) and in "real" art collages (very much used in his *Work Journals*, Brecht, 1972/1993). For Brecht, collage formed part of his holistic thinking about the idea of a work being in constant progress;

this idea is composed of processes of reflection, imagination, seeking, and finding, respectively. Brecht found in the heterogeneity of cutting and gluing "the body and flow of his associative thinking" (Didi-Huberman, 2018, p. 17). For the playwright, collage was a question of destroying and recomposing, an interruption of the continuity of official narratives and authorized narrations. This method facilitates a glimpse of displacement, discontinuity, delay, an insight into differences, incoherencies, the disorder of the world with its contradictions—in short, a critical view of historicity. Collage allowed him to transform tangible and mental material which themselves produced new ideas, associations, and thoughts. Collage has a distancing effect because it creates intervals where unity is seen, recompositions forge new adjunctions. This technique operates through a double optic: The familiar is deconstructed and the uncanny appears, which then becomes comprehensible, understood in a new way, in the form of a renovated unity of seemingly contradictory terms. A new comprehension beyond the officially approved facts is possible, as is an insight into pre and post-history. It deconstructs chronology in favor of anachronism. It is consistent with the faculty of the arts for bridging supposed opposites that would be unbearable for logical thinking (Fiorini, 2010). Art does not have to show facts as if they were evident but rather comprehensible although still not fully understood (Didi-Huberman, 2018).

Not in vain, Brecht's most important contributions "on distancing date from his years in exile, as though his aesthetic position on strangeness/foreignness, on the uncanny, went together with his situation as a foreigner in political exile" (Didi-Huberman, 2018, p. 62). The emigrant and exiled finds themselves in the perfect condition for the distanced view and the transformation of authorized life versions. Their position renders the recomposition of narratives almost inevitable since they have been obliged to overstep frontiers. Collage is a perfect artistic means for the composition of alternative narratives.

Concurrently, collage can alleviate anxieties about producing aesthetically correct images, since the images themselves pre-exist and do "not require the production of original imagery or mastery of difficult skills" (Hyland Moon, 2010, p. 18, with further references; also Marxen, 2011; Linesch, 1988). This is of great value in the described adolescence context, since in the first phase, it is necessary to avoid early frustrations amongst participants with more manageable processes such as collage.

Finally, this technique "offers the opportunity to engage with cultural messages and stereotypes conveyed through mass media," a privileged aspect in the context of multiculturalism. Of course, the art therapist is responsible for providing an appropriate choice of materials—such as newspapers, magazines, journals, and maps—that includes different minorities, persons, varieties of people from different places, backgrounds, social classes, gender, etc. (Hyland Moon, 2010, p. 19; Matto, 1997). In the selection of recycled materials for the collage, it is also important to take into account the interests of young people with regard to music, sports, clothing, and, in general, youth cultures.

Regarding additional materials needed for the collaging process, I recommend avoiding the use of craft knives, fine-tipped scissors, or glue with solvents; that is, all those materials that might be turned into weapons. To expand the works during the collaging phase, pencils, colored pencils, rubbers, rulers, sharpeners, thin and thick markers, as well as crayons and pastels can be offered. As a support, cardboard and sheets of different sizes, colors, and textures of paper should be supplied.

In my experience, the mentioned adolescents expressed on numerous occasions the need to confirm or to challenge boundaries, both in verbal and behavioral ways, as well as on an artistic level. For the latter, materials that are useful are those that allow participants to trace marked contours, such as charcoal and thick markers (Marxen, 2011). Often, in the first sessions, instead of or in addition to completing the collages, teens want to decorate their portfolios with black markers and other materials.

Normally, these are teens who, at least at the beginning of the activity, need some structure. For this reason, it is convenient to start with some themes and a series of techniques that serve as a structure onto which they can hold. These themes should be sufficiently open to offer some freedom and individuality. For example, as a first topic, I propose participants to create a collage with images that attract them, that they like, and with which they identify. In this context, I favor starting with topics of these characteristics and further structuring the activity through techniques and materials, to gradually achieve a less directive group dynamic until eventually arriving at a non-directive dynamic.

In the first session, the group leader introduces themselves and explains in detail the process and objectives of the activity: Regarding the work, no notes will be given,[2] the expression will be valued, but there will be no judgments. Typically, the participants will have already heard about the activity by the older students, via an institutional tradition whereby one group informs its successor about the activity. As this information often reaches novices in the form of rumors, it is important for the group leader to clearly explain the principles of the activity themselves: the boundaries, the materials, the storage of the portfolios with the works, the duration of the sessions, and the objectives of the activity itself. It is also essential that youth are allowed to not participate if it is done in a peaceful manner and that there is no obligation to finish a work, with options to leave it unfinished in the folder or to complete it later, if it is desired. In the beginning, it is important to respect possible ambivalence shown by youth to the activity, including its rejection, which is to be interpreted at a later stage. These expectations sometimes clash with other norms of the institution and thus bare repeating at the start.

The first sessions are ultimately decisive, since they can be treated as repetition of prior attempts at affectionate relationships in early childhood that can be used therapeutically. These beginnings require from the professional an active waiting capacity and an adequate distance-closeness proximity regulation. This means on the one hand not to impose one's ideas, judgments or statements. On the other hand, it requires an empathic *being with* the participants. For this attitude, the professional's own previous psychotherapy is crucial. Also, one must know how to intervene in different levels: at the relational level and at the medial level, that means in the artistic work itself, or in both, according to what the situation requires (Domma, 1999).

In this first phase, sometimes, the teenagers choose from the magazines images of extreme violence, produce them, or manipulate preexisting ones toward this end. Often, the violence is praised by peers and taken as an example to follow. In these situations, the ideas of aesthetic countertransference are relevant. Obviously, the images have an effect on the professional, on the author, and on the other participants. The concept of countertransference gives account of the effect the artwork produced by the client has on the therapist and the other group members. It is the therapist's responsibility to become aware of their aesthetic feelings and reactions in order to analyze but never to act them out with the client. At the point of the violent images, the worst reaction on the part of the group leader would be to scandalize the issue. If the situation allows it, and if there is enough familiarity in and with the group, it is convenient to elaborate this violence verbally or symbolically, modifying, expanding, or continuing the subject with the same image or with others (Marxen, 2011). It is worth bearing in mind that the supposed brutality in this context is a mechanism in which the inner suffering and despair are expelled outward in order to feel the relief of projecting it towards the external world instead of bearing it inside. The psychopathic opposite would be to feel pleasure and get positively stimulated with the violent images, something I have hardly ever observed in the UEC setting.

Equally frequent are the images linked to drug addiction, specifically joints. In these cases, the joints appear in the paintings as a support, which usually has to do with the consumption habits of the teens, considering drugs exist as a sustaining pillar in their lives. In this context, they usually ask or question the professional about their own habits around drug addiction. Here, the art therapist must demonstrate in the long term—that is, during the course—that they have resources, strength, and satisfaction at work that precludes the consummation of any drugs. This is because behind these repeated questions on the part of the teens are the doubts of how to live without drugs and corresponding resource, something that perhaps they do not know about from their own backgrounds (Figure 2.3).

At the beginning of the groups, some participants may show manifestations of a negative transference, to the extent of feeling distrust towards the professional adult. This should not be considered strange if we take into account once again the family background and the past schooling of the children: In the vast majority of cases, they did not have stable adults who would sympathize with them or demonstrate a certain fondness for them. In this sense, it is beneficial that the children express this negative transference towards the professional. To address this lack of confidence in a long process, the activity must have enough months to last. By this, I mean that the dynamics require

Figure 2.3 Art therapy practice, special school unit, UEC, Barcelona, 2009.

that the group must be long enough to initially experience negative transference and then a corrective attachment relationship with the professional. For this purpose, it should have a duration of at least six months, with one session per week.

In one of my groups, e.g., a boy barely participated in the initial phase of collages or other works on paper; he did not decorate his folder either. Instead, he created what I described as "ephemeral art" on the blackboard that was in the classroom. At the beginning, he did not know this concept, but then, after my explanation, he said: "Yes! Exactly, to be able to erase it, so that no one is left with this." Of course, I did not object to that. He continued to draw on the board and I limited myself to commenting that such art would always be ephemeral, unless it was documented with a camera. "If you take a picture of my work with your camera, I'll kill you!" he answered. I replied that I would never take a picture without prior permission from the author. A few months passed until I was able to establish a relationship of minimum confidence. In the end, this was possible thanks to what Aichhorn has called "the cure in transference" (1965) and what I would call an "art therapy of attitudes" (Marxen, 2011). During the process, he was able to perceive little by little, through my attitude, that I respected him and also his artwork. Thus, he was able to slowly lessen his distrust, without losing it altogether. When the course and the group had finished, he still had one year left in the institution, so that sometimes I crossed paths with him when I was with groups. Even then, I was not exempted from proving my reliability: "Show me my work x and my work y. Surely they are not there and you have thrown them away!" Here we see further proof of the importance of safe storage of the works: I could show him his works that were three-dimensional and, while difficult to keep, were in good condition. "You know what?" he told me. "Now I can tell you: in the end I had a great time in the group, with you."

In this way, the attitude of the professional during the first phase of a group is very important, as they must have enough personal strength to not be provoked by the teens and their rejections. Simultaneously, they must show a real interest in the participants, a lot of empathy, and an attitude that lacks prejudice. Otherwise, young people will act immediately against them, since they detect adult failures and weak points immediately. A good dose of humor and calm serenity is always advantageous. Critically, a positive beginning helps the participants to become familiar with the activity and with the group leader.

Independent of the techniques, it is essential in working with uprooted young people to offer them a means to build a narrative of their experiences, be it through art, music,[3] writing, or oral history. Moreover, it is about them finding a feeling of continuity within these activities, which translates in art therapy to the safe storage of portfolios with works and materials.

Fire Test and Catharsis

The second and third phases tend to be the most critical, because that is when the adolescents will try with all their strength to push boundaries and challenge the resistance of the professional, who must face frequent humiliations, criticisms, and intimidations. Attending consistent personal therapy, as well as good supervision, is essential to be able to face these phases. The participants usually submit the adult to several tests, which I will call "fire test," to see if the professional will resist or not; if they can kick them out or not. Dodging the negative transferor prohibiting it would be counterproductive; on the contrary, it must be produced, so that it can be worked upon. The ideas of Winnicott (1984) on the importance of holding among teens with alleged antisocial tendencies are relevant. If the work is successful, the participants will try to recover the holding that they were given in childhood and adolescence, testing the boundaries to the maximum to provoke an adult reaction. This has as a consequence, a certain exhaustion of the professional, since they carry out the educational work in a way that caregivers, in their time and often the result of belonging to an extremely disadvantaged social group, have not been able to fulfill (Menzen, 1999). This can translate, e.g., into a considerable physical fatigue of the therapist once a group session ends.

In these two phases, verbal violence is almost the order of the day. Physical violence, on the other hand, would be more of an exception and cannot be allowed. One of the responsibilities of the facilitator is to set boundaries to avoid physical violence, so that the group engages in a constructive and safe experience for adolescents. As for the verbal violence towards the professional, in the first two phases, it is about taking it to a certain point, making it clear that one does not allow oneself to be frightened by it. Then, if it is appropriate, one should pause to show the teens the impact of their violence and their humiliations, e.g., by saying: "How would you feel if you were to be received early in the morning with these words?" Again, the advantage of working with art lies in the opportunity to approach subjects of violence in a symbolic and non-direct way. A good solution for establishing a non-violent setting is to emphasize respect towards the work of the other, that is, to prohibit that one mocks or destroys the work of others, explaining that all works are accepted here. This is much less direct than stressing the non-violence against each other, something frequently ridiculed by the participating adolescents.

Now, with regard to violence in relation to adolescence in general, it is good to consider the social context of youth. In this sense, violence can meet the "very deep emotional needs of both adolescents and society" (Quaglia, 2001; p. 104; translated from Spanish). A critical attitude must be adopted so as not to mix or associate violence and crime with adolescence (Fize, 2007). For the same reason, it is advisable to know how to discriminate what violence is being talked about in societies that allow extreme social exclusion situations to occur as well as difficulties in accessing an adequate living and the working world, and where certain adults, professionals, politicians, and relatives abuse their power over young people (Fize, 2007).

Before classifying the adolescents' acts as violent, it must be kept in mind that users of the UEC repeatedly tend to act before reflecting, sometimes because of a low frustration tolerance that prevents them from working at a slower pace and from asking questions verbally. According to Aichhorn (1965), they often follow the principle of pleasure rather than the principle of reality. That is the reason why it is difficult for them to understand that by renouncing immediate pleasure or relief, they can later achieve a more prolonged pleasure. Regarding symbolization, "we enter a field where the relationship with the word is complicated; we are before patients [participants] who come to show us what makes them act" (D'Angelo, 2000, p. 86; translated from Spanish). Blos (1979) speaks of a gestural communication instead of a linguistic one. It is a defense mechanism that protects the ego from the elaboration of a conflict that lies in the action with the external world. Now, according to Freud, *agieren* is also a way of repeating the repressed, not as a memory but as an action (Freud according to D'Angelo, 2000). D'Angelo (idem: p. 87) concludes that these people "start from the answer, not the question; especially from the response that ensures the consistency of the Other..." So, we return to the importance of the holding described by Winnicott (1984) and experienced by the adolescents through the adults' reaction.

In any case, the preference for action over the verbal articulation is selective and no longer constitutes a generalized language or thought disorder (Blos, 1979). It should not even be considered that all children with disruptive behavior have a psychological problem; sometimes they simply lack a part of the corresponding social education, so they find it difficult to renounce instantaneous satisfactions.

Nor do I recommend to consider these forms of *agieren* exclusively in a negative way. It is a way of communication that can reach a high degree of creativity and humor. Sometimes this communication comes to acquire artistic functions, if art is understood as the deconstruction of conventional forms to create new ones (Fiorini, 2010), and, also, the art as a reaction to what the teens have previously lived.[4]

In respect to materials, in the second and third phases, we shift from collage to painting. The latter material offers less control and, at the same time, is more regressive. It is essential to offer it in small amounts, since a problem in these groups is usually the difficulty to find the adequate measures and to respect the limits and boundaries. I prefer to offer only the primary colors, in addition to white and black. All other colors are mixed, which also extends the learning process.

As for the infrastructure, it is slightly more complicated with paint because it needs to dry and cannot be stored as easily or compactly as dry media. That is why we need a safe space where the works can dry without being exposed to the gaze of other people. Painting can be used to mark the boundaries at the pictorial level (Figure 2.4).

In this sense, one participant outlined all the contours of his picture with strong red lines. In his case, a confusion with boundaries could be observed to the extent that he considered me more of a friend than a professional. Sometimes these attitudes are mixed with eroticism and seduction, which turns the professional into an object to seduce. Obviously, this confusion must be corrected, since a transference position of accomplice complicates the intervention and the respect of the professional (Rassial, according to Hartmann, 2000b).

Figure 2.4 Art therapy practice, special school unit, UEC, Barcelona, 2006.

It has happened that the participants paint in such a way that they superimpose several layers of paint on the same sheet, mixing all the colors they have with their disposal, which normally results in a brown tone. As a consequence, these works are easily associated with anal aspects. The texture of the material can also work to intensify this sensation. It is helpful to set limits before the process becomes too destructive or defense mechanisms are too quickly dismantled, since in these situations they find quick parallels with moments of despair in their lives. However, in some cases, with these "anal" works, they have been able to develop quite constructive techniques with which, afterwards, they have given rise to works of interesting color combinations and contents.

A theme to work with painting can be the city and subjects related to the urban context. In several groups, the participants associated their urban life directly with "excrement." A potential solution can be found in painted elements of the countryside or of an excursion or a trip from the city to a rural setting. With this theme, they could deepen on a pictorial and verbal-level engagement with their multiple social problems, located mainly in the same urban environment.

Dissolution

After getting familiar with painting, we then move on to clay and three-dimensional work. Frequently, the adolescents ask for new materials, with more variety, quantity, and better quality, thus transferring their real-life shortcomings to the art materials.

I recommend working with clay towards the last sessions, when the participants already know the activity and the adult professional. Clay is a material that has no structure by itself; it is the participant who has to give it structure. This might be translated for some into a lack of control and helplessness. In the context of the UEC, this is often contested by manic defenses that translate into actions such as throwing the clay on the ground, to peers, to the ceiling, to the wall, etc. More often, however, this material tends to be quite attractive for teenagers. In addition, it is an essential step before arriving at the expanded three-dimensional work, which includes clay, plasticine, wire, belts, yarns, and different three-dimensional recycled materials, such as boxes and tubes, among others.

It is with these materials, in the last phase, with which a dissolution and a change from a negative to a positive transfer is usually achieved. Occasionally, the teens who were the most reluctant in the beginning now show the greatest interest in linking themselves to the activity and the professional. For clay, I propose themes such as the production of objects that have some utility and attractiveness for the adolescents, e.g., the production of ashtrays and key rings (Domma, 1999), since the use of "functional ceramics" allows defenses to manifest for people who do not want to delve too deeply into their internal thoughts (Dannecker, 1999). At the end, group work can be proposed such as shaping a city with parks, houses, cars, people, lampposts, walkers, etc., so that each participant can contribute one or several elements.

In almost all groups, I have been fascinated by the skills shown by the teens in this last phase. They know how to recycle and take advantage of the most basic materials to convert them into furniture, carpets, televisions, staircases, gardens for their models of houses, rooms, lots or parks. This is even more surprising when one considers that, at first, their demands were more consumption driven. In fact, I have seen in these groups models of a sophistication that would allow participants to access a college of art and design. Often, the teens themselves sprout their ability. They had almost never considered, e.g., the possibility of following professional training in art or design, among other reasons because they have always been labeled as failures. Also social barriers play against them. In this respect, a teen told me that art was only for "the posh and fancy." This is further proof of the need to redefine art in social terms and to lower it from its elitist platform, as proposed by the MACBA through the described line of work.

Yet, it is frustrating to sometime see teens who are just unable to feel successful. This happens frequently because they have been so constantly programmed and labeled as failures that they self-fulfill the label, in a way of self-labeling (Bergalli, 1980; Matza, 1969; Becker, 1963/1997). On one occasion, a participant used to destroy his excellent drawings, paintings, and models, saying that all of it is "a shit." This self-evaluation was not influenced by the fact that his mates asked him for copies, liking his artworks so much. Here, the destruction shows a very low self-esteem, not congruent with reality at all. The message and label of failure have been so profoundly ingested that it is difficult to change in a one-course-activity. In order to de-label and to avoid re-labeling, the art therapist should not just tell but show with their attitude that they do appreciate the artwork; for example, eventually retrieving it from the trash.[5]

In psychoanalytic terms and according to Lacan, it is a question of breaking up the imaginary identification with the group of counterparts,[6] all segregated in the group of one determined symptom (here: carriers of social and educational failures in the UEC). This segregation leads to an identification with that symptom. The supposed homogeneity of the group is also imaginary. The analytical task is not to reinforce this identification but the opposite: to make the particularity of each subjectivity unfold. It is a question of freeing the subject of this imaginary homogeneity and to re-activate its position of alterity. Finally, a different relationship with the real in Lacanian terms is possible. That means to find a different way to encounter what seems impossible or difficult to bear and to symbolize (Recalcati, 2007).

With everything in the last phase, the concentration potential of the teens increases in an almost magical way. Whereas before it was difficult for them to dedicate 40 minutes to artistic work (and any other activity at school), now they find it easy to work for 60 minutes without appreciating the passage of time, sometimes wanting to continue for longer. In my opinion, it is useful to give them the opportunity to work with the new ambition and concentration for a longer time and not to insist on the fixed schedule, if the infrastructure of the institution allows it.

In their educational institutions, many teachers and educators had tried to refer the mentioned adolescents to mental health institutions for treatments and medications according to the supposed Attention Deficit Hyperactivity Disorder (ADHD). The adolescents' very strong resistance towards mental health treatments has already been stressed as a possible intuition of refusing to be institutionalized by the dominant medical discourse.[7] Likewise, it is a fact that after one school-term of the described art therapy process and without any medication, their attention does not show any deficit or dysfunction (see for the deconstruction of the ADHD and a very critical view on overmedication Valverde Eizaguirre, 2015; Knobel Freud, 2013; Horwitz, 2010).

As will be explained in the next chapter, the art therapy practice should be freed from the dominant discourse, of hegemony, and its penetration in Gramsci's sense: This means, e.g., not to accept uncritically the dominant medical discourse and its diagnosis (i.e. the ADHD; Marxen & Greteman, 2019).

Obviously, the sophisticated three-dimensional models of the last phase in art therapy symbolize the holding that we may have exonerated at those moments. One could speak of a "architecture-therapy." In this sense, one participant created a loft with a very sophisticated interior design. Two others elaborated a duplex with terraces and plants, where details such as stairs, chairs, televisions, and other furniture, including the blanket and cushion for the bed, were not lacking. In another group, a boy designed a one-storied park with grass, a merry-go-round, animals, and a cafe with terrace, tables, and chairs, saying: "Here in this park, we can spend a good time on Sunday."

At the verbal level, a change towards dissolution or improvement can be observed at the end of the work with clay, when the teens begin to insistently ask about the therapist's personal life in a non-derogatory way. Of course, it would not be beneficial here to reveal everything about private life, and even less the intimate aspects, but I recommend interpreting this insistence with the interest that adolescents, in these moments, are developing what life can be beyond the social exclusion, about which they do not know much. It can also be a sign that they have begun to take this adult seriously and trust them, because they have demonstrated strength, loyalty, and above all, empathy. At this moment, they begin to understand the impending separation with the therapist, perceiving them as a person who lives in a world outside their own. This aspect is very important for those children who have previously had difficulties with boundaries, in the sense of considering the therapist as one of their own.

Another index for change can be seen when the teens want to proudly show their work to respected educators. This last phase can be extremely enriching, both for teens and adults, since the positive aspects of the adolescents manifested in qualities such as freshness, agility, humor, their technical skills with art, their pleasure and, finally, their health.

At that moment, they can demonstrate their desire to prolong the activity beyond the span of the group and to continue the next course. According to my experience and after prolonged conversation with some groups, I do not recommend giving in to those desires. The extension does not suspend the need to confront at some point the termination. I suggest finishing on the set dates and with the extended three-dimensional work, which in my case has almost always coincided with the enthusiasm of the teens. By this phase, they have understood that they can gain strength through the introjection of a new good experience in form of completing successful work—both at a creative level and at an emotional level. Of course, the termination must be announced repeatedly and be prepared in advance, putting emphasis on the positive experience that always remains "inside one," as a memory nobody can take away.

In order to achieve the resolution, the concept of "the cure in transference" of Aichhorn (1965) becomes relevant again, which implies a harsh process, not only for the professionals but also for the participants, since before dissolution, they must face hard and violent moments and processes where perhaps the affect attunements of early childhood are repeated, with all its problems and associated shortcomings (Stern, according to Domma, 1999).

Concluding Remarks About the Practice

Working with adolescents with behavioral problems, there are multiple advantages of art therapy that have been studied by several authors (Marxen, 2016, 2011, 2009; Camilleri, 2007; Sudres, 2005; Hampe et al., 1999; Riley, 1999; Kramer, 1998, 1993, 1958; Linesch, 1988). The issues of social behavior, coexistence, and communication can be addressed indirectly through the creative process, since it is necessary for participants in groups to share space, materials, adult attention, and respect the works of others. In addition, the creative process is an appropriate vehicle to address frustration tolerance, something that tends to be low among this group of young people. Creative activities require many decisions at the cognitive level and can lead to some frustration if the result does not match the initial idea and expectations. The concept of process has to be internalized, as opposed to one of magical solutions. All these issues are worked on a symbolic level, provided the adolescent has established a relationship of trust with the art therapist, who must maintain an empathic listening space and therapeutic holding, in the sense of the potential space described by Winnicott (1971). It allows creative play, wherein the participants can pass from action to symbolization and reflection (Domma, 1999). Again, we must bear in mind that the teens, in most cases, have not had this experience during their childhood.

In this potential space, artistic expression reaches a personal meaning and a form of constructive communication. Making art in this context helps the participants control their possible aggressive feelings because they can be converted into a form that in turn can be developed, transformed, changed, and stored in a secure environment. The impulses can be moderated and conflicts are given a form, so that the participant experiences how they can control their aggressions through symbolization. Aggressions can be expressed and transformed without this having effects in and for the real world. I recommend performing the interpretations from the creative process and its possible challenges, not regarding the finished works and even less about the participants' personalities.

In an adequate setting of holding, the activity also helps to encourage creativity and increase self-esteem. I have already referred, in this sense, to the amazing talents shown by some of the teens.

Otherwise, if a secure and empathetic environment is not created, the activity quickly becomes destructive. It would be a mistake to maintain the illusion that art itself is therapeutic, since it cannot be assumed that they use the materials constructively by default. On the contrary, especially at the beginning, there are frequent attempts to avoid or boycott the activity through various forms of aggression, including active or passive destruction (Bröcher, according to Domma, 1999).

However, the ideas of Edith Kramer on sublimation are relevant: Art therapy or art workshops offer a concrete resource to stimulate and amplify the capacity of sublimation. Aggressive impulses are channeled into the creative process and sublimated (Klosinski, 1999; Kramer, 1998, 1993, 1958). This is a resource that verbal therapy or analysis does not count (Hartmann, 2000a). It's exciting to see the teens take a step from hands that destroy to hands that produce and create. In some cases, teens adhere to the artistic activity in such a way that they undertake a creative process of their own outside the institution. This has been considered in art therapy to be a step of the process of becoming independent from the therapist (see the ideas of Naumburg in this regard, 1980).

After having developed the groups for eight consecutive courses at the UEC and the public high school, I can conclude that the art workshops have been a resource highly valued both by the staff of the institutions and by the teens themselves. Thus, every year, many students who do not participate in the groups wish to be to such a degree that they claim to be accepted in the art groups in the following year.

In summary, MACBA financed and supported services for certain adolescents who preferred not to use mental health services. The museum offered a resource beyond those offered in the fields of Health and Education. Of course, both programs, the one carried out by Montse Rodríguez and Eva Marxen, were part of the museum's policies to expand its functions and reconsider art in a social and political way. The objective of the museum was not limited to the production of exhibitions, but instead extended to offer different types of services aimed at a variety of potential users.

Starting from these museum policies, we determined to conduct a contemporary rereading of aesthetic ideas as well as a rupture with the margins established for and by the arts to undo its limits and act on their tensions: between art and politics, between art and community, between art and clinic.

Research and Evaluation

Both programs, the Lacanian psychoanalysis applied to the museum and the art therapy of a psychoanalytical orientation and an anthropological understanding, were finished off in the MACBA museum with a research seminar *Alleged opposites: On the public sphere, art and the clinic. A research working group based on a critique of the analytical and art-therapeutic devices implemented at MACBA since 2002* (2012–2013; https://www.MACBA.cat/en/alleged-opposites).

Before describing the details and objectives of the seminar, it is important to stress that both practices were and are not intended for exhibition. Along with the museum's policies, one of the main goals was to facilitate a work of subjectivity, going "beyond the regime of visibility, whose paradigm is the exhibition" (Ribalta, 2004, p. 9, above). "An exhibition space," however, "converts practices into objects." There is a contradiction between "antagonistic, process-based and experimental practices that seek to explode the established institutional frameworks and their implicit disciplinary divisions—that is, between subjective forms of appropriation and practice of methods and artistic knowledge and the exhibitionary-institutional monumentalisation of these practices" (Ribalta, 2010, pp. 254–255).

The processes, to be described as subjective and which, by intention, cannot be represented, will become fossilized or sterilized by the "institutional exhibitionary framework." Therefore, it is about breaking the logic of "sovereign, disciplinary and liberal devices of power" and questioning the presentation in exhibitions as "when the artistic project is valorized in our society" (Holmes, 2006, pp. 430, 412). And it is exactly this logic in which the practices carried out by Marxen and Rodríguez are located.

According to Ribalta (2010, p. 229), who initiated the practices, "the museum has to accommodate different and equal uses for these different publics, which are neither limited to the exhibition space nor excessively determined by the imperative of visibility." It was about finding

> a space for art that temporarily suspends pre-constituted institutional autonomy and investigates new forms of interaction with the social, though without seeking to overstage this process. We saw the museum as a space for this experimentation, not solely or principally to exhibit it. We tried to find ways in which art could make a significant contribution, based on its specificity, to a multiplication of public spheres.
>
> (ibid., p. 252)

What he aspired to develop was a different relationality, "another relationality," oblivious to charitable or capitalist instrumentalizations, at the same time with a critical analysis of everything that implies "the relational." The intention was to go beyond a "communitarianism" that annulled "the positions of differentiation and the visualization of antagonism," as well as the conflict with the other and "the potential for difference of the artistic space."

Furthermore, it implied a rejection of the "relational aesthetic" developed by Bourriaud (1998), since this is understood as "a perverse objectification of both political activism and the new forms of immaterial, affective, communicative and relational production of post-Fordism;" in short, an aestheticization of social processes, imposing the expository or even a marketing operation aimed at entertaining and seducing customers (García Canclini, 2014; Ribalta, 2010, pp. 251, 253).

This is even more evident when considering the contemporary instrumentalization of the arts, whether of a capitalistic or institutional nature. In the former case, publicity and symbolic capital are accumulated in the form of "good press" accrued to the sponsor; in the latter case, public acknowledgment of the institution is the intention, marketing supposedly creative activities in an effort to distract from its reactionary institutionality, such as with detention centers and jails. Both of these instrumentalizations usually follow capitalist logic by overvaluing the final, tangible result, as well as its subsequent commodification. The subjective process, however, requires privacy and intimacy beyond public exposure. As such, resistance against these exhibitionary instrumentalization dynamics is necessary (Marxen, 2018; Bourdieu & Haacke 1995).

Although coming from different professional fields, all three professionals implied (Rodríguez as a Lacanian psychoanalyst, Ribalta as MACBA's public program director, and Marxen as an anthropologist and art therapist) agreed on the non-exhibition principle as an institutional critique and resistance against the commodification of subjectivity.

Yet, starting in 2009/2010, already with Ribalta's successors Marta García and Yaiza Hernández, the idea was intensified to reflect publicly on the practice, which by then in its eighth year. Much experience, observations, and critiques had been developed by then that could be of good use for institutions, professionals, and other people. Additionally, both practices had been financed mainly by public money through the museum's public funding at the time. So, the idea was also to find a way to return our gained knowledge to the public.

Since then, the museum has undergone a massive privatization process. Under Borja's follower, Bartomeu Marí (2008–2015), MACBA has resumed the neoliberal and taming model (Mahony, 2016 and my own observations). This process, together with a complete change of direction and abandonment of MACBA's previous policies, led to the end of the practices in 2011. During this time, it diminished significantly the budget of a previously very ambitious research seminar proposal, e.g., funding to bring relevant guest speakers from abroad was completely cut.

Yet, we could organize a seminar of nine sessions, each of two hours. The seminar was at a very affordable price: 20 euros all sessions included and a discount for students and the unemployed of ten euros. The interest was so huge that we had to operate with a waiting list.

The official Internet presentation of the seminar (still available at: http://www.MACBA.cat/en/alleged-opposites) was preceded by internal working documents elaborated by Marxen and Rodríguez (2009–2012), such as the following:

> In 2002, the MACBA launched a clinical device reflecting on artistic productions and developed by professionals in the psychoanalytic, art-therapeutic, and anthropological fields. This clinic has been developed for ten years in an urban and public space, the MACBA, which does not belong to the field of mental health. From this transgressive drift emerges the need to question a practice that comes from the exercise of a "poetic-artistic logic" and a deconstruction-reconstruction on an institutional level (from the clinic to the artistic institution).
>
> The foundation of this project is to investigate the processes of construction of the image and the social formations that come from these applications.
>
> The purpose of our practice was to tap into the insight that comes from the fields of Lacanian psychoanalysis, related aesthetic studies, and the analysis of the mechanisms of language production (Rodríguez's program). Another opening takes place from a psychoanalytically oriented art therapy work that, with an anthropological understanding, aims to sustain the ability of symbolization (Marxen's).
>
> Both applications pose forms of subjective appropriation of artistic methods and productions beyond the exhibition regime, and in both of them we find the encounter with the following: the use of visual productions, the development of work with collectives that the political places in the periphery of the social (mental patients and adolescents labeled as "in a social risk situation"), the rigorous continuity during a decade, the public institutional development of the work, and its definition as practices of subjectivity oriented by psychoanalytic discourses. In both cases, they have been developed at the institutional level in a museum of contemporary art; and it is about different forms of subjective appropriation of artistic methods, beyond the expository regime.
>
> We articulated this research with *Words in Progress*, by Ignasi Aballí, and *Works in Progress*, by Dora García. Both artists, internationally recognized, have participated in the seminar with their words and their work, illustrating the assumptions and asking the questions that formulate these clinical applications.
>
> We have constructed a new political and clinical knowledge, one in opposition to the dominant discourses of Psychiatry and Education; a discourse that excludes domination. Finally, we show the confluences that are currently constituted from the clinical, theoretical, and artistic knowledge.

Both Rodríguez and Marxen held four consecutive sessions about their practices after having started with one common introduction. The artist invited by Rodríguez was Ignasi Aballí, while Marxen hosted Dora García. Both speakers are considered representative for the practices of their respective hosts. Furthermore, the Lacanian psychoanalyst Shula Eldar participated in Rodríguez's part and activist-writer "Bifo" (Franco Berardi) in Marxen's.

Several publications have resulted from the decade of practice and the research seminar, most notably Rodríguez's book *Esquizofrenias y otros hechos de lenguaje. De la clínica analítica del MACBA (2002–2013)* [Schizophrenia and other facts of language. About the analytical MACBA clinic (2002–2013)] and the present book by Marxen (see also the related articles by Marxen & Greteman, 2019; Marxen, 2018, 2016; Sajnani et al., 2017).

Rodríguez carried out the first part, entitled *Political Uses of Aesthetics. A Psychoanalytic Application with Subjects Diagnosed with Serious Mental Pathologies*. It dealt with the research on the mechanics of language creation processes, the consistency of artistic production and the logic of underlying social ties, arising from psychoanalytic practice with clients of mental health centers (2002–2011).

Her seminar part consisted of the following agenda:

1 Presentation of the device and related bibliography to work with the following pairs of concepts: Political-clinical; use/purpose-meaning; production-device; ethics-aesthetics; body-language; subjectivity-discourse; desire-demand; psychoanalysis-psychotherapy; representation-denomination.
2 The MACBA research: An approach to the device concept: Agamben and Deleuze; readings of Foucault and Lacan; research protocol and its documentation; transmission and use of the device; about the interval of artistic formations and the work processes with people who are clients of the mental health centers; the subject as an institutional production; subjectifying the production, current conditions of the emergence of subjective productions. Clinical examples.
3 Discourse and clinics today: Artistic devices; psychotherapies and psychoanalysis; ethics and politics of otherness in the uses of the artistic, political, and clinical; the analytical space as verbal construction: Lacan's Joyce.
4 The consistency of the social bond effect of this practice and the mechanics of its construction: The naming and the invisible; towards a policy that works with the presence of the irreducible. Clinical notes. Identity-identification: A reading of "The Mirror Stage" by Lacan, with Shula Eldar.
5 The art work of Ignasi Aballí: Significant paths in his work with film screening, by and with Ignasi Aballí[8] (Figure 2.5).

The details of this theoretically dense work is beyond the scope of the present, see for the details of her work Rodríguez, 2015.

The second part of the seminar was entitled *Deconstructions and Renovations: Ar/ctivate Potentials* and held by Eva Marxen.

Her project was based on the use of art therapy with a psychoanalytic slant and an anthropological understanding. It began in 2003 at educational

Figure 2.5 Ignasi Aballí "Rétol," 2005; as exhibited during his show *0–24h* at the MACBA museum.

centers in the Raval with teenagers who had been labeled "at risk of social exclusion." The project started with the creation of the necessary conditions (Winnicott's "potential space") for subjective work, aimed at maintaining the capacity for symbolization.

The aim of *Deconstructions and Renovations* was to conceptualize and theorize the practices of the MACBA and to link them with the reflections and qualitative research of the social sciences. For this, a critical analysis as the basis of thought is considered crucial. It means to question the meta-narratives of the different disciplines, especially the ones related to the "psych disciplines": psychology, psychiatry, psychotherapy, as well as different forms of "therapy," and to locate them in their political context.

The social and political function of the museum and art are of interest. In the context of this seminar, it was analyzed how the museum is not only a producer of exhibitions but also how it can operate as a provider of different types of services aimed at different groups and people (Ribalta, 2004). With the last modality, it becomes a "nomadic museum." In short, it is about taking the museum beyond its walls and to address groups that do not necessarily go to a contemporary art museum.

The agenda was the following:

1 Psychoanalytic theories: Winnicott ("potential space"), Fiorini ("tertiary processes"), M. Klein ("play technique") and the use of their concepts in the "psych" practices of MACBA. Bion: The reaction of the establishment to the new idea; the communicability of the idea. Ethical and continuity issues.

These subjects are explained in detail in the present chapter and have partly been published in previous versions (Sajnani et al., 2017; Marxen, 2016, 2011, 2009).

2 Question of the "psych" theories; fostering narratives and agency; critical review of creative therapies; Labeling approach.

Parallel: projection of Dora García's videos: *Mad Marginal* series and others.

These topics are explained in detail in the second, third, and fourth chapter of the present book.

3 Institutional work with public and private institutions in Health, Education, Social Work, and the Penitentiary; the concept of the "total institution" by Goffman.

With Dora García.

This part is mainly elaborated in Chapter 6.

4 Ethnographic narratives and their use in the clinic: The reification and resistance approach; deconstructions of institutionalized lives and modifications of situations of domination, imposed by dominant identities, dominant subjectivations.

All these points are further explained in Chapters 3, 4, and 6.

5 The ethics of financing: the symbolic capital of Bourdieu and its relevance for the institutions of art and culture.

The relevance of symbolic capital for artistic practices is described in Chapters 2, 4, and 5.

As mentioned in the Internet text, "the objective of the seminar was to give certain visibility to both projects, question them, and theoretically adapt the results arising from these applications" (http://www.MACBA.cat/en/alleged-opposites). For this purpose, we opted methodologically to first lecture followed by open discussion, a co-construction of meaning with a free verbal association among all participants. Continuously, reference lists for readings were provided. In no way was the seminar meant to provide recipes or formulas of practices. We aimed at a transversal diffusion of our work, thus creating new works and situations. For this, we thwarted the totalizing and infantilizing "separation of production and reception and its multiply tiered hierarchy." The goal was to engage participants informed discussions and further responsible developments of the treated subjects of the seminar (Raunig, 2014, p. 12; referring to Brecht and Benjamin). The point is to explain what has been done and to verify the reality of these actions. As opposed to "the absorption of one mind by another, it allows their interrelation, at the same time maintaining the identity of each." The inclusion of the two artists and their works offers new insights "and expands our field of epistemological appropriations" (Borja-Villel, 2010, pp. 38–39).

As already said, both practices aimed at the work of subjectivity. The process and its results are not generalizable or quantifiable; in no way is it a question of establishing success criteria in advance. For this reason, qualitative research, as opposed to quantitative research, is definitely more appropriate.

In the museum context, a discourse of accessibility has been expanded in favor of increasing the amount of people to attract. This has been criticized within the function of control official institutions like museum exercise over the population (Bennett, 2009; Foucault, 2008, 2007). Accessibility is mainly measured in quantitative terms without considering the intensity or quality of the *experience* related to the museum as a cultural space. The experience is reduced to quantitatively registered visits and to a commodified spectacle as well as a consumption that neutralizes any critical thinking. The public is seen as a preconfigured, measurable, and finally controllable entity waiting to be addressed by activities predesigned for them. The result is "a progressive trivialization and impoverishment of experience, in which the critical, emancipatory dimension of cultural experience is eliminated in favour of false participation" (Ribalta, 2010, p. 230).[9]

In general, supposed "objective quantification" implies a "self-proclaimed objectivity of an institution," at the same time dismissing "any expression of the conflicting point of view or opinion as subjectivity (in other words sensibility, the qualitative and anything else that might be influenced by personal interests)" (Sayad, 2004, p. 197).

Yet, a form of resistance on an institutional level in ways of antagonistic, counter-hegemonic cultural practices against the neutralization and commodification of the cultural experience is possible (see Mouffe, 2017, 2012 and in Chapter 3). An extensive quote by Ribalta follows to give space for his own words:

> As opposed to the spectacularised, instrumentalised, trivial conception (governed by a soft model of participation based on statistics and consumption) …the MACBA's experience in the last decade [1999–2009] has represented a counter-model, characterised by a search for a critical anchorage in the tradition of modern art institutions. … [Its model constituted] a singular understanding of the museum as a space for debate and conflict, and a critical re-reading of the modern tradition that brings together artistic methods, social knowledge and action in the public sphere as a way of reinventing the field of art and according it a new significance and social legitimacy. This has been a fundamental aspect of the MACBA during this period: its capacity for institutional experimentation. The Museum has moved forward in this respect with no institutional interlocutor of the same characteristics at the international scale.… [For this purpose], the MACBA's activities (visibly materialised in the construction of a collection, a programme of temporary exhibitions and a programme of activities) have sought to promote a different narration of the art of the second half of the twentieth century. They also aim to table the relation between modern art and modernity by establishing Barcelona's peripheral role in the configuration of the dominant discourses about modern art. Inspired by feminist and post-colonial studies, this line of work was based on the recognition of the fact that forms of knowledge and power structures are totally inseparable. The concept of periphery

is semantically inverted here; rather than what might be considered a culturally subordinate position, it adopts a process of self-recognition and the construction of a viewpoint that challenges the central power/knowledge structures, in opposition to which it is defined. In this way, it seeks to identify and understand the specific cultural processes that make Barcelona a peripheral centre of modernity (and I stress the contradiction of 'peripheral centre').

(Ribalta, 2010, pp. 225–226)

Notes

1 The direct translation would be Chinatown. Yet, the reference of naming over a hundred years ago, was not so much China but "the remote other."

2 Instead of numeric marks and as mentioned above, at the end of the school year, one by one interviews of evaluation can be held with the participants.

3 There are interesting music therapy experiences in France where rap workshops are offered in jails for minors led by three professionals: a professional rap musician for the music know-how and two music therapists in charge of providing the therapeutic holding in Winnicott's sense. Furthermore, writing the texts is a narrative technique. At the same time, the rhythm of the music, "flow," represents a way to find a personal style and identity. The following combination of music and text serves to combat binary thinking. The recording of the music warrants the mentioned continuity of and through the created artworks (Aubert & Lehousse, 2007).

4 I owe this insight to the artist Hans Peter Feldmann in a personal conversation (2007).

5 This measure is of course not translatable to other contexts. For a psychotic client, the destruction of an artwork can be seen as a literal liberation of painful aspects of themselves. Retrieving the artwork from the bin would be experienced as extremely hurtful (see Killick, 2017, 1997; Schaverien, 1997).

6 Translation of the Lacanian term "semblable," a person perceived by the subject as similar, mainly in a visual sense (Evans, 1996; Lacan, 1938).

7 Fernand Deligny (2009, p. 102; translated by myself from Spanish) had carried out "anti-psychiatry" and "anti-pedagogy" projects with adolescents, most notably on the autistic spectrum. He described this resistance as

> at the margin of the *ideological apparatus of the State*: a small gang organizes itself the best they can and persists in spite of all, relatively freer in movements and intention than anything that is "institution"—infallibly ideological apparatus of the State.

8 For an excellent account for the relevance of Aballí's artwork in a Lacanian context (see Wajcman, 2006).

9 See Chapter 5 in how far this "false participation" hinders the creation of spaces of subjectivity.

References

Aberastury, A., & Knobel, M. (2001). *La adolescencia normal* [The normal adolescence]. Buenos Aires, Argentina: Paidós.

Achotegui, J. (2000). Los duelos de la migración: una aproximación psicopatológica y psicosocial [The migration loss: A psychopathological and psychosocial approach]. In E. Perdiguero, & J.M. Comelles (Eds.), *Medicina y cultura. Estudios entre la antropología y la medicina* [Medicine and culture. Studies between anthropology and medicine] (pp. 83–100). Barcelona, Spain: Edicions Bellaterra.

Aichhorn, A. (1965). *Wayward youth*. Crawfordsville, IN: Penguin Books.

Aragon, L. (2001). *Los colages* [The collages]. Madrid, Spain: Editorial Síntesis.

Aubert, J.P., & Lehousse, C. (2007). *A Rap and Slam workshop in prison*. Paper in the IX ECARTE Conference. Tallinn, Estonia: University of Tallinn.

Banal, I., & Canudas, J. (2005). *Hospital 106, 4t 1a. El lugar y el tiempo* [Hospital 106, 4t 1a. The place and the time]. Barcelona, Spain: Actar.

Becker, H. (1963/1997). *Outsiders: Studies in the sociology of deviance*. New York, NY: The Free Press.

Bennett, T. (2009). Museo [Museum]. In M.J. Borja-Villel, & J. Ribalta (Eds.), *Ideas concebidas* [Conceived ideas] (pp. 179–195). Barcelona, Spain: MACBA.

Bergalli, R. (1980). Origen de las teorías de la reacción social. Un aporte al análisis y crítica del labelling approach [Origin of the theories of social reaction. A contribution to the analysis and critique of the labelling approach]. *Papers: Revista de Sociologia* [Papers: Journal of Sociology], 13, 49–96.

Bion, W. (1995). *Attention and interpretation*. Ithaca, NY: Rowman & Littlefield Publishers.

Bion, W. (1991). *Experiences in groups*. London, UK and New York, NY: Routledge.

Blos, P. (1979). *The adolescent passage: Developmental issues*. New York, NY: International Universities Press.

Borja-Villel, M.J. (2010). The museum questioned. In: M. Borja-Villel, K. Cabañas, & J. Ribalta (Eds.), *Relational objects. MACBA collection 2002–2007* (pp. 19–39). Barcelona, Spain: MACBA.

Bourriaud, N. (1998). *Relational aesthetic*. Dijon, France: Les presses du réel.

Brecht, B. (1972/1993). *Arbeitsjournal*. Frankfurt, Germany: Suhrkamp [English version: (1993). *Journals 1934–1955. Diaries, letters and essays*. York, UK: Methuen Drama].

Brecht, B. (1963). *Schriften zum Theater*. Frankfurt: Suhrkamp. [English version: (2014). *Brecht on theatre*. London, UK: Bloomsbury Academic].

Bourdieu, P., & Haacke, H. (1995). *Free exchange*. Cambridge, UK: Polity Press.

Bröcher, J. (1999). Lebenswelt und Didaktik-Unterricht mit verhaltensauffälligen Jugendlichen auf der Basis ihrer (alltags-) ästhetischen Produktionen [Living environment and didactics lessons with behavior-sensitive young people based on their (everyday) aesthetic productions]. In R. Hampe, D. Ritschl, & G. Waser (Eds.), *Kunst, Gestaltung und Therapie mit Kindern und Jugendlichen* [Art, creation, and therapy with children and adolescents] (pp. 370–379). Bremen, Germany: University of Bremen.

Camilleri, V.A. (Ed.). (2007). *Healing the inner city child. Creative arts therapies with at-risk youth*. London, UK and Philadelphia, PA: Jessica Kingsley Publishers.

Case, C., & Dalley, T. (2014). *The handbook of art therapy*. London, UK and New York, NY: Routledge.

Case, C., & Dalley, T. (Eds.). (1999). *Working with children in art therapy*. London, UK and New York, NY: Routledge.

D'Angelo, M. (2000). Caso clínico. Límites de una intervención [Clinical case. Limits of an intervention]. In A. Hartmann, C.T. Quaglia, & J. Kuffer (Eds.), *Adolescencia: una ocasión para el psicoanálisis* [Adolescence: An occasion for psychoanalysis] (pp. 81–95). Buenos Aires, Argentina: Miño y Dávila editores.

Dannecker, K. (1999). Horror in der Kunst-Horror Vacui? Angst in der Kunst von Kindern und Jugendlichen [Horror in art - horror vacui? Anxiety in the art of children and adolescents]. In R. Hampe, D. Ritschl, & G. Waser (Eds.), *Kunst, Gestaltung und Therapie mit Kindern und Jugendlichen* [Art, creation, and therapy with children and adolescents] (pp. 206–222). Bremen, Germany: University of Bremen.

Delgado, M. (2005). *Elogi al vianant. Del 'model Barcelona' a la Barcelona real* [Praise the pedestrian. From the 'Barcelona model' to the real Barcelona]. Barcelona, Spain: Edicions de 1984.

Delgado, M. (2002). *Disoluciones urbanas* [Urban dissolutions]. Medellín, Colombia: Editorial University of Antioquia.

Delgado, M. (1998). *Diversitat i integració* [Diversity and integration]. Barcelona, Spain: Empúries.

Deligny, F. (2009). *Permitir, trazar, ver* [To allow, to trace, to see]. Barcelona, Spain: MACBA.

Didi-Huberman, G. (2018). *The eye of history. When images take position.* Providence, RI: RIC Books.

Domma, W. (1999). Ästhetische Erziehung mit verhaltensauffälligen Schülern - konzeptionelle Überlegungen am Beispiel der Kunstwerkstatt [Aesthetic education with behavioral students - conceptual considerations using the example of the art workshop]. In R. Hampe, D. Ritschl, & G. Waser (Eds.), *Kunst, Gestaltung und Therapie mit Kindern und Jugendlichen* [Art, creation, and therapy with children and adolescents] (pp. 380–394). Bremen, Germany: University of Bremen.

Evans, D. (1996). *An introductory dictionary of Lacanian psychoanalysis.* London, UK and New York, NY: Routledge.

Feixa, C. (2006). *De jóvenes, bandas y tribus* [About young people, gangs, and tribes]. Barcelona, Spain: Ariel.

Feixa, C., Porzio, L., & Recio, C. (2006). *Jóvenes 'latinos' en Barcelona. Espacio público y cultura urbana* [Young 'latinos' in Barcelona. Public space and urban culture]. Barcelona, Spain: Anthropos and Ayuntamiento.

Fernández González, M. (2014). *Matar al chino: entre la revolución urbanística y el asedio urbano en el barrio del Raval de Barcelona* [Kill the Chino: Between urban revolution and the urban siege in the Raval neighborhood of Barcelona]. Barcelona, Spain: La Llevir-Virus.

Fernando, S. (2010). *Mental health, race and culture.* Basingstoke, UK: Palgrave.

Fiorini, H.J. (2010). *The creating psyche: Theory and practice of tertiary processes.* Vitoria-Gasteiz, Spain: Agruparte.

Fize, M. (2007). *Los adolescentes* [The adolescents]. Mexico City, Mexico: Fondo de Cultura Económica.

Foucault, M. (2008). *The birth of biopolitics: Lectures at the Collège de France, 1978–1979.* London, UK: Palgrave Macmillan.

Foucault, M. (2007). *Security, territory, population: Lectures at the Collège de France, 1977–1978.* London, UK: Palgrave Macmillan.

Foucault, M. (2006). *History of madness.* New York, NY: Routledge.

Foucault, M. (1975). *Discipline and punish: The birth of the prison.* New York, NY: Random House.

Foulkes, S.H. (2018). *Group-analytic psychotherapy.* London, UK and New York, NY: Routledge.

Frost, P.J. (1985). *Organizational culture.* London, UK: Sage.

Gadamer, H.G. (1997). Ästhetik und Hermeneutik. In H.G. Gadamer (Ed.), *Gadamer Lesebuch* (pp. 112–119). Tübingen, Germany: J.C.B. Mohr (Paul Siebeck). [English version: (2007). *The Gadamer reader: A bouquet of the later writings*. Evanston, IL: Northwestern University Press].

Gadamer, H.G. (1960/1990). *Wahrheit und Methode*. Tübingen, Germany: J.C.B. Mohr (Paul Siebeck). [English version: (2004). *Truth and method*. London, UK, and New York, NY: Continuum].

García Canclini, N. (2014). *Art beyond itself. Anthropology for a society without a story line*. Durham, NC: Duke.

Geertz, C. (1974). 'From the native's point of view': On the nature of anthropological understanding. *Bulletin of the American Academy of Arts and Sciences*, 28(1), 26–45.

Giddens, A. (1979). *Central problems in social theory: Action, structure, and contradiction in social analysis*. Berkeley and Los Angeles, CA: University of California Press.

González Virós, I. (2005). Lecciones aprendidas desde el urbanismo [Lessons learnt from urbanism]. In I. Banal, & J. Canudas (Eds.), *Hospital 106, 4t 1a. El lugar y el tiempo* [Hospital 106, 4t 1a. The place and the time]. Barcelona, Spain: Actar.

Grinberg, L., Sor, D., & Tabak de Bianchedi, E. (1991). *Nueva introducción a las ideas de Bion* [New introduction into the ideas of Bion]. Madrid, Spain: Tecnipublicaciones.

Haacke, H. (1975). *Framing and being framed*. Halifax, NS: Press of Nova Scotia College of Art and Design.

Hampe, R., Ritschl, D., & Waser, G. (Eds.). (1999). *Kunst, Gestaltung und Therapie mit Kindern und Jugendlichen* [Art, creation, and therapy with children and adolescents]. Bremen, Germany: University of Bremen.

Hartmann, A. (2000a). Acting out-Pasaje al acto. In A. Hartmann, C.T. Quaglia, & J. Kuffer (Eds.), *Adolescencia: Una ocasión para el psicoanálisis* [Adolescence: An occasion for psychoanalysis] (pp. 81–94). Buenos Aires, Argentina: Miño y Dávila editores.

Hartmann, A. (2000b). La dirección de la cura en el límite de la subjetividad [The direction of cure on the limits of subjectivity]. In A. Hartmann, CT. Quaglia, & J. Kuffer (Eds.), *Adolescencia: Una ocasión para el psicoanálisis* [Adolescence: An occasion for psychoanalysis] (pp. 159–166). Buenos Aires, Argentina: Miño y Dávila editores.

Hartmann, A., Quaglia, C.T., & Kuffer, J. (2000). *Adolescencia: Una ocasión para el psicoanálisis* [Adolescence: An occasion for psychoanalysis]. Buenos Aires, Argentina: Miño y Dávila editores.

Heidegger, M. (1927/1986). *Sein und Zeit*. Tübingen, Germany: Max Niemeyer Verlag. [English version: (1962). *Being and time*. San Francisco, CA: Harper and Row].

Holmes, B. (2006). The artistic device, or, the articulation of collective speech. *Ephemera*, 6(4), 411–432.

Horwitz, A.V. (2010). Pharmaceuticals and the medicalization of social life. In D.W. Light (Ed.), *The risks of prescription drugs* (pp. 92–115). New York, NY: Columbia University Press.

Hyland Moon, C. (2010). A history of materials and media in art therapy. In C. Hyland Moon (Ed.), *Materials & media in art therapy. Critical understandings of diverse artistic vocabularies* (pp. 3–47). New York, NY and Hove, UK: Routledge.

Killick, K. (Ed.). (2017). *Art therapy for psychosis: Theory and practice.* London, UK and New York, NY: Routledge.
Killick, K. (1997). Unintegration and containment in acute psychosis. In K. Killick, & J. Schaverien (Eds.), *Art, psychotherapy and psychosis* (pp. 38–51). London, UK and New York, NY: Routledge.
Klein, M. (1955/1975). The psycho-analytic play technique: Its history and significance. In P. Heinemann, & R. Money-Kyrle (Eds.), *New directions in psycho-analysis. The significance of infant conflict in the pattern of adult behaviour* (pp. 122–140). London, UK: Tavistock [reprinted New York, NY: Free Press].
Klosinski, G. (1999). Chancen und Grenzen der Kunsttherapie bei Pubertierenden und Adoleszenten aus der Sicht des Jugendpsychiaters [Opportunities and limits of art therapy among adolescents from the perspective of the adolescent psychiatrist]. In R. Hampe, D. Ritschl, & G. Waser, (Eds.), *Kunst, Gestaltung und Therapie mit Kindern und Jugendlichen* [Art, creation, and therapy with children and adolescents] (pp. 290–302). Bremen, Germany: University of Bremen.
Knobel Freud, J. (2013). *El reto de ser padres* [The challenge of being parents]. Barcelona, Spain: Ediciones B.
Kohut, H. (1984). *How does analysis cure?* Chicago, IL: University of Chicago Press.
Kohut, H. (1977). *The restoration of the self.* Chicago, IL: University of Chicago Press.
Kramer, E. (1998). *Childhood and art therapy: Notes on theory and application.* Chicago, IL: Magnolia Street Publishers.
Kramer, E. (1993). *Art as therapy with children.* Chicago, IL: Magnolia Street Publishers.
Kramer, E. (1958). *Art therapy in a children's community.* Springfield, IL: Charles C. Thomas Publisher.
Lacan, J. (1938). *Les complexes familiaux dans la formation de l'individu. Essai d'analyse d'une fonction en psychologie* [Family complexes in the formation of the individual. An attempt of analysis of a function in psychology]. Paris, France: Navarin.
Laddaga, R. (2006). *Estética de la emergencia* [Aesthetics of emergence]. Buenos Aires, Argentina: Adriana Hidalgo Editora.
Lefley, H.P., & Pedersen, P.B. (1986). *Cross-cultural training for mental health professionals.* Springfield, IL: Charles C. Thomas Publisher.
Linesch, D. (1988). *Adolescent art therapy.* New York, NY: Brunner/Mazel.
Loewenthal, D. (Ed.). (2015). *Critical psychotherapy, psychoanalysis and counselling. Implications for practice.* Basingstoke, UK: Palgrave Macmillan.
Mahony, E. (2016). The uneasy relationship of self-critique in the public art institution. *Curator: The Museum Journal*, 59(3), 219–238.
Malchiodi, C.A. (2002). *The soul's palette: Drawing on art's transformative powers for health and well-being.* Boston, MA: Shambhala.
Marginyà, F., & Maza, G. (2001). Inmigración y huecos en el centro histórico de Barcelona (1986–2000) [Immigration and holes in the historical center of Barcelona (1986–2000)]. In Migración y cambio social [Migration and social change]. Número extraordinario dedicado al III Coloquio Internacional de Geocrítica (Minutes of the colloquium). *Scripta Nova. Revista electrónica de Geografía y Ciencias Sociales* [Scripta Nova. Electronic Journal of Geography and Social Sciences], 94(62).
Marxen, E. (2018). Artistic practices and the artistic dispositif – A critical review. *Antípoda. Journal of Anthropology and Archeology*, 33, 37–60.

Marxen, E. (2016). La expresión veraz de los saberes corporeizados [The fearless expression of embodied knowledges]. In I.A. Hernández, F. Grijalva Maza, & A.R. Gómez Rossi (Eds.), *Más allá del texto. Cultura digital y nuevas epistemologías* [Beyond the text. Digital culture and new epistemologies] (pp. 67–78). Mexico City, Mexico: Editorial Itaca.

Marxen, E. (2012). 'La comunidad silenciosa'. Migraciones filipinas y capital social en el Raval (Barcelona) ['The silent community'. Filipino migrations and social capital at Raval (Barcelona)]. PhD thesis. On-line publication: Tarragona, Spain: University Rovira i Virgili. http://www.tdx.cat/bitstream/handle/10803/96667/TESIS.pdf?sequence=1 [Accessed 20 October 2019].

Marxen, E. (2011). *Diálogos entre arte y terapia. Del 'arte psicótico' al desarrollo de la arteterapia y sus aplicaciones* [Dialogues between art and therapy. From 'psychotic art' to the development of art therapy and its applications]. Barcelona, Spain: Gedisa.

Marxen, E. (2009). Therapeutic thinking in contemporary art. Psychotherapy in the arts. *The Arts in Psychotherapy*, 36, 140–147. doi: 10.1016/j.aip.2008.10.004.

Marxen, E. (2005). Case study: Improvement through art therapy. In L. Kossolapow, S. Scoble, & D. Waller (Eds.), *European arts therapy. Different approaches to a unique discipline. Opening regional portals* (pp. 268–275). Münster, Germany: LIT.

Marxen, E. (2004a). Arteterapia e inmigración [Art therapy and immigration]. *Revista de Trabajo Social* [Journal of Social Work], 173, 71–76.

Marxen, E. (2004b). The benefits of art therapy in the immigration field. Retrieved from: http://www.evamarxen.com/Eva-Marxen/Eva-Marxen_Articles_files/the-benefits-of-art-therapy.pdf [Accessed 1 October 2019].

Marxen, E., & Greteman, A. (2019). Ingesting power. *RECIE. Electronic Cientific Review of Educational Research*, 4(2), 875–886.

Matto, H.C. (1997). An integrative approach to the treatment of women with eating disorders. *The Arts in Psychotherapy*, 24(4), 347–354.

Matza, D. (1969). *On becoming deviant*. Englewood Cliffs, NJ: Prentice Hall.

Maza, G., McDonogh, G., & Pujadas, J.J. (2002). Barcelona, ciutat oberta: Transformacions urbanes, participació ciutadana i cultures de control al barri del Raval [Barcelona, open city: Urban transformations, citizen participation and cultures of control in the Raval district]. *Revista d'Etnologia de Catalunya* [Journal of Catalan Ethnology], 21, 114–131.

McDonough, G. (2005). Discourses of the city: Policy and response in post-transitional Barcelona. In S.M. Low (Ed.), *Theorizing the city. The new urban anthropology reader* (pp. 342–376). New Brunswick, NB: Rutgers University Press.

Menzen, K.H. (1999). Neue Paradigmen jugendlicher Entwicklung [New paradigms in adolescent development]. In R. Hampe, D. Ritschl, & G. Waser, (Eds.), *Kunst, Gestaltung und Therapie mit Kindern und Jugendlichen* [Art, creation, and therapy with children and adolescents] (pp. 44–57). Bremen, Germany: University of Bremen.

Molloy, T. (1997). Art psychotherapy and psychiatric rehabilitation. In K. Killick, & J. Schaverien (Eds.), *Art, psychotherapy and psychosis* (pp. 237–259). London, UK and New York, NY: Routledge.

Moro, M.R. (2002). *Enfants d'ici venus d'ailleurs* [Children from here coming from abroad]. Paris, France: La Decouverte.

Moro, M.R. (1998). *Psychothérapie transculturelle des enfants de migrants* [Transcultural psychotherapy with migrant children]. Paris, France: Dunod.

Moro, M.R., De La Noë, Q., & Mouchenik, Y. (2004). *Manuel de psychiatrie transculturelle. Travail clinique, travail social* [Handbook of transcultural psychiatry. Clinical work, social work]. Grenoble, France: La Pensée Sauvage.

Mouffe, C. (2017). An agonistic conception of the museum. In Fictilis (Ed.), *Museum of capitalism* (pp. 78–79). New York, NY: Inventory Press.

Mouffe, C. (2012). Alfredo Jaar: The artist as organic intellectual. In A. Jaar (Ed.), *The way it is. An aesthetics of resistance* (pp. 264–281). Berlin, Germany: Realismus-Studio of NGBK, New Society for Visual Arts.

Naumburg, M. (1980). Art therapy: Its scope and function. In E.F. Hammer (Ed.), *The clinical application of projective drawings* (pp. 509–517). Springfield, IL: Charles C. Thomas Publisher.

Payne, M. (1996). *What is professional social work?* Birmingham, UK: Venture Press.

Quaglia, C.T. (2001). La violencia, a la retaguardia del orden establecido [Violence, the rear of the established order]. In A. Hartmann, C.T. Quaglia, & J. Kuffer (Eds.), *Adolescencia: una ocasión para el psicoanálisis* [Adolescence: An occasion for psychoanalysis] (pp. 103–118). Buenos Aires, Argentina: Miño y Dávila editores.

Raunig, G. (2014). *The machinics of political art. Another twelve theses on the actualization of Walter Benjamin's 'The author as producer'*. Bilbao, Spain: Consonni.

Recalcati, M. (2007). *Lo homogéneo y su reverso. Clínica psicoanalítica de la anorexia-bulimia en el pequeño grupo monosintomático* [The homogeneous and its reverse. Psychoanalytic clinic of anorexia-bulimia in the small monosymptomatic group]. Malaga, Spain: Miguel Gómez Ediciones.

Rechtman R. (1997). Transcultural psychotherapy with Cambodian refugees in Paris. *Transcultural Psychiatry*, 34, 359–375.

Reguillo, R. (2012). *Culturas juveniles. Formas políticas del desencanto* [Youth cultures. Political forms of disenchantment]. Mexico City, Mexico: Siglo XXI Editores.

Ribalta, J. (2010). Experiments in a new institutionality. In M.J. Borja-Villel, K. Cabañas, & J. Ribalta (Eds.), *Relational objects. MACBA collection 2002–2007* (pp. 225–265). Barcelona, Spain: MACBA.

Ribalta, J. (2004). Mediation and construction of publics. The MACBA experience. Retrieved from: http://www.republicart.net/disc/institution/ribalta01_en.pdf [Accessed 20 October 2019].

Riley, S. (1999). *Contemporary art therapy with adolescents*. London, UK and Philadelphia, PA: Jessica Kingsley Publishers.

Rodríguez, M. (2015). *Esquizofrenias y otros hechos de lenguaje. De la clínica analítica del MACBA (2002–2013)* [Schizophrenia and other facts of language. About the analytical MACBA clinic (2002–2013)]. Madrid, Spain: Brumaria.

Rosler, M. (2013). *Culture class*. Berlin, Germany: Sternberg Press.

Sajnani, N., Marxen, E., & Zarate, R. (2017). Critical perspectives in the arts therapies: Response/ability across a continuum of practice. *The Arts in Psychotherapy*, 54, 28–37. doi: 10.1016/j.aip.2017.01.007.

Sayad, A. (2004). *The suffering of the immigrant*. Cambridge, UK and Malden, MA: Polity Press.

Schaverien, J. (2000). The triangular relationship and the aesthetic countertransference in analytical art psychotherapy. In A. Gilroy, & G. McNeilly (Eds.), *The changing shape of art therapy* (pp. 55–83). London, UK and Philadelphia, PA: Jessica Kingsley Publisher.

Schaverien, J. (1997). Transference and transitional objects in the treatment of psychosis. In K. Killick & J. Schaverien (Eds.), *Art, psychotherapy and psychosis* (pp. 13–37). London, GB and New York, NY: Routledge.
Smith, N. (2009). Son los museos tan solo un vehículo al servicio del desarrollo inmobiliario? [Are museums just a vehicle at the service of real estate development?] In M.J. Borja-Villel, & J. Ribalta (Eds.), *Ideas concebidas* [Conceived ideas] (pp. 130–149). Barcelona, Spain: MACBA.
Smith, N. (2000). Del Lower East Side al Raval [From the Lower East Side to Raval]. *La Vanguardia*. 8 December 2000.
Smith, N., Observatorio Metropolitano, Rolnik, R., Ross, A., & Davis, M. (2009). *Después del neoliberalismo: ciudades y caos sistémico* [After neoliberalism: Cities and systemic chaos]. Barcelona, Spain: MACBA.
Subirats, J., & Rius, J. (Dir.). (2006). *Del Chino al Raval. Cultura y transformación en la Barcelona central* [From Chino to Raval. Culture and transformation in central Barcelona]. Barcelona, Spain: Centre de Cultura Contemporània de Barcelona.
Sudres, J.L. (2005). *Soigner l'adolescent en art-thérapie* [Curing the adolescent in art therapy]. Paris, France: Dunod.
Valverde Eizaguirre, M.A. (2015). El arte de hacer visible lo invisible: el marketing en el TDAH [The art of making the invisible visible: The ADHD marketing]. *Norte de Salud Mental*, 13(52), 11–26.
Wajcman, G. (2006). Memoria, visión, espera [Memory, vision, wait]. In *Ignasi Aballí 0–24 H* (pp. 235–288). Barcelona, Spain: MACBA. Retrieved from: https://www.macba.cat/uploads/publicacions/0_24h_ignasi_aballi/Aballi_wajcman.pdf [Accessed 20 October 2019].
Wengrower, H. (2001). Arts therapies in educational settings: An intercultural encounter. *The Arts in Psychotherapy*, 28, 109–115.
Winnicott, D.W. (1984). *Deprivation and delinquency*. London, UK and New York, NY: Tavistock.
Winnicott, D.W. (1971). *Playing and reality*. London, UK and New York, NY: Tavistock/Routledge.
Zito Lema, V. (1990). *Conversaciones con Enrique Pichon Rivière. Sobre el arte y la locura* [Conversation with Enrique Pichon Rivière. About art and madness]. Buenos Aires, Argentina: Ediciones Cinco.

3 Spaces beyond Hegemony

Gramsci and a Critical Review on Psychopathology and Art

In art therapy, the institutional discourses of the art and therapy fields come together. Art therapists need to undertake a critical analysis of both so as to avoid the unchallenged influence of hegemonic discourses concerning both the making and perception of art, as well as the dominant discourse of psychopathology. For both the critical analysis of therapy and art, Gramsci and his followers are useful sources.

Their work can help us to achieve this critical analysis in order to facilitate spaces beyond stereotyping and labeling. The art therapy practice—as any other therapy practice—should be freed as much as possible from the dominant discourse of hegemony and its penetration in Gramsci's sense. This implies, for example, not accepting uncritically the dominant medical discourse, including diagnosis.

The attitude of the art therapist and their critical stance towards dominant discourses in art and therapy are paramount. This includes the serious and radical acceptance of the knowledge of the participants with whom they work, including their style of verbal and artistic expression.

Gramsci had already considered disease as a social-political process, as an incorporation of inequality. Following his reasoning, the body constitutes a terrain of hegemonic conflicts. Furthermore, and like Goffman (1961) as well as Foucault (2006), he unmasked psychopathology as a social and political construct intended to limit marginalized people's social action and participation (Pizza, 2005a; Gramsci, 1971).

A critical analysis also has to be undertaken with the arts. This is to say that a critical perspective in art therapy should be ingrained within the social context of art. No artistic practice takes place in an autonomous space. Nor can it offer a neutral experience; rather, artistic practices are embedded in the structural logics of society and connected to its governmental, dominant discourse. Only through an epistemological broadening of the body of knowledge, following critical analysis of the interconnection of art and society, as well as a posterior awareness on the part of the professional, are the arts in therapy able to challenge these mechanisms of control and oppression; otherwise they reify them.

Hegemony and Counter Hegemony

In Gramsci's thinking, the concept of hegemony is the most crucial. Among contemporaries and neo-Gramscists, political scientist Chantal Mouffe has certainly contributed to the applications of Gramsci's thoughts in the political (Laclau & Mouffe, 1985) as well as in the cultural and artistic arena (2012, 2007)[1].

For Mouffe, hegemony means a double Marxist inversion: turning ideological superstructures over economic ones on the one hand and the primacy of the civil society over the political on the other. Regarding the latter, Gramsci had very well detailed how hegemony is not only imposed and maintained through relations of forces, including laws, parliament, legislative, juristic, military, etc., but even more so through the operations of consensus and agreements on the supposed "common sense" in what he called "civil society." This is "a specific understanding of reality … and determines what is possible and legitimate at a given moment" (Mouffe, 2012, p. 268). It also provides "the terrain in which specific forms of subjectivity are constructed." Culture plays a prominent role in this construction (Mouffe, 2017, p. 78).

Hegemony penetrates society by channels of the "common sense," mainly through cooption, domination, and coercion. In this sense, the civil society is the instance of consensus production.

The first inversion (economic) serves to escape Marxist overdetermination of the economic sphere and the second to escape Leninist authoritarianism (Villacañas Berlanga, 2018).

Gramsci formed part of a past and present form of Marxism that has distinguished itself from Soviet communism. In this sense, de Martino spoke of a "creative Marxism" that is dynamic and in constant movement as opposed to a "dogmatic" one (de Martino, 2008, pp. 74–75;[2,3] translated by myself from Spanish). Geographically, the dynamic and creative developments of Marxism can be located in the Mediterranean as opposed to Soviet adaptions of Marx. Especially in Italy, Gramsci and de Martino were followed by numerous thinkers such as Negri, Agamben, Virno, Berardi, Lazzarato, Vattimo.[4] At the same time, critiques were raised against the dogmatism of the Italian Communist Party most prominently by Pasolini throughout his art and writing (for a summary Ameri & Abril, 2009).

According to Gramsci, the raw economic facts could difficultly be understood as the "maximal factor of history." He rejected "a mechanic vision of materialism that reduces social and cultural life to issues of the relations of productions" (Pizza, 2005a, p. 19; translated by myself from Spanish).

Moreover, he distinguished between "economy style" and "economic system." The latter means the economy determined by economic structures like the relations of productions. Yet, economy has also been defined by styles that are directly and dynamically developed by forms of social lives, creative practices, cultural traditions, social and collective will, and forms of collective resistance. Societies and communities understand economic facts in their own way, adapting and creatively shaping them to their needs. The understanding of economy is impossible without including history. History interlaces with new realities and together they develop the productive system and the popular economy (Villacañas Berlanga, 2018).

Gramsci certainly found ways to escape economic overdeterminism. Yet, economy still plays an important role in civil society. Economy is not the only reason of politics but *a* necessary condition of it. Hegemony is an "ethic-political dispositif" that *also* implies economy. If it is "interpreted in the light of cultural traditions," then it can generate an ethic-political content that can transform a state based on domination and coercion into a leadership of popular will. Finally, hegemony becomes emancipatory (Villacañas Berlanga, 2018, pp. 18, 20).

Furthermore, hegemony always includes "a certain definition of reality," this definition being academically housed in Philosophy. The struggle for hegemony is additionally a struggle for reality. This reality is not so much an abstract analysis of texts but it rather implies human relationships (Villacañas Berlanga, 2018, p. 23; de Martino, 2008; Pizza, 2005a).

For Gramsci's follower de Martino, history and reality are both crucial for the comprehension of the *dialectics between hegemony and subalternity* (Feixa, 2008).

For a contemporary understanding of subalternity, an essentialist comprehension is rejected in favor of a dynamic and relational one. It is rather a question of the type of relation, if the subject affirms their subalternity or if they exit their subaltern position under domination of hegemony. At the same time, Spivak's (1997) and Asensi's (2009) indications are important not to delude the term "subaltern" by being used exclusively in a relational sense. Following Asensi (2009, pp. 35–36), and without dismissing the relational sphere, the difficulty of the subaltern should be stressed to enter "the category of the relational" itself. It is a position of being continuously exposed to a threat of the very possibility of their literal and symbolic life (Marxen, 2016; Butler, 2004).

The relationship between hegemony and subalternity is never static. Both are related by bidirectional relations of penetrations, domination, and resistance. For Gramsci, subalternity was a counter position, whereas de Martino went further, considering it an opposition and possible resistance against hegemony (de Martino, 2008; Feixa, 2008; Gramsci, 1975).

Resistance, Counter and New Hegemonies

Following Marx (1988) and Gramsci (1971; Pizza, 2005a), human beings are considered to be socially constructed but at the same time they themselves construct society and its structures by their practices. All current hegemonies are results of previous hegemonies (Mouffe, 2007), in the same way as Marx had explained the current structures of societies and production as being inherited by previous generations. Yet, neither Marx nor Gramsci considered structures or hegemony to be immovable. On the contrary, there are always possibilities of agency and resistance that "can influence and modify social and political structures," at the same time the very structures "condition and dominate the capacity of the subjects" (Pizza, 2005a, p. 18; see for details of resistance also Foucault as outlined in Chapter 4).

It is a question of unsettling "accepted views and to undermine the dominant hegemony" (Mouffe, 2012, p. 279).

All politics focuses on the reproduction or deconstruction of hegemony, the latter being "always in relationship with a potentially counter-hegemonic order" (Mouffe, 2007, p. 26). Any political order is "based on some form of exclusion," in the sense of some different

> possibilities that have been repressed and that can be reactivated … Any hegemonic order is susceptible to impugnation by counter hegemonic practices, namely practices that try to disarticulate the existing order with regards of installing a different form of hegemony.
>
> (Mouffe, 2007, p. 63)

Gramsci had elaborated the idea of the organic intellectual who is crucial for "untooling" current hegemony and to work on new forms of future and becoming; in short, counter hegemony.

The organic intellectual in Gramsci's sense is in no way an objective arbitrator of history, in charge of dissolving contradictions. Rather, they form part of uncertainties and the search of new meanings, without pretending to find easy and clear solutions or answers. They should contribute to society by new modes of thought, "an intellectual committed to devising and creating new forms of society," contributing "to the fostering of agonistic public spaces through very different modes of interventions" (Mouffe, 2012, p. 279).

Organic Intellectuals in Latin America

Some very effective practices undertaken by "organic intellectuals" in Gramsci's sense can be found in Latin America. There, already in the 60s "many revolutionary battles… were waged on the cultural front, where intellectuals and artists acknowledged the relationship between illiteracy and social and economic exclusions with the perpetuation of exploitative colonial modes of production" (González, 2018, p. 52). Brazilian Paulo Freire has been crucial in this sense, especially with his method of "epistemic disobedience …based on a profound assessment of the situations of exclusion, maintained in place by rhetoric of development." Only by opposing this rhetoric, in favor of "an acknowledgement of underdevelopment," does a process of critical consciousness become possible (González, 2018, p. 52).

Furthermore, Freire's approach was dialogical, which means that instructors and students would learn from each other, with the instructor undergoing a transformative process. Freire aimed at an internal liberation of the oppressed, starting with "becoming aware of a condition … and through this awareness to become empowered and act upon the situations" Within this process, the identification and conception of solutions by the oppressed were paramount. It has never been a question of hierarchical assessment of how to overcome oppression. Freire opposed "the traditional top-down pedagogical model which he described as 'banking education'" (González, 2018, p. 52).

The ideas of empowerment can be directly connected to Gramsci's. For him, the relation of the subaltern with hegemony is necessarily pedagogical. The popular culture of the subaltern should be "re-historized," in the sense of analyzing its components, its potential of resistance, and its symbolic power, in a process of empowerment.

Far away from being clearly defined terms, "popular," "popular culture," and "popular art" are used in many different ways and contexts. Here it is used as equitable or coming from the subaltern in Gramsci's sense, which means to be in opposition to the hegemonic or dominant.

In the Latin American context, Escobar (2008) has explained the inclusion of the indigenous and mestizo into the category of the popular. They constitute the subaltern in the relation of exclusion established by the Conquista, developed and maintained during the colonial and postcolonial period.

Many artists in Brazil and other Latin American countries have incorporated "the vocabulary of the popular" and Freire's ideas of consciousness-raising, dialogism, and identification with the excluded (González, 2018, p. 53). In this vein, Brazilian artists like Lygia Pape and Hélio Oiticica, architect Lina Bo Bardi and filmmaker Glauber Rocha with his *Cinema Novo* [New Cinema] had strongly engaged with learning from the popular. In the words of the mentioned architect:

> We recognize a constructive tropism in Brazilian art that easily refers to indigenous and African origins in the recycled objects of the Northeast, in the permanence of geometric elements of carnival, in the patchwork blankets of Minas, in popular ceramics, in the spontaneous architecture of the seaside.
> (González, 2018, p. 54)

Oiticia embraces in his work the local Brazilian lifestyle, addressing stereotypes of tropical cultures through the inclusion of palm trees and live birds, as in *Tropicalia* (1967). This decisive work in Oiticica's career became the name of a movement that transcended the defined contours of music, literature, theater, and film. He stressed the creative will of culture and called for a "refounding" of Brazilian culture based on the local and popular, rejecting North American and European culture but without claiming for purity, since purity for him was a myth. He rather followed the ideas of anthropophagy, previously developed by Oswald de Andrade in 1928 (2017) and manifest in artworks such as *Abaporú* (1928) or *Anthropophagy* (1929) by Tarsila do Amaral. Impositions by colonialist culture is opposed by a new approach of ingesting it to produce something new, based on local cultures, like the Brazilian indigenous and Afro Brazilian. The final objective is to create something original by breaking with fixed places, as well as spatial, cultural, and social boundaries.

The most erudite Latin American avant-garde and also contemporary art "share with popular traditional [art] parallel scenarios; nowadays, those seem to constitute the most auspicious spaces where to resist the concerted aestheticism of global hegemonic culture" (Escobar, 2008, p. 16, translated from Spanish by myself).

Artists like Hélio Oiticia, Lygia Pape, and Lygia Clark

> shared the engagement with popular forms of knowledge and cultural production that characterized good part of the Brazilian avant-garde at that moment, but at the same time, their commitment to what Oiticica would continually refer to as the *vontade construtiva* (constructive will) and its imperatives of invention and emancipation through the non-objective form

was crucial. For this, they inquired into "popular imaginaries and visual vocabularies" (González, 2018, p. 35). These ideas are particularly manifest in Oiticica's works such as the *Parangoles*, related to his own engagement with favela [shanty town] culture, especially his dedication to and study of Samba dance as well as his friendships with favela habitants (Small, 2016).

Within contemporary Brazilian art, Jonathas de Andrade is a good example for the aforementioned appreciation of popular culture, most prominently in his video *Jogos dirigidos* [Directed games] (2019). It shows a rural community wherein the hearing-impaired part of the population had developed their own sign language, using it in the video in a highly playful way. He draws directly from Freire and his *Pedagogy of the Oppressed* (1968), refiguring "the top-down hierarchy between teachers and students as a mutually beneficial exchange. If not all voices are recognized as authoritative, can we learn to listen differently and communicate the unspeakable?" (Esparza Chong Cuy, 2019, p. 101).

Movements and ideas related to the Pedagogy of the Oppressed spread through various Latin American countries, such as Mexico (still today prominent at the Institute for Critical Pedagogy at Chihuahua: http://ipec.edu.mx/), Peru, Columbia, and Chile.

In the latter country, it was very much fostered during the government of Salvador Allende and the Popular Unity. Among many cultural and educational movements, the Museum Solidarity Salvador Allende (MSSA) should be emphasized. The museum was, from its very beginning, in an organic relationship with the revolutionary process of the country. As mentioned above, the cultural and revolutionary battles were organically interwoven and inseparable. As Pedrosa (2017, p. 134) said, "In its essence, the struggle for socialism is the struggle for culture."

Curated by the Brazilian Mário Pedrosa, the museum was set up for the people. Artistic creations should not be circulating among the privileged collectors in metropolitan areas of the global North. Very much in line with Walter Benjamin's ideas expressed in "The Author as Producer" (1998), the artists and curator changed the institutional circulation modus of art itself. Without referring directly to Gramsci, Pedrosa coincided very much with the ideas of the organic intellectual who would actively contribute to the transformation of society through counter-hegemonic cultural practice; in his case, curatorship.

The museum collection should reflect art as a collective necessity and account for artistic solidarity in a specific historical moment. This solidarity went on during the dramatic history of the museum: Brutally interrupted by the military coup (1973) and regime (1973–1990), the museum was forced to exile. There, the solidarity of artists made its survival possible as a nomadic museum (MSSA, 2016). Nowadays, the museum continues its collections, exhibitions, and especially its public programming in the same spirit, the latter very much orientated towards its popular neighborhood (http://mssa.cl/; García Saavedra, 2017; Figures 3.1 and 3.2).

Figure 3.1 Exhibition opening MSSA, 30 March 2019, Avenida República, Santiago. Courtesy: MSSA.

Figure 3.2 Neighbor meeting. Body map of the neighborhood. MSSA, 2017. Courtesy: MSSA. Map elaborated by the neighbors themselves.

De Martino's Progressive Folklore

For Gramsci, it was essential for the artist to be in direct contact with popular culture as the new culture to come should exclude the fracture between elite and popular culture. As such, intellectuals and artists should overcome their elitist position for the construction process of a new culture for a new society.

Gramsci's follower, ethnologist Ernesto de Martino (1908–1965), went several steps further. In the same advocacy for popular culture, he stressed its potential of resistance, contest, and reaffirmation of their own social class. During his extensive fieldwork in Southern Italy, he highlighted the rebellious elements he found there, for example, in the texts of peasants' songs. Peasants were able to articulate daily struggle by words, sound, music, gestures, meanings, and oral culture.[5] This happened in permanent connection with the ongoing class oppression and struggle.

De Martino's inquiry (2008) aimed at re-historicizing popular culture, giving it a place of contest against hegemony and colonialism. Far away from equating the popular with superstition, primitive or retarded, he considered it an active creation of resistance. For him, folklore was progressive, in the sense that it illuminated the past but at the same time reflecting the present and showing new ways for the future.[6]

Following Ticio Escobar (2008, pp. 13–14) in the Paraguayan context, popular art constructs history, produces spaces of subjectivity, and affirms difference. It serves also for collective identification, social cohesion, and political contest.

This potential, however, is always in danger of being co-opted by the dominant class, in a frankly reactionary way, to maintain their threatened hegemony. Already Gramsci had analyzed the stunning capacity of hegemony to absorb protests and claims of the subaltern in order to maintain their position of power by supposed concessions.

For Walter Benjamin, real political art would be unassimilable for capitalism (Marxen, 2018; Benjamin, 1998, 1968). Instead of insisting on the question whether these "real unassimilable art forms," "unsubmissive zones," or "unpolluted areas" exist, for Escobar (2008, p. 17) an analysis of "contingent location points" should rather be undertaken.

Regarding the relation of hegemony and subalternity, de Martino had always stressed its mutual directions. For instance, let's understand folklore as the cultural productions of the subaltern. By no way should folklore be considered a mere adaptation and reception of hegemonic culture. Within the influence of hegemony towards subalternity, there is also always a creative and active element of readaptation. At the same time, the direction is never unilateral. The subaltern has always influenced hegemony as well. In the opposite direction, progressive folklore sets boundaries against the penetration of bourgeois culture and values as a form of resistance.

In the revolutionary process, progressive popular culture has to be given a prominent status, relating it with the political and social emancipation of the people.

De Martino (2008, p. 52) had shown the importance of "parallel anthropology" in the Italian context and how artists and intellectuals have approached and highly appreciated popular culture: the re-editing of popular tales and stories by Italo Calvino and Cesare Pavese, the writings by Leonardo Sciascia and Primo Levi, the film and written work by Pier Paolo Pasolini and his preference to write in his maternal dialect as opposed to hegemonic Italian, the theater of Dario Fo, and particularly the neorealist cinema of Roberto Rosselini, Luchino Visconti, Michelangelo Antonioni, Vittorio De Sica. For this cinema school that can be historically located from the mid-forties to the very beginning of the sixties, films should give protagonism to marginalized realities. As a direct contest against the illusion of fascist representation, the neorealist filmmakers strived to show the social and political realities of postwar Italy beyond fascist institutions and facades.

Coming back to the Brazilian context, the exchange between filmmakers Rocha and Rosselini as across the continents should be mentioned (Rocha & Xavier, 2018; Rocha, 2011). Like the Italian neorealists, the Cine Novo and Glauber Rocha also put into evidence social inequalities, miseries caused by the Second World War and fascism (Italy) or colonialism and dictatorships (Brazil). Both strived for social and political denouncement and to rewrite historical memory (Ripalda, 2005).

The mentioned artists have certainly contributed to the re-evaluation of popular culture through the creation of impressive artworks. Yet, Umberto Eco (1977) has warned against the nostalgic and consumerist recuperation of folklore in the form of a capitalist recycle and co-option of what the same imperial capitalist system previously had eradicated.[7]

Disarticulation of Hegemony through Art

Gramsci had stressed the importance of intellectuals in the reification "or disarticulation of a given hegemony" (Mouffe, 2012, p. 268). Chantal Mouffe (2012, 2007) has outlined the importance of cultural and artistic practices within this task. Artists have an important role to subvert the dominant hegemony. Yet, they must always be aware that the arts are vulnerable to be abused to reify the dominant discourse by imposing the aesthetic canon and reifying domination.

Following the Gramscian hegemony approach, "the relation between art and politics cannot be visualized in terms of two separately constituted fields—art on one side and politics on the other—between which a relation would need to be established" (Mouffe, 2012, p. 268). This would lead to a mistaken topology. All art embraces a political dimension, since it reflects a given symbolic order. At the same time, politics always embraces an aesthetic dimension in the symbolic order of social relationships. The arts never exist in a cultural vacuum. They are always interconnected with the structures of a society, which they can either reify or challenge. The latter oppose society's mechanisms of control and oppression, defying the hegemonic societal discourse in Gramsci's sense, facilitating spaces for resistance, alternatives, and, eventually, a potential for change.

Because of the inseparable topology of art and politics and in accordance with political scientist Chantal Mouffe, the term "critical art" is given preference over "political art." The latter is considered redundant and inevitably leads to an incorrect topology.

Chantal Mouffe (2012, 2007), Ana Longoni (2011, who discusses a "politicity" in the arts [Sp. "politicidad"]), and Eva Marxen (2019, 2018, 2016, 2013) have all identified different forms and possibilities in critical art practice, with "activist art" being the most obvious, but not the only way, of using art to oppose oppression (see for details of the different forms of critical art Chapter 5).

Any form of critical art, in one way or another, contributes to Gramsci's "war of position." It means to engage with the crucial institutions of art and culture in order to profoundly change their functioning. Nowadays, the objective "aims at targeting the nodal points around which the neoliberal hegemony has been established, so as to disarticulate the key discourses and practices through which it is sustained and reproduced" (Mouffe, 2012, pp. 270–271). These discourses include the economic, social, political, cultural, legal, and environmental.

One of the challenges in this struggle for change is to show how incompatible contemporary capitalism is with democracy. In addition to an ever-present exploitation of humans over humans, now the ruling of an anonymous finance dispositif has been able to reduce human existence to precariousness and poverty worldwide. This exploitation is not linked to the power of the state anymore but appears as a disguise of power, completely diluted in its tangibility (Villacañas Berlanga, 2018). "Today … the state exposes people to the powers of the market, rather than protecting them from it" (Weibel & Latour, 2007, p. 105).

Culture can offer important spaces of resistance "in this war of position because …this is where the common sense is established and subjectivities are constructed." Particularly, critical art should foster dissent and "agonistic confrontation…. [challenging] the dominant consensus by making visible what it tends to obscure and obliterate" (Mouffe, 2012, p. 271).

The position of war implies a variety and multiplicity of engagement with many institutions of different kinds. It is opposed to the "withdrawal from" standpoint elaborated among others by Hardt and Negri (2009). They defend an "exodus" from all institutions and refuse any engagement with the state: "This strategy of evacuation of the places of power is justified by the claim that, under post-Fordist conditions of cognitive capitalism, desertion is the only form of resistance to the immanence of biopolitical capitalism" (Mouffe, 2012, p. 270).

"Cognitive capitalism" means the co-option of the so-called creative and independent work. Over the past decades, capital has shown a "progressive decomposition": variable capital, including labor force has more and more separated from constant capital (Hardt & Negri, 2009, p. 150)[8]. Labor force is not bound to a specific site anymore, as it was to the factory in Fordist capitalism. Although this open relation of capital offers new possibilities of flexibility and creativity, political awareness and organization are necessary to oppose exploitation and co-option (Hardt & Negri, 2009). Artists have become an important element of post-Fordist production. Important strategies of cultural work such as self-management and creativity, as well as supposed anti-hierarchical and flexible labor structures have all substituted the disciplinary regime of the Fordist period in order to be converted into the necessary conditions of contemporary capitalism. Artists are the ideal work force with their enthusiasm, astonishing self-motivation, flexibility, resourcefulness, and at the same time without financially great expectations. Enthusiasm and creativity are perverted from "a site of resistance, to its becoming a central driver of 'official culture' and the very source of the refreshment of contemporary capital" (Cummings & Lewandowska, 2007, p. 143).

Thus, the system easily neutralizes those practices that initially were conceived to oppose it.

The exodus strategy includes art institutions, since the art world has been "totally instrumentalized by 'the creative industries.' They have become complicit with capitalism and cannot any more provide a site of resistance" (Mouffe, id, referring to Hardt & Negri; see also Chapter 4 and 5; and Cauwet, 2017). Yet, exodus does not mean "a refusal of the productivity of biopolitical labor power" but "a process of *subtraction* from the relationship with capital by means of actualizing the potential autonomy of labor-power" (Hardt & Negri, 2009, p. 152, italics in the original).

For Gramsci and neo-Gramscian Mouffe, however, it is evident that hegemony has to be untooled from inside of the existing institutions, not by exiting them, in order to trigger agonistic debates. In this vein, agonistic art practices have to be two-folded: In the first place, they must "unsettle accepted views" in order to "undermine the dominant hegemony" (Mouffe, 2012, p. 279). This, however, is not sufficient. After the disarticulation of dominant hegemony, a new articulation of a counter-hegemony must follow. Otherwise a void is left that can easily be filled by fascist discourses.

This is also valid for the museum as an institution. From its very beginning in the 18th century, it has served as an institution to reflect, celebrate, and maintain Western bourgeois hegemony (Mouffe, 2017; Mignolo, 2014). Nowadays, many museums serve neoliberal hegemony by the total commodification of the aesthetic experience through blockbuster exhibitions and their shops full of art gadgets, thus "contributing to the commercialization and depoliticization of the cultural field." The public has been transformed from reasoning into "culture-consuming." Already in 1962, Habermas observed the public to have shifted "from active sovereign into passive consumer" (Weibel & Latour, 2007, p. 101).

Yet, "the task for radical politics is to engage with them, ...converting the museums into sites of position to neoliberal hegemony and of transforming them into agonistic public spaces where this hegemony is openly contested"

(Mouffe, 2017, pp. 78–79: also Ribalta, 2010 and Chapter 2). According to Manuel Borja, former director of the MACBA and current director of the Reina Sofia Museum in Madrid, it is a question of establishing dynamic relationships with the public and the territory in which the museum is located. Overcoming social, economic, symbolic, racial barriers is an ongoing challenge within the task to establish bonds with the broader population. Then, spaces of dissent, of critical contest, and conflicting debates of history and society can emerge. Finally, the museum can become an agonistic public space where hegemony is contested in order to unsettle and reconstruct the common sense and social imaginary.

> By providing people with a different kind of experience than the one they find in their role as consumers, and making them aware that aesthetics experience cannot be reduced to the mere act of consuming, museums and cultural institutions can also become spaces of resistance to the process of commodification of culture brought about by the development of cultural industries.
>
> (Mouffe, 2017, p. 79)

For Mouffe (2012, p. 273), Afredo Jaar is an excellent example of Gramsci's organic intellectual/artist. Operating on a "multiplicity of sites" (art world, public spaces, memorials, educational centers), he has developed an "aesthetics of resistance informed by the hegemonic strategy of war of position." He provides possibilities of "counter-information" or "counter-environment" (Mouffe, 2012, p. 275, referring in the first option to Didi-Huberman and in the second to Valdés). By engaging with a variety of sites, Jaar also highlights the fact that the war of position has to be fought in many of the terrains where hegemony is ruling; the artist cannot afford to recluse in the art world. The multi-site of artistic interventions serves to combat the total social mobilization of capitalism (Mouffe, 2007; Krauss, 1990).

> Art can offer a chance for society to reflect collectively on the imaginary figures it depends upon for its very consistency, its self-understanding. But this is exactly where our societies are failing, and failing miserably, as a result of the way artistic invention and display has been instituted as a central function over the last twenty years.
>
> (Holmes, 2004, p. 549; see in this context also the concept of the artistic dispositif, explained in the introduction)

Most concretely, Jaar has given expression to these Gramscian ideas in his work *The Gramsci Trilogy* (2004–2005), in which he brings together Gramsci, Pasolini, and to a certain extent Negri (Jaar, 2005). He inquires in the intellectual's and artist's role in society, "examining their modes of resistance in facing the forces of power" (Mouffe, 2012, p. 275). He questions how the artist can maintain their capacity of dialogue without losing themselves to the art world of glamor. The relation of the intellectual and artist with power and institution must be problematized. Intellectuals and artists usually belong to society's superstructure, remote from the popular. Jaar expresses this issue by an installation of a mirror in what was Gramsci's prison cell (Jaar, 2005), thus providing a reflection of our own image and position.

Critical artistic practices unsettle hegemony and at the same time they serve for the construction of *new subjectivities* (Mouffe, 2007).

The power of art is grounded in its greater potential for freedom. Artistic language condenses different tenses in one single work, beyond the rigid authority of one concrete signification. This allows art to call out social unease, while simultaneously opening new horizons and exploring possible alternatives for the future (Marxen, 2018, 2016; Sajnani, Marxen, & Zarate, 2017; Vattimo, 2005; Gadamer, 1997).

Arts "allows us to participate in new experiences through imagination and the emotions they evoke and to establish forms of relationships different than the ones we are used to" (Mouffe, 2012, p. 280, referring to John Dewey). For Mouffe (id), art achieves this by working on our sensations and affects. It is not a question of working on already constituted subjects but on "the inscription of the social agent in practices that will mobilize its effects in a way that subverts a given frame of identification to allow for other modalities of subjectivity" (Mouffe, 2012, p. 272).

Claire Bishop's consideration on participatory art are also helpful for this understanding. She says it has

> a double ontological status: it is both an event in the world and at one remove from it. As such, it has the capacity to communicate … the paradoxes that are repressed in every day discourse, and to elicit perverse, disturbing, and pleasurable experiences that enlarge our capacity to imagine the world and our relations anew.
>
> (Bishop, 2012, p. 82)

In this sense, critical art is not meant to transmit "'true reality.' This would be completely at odds with the anti-essentialist premises of the theory of hegemony which rejects the very idea of 'true consciousness' and asserts that 'identities' are always the result of processes of identification" (Mouffe, 2012, p. 272).

Hegemony and Therapy

Regarding "therapy," medical anthropology can give us important clues and references for a critical analysis of this term, especially those authors who have aligned with what has been called Marxist medical anthropology. Within this broad group, some have developed important elaborations, thoughts, and critiques about health and illness, referring to Antonio Gramsci and his follower Ernesto de Martino.

In the first place, the distinction between biomedicine[9] and psychology on the one hand and social science on the other should be stressed when it comes to the consideration of health and illness. The first have always tended to individualize illness and to examine its physical and mental conditions in the individual. By contrast, social sciences, in form of medical anthropology or sociology, consider the economic political conditions of mental or physical illness, undertaking a macrosocial analysis of the processes related to health, affliction, and medical attention/service (Jenkins, 2015). Marxist medical anthropologists have looked at disease as a result of exploitation. They examine in detail the social relation of inequalities and unease as well as the injustice regarding the availability of medical services (Martínez, 2008; in the migration context see Sayad, 2004; Kareem & Littlewood, 1992). Biomedicine is denounced as an instrument of capitalism and imperialism, functioning under their principal of global capital accumulation (Baer, 1982). It hides realities of poverty and misery by individualizing disease and decontextualizing it from its socioeconomic conditions that are the actual determinants of the unease (Sayad, 2004). Thus, signifiers in form of biomedical categories (such as the Diagnostic and Statistic Manual of Mental Disorders, short DSM-5, now in its 5th edition) veil social inequalities and relationships between hegemony and subalternity. Biomedicine refies disease by its knowledge and practices (Martínez, 2008; Taussig, 1992).

Another fundamental difference between biomedicine and psychology on one side and social science on the other is highly relevant for both clinical practice and research: Biomedicine follows the model of the professional as a subject in a position of knowing, "the subject supposed to know," such as in psychoanalysis elaborated by Lacan (1977). This position supposedly allows the professional to read, decipher, or interpret the patient's ways of expression. The own senses of the patient are "handed over to the professional who has become the guardian or banker of [their] mind." The result is the capturing of subjectivity by the professional, "the alienation of the patient's self-understanding and capacity" as well as their "loss of autonomy and cultural lobotomization" (Taussig, 1992, pp. 96–97).

Social science that is based on interpretive ethnography as the main research method, however, does not consider the professional to have that knowledge and control. It lies rather in the affected person's narrative and not in a technical jargon or hierarchically established code. The ethnographic position implies an openness to the meanings and social relations expressed in the afflicted person's narrative. It is a question of discovering the social in the individual and re-relating the personal to the political (Denzin, 2014, 1997). In contemporary art, Jo Spence has carried out these dialectics in her work *Pictures of Health* (1982–1986), both in words and images. Collocating art "in a socialist context" (Roberts, 2005), she aspired to a global sphere, starting from her own or her clients' personal situation. She connected the individual image and story to a broader institutional and political context (Spence, 2005). "She strove to reunite social and personal identities, politicizing personal narratives and personalizing politics" (Marxen, 2011, p. 240, referring to Grover, 2005).

The condition of possibility of ethnography, whether in texts or images, implies "the position of not knowing of the ethnographer or its oscillation between a self-knowledge 'suspended' and a local knowledge to know." It is an "intrinsic position of the ethnographer as a liminal territory between professional knowledge and the social world" (Marxen, 2012, p. 83).

Within Marxist anthropology, Morgan (1987) has well distinguished several currents. What they all share in common is to consider their approaches not as a remote academic philosophy but as a way to change conditions, in line with Marx, Gramsci, and contemporaries as Negri. Gramsci had already outlined the importance of an "alive theory" that reflects the experience of real life, a theory that is a "practical activity," a "dialogue of transformation," contributing to the "transformation of culture and society" (Pizza, 2005a, pp. 20, 18). Only by "real" experience, they can join the transforming praxis (Pizza, 2005a, p. 22).

"Theory reflects the relations of force" (Pizza, 2005a, p. 22). That is why researchers, academics, and scientists should become aware of their implication in their own power structures. Gramsci had already seen the importance of a critical methodology, which at the same time must be reflexive of its institutionality and its relation to the state. In science, namely in academia, structural forces are at stake that transform people, anthropologists included, and commodify life in general and academic activities in particular.

De Martino (2008) aimed at a true commitment of the intellectual with society. He criticized the condition of the intellectual co-opted by the dominant group to fulfill functions of hegemony.[10] For him and his followers, like Marxist anthropologist Eduardo Menéndez in Mexico, ethnographic fieldwork should not be a duty for future publications and academic careers but a practical imbursement into the culture one studies. Among other tasks, this implies the severe studies of people's histories and languages.

Different Approaches in Marxist Medical Anthropology

Regarding the different approaches in Marxist medical anthropology, in the very *first* place, there is Orthodox Marxism. This means to analyze issues of health and illness etiologically as a direct result of capitalist production relations. The capitalist system provokes disease and reinforces it by its consequent inequalities of access to treatments that are called "therapeutic." Health is considered as "a profoundly political reality" (Martínez, 2008, p. 155, translated by myself from Spanish).[11]

The *second* approach, Cultural Critiques or Critical Culturalism, deserves a detailed consideration because of its abundant links and references to cultural anthropology. It focuses more on subjects of social control and coercion of biomedicine. Orthodox concepts of social class and production relations are substituted or supplemented by power and control (Scheper-Hughes, 1992; Taussig, 1992). Although for Morgan they form a fourth group, poststructuralist authors are important for subjects of health and control, such as Foucault (2006, 1994, 1978, 1975) as well as feminist anthropologists like Esteban (2014) and Juliano (2002). In art, once more, Jo Spence's (2005) work is highly relevant in this context too because of her focus on health and gender. The Cultural Critiques allow for the integration of cultural dimensions with references to Lukács, Gramsci, the Frankfurt School, and in the case of Michael Taussig with abundant links to Walter Benjamin. Taussig (1992) is an especially good example of how to relate macro economy with specific processes of the affected people in their clinical communication and their sickness experience or embodiment. He and other representatives of this current, like Nancy Scheper Hughes (1992), draw bridges between political economy and culture, Marxism and hermeneutics. Instead of following an orthodox Marxist approach of an overdetermination by economy, the affected person's culture is on stake and the representation of disease.

In an impressive case study of a woman suffering from polymyositis, Taussig (1992) shows how symptoms are signs of social relationships disguised as natural things, to be objectively deciphered by the biomedical profession. In alignment with the first group of Orthodox Marxism, biomedicine is unmasked to uproot social relationships, to dehistoricize and dissocialize the experience of unease. The latter is reified in order to reproduce a social order: capitalism. Referring to Lukács (1922/1971), the political ideology of capitalism is reproduced as a phantasmatic objectivity, the science of facts and evidence. The award is the illusion of a stable world, security is given in return for obedience, certainty in return for submission of both clients and professionals under the established common sense, the supposed stable structures of conventional meanings.

> In the name of the noble cause of healing, the professionals have been able to appropriate this mutuality and in a very real sense exploit a social relationship in such a way that its power to heal is converted into the power to control.
>
> (Taussig, 1992, p. 101; also Foucault, 1967)

As opposed to Talcott Parson's "analysis whereby the 'collectivity orientation' of the medical profession was opposed to the business ethic of self-interest," now health has become a commodity. It is market driven and paced by insurance companies, pharmaceutical and related industries. "It is the medication of business applied to the business of medicine" (Taussig, 1992, pp. 102, 105; Parson, 1964).

Within the discussion of cultural competencies, Taussig uncovers them as pure manipulation of the patient in the medical context. Criticizing Kleinman, Eisenberg, and Good (1978), he unmasks that the "culturally different" client is in the first place included in the noncompliant patient group that is always accused to raise costs in the medical business. For Taussig (1992, pp. 108–109), it is scandalous and "self-defeating to appeal to Anthropology for evidence as to the power of concepts like the 'patient's model' and the difference between the 'how' and the 'why' of 'disease' and 'illness.'"[12] As opposed to Kleinman et al. (ibid), it is not a question of analyzing the "cultural construction of clinical reality" but of untooling how the "commoditized reality" is reconstructed in the clinic and in therapy.

Following the already mentioned Gramscian idea that sickness is the incorporation or embodiment of inequality, the insistence on supposed cultural difference obviously hides the real condition and perpetration of social inequality (Pizza, 2005a). It might lead to "culturalization" of social problems (Fernando, 2010; Delgado, 1998; Rechtman, 1997) and a "fetishisation of difference" (Kareem & Littlewood, 1992, p. 12).[13]

Regarding the "commoditized reality," "the medical anthropology of so called 'primitive' societies also teaches us that medicine is preeminently an instrument of social control." They teach us "to examine the social and moral causes of sickness, and that those causes lie in communal and reciprocal inter-human considerations which are antithetical to the bases of modern social organization patterned on the necessities of capitalist and bureaucratic prerogatives."

Taussig (1992) quotes Turner (1967) and his reference to the Ndembu doctor in rural Zambia:

> It seems that the Ndembu 'doctor' sees his task less as curing an individual patient than as remedying the ills of a corporate group. The sickness of the patient is mainly a sign that "something is rotten" in the corporate body. The patient will not get better until all the tensions and aggressions in the group interrelations have been brought to light and exposed to ritual treatment.
>
> (109)

As opposed to an individualized treatment, traditional medical practices consider the unease a "social myth" (Levi-Strauss, 1976). Yet, in our contemporary, postindustrial societies, the therapeutic process is paced by fragmentation, isolation, and commodification, all under the rule of cost efficiency. Instead of cutting the therapeutic process agonizingly short,

> The real task of therapy calls for an archeology of the implicit in such a way that the processes by which social relations are mapped into diseases are brought to light, de-reified, and in doing so liberate the potential for dealing with antagonistic contradictions and breaking the chains of oppression.
>
> (Taussig, 1992, p. 93)

As Gramsci (1918) had already said:

> Life, all life, not only the mechanical activity of the extremities, but the same physiological aspect of the activity detaches itself from the soul and become barter goods; it is the destiny of Mida, of the enchanted hands, symbol of modern capitalism.

For the Marxist anthropologist Menéndez (1994), becoming sick, dying, treating sickness, and death are all processes of social facts towards which any society needs to develop actions, techniques, and ideologies. Some of these are organized as official professional practices. Moreover, health, sickness, and its treatments have been perceived in a historic process: "This historic process is characterized by relations of hegemony/subalternity that operate in social sectors [...] of a determined society." These sectors are in permanent relationship with others, including their technical knowledge related to health and sickness (Menéndez, 1994, p. 72; translated from Spanish by myself). In this sense, hegemony-subalternity relations are not to be understood as dichotomous but relational, yet the hegemonic forces imposing facts and situations on the subaltern that forces the latter to react and act. Biomedicine has occupied a hegemonic position towards traditional medicine; however, it has never been able to eliminate other cultural systems that define and attend processes of health and illness in a different way, not accepted by biomedical entities (Menéndez, 1994).

In general, in every society, sickness and afflictions have been major areas of "social control and ideology, both on a macro and micro level." This happens due to three processes:

> The existence of sufferings that refer to negative collective meanings; the development of behaviors that need to be stigmatized and/or controlled; and the production of institutions that take care of the mentioned meanings and collective control, not only in technical but [also] socio-ideological terms.
>
> (Menéndez, 1994, p. 72)

It would be highly ethnocentric to apply the aforementioned only to a certain time period or culturally defined area.

Scheper Hughes (1992) has shown in her ethnography in Northeastern Brazil how state agents and biomedical professionals convert hunger into a disease, thus disguising and masking its social conditions and economic causes. *Hegemony in the sense of Gramsci is manifest by the penetration of the dominant ideology in the most deprived groups of the country, establishing a coercion of clients by professionals* (Martínez, 2008).

The *third* group of Marxist anthropology is known as Theory of Dependence and examines inequalities of health and disease on a global level. Their first concern is how first world countries expropriate and exploit peripheral and semi-peripheral nations in the global capitalist system (Elling, 1981). Biomedicine organizes diseases and treatments under a commodity logic, adapting them to the global configuration of inequalities that are at the same time reinforced/reified by it (Martínez, 2008).

For Gramsci, the interaction between physical and mental well-being and political economy was highly important. According to him, in the global health system, the well-being of some is only possible at the expense of the afflictions of others (Pizza, 2005a).

Medical Marxist Anthropology in the Peripheries

Gramsci's ideas are reflected, explicitly and implicitly, in all the different groups of Marxist anthropology. He has been of special importance for (medical) anthropology in Italy and Mexico. As Feixa (2008) has put into evidence, the distinction of hegemony and subalternity is also of importance in academia, here namely in Anthropology. In the global system, Italian and Mexican schools have only gained a peripheral place, and have absolutely been ignored by Anglo-Saxon anthropology. This is once more evident in their lack of referrals or translations from Spanish into English,[14] something that has not happened with French anthropology or social science (Martínez, 2008).

Yet, there are various similarities between the so-called peripheral medical anthropology and the second current of Cultural Critiques or Critical Culturalism, especially as represented by Taussig and Scheper Hughes.

For Gramsci, the comprehension of the hegemonic relations required a concrete analysis of the relations of force. They act not so much on the already constituted subject but rather upon the construction of subjectivity. In this vein, Gramsci (1971) understood (mental) "disease as a process of embodiment/incorporation of the historic contradictions determined by the relations of force" (Pizza, 2005a, p. 22).

It is crucial to understand the subjective aspects of these forms of incorporation. They lead to an embodiment of the hegemony-subalternity processes and conflicts in the broader sense of social reality (Scheper Hughes, 1992). The meaning of this transformation is not psychological but rigorously political. The political aspects of embodiment make us question the health-illness dichotomy and to conceive it as a socio-political process (Pizza, 2005a, p. 16; de Martino, 1977).

Gramsci had already outlined how Fordist capitalism conditioned a new type of human being, completely paced for Fordism's own benefits (see for post-Fordism Negri & Hardt above and Chapter 4).

At the same time, there has always been space for agency and thus resistance. People are conditioned by structures but also condition the structures (above). This agency and possibility of resistance also work in the processes of health and sickness. There is a resistance against the structural violence that produces inequality and suffering as well as against the social control that aims at the maintenance of the status quo. In this sense, Gramsci has shown us how much health there is in disease and how much sickness there is in health (Pizza, 2005a, p. 27; Taussig, 1992, above).

Later, these Gramscian thoughts have been similarly articulated by Rolnik and Deleuze in their reasoning of the "'big dominant health' limited to the functional and pragmatic order, enslaving the subject to the 'map of the prevailing sense' and thus producing pathologies" (Sajnani et al., 2017, p. 29; Rolnik, 2001, pp. 5–6; Deleuze & Parnet, 1987).

On a global level, this resonates with the Theory of Dependence (above). It describes how economically dominant countries enslave other countries to their map of prevailing senses and produce pathologies of exploitation and dependence.

After Gramsci, his follower de Martino has integrated the former's theories, mainly about hegemony and subalternity relations, into existential phenomenology, and the philosophy of Croce, including the history of popular religions and traditions with an emphasis on magic and psychopathology. As a result, his approach can be considered "an intersection between Marxism, historicism, and existentialism" (Martínez, 2008, p. 163).

In his detailed research in the south of Italy (1977; and his trilogy *Sud e Magia* [South and magic], 1958, 2005, 2015), de Martino focused on the interaction between magic or magical beliefs of the South Italian peasant and disease. For de Martino, magic is a resource of the peasant to encounter the existentialist uncertainties caused by hunger, the uncontrollable forces of nature, the exploitation by the dominant class, the landowners, untreated diseases, and high death rates. Magic serves

> to rescue the subject and the social order from their crisis of vulnerability by the anticipation and dehistoricization of the occurrence. Magic thus is a popular resource in the face of misfortune that has been grounded within a historic tradition.
>
> (Martínez, 2008, pp. 163–164)

The extreme conditions of vulnerabilities and existentialist uncertainties have been called by de Martino as "the crisis of presence" (*crisis de la presencia*). It describes the risk of losing the relation of oneself with the world, of feeling annulled by a situation without control against the forces of nature on the one hand and cultural and social oppression by society's elites on the other. Being faced with this risk of disintegration, the magic-religious symbolism seems to rescue the individual as well as collective life (Feixa, 2008, p. 35). The sensation of disintegration and existentialist annulment is even worse considering that the subaltern and their knowledge have been officially dehistoricized, which means annulled by the official discourse of history. This has led to a deep sensation of alienation and abandonment. The consequent anxiety becomes unbearable or even explodes in the most critical moments of existence: facing pain, hunger, loneliness, and all the more death (Feixa, 2008).

In this context, psychopathology is understood as a "symptom of a social order that has to be read starting with historic and dialectical clues of social class where ideology holds a special role within the reproduction of social practices" (Martínez, 2008, p. 164). This happens in favor of the controlling, dominant class (Taussig, 1992, above). The big problem is that the dehistoricization of and by magic perpetuates the further domination of the dominant class. This helps them to manipulate magic and myths, impoverishing, essentializing, mystifying rather than mythologizing them for their own purpose and in order to advantage of their discourse of domination (Escobar, 2008).

At this point, Gramsci's theories about hegemony are once again important: In order to establish and maintain power, the elites do not only need formal channels of power like the parliament, the legislative, etc. Rather, they utilize an informal control by penetrating the subalterns' minds and identification with the elite's values. Hegemony is thus a sum of "beliefs, values, ideologies, tastes, preferences, habits, norms, principles and knowledge, a *Weltanschauung* that permeates the civil society until it is installed in the subaltern classes as 'common sense'" (Martínez, 2008, pp. 164–165; see for common sense also Bourdieu, 2000, 1987 and Mouffe, above).

Since Gramsci had already considered any relation with hegemony to be also necessarily a pedagogic relation, de Martino further elaborated alternatives in the form of a rehistorization of the "archaic": This means a historization of popular culture, analyzing its components, its potential of resistance, and its symbolic power, in a process of empowerment. This project is also for de Martino at the same time scientific and political (Martínez, 2008, p. 165).

With the help of de Martino's writings, in Italy (Pizza, 2005a, 2005b; Seppilli, 1996, 1989, 1984; Bartoli, 1989) and Mexico (Menéndez, 1994, 1990, 1984, 1981), medical anthropology could reconcile and combine disease as meaning and experience with its political aspects of domination and exploitation. In Italy and Mexico, both approaches have been at the same time of critical thinking and applied to practice. For example, in the Centro Sperimentale di Educazione Sanitaria [Experimental Center of Health Education] in Perugia, Italy, the objective is not being accomplice with biomedicine by promoting "cultural competencies." Once again, this requires the manipulation of clients in favor of perpetuating power relationships for commodified biomedicine services. Those rely on an advisory of dominant services to help them their mission of compliance and inculcation (see Taussig, 1992, above). On the contrary, the objective of medical anthropology based on Gramsci and de Martino is to show how hegemony dominates health and its services, how it overrules popular knowledge in questions of health and sickness, especially traditional medicine. It does not follow blindly the developmentalist discourse (see above Freire). It is at the same time critical, analytical, and applied because it has developed services where the subaltern groups are empowered in their rehistorized knowledge as well as their capacity of resistance, in short agency. At the same time, they are actively included in the planning and transformation of services (Martínez, 2008).

The MACBA art therapy practices described in Chapter 2 followed these lines exactly: They offered spaces where the adolescent participants' capacity of agency, which should be understood as a capacity of auto-determination, was strengthened.

Previously, Marxen (2016), in alignment with Foucault (2001) and Negri and Guattari (1996), has shown the capacities of marginal subjects, belonging to subaltern groups, to challenge the dominant and hegemonic discourse. Their knowledge is embodied by lived experience rather than the result of a formal and textual learning. For Negri and Guattari (id), marginal subjectivities are the best analysts of the capitalist domain. Their language, images, and expression are not ideological but embodied/incorporated. They are subjectivities in possible rebellion, prone to find new forms of expression and creation. They have an embodied, lived knowledge about the failures of the capitalist system and society. As with Gramsci and de Martino, there is a lot of health in supposed sickness. In this context, the young people's strong resistance towards mental health treatments should be seen as a possible refusal to be institutionalized by the dominant medical discourse (Marxen & Greteman, 2019; Chapter 2; Marxen, 2018).

Due to their critical and symbolic efficacy, the arts are especially appropriate to represent and to express these experiences beyond the mainstream. Through artistic expression the dominant discourse can be refracted. If the artistic practices go beyond a mere "spectacle of (sub)alternity" and offer alternative narratives, then they can offer spaces of resistance and agency (Marxen, 2016, p. 76). In line with the ideas of Deleuze and Guattari (1986) on minor language located at the edge of the dominating discourse, art therapy is a potential space where the participants' narratives can activate their hidden potential beyond the majority thinking and its mechanisms of marginalization, labelling, and control (for further details see Chapter 4).

In therapy and art therapy, Gramsci and de Martino's work allow us "a rigorous analysis of the social and economic conditions of disease" where culture, political economy, ideology, and material life are understood in a dialectical manner (Martínez, 2008, p. 169).

Notes

1 Mouffe's book *Artistic Practices and Agonistic Democracy* (2007) was co-edited by the MACBA museum and underlines the museum's interest into Gramsci's ideas applied to arts and culture by then.
2 Like Mouffe's 2007 book also de Martino's *Progressive folklore* (2008) was co-published by MACBA and shows once again the museum's commitment with the described subjects of subalternities and forms of resistance.
3 See for the importance of constant movement in anarchism Ibáñez (2014).
4 See also French philosophers like Guattari, Badiou, Nancy, among others.
5 Until today, contest is to be found in songs and sound: the songs of the working class, of house, of hip hop, etc. The Italian journal *I Giorni Cantati* [The sung days] was dedicated to the analysis of this subject.
6 The estimation of folklore by Gramsci and even more so by de Martino is another important divergence from Soviet communism. Within the latter, big deal of popular culture was considered retarded or even an obstacle for the country's progress and development.

7 See for the consumerist appropriation of subaltern culture by hegemony Martín-Barbero (1987) and García Canclini (1995).
8 Earlier, Holmes (2006, p. 414) had summarized cognitive capitalism as "the rise of intellectual or 'immaterial' labour based on cooperation and open resource-sharing, and by the commodification or 'enclosure' of knowledge in the form of intellectual property, which is then deployed as a source of rent."
9 As a broad definition of biomedicine, the Oxford Dictionaries offer the following: "The branch of medicine concerned with the application of the principles of biology and biochemistry to medical research or practice" (https://en.oxforddictionaries.com/definition/biomedicine).
10 See also Bourdieu's statement (1990, p. 145) about artists and intellectuals as

> a dominated fraction of the dominant class. They are dominant, in so far as they hold the power and privileges conferred by the possession of cultural capital ... but ... dominated in their relations with those who hold political and economic power.

11 The parallel to art is striking: For Mouffe (2012, 2007, above) also art is a profoundly political reality.
12 For Kleinman (1991, p. 7), "illness refers to the patient's perception, experience, expression, and pattern of coping with symptoms, while disease refers to the way practitioners recast illness in terms of their theoretical models of pathology."
13 See for a relevant case study in art therapy Marxen (2005).
14 An exception would be the work of cultural anthropologist Néstor García Canclini, Argentinean born and based in Mexico, most notably his book about contemporary art and anthropology (García Canclini, 2010, 2014), quoted throughout this book.

References

Ameri, S., & Abril, J.C. (2009). Prefacio [Preface]. In P.P. Pasolini, *Las cenizas de Gramsci* [The ashes of Gramsci] (pp. 7–19). Madrid, Spain: Visor Libros.

Asensi, M. (Ed.). (2009). La subalteridad borrosa. Un poco más de debate en torno a los subalternos [The subalternity blurred. A little more debate about the subaltern]. In G.C. Spivak, *¿Pueden hablar los subalternos?* [Can the subaltern speak?] (pp. 9–39). Barcelona, Spain: MACBA.

Baer, H. (1982). On the political economy of health. *Medical Anthropology Newsletter*, 14(1–2), 13–17.

Bartoli, P. (1989). Antropología en la educación sanitaria [Anthropology in health education]. *Arxiu d'Etnografia de Catalunya* [Archives of Ethnography of Catalonia], 7, 17–24.

Benjamin, W. (1998). *Understanding Brecht*. London, UK: Verso.

Benjamin, W. (1968). The work of art in the age of mechanical reproduction. In H. Arendt (Ed.), *Illuminations: Essays and reflections* (pp. 217–251). New York, NY: Schocken Books.

Bishop, C. (2012). Participation and spectacle: Where are we now? In D. García (Ed.), *Klau mich. Mad Marginal. Cahier #3*, (pp. 63–83). Cologne, Germany: Verlag der Buchhandlung Walther König and Documenta 13.

Bourdieu, P. (2000). *Pascalian meditations*. Stanford, CA: Stanford University Press.

Bourdieu, P. (1990). *In other words. Essays towards a reflexive sociology*. Stanford, CA: Stanford University Press.

Bourdieu, P. (1987). *Questions of sociology*. Middletown, CT: Wesleyan University Press.

Butler, J. (2004). *Undoing gender*. New York, NY: Routledge.

Cauwet, L. (2017). *La domesticación del arte. Política y mecenazgo* [The domestication of art. Politics and patronage]. Barcelona, Spain: Incorpore.

Cummings, N., & Lewandowska, M. (2007). From *Capital* to enthusiasm: An exhibitionary practice. In P. Basu, & S. Macdonald (Eds.), *Exhibition experiments* (pp. 134–153). Oxford, UK: Blackwell Publishing.

De Andrade, O. (2017). Manifesto of anthropophagy. In S. D'Alessandr, & L. Pérez Orama (Eds.), *Tarsila do Amaral. Inventing modern art in Brazil* ((exh. cat.) pp. 176–178). New Haven, CT: Yale University Press.

De Martino, E. (2015). *Magic: A theory from the South*. Chicago, IL: Hau Books.

De Martino, E. (2008). *El folclore progresivo y otros ensayos* [The progressive folklore and other essays]. Barcelona, Spain: MACBA/Bellaterra: Universidad Autónoma de Barcelona.

De Martino, E. (2005). *The land of remorse: A study of Southern Italian Tarantism*. London, UK: Free Association Books.

De Martino, E. (1977). *La fine del mondo. Contributo all'analisi delle apocalissi culturali* [The end of the world. Contribution to the analysis of cultural apocalypses]. Torino, Italy: Einaudi.

De Martino, E. (1958). *Morte e pianto rituale nel mondo antico: Dal lamento funebre antico al pianto di Maria* [Death and ritual mourning in the ancient world: From the ancient funeral lament to the weeping of Mary]. Torino, Italy: Einaudi.

Delgado, M. (1998). *Diversitat i integració* [Diversity and integration]. Barcelona, Spain: Empúries.

Denzin, N. (2014). *Interpretive autoethnography*. Thousand Oaks, CA: Sage.

Denzin, N. (1997). *Interpretative ethnography. Ethnographic practices for the 21st century*. Thousand Oaks, CA: Sage.

Deleuze, G., & Parnet, C. (1987). *Dialogues*. New York, NY: Columbia University Press.

Deleuze, G., & Guattari, F. (1986). *Kafka: Toward a minor literature (Theory and history of literature)*. Minneapolis, MN: The University of Minnesota Press.

Eco, U. (1977). *Dalla periferia dell'impero* [From the periphery of the empire]. Milan, Italy: Bonpiani.

Elling, R.H. (1981). The capitalist world system and international health. *International Journal of Health Services*, II, 21–51.

Escobar, T. (2008). *El mito del arte y el mito del pueblo. Cuestiones sobre arte popular* [The myth of art and the myth of people. Questions about popular art]. Santiago de Chile: Ediciones Metales Pesados.

Esparza Chong Cuy, J. (2019). Voice. In J. Esparza Chong Cuy (Ed.), *Jonathas de Andrade* (exh. cat.) (pp. 100–101). Chicago, IL: MCA.

Esteban, M.L. (2014). *Antropología del cuerpo. Género, itinerarios corporales, identidad y cambio* [Anthropology of the body. Gender, body itineraries, identity, and change]. Bellaterra, Spain: Ediciones Bellaterra.

Feixa, C. (2008). Más allá de Eboli: Gramsci, de Martino y el debate sobre la cultura subalterna en Italia [Beyond Eboli: Gramsci, de Martino, and the debate about subaltern culture in Italy]. In E. de Martino, *El folclore progresivo y otros ensayos* [The progressive folklore and other essays] (pp. 13–66). Barcelona, Spain: MACBA/Bellaterra: Universidad Autónoma de Barcelona.

Fernando, S. (2010). *Mental health, race and culture.* Basingstoke, UK: Palgrave.
Foucault, M. (2006). *History of madness.* New York, NY: Routledge.
Foucault, M. (2001). *Fearless speech.* New York, NY: Semiotext(e).
Foucault, M. (1994). *The birth of the clinic.* New York, NY: Vintage Books.
Foucault, M. (1978). *The history of sexuality. Volume I: An introduction.* New York, NY: Random House.
Foucault, M. (1975). *Discipline and punish: The birth of the prison.* New York, NY: Random House.
Foucault, M. (1967). *Madness and civilization.* New York, NY: Mentor Books.
Freire, P. (1968). *Pedagogy of the oppressed.* New York, NY: Seaburry Press.
Gadamer, H.G. (1997). Ästhetik und Hermeneutik. In H.G. Gadamer (Ed.), *Gadamer Lesebuch* (pp. 112–119). Tübingen, Germany: J.C.B. Mohr (Paul Siebeck). [English version: (2007). *The Gadamer reader: A bouquet of the later writings.* Evanston, IL: Northwestern University Press].
García Canclini, N. (2014). *Art beyond itself. Anthropology for a society without a story line.* Durham, NC and London, UK: Duke University Press.
García Canclini, N. (2010). *La sociedad sin relato. Antropología y estética de la inminencia.* Buenos Aires, Argentina: Katz [English version: (2014). *Art beyond itself. Anthropology for a society without a story line.* Durham, NC and London, UK: Duke University Press].
García Canclini, N. (1995). *Consumidores y ciudadanos. Conflictos multiculturales de la globalización* [Consumers and citizens. Multicultural conflicts of globalization]. Mexico City, Mexico: Grijalbo.
García Saavedra, S. (2017). Co-creaciones barriales: transformaciones recientes del Museo de la Solidaridad Salvador Allende y el barrio República en Santiago, una experiencia de descentralización museal [Neighborhood co-creations: Recent transformations of the Salvador Allende Solidarity Museum and the Republic neighborhood in Santiago, a museum decentralization experience]. *Revista de Gestión Cultural* [Journal of Cultural Administration], 10, 26–29.
Goffman, E. (1961). *Asylums. Essays on the social situation of mental patients and other inmates.* New York, NY: Anchor Books/Random House.
González, J. (2018). Memories of underdevelopment: Art and the decolonial turn in Latin America, 1960–1985. In P. Coleman (Ed.), *Memories of underdevelopment: Art and the decolonial turn in Latin America, 1960–1985* (exh. cat.) (pp. 25–57). San Diego, CA: Museum of Contemporary Art San Diego.
Gramsci, A. (1975). Osservazioni sul folklore [Observations about folklore]. In A. Gramsci, *Letteratura e vita nazionale* [Literature and national life] (pp. 267–268). Rome, Italy: Editori Riuniti.
Gramsci, A. (1971). *Selections from the Prison Notebooks.* New York, NY: International Publishers.
Gramsci, A. (1918). Merce [Commodities]. *Avanti!* 6 June 1918.
Grover, J.Z. (2005). Fototerapia: la vergüenza y las trampas de la memoria. In J. Spence, *Más allá de la imagen perfecta. Fotografía, subjetividad, antagonismo* [Beyond the perfect image. Photography, subjectivity, antagonism] (exh. cat.) (pp. 388–409). Barcelona, Spain: MACBA/Actar [Original version (1990). *Afterimage,* 18, 1 (Summer 1990)].
Habermas, J. (1962). *The structural transformation of the public sphere.* Cambridge, UK: Polity Press.
Hardt, O., & Negri, T. (2009). *Commonwealth.* Cambridge, MA: Belknap Press.

Holmes, B. (2006). The artistic device, or, the articulation of collective speech. *Ephemera*, 6(4), 411–432.

Holmes, B. (2004). Artistic autonomy and the communication society. *Third Text*, 18(6), 547–555.

Ibáñez, T. (2014). *Anarquismo es movimiento. Anarquismo, neoanarquismo y postanarquismo* [Anarchism is movement. Anarchism, neo-anarchism, and post-anarchism]. Barcelona, Spain: Virus Editorial.

Jaar, A. (2005). *The aesthetics of resistance*. Barcelona, Spain: Actar.

Jenkins, J.H. (2015). *Extraordinary conditions. Culture and experience in mental illness*. Oakland, CA: The University of California Press.

Juliano. D. (2002). *La prostitución: el espejo oscuro* [Prostitution: the dark mirror]. Barcelona, Spain: Icaria.

Kareem, J., & Littlewood, R. (1992). *Intercultural therapy. Themes, interpretations and practice*. London, UK: Blackwell Science.

Kleinman, A. (1991). What is a psychiatric diagnosis? In A. Kleinman, *Rethinking psychiatry: From cultural category to personal experience* (pp. 5–17). New York, NY: Simon and Schuster.

Kleinman, A., Eisenberg, L., & Good, B. (1978). Culture, illness and care: Clinical lessons from anthropologic and cross-cultural research. *Annals of Medicine*, 88, 251–258.

Krauss, R. (1990). The cultural logic of the late capitalist museum. *October*, 54, 3–17.

Lacan, J.J. (1977). *The Seminar. Book XI. The four fundamental concepts of psychoanalysis*. London, UK: Hogarth Press and Institute of Psycho-Analysis.

Laclau, E., & Mouffe, C. (1985). *Hegemony and socialist strategy: Towards a radical democratic politics*. London, UK: Verso.

Lévi-Strauss, C. (1976). The effectiveness of symbols. In C. Lévi-Strauss, *Structural anthropology* (pp. 186–205). New York, NY: Basic Books.

Longoni, A. (2011). Experimentos en las inmediaciones del arte y la política [Experiments in the immediacies of art and politics]. In R. Jacoby (Ed.), *El deseo nace del derrumbe. Acciones, conceptos, escritos* [Desire arises from collapse. Actions, concepts, writings] (pp. 5–29). Barcelona, Spain: La Central.

Lukács, G. (1922/1971). Reification and the class consciousness of the proletariat. In G. Lukács, *History and class consciousness: Studies in Marxist dialectics* (pp. 83–222). London, UK: Merlin Press.

Martín-Barbero, J. (1987). *De los medios a las mediaciones. Comunicación, cultura y hegemonía* [From media to mediations. Communication, culture, and hegemony]. Mexico City, Mexico: Gustavo Gili.

Martínez Hernáez, A. (2008). *Antropología médica. Teorías sobre la cultura, el poder y la enfermedad* [Medical anthropology Theories about culture, power, and disease]. Barcelona, Spain: Anthropos.

Marx, K. (1988). *Contribution to the critique of political economy*. New York, NY: International Publishers Company.

Marxen, E. (2019). Transforming traditions: Walter Benjamin, art, and art therapy. In R. Hougham, S. Pitruzzella, & W. Wengrower (Eds.), *Traditions in transition: New articulations in the arts therapies* (pp. 251–271). London, UK: Ecarte (European Consortium of the Arts Therapies).

Marxen, E. (2018). Artistic practices and the artistic dispositif – A critical review. *Antípoda. Journal of Anthropology and Archeology*, 33, 37–60.

Marxen, E. (2016). La expresión veraz de los saberes corporeizados [The fearless expression of embodied knowledges]. In I. A. Hernández, F. Grijalva Maza, & A.R. Gómez Rossi (Eds.), *Más allá del texto. Cultura digital y nuevas epistemologías* [Beyond the text. Digital culture and new epistemologies] (pp. 67–78). Mexico City, Mexico: Editorial Itaca.

Marxen, E. (2013). Deshaciendo fronteras: el arte como denuncia [Undoing frontiers. Art as denouncement]. In P. Laverde (Ed.), *No nos cabe tanta muerte* [We do not accept so much death anymore] (exh. cat.). Barcelona/Granollers, Spain: Roca Umbert.

Marxen, E. (2012). 'La comunidad silenciosa'. Migraciones filipinas y capital social en el Raval (Barcelona) ['The silent community'. Filipino migrations and social capital at Raval (Barcelona)]. PhD thesis. On- line publication: Tarragona, Spain: University Rovira i Virgili. Retrieved from: http://www.tdx.cat/bitstream/handle/10803/96667/TESIS.pdf?sequence=1 [Accessed 20 October 2019].

Marxen, E. (2011). Pain and knowledge: Artistic expression and the transformation of pain. *The Arts in Psychotherapy*, 38, 239–246. doi: 10.1016/j.aip.2011.07.003.

Marxen, E. (2009). La etnografía desde el arte. Definiciones, bases teóricas y nuevos escenarios [Ethnography from art. Definitions, theoretical bases and new sceneries]. *Alteridades* [Alterities], 19(37), 7–22.

Marxen, E. (2005). Case study: Improvement through art therapy. In L. Kossolapow, S. Scoble, & D. Waller (Eds.), *European arts therapy. Different approaches to a unique discipline. Opening regional portals* (pp. 268–275). Münster, Germany: LIT.

Marxen, E., & Greteman, A. (2019). Ingesting power. *RECIE. Electronic Cientific Review of Educational Research*, 4(2), 875–886.

Menéndez, E. (1994). La enfermedad y la curación. ¿Qué es la medicina tradicional? [The disease and the cure. What is traditional medicine?]. *Alteridades* [Alterities], 4(7), 71–83.

Menéndez, E. (1990). *Antropología Médica. Orientaciones, desigualdades y transacciones* [Medical Anthropology. Orientations, inequalities, and transactions]. Mexico, Mexico City: CIESAS.

Menéndez, E. (1984). *Hacia una práctica médica alternativa. Hegemonía y autoatención (gestión) en salud* [Towards an alternative medical practice. Hegemony and self-care (management) in health]. Mexico City, Mexico: CIESAS.

Menéndez, E. (1981). *Poder, estratificación y salud. Análisis de las condiciones sociales y económicas de la enfermedad en Yucatán* [Power, stratification, and health. Analysis of the social and economic conditions of disease in Yucatán]. Mexico, Mexcio City: Ediciones de la Casa Chata.

Mignolo, W. (2014). *Activar los archivos, descentralizar a las musas* [Activate the archives, decentralize the muses]. Barcelona, Spain: MACBA.

Morgan, L.M. (1987). Dependency theory in the political economy of health. *Medical Anthropology Quarterly*, 1(2), 131–154.

Mouffe, C. (2017). An agonistic conception of the museum. In Fictilis (Ed.), *Museum of capitalism* (pp. 78–79). New York, NY: Inventory Press.

Mouffe, C. (2012). Alfredo Jaar: The artist as organic intellectual. In A. Jaar (Ed.), *The way it is. An aesthetics of resistance* (pp. 264–281). Berlin, Germany: Realismus-Studio of NGBK, New Society for Visual Arts.

Mouffe, C. (2007). *Prácticas artísticas y democracia agonística* [Artistic practices and agonistic democracy]. Barcelona/Bellaterra, Spain: MACBA/Universidad Autónoma de Barcelona.

MSSA – Museo de la Solidaridad Salvador Allende. (2016). *Museo Internacional de la Resistencia Salvador Allende 1975–1990* [International Museum of Resistance Salvador Allende 1975–1990]. Santiago de Chile: MSSA.

Negri, T., & Guattari, F. (1996). *Las verdades nómadas* [Nomadic truths]. Irun, Spain: Iralka.

Parson, T. (1964). *The social system*. Oxon, UK: Routledge.

Pedrosa, M. (2017). *De la naturaleza afectiva de la forma* [Of the affective nature of the form]. Madrid, Spain: MNCARS.

Pizza, G. (2005a). Antonio Gramsci y la antropología médica contemporánea. Hegemonía, 'capacidad de actuar' (agency) y transformaciones de la persona [Antonio Gramsci and medical anthropology today. Hegemony, agency and transforming persons]. *Revista de Antropología Social*, 14, 15–32.

Pizza, G. (2005b). *Antropologia medica. Saperi, pratiche e politiche del corpo* [Medical anthropology. Knowledge, practices, and policies of the body]. Rome, Italy: Carocci.

Rechtman R. (1997). Transcultural psychotherapy with Cambodian refugees in Paris. *Transcultural Psychiatry*, 34, 359–375.

Ribalta, J. (2010). Experiments in a new institutionality. In M.J. Borja-Villel, K. Cabañas, & J. Ribalta (Eds.), *Relational objects. MACBA collection 2002–2007* (pp. 225–265). Barcelona: MACBA.

Ripalda, M. (2005). *El neorrealismo en el cine italiano. De Visconti a Fellini* [Neorealism in Italian cinema. From Visconti to Fellini]. Madrid, Spain: Ediciones Internacionales Universitarias.

Roberts, J. (2005). Entrevista con Jo Spence. In J. Spence, *Más allá de la imagen perfecta. Fotografía, subjetividad, antagonismo* [Beyond the perfect image. Photography, subjectivity, antagonism] (exh. cat.) (pp. 88–103). Barcelona, Spain: MACBA/ Actar [Original version (1992). *Selected errors*. London, UK: Pluto Press].

Rocha, G. (2011). *La revolución es una eztétyca* [The revolution is an eztétyca]. Buenos Aires, Argentina: Caja Negra.

Rocha, G., & Xavier, I. (2018). *On cinema*. London, UK: I.B. Tauris.

Rolnik, S. (2001). *¿El arte cura?* [Does the art cure?]. Barcelona, Spain: MACBA.

Sajnani, N., Marxen, E., & Zarate, R. (2017). Critical perspectives in the arts therapies: Response/ability across a continuum of practice. *The Arts in Psychotherapy*, 54, 28–37. doi: 10.1016/j.aip.2017.01.007.

Sayad, A. (2004). *The suffering of the immigrant*. Cambridge, UK and Malden, MA: Polity Press.

Scheper-Hughes, N. (1992). *Death without weeping*. Berkeley, CA: University of California Press.

Seppilli, T. (1996). Antropologia Medica: Fondamenti per una strategia [Medical Anthropology: Foundations for a strategy]. *Rivista della Società italiana di antropologia medica* [Journal of the Italian Society of Medical Anthropology], 1–2, 7–22.

Seppilli, T. (Ed.). (1989). *Le tradizioni popolari in Italia: Medicine e magie* [Popular traditions in Italy: Medicine and magic]. Milan, Italy: Electa.

Seppilli, T. (1984). La medicina popolare in Italia [Popular medicine in Italy]. *La Ricerca Folklorica* [Folkloric Research], 8, 3–7.

Small, I. (2016). *Hélio Oiticica. Folding the frame*. Chicago, IL: The University of Chicago Press.

Spence, J. (2005). *Más allá de la imagen perfecta. Fotografía, subjetividad, antagonismo* [Beyond the perfect image. Photography, subjectivity, antagonism] (exh. cat.). Barcelona, Spain: MACBA.

Spivak, G.C. (1997). El boom del subalterno [The boom of the subaltern]. *Revista de Crítica Cultural* [Journal of Cultural Critique], 15, 48–53.

Taussig, M. (1992). Reification and the consciousness of the patient. In M. Taussig, *The nervous system* (pp. 83–109). London, UK, and New York, NY: Routledge.

Turner, V. (1967). A Ndembu Doctor in practice. In V. Turner, *The forest of symbols: Aspects of Ndembu ritual* (pp. 359–393). Ithaca, NY: Cornell University Press.

Vattimo, G. (2005). Art beyond aesthetics: Alfredo Jaar. The commitment rediscovered. In A. Jaar (Ed.), *The aesthetics of resistance.* Barcelona, Spain: Actar.

Villacañas Berlanga, J.L. (2018). Gramsci, un hombre para todas las estaciones [Gramsci, a man for all seasons]. In A. Gramsci, *Pasado y presente. Cuadernos de la cárcel* [Past and present. Prison Notebooks] (pp. 11–27). Barcelona, Spain: Gedisa.

Weibel, P., & Latour, B. (2007). Experimenting with representation: Iconoclash! and making things public. In P. Basu, & S. Macdonald (Eds.), *Exhibition experiments* (pp. 94–108). Oxford, UK: Blackwell Publishing.

4 The Nomadic Museum

Arts and Subjectivities

We continue here from the embeddedness of the art therapy practices in the broader institutional context of the museum, as explained in Chapter 2. Over the mentioned period, and leaning on MACBA's policies and activities, it was possible to redefine art and art therapy in critical, political, and social terms, going beyond bourgeois, romantic, and expressionist conceptions. In pursuit of this definition, we drew upon Benjamin's and Brecht's ideas regarding the secularization and proletarianization of the arts, as well as their techniques of shock and the distancing effect.

My art therapy practice formed part of the institutional logics of the museum during a time when MACBA's aim was not only to set up exhibitions but also to provide different types of services for a variety of groups in the city. In this sense, the public should be considered an active transformer, rather than a passive contemplator.

Going beyond the concrete MACBA experience, the possibilities of such an institution will be analyzed and interrogated as to how far it can allow a specific social relation between the arts and the subject. Can it provide an experience of subjectivity, a field for and of the creating subject? Breaking the fiction of art's autonomy, protected traditionally by the museums' walls, these efforts also involve amplifying the experience of subjectivity out of the actual building. The "nomadic" museum facilitates this experience of resistance within and beyond its walls in order to probe society and its institutions with its poetic needles beyond a mere quantitative discourse of "accessibility."

The Past: Walter Benjamin and Bertolt Brecht

The continuous insertion of art into the social and political field, as well as in therapy and research activities, has been observed at least since the last century. Yet, two primary thinkers who had developed their ideas and thoughts in the first half of the 20th century should serve as critical references: Walter Benjamin and Bertolt Brecht (Marxen 2009a, 2009b; Vattimo 2005).

Walter Benjamin intensively and unremittingly inquired about the change in the relation of production in art and literature. For him, the social and revolutionary transformation of art was primarily based on its technical industrialization, especially in the form of film and photography. The "uniqueness" vanished in favor of multiple fabrications. "Once the criteria of authenticity have disappeared, it is the social and political context which determines the sense of an artwork" (Rendueles & Useros, 2015, p. 41; translated by myself from Spanish). This allowed a complete change in access to art, shifting from a social and economic privilege to favor a new relationship with the broader population. In this vein, the arts achieved a social and political function to promote change in society. Yet, Benjamin was also extremely aware of the simultaneous vulnerability of the arts, at once necessary for the affirmation and enforcement of democratic rights but at the same time always in danger of manipulation and abuse by power and domination whatever their creed, including fascism. Tragically, Benjamin himself endured the consequences of the latter via exile and death (Figure 4.1).

The relation of production in the arts which Walter Benjamin aspired to involved "the liquidation of art in its traditional bourgeois form" (Buck-Morss, 2005, p. 81, translated from Spanish), which focused on a new clientele: the working class who were at that time usually excluded from art world conversations.

According to Benjamin, technical industrialization would radically change the relationship of the masses with art, allowing for far greater

Figure 4.1 Walter Benjamin Memorial *Passages* by Dani Karavan, Portbou, Catalonia/Spain. After seven years of exile in different parts of Europe fleeing the Nazis, the last passage of Benjamin was to Portbou at the French-Spanish border. Being denied the Spanish transit visa on his way to New York, he committed suicide in 1940 rather than continue struggling against the ongoing threat of his extermination. He was hastily buried in the city's cemetery. The title of the monument also refers to his last unfinished work, *Passagenwerk* (Arcades Project). Foto: Marxen, 2018.

social significance. The immense technical possibilities of reproduction will decrease—or even completely eliminate—the aura and magic of art, which, once secularized, can achieve social and political function. Here, the concept of "authenticity" is questioned; the frontier between original and copy is blurred. This hinders—or at least hampers—the traditional contemplation of the artwork and its conversion into property, surplus value, and fetish (Rendueles & Useros, 2015; Benjamin 1968).

In the 1920s and 30s, the production mechanisms of art were undergoing a radical change. Once hoarded in the hands of the wealthy and elite, who controlled its consumption and viewing, art moved into the social and political sphere, offering the general public an opportunity to engage more closely. Art stepped out of the "cult of beauty" (Benjamin, 1968, p. 6) and the mission of the artist became contribution to social transformation. Artistic practice itself, it was theorized, should engage with and reflect the relations of production and meet contemporary conditions of society. The conditions and megastructures of production, access, and dissemination of the arts have to change entirely in a society in order to entirely change that society (Benjamin, 1998).

The loss of artistic mystique and uniqueness is more than compensated for by the technical possibilities of mass distribution which bring art into the public arena. The uniqueness of the artwork—its "aura"—is replaced by popular access. Critically, people's living situations, working conditions, and views of their own oppression are voiced as a result (Benjamin, 1968).

As the production mechanisms themselves are radically changed, the social function of art is turned upside down: It's grounding in "rituals" is replaced by its grounding in politics. As a result, "outdated concepts" like "creativity," "genius," "eternal value," "mystery," or "spiritual renewal" are put aside, all terms whose uncontrolled use easily serve "fascism" (Benjamin, 1968, p. 2, 1998, p. 93).

Furthermore, the technical reproduction of art showcases innovative values and forms. So, the issue is not in questioning the loss of quality or aesthetics, but instead, stressing the innovative function of art to transmit critical messages. This is an enrichment rather than an impoverishment of art. In its criticality, this "new" form of art achieves important aesthetic consequence. In this sense, Benjamin (1968) referred to his contemporaries pursuing Dadaism in art, and Charlie Chaplin's contributions to cinema. At the same time, Benjamin dedicated an extensive analysis of Brecht's "Epic Theater," as an important example of politically committed art (Benjamin, 1998). The playwright highlighted the proletarianization of the bourgeois writer in order to show solidarity with the proletariat. In his concept of "Epic Theater," Brecht sought to remove theater from its bourgeois pedestal and close the gap between the public and artists. That is, he wanted to turn the stage into a podium where viewers could adopt a critical and active position and both actors and spectators could work together to alter the conditions of human coexistence (Brecht, 2014; Benjamin, 1998, 1968). He changed the dynamics of artistic production by converting the previously passive contemplator into an active agent.

This is not a "theater of experience" *(Erlebnis)*, but a "theater of knowledge" *(Erkenntnis)* (Brecht, ibid.). In taking this step from the Aristotelian Theater toward the Epic Theater, Brecht was served by a variety of techniques, as well as the intervals between actions, songs, signs in the scenery, and so on. Thus, he intended to stop both the spectator and the actor from identifying with the characters and create a distance that would permit the adoption of a critical attitude toward the work, its contents, and, above all, its political-social context. The different sequences of the play collide and, for Brecht, this clash is an essential element of his theory of theater (Marxen, 2012; Benjamin, 1998).

It is precisely the idea of collision or shock, developed by Brecht in theater, which Benjamin expands with his "dialectical images" in, for example, *The Arcades Project* (2002). The pedagogical objective of this work is none other than, according to the author, to make a "collective psychotherapy for a revolutionary class." (Buck-Morss, 2005, p. 32). In this sense, the method of shock is used to awaken the collective dreamer. This shock is produced by the "dialectical images," which arise at the same time past and present, and are defined as the involuntary memory of redeemed humanity (Benjamin, 2002). A critical part of the past is unleashed in the present. This image untangles past repressions and offers at the same time new possibilities for the present. For Benjamin, the artist's and intellectual's task is to operate with the dialectical image, becoming a psychoanalyst who treats the collective neurosis (Marxen, 2019; Witte, 1976).

Intersection of Art, Politics, and Subjectivities: MACBA 1999–2009

In Barcelona and from 1999 to 2009, the MACBA pursued the intersection of art, community, politics, and subjectivities. On the one hand, this was reflected in the exhibition programming. Many exhibitions had political content, such as the individual show by William Kentridge, a prominent antiapartheid activist in South Africa; the exhibitions by the Austrian artists Günther Brus and Peter Friedl with their anti-establishment performance art; and the exhibitions *Disagreements: On Art, Politics and the Public Sphere in the Spanish State*, which proposed the construction of "a counter narrative and counter structure of contemporary art in Spain," and *Antagonisms*, "which presented a series of case studies of moments or situations in which there have been a confluence of artistic practices and political activity in the second half of the twentieth century" (Ribalta, 2004, p. 6). Yet, a big part of the museum's activities and budget were destined to create new ways of socialization between the museum and the city.

From 1999 to 2008, under the direction of Manuel Borja-Villel,[1] MACBA's programming included short- and long-term training and socialization activities, such as conferences, workshops, seminars, and "relational spaces" aimed at different types of professionals and collectives. Instead of the term "education," the concept of mediation was preferred (Ribalta, 2003). The museum aspired to a pedagogical model that involved experimentation with forms of self-organization and self-learning. The objective of this method was to produce new structures that could give rise to unprecedented forms of articulation of artistic and social processes. The aim was to give the public "agency," to favor its capacity for action and to overcome "the limitations of the traditional divisions of actor and spectator, producer and consumer." Ultimately, the public must be considered as the transforming agent and not as a passive contemplator (Marxen, 2009a, 2009b; Ribalta, 2006, p. 29). The idea of "empowerment" is highly important here, "that is, giving publics power and autonomy, in keeping with the idea of plurality of productive forms of appropriation of the museum," precisely by the same publics (Ribalta, 2010, p. 234). The ideas of agency and empowerment were later reiterated by Warner (2005), Fraser (1997), and Mouffe (1993) in form of counter-publics (Ribalta, 2010, who refers to the three authors when elaborating on the MACBA experience). Yet, much before, already in 1968, the Tucumán Arde collective in Argentina, for example, chose the print media union's headquarters in Rosario and Buenos Aires as their exhibition spaces in order to reach out to alternative publics, as opposed to or besides the typical art world consumers (Longoni and Mestman, 2010).

Regarding the subjects of therapy and subjectivity, the museum's activities included, for example, those devoted to "art and therapy," anti-psychiatry (the "Still Remember: Anti-Psychiatry" series of conferences in 2006 is a good example; the publication on the "anti-psychiatric" work of Deligny *To Allow, to Trace, to See*, 2009, see Chapter 6), and of art and psychoanalysis (such as a seminar that took place in 2003: "Image, Gaze, Appearance. Consequences of Lacanian Theory"), sometimes accompanied by exhibitions: the Prinzhorn Collection, Zush, Jo Spence or Robert Frank, among others.

In addition, a series of activities have been carried out with the intention of re-articulating the relationship between the museum and the city, with the objective of institutional criticism. This is the case of the project "How Do We Want to be Governed?" (2004), whose curator was Roger Buergel and which consisted of an exhibition in the peripheral Poblenou-Besòs area, of which the population of the area formed part of "from below" (Ribalta, 2004). The project critiqued and opposed the massive Forum 2004, an event similar to a World Exhibition. In the local context, it was an expansion of official gentrification beyond the city center, along the peripheral seaside of Barcelona, with the ultimate goal of an extended real estate speculation. Previously, the workshop "Direct Action as One of the Fine Arts" (2000) was organized in which different groups of artists joined various social movements to work together on five themes: new forms of underemployment and precarious work, frontiers and migrations, urban speculation and gentrification, creation of alternative media, and direct action policies (see Ribalta, 2004). Later, *Las Agencias* (The Agencies) struggled together with activists groups against the World Bank Summit (2001). This project led to considerable tensions between the activist groups and the museum on the one hand. The issues were of institutional nature and dealt with ownership, power mechanisms, and representationality of the struggles. On the other hand, the general museum and public program directors faced severe attacks by funding authorities "who do not espouse anti-capitalist values" (Mahony, 2016, p. 227). The politicians, the museum board, and sponsors accused Borja and Ribalta to have abused funds and transgressed their institutional limits.

As a "relational space," on the other hand, the program "Good Roll. Policies of Resistance and Musical Cultures" (2002) stood out, which was presented "as an analysis of musical subcultures understood as generating subaltern public spheres." According to the above, the museum sought to contribute to a radical redefinition of the artistic relationship and how art can be an essential part of the political sphere (Ribalta, 2004). For this reason, institutional criticism is part of the "artistic practices within the museum... which have aspired to make transparent the conditions of the work of the institution and the relations of power implicit in it, particularly to the expository form" (Ribalta, 2006, p. 29).

Moreover, conferences and workshops were held about the possible reorganization of the museum in a postindustrial, postcolonial, and postmodern era, as well as about the decentralization of art activities, as in the seminar and in the workshop "Musée d'Art Ancient, Département d'Art Moderne" (2008). It aimed at rethinking the cultural organizations considering the new relations between art and economy, organized among others by George Yúdice and the participants of the network Transform and Translate.

The museum is also conceived as a forum for popular education in which the gap between the contemporary arts and society must be put into evidence. In this sense, attempts were discussed and investigated regarding how art and artists can be articulated socially in the different spheres of society (Ribalta, 2006). In this context, the Independent Studies Program (PEI) has been initiated and developed, a long-term training that includes writing and critical theory, gender technologies, therapy criticism, urban history, political imagination, and anti-system movements as well as political economy. With these teaching spaces, it was hoped to offer a new form of political education to citizens and, at least in its beginnings, an alternative to local universities (Ribalta, 2006).

Gender technologies have been one of the main subjects of the museum; as a result, the seminars, workshops, and conferences have involved internationally recognized academics and representatives from feminist movements who are not frequently invited to Catalan or Spanish universities (with the exception of Dolores Juliano), such as Angela Davis, Beatriz now Paul Preciado, Gayatri Spivak, Donna Haraway, Judith Butler, and Hélène Cixous.

In other words, we are faced with a different way of considering art and its use; that is, of conceiving its usefulness in the political, the social, and the therapeutic. It is not about offering "nice" expositions for bourgeois, where they can spend a few hours of contemplation on Sunday, but to choose activities and exhibitions that go "beyond the perfect image" (the title of the exhibition of Jo Spence, with the eponymous catalog, 2005). The hope is to differentiate art from its appearance of beauty (Benjamin, 1998, 1968), to fight the bourgeois production of states of illusion (Brecht, 2014).

In 2005, the seminar "Critique and Daily Life. Discourse Theory and Art Critique" was held by Xavier Antich and Manuel Asensi. It served as the predecessor of the PEI program (see above).

Ironies of life, the seminar dealt with—among many other subjects—the *Arcades Project* by Walter Benjamin and its relevance for contemporary Barcelona's Raval.

Benjamin worked on the Arcades from 1927 until his death, describing the urban politics of Georges-Eugene Hausmann (Figure 4.2). He conceived his massive restructuring plans for Paris by the middle of the 18th century when he worked for Napoleon III, both opening the city to private investments and speculations. He declared himself "artiste démolisseur" (demolition artist).

Figure 4.2 Walter Benjamin Memorial *Passages* from inside. Benjamin quotation on the glass panel at the bottom of the monument in direct contact with the waves: "It is more arduous to honour the memory of the nameless than that of the renowned. Historical construction is devoted to the memory of the nameless." Foto: Marxen, 2018.

His principal actions consisted in demolishing buildings in order to convert narrow streets into ample boulevards. The former was difficult to control, in a time of constant riots or even coming revolutions. Haussmann's urbanism served to prevent the construction of barricades of the rebellious, while at the same time benefiting bourgeois speculations (Harvey, 2012; Buck-Morss, 2005; Benjamin, 2002). As a consequence of Hausmann's counterrevolution, the rents in Paris' city center raised in such a way that the working class was forced to move to the suburbs. Finally, the growing influence of the bourgeoisie led to an equally growing concern for the vigilance and control of the common population, a phenomenon Hausmann called "strategic embellishment" (Buck-Morss, 2005, pp. 44–45).

Benjamin's objective in the *The Arcades Project* was "to show the other side of the urban world: the nineteenth century as hell" (Buck-Morss, 2005, p. 228).

The parallels between Benjamin's Arcades and the contemporary gentrification of Barcelona's Raval is striking (see Chapter 2 with references to Fernández González, 2014; Marxen, 2012, 2009; Subirats & Rius, 2006; McDonough, 2005; Delgado, 2005, 2002; González Virós, 2005; Maza, McDonogh, & Pujadas, 2002; Marginyà & Maza, 2001; Smith, 2000; as well the films by Guerín, 2001 and Jordà, 2003).

In the same way, Hausmann pretended to organize and arrange Paris during the 19th century, Catalan architect Oriol Bohigas has been working on it in Barcelona before and after its Olympic Games (1992): perfecting society, ordering architecture and public space while at the same time impeding the democratization of social and urban relationships (Buck-Morss, 2005). All these subjects formed part of the discussion held in the heart of Raval, in a building which itself formed part of the most important local embellishment plans....

As already mentioned in Chapter 2, the MACBA experience focused on "forms of subjective appropriation of artistic methods in processes outside the mainstream and outside the museum" going "beyond the idea of visibility whose paradigm is the exhibition" (Ribalta, 2004, p. 9). Some of the museum projects and programs have been described in order to achieve this work of subjectivity. The art therapy and psychoanalytic devices as explained in Chapter 2 definitely formed part of that effort.

Going beyond the concrete MACBA experience, the possibilities of such an institution should be analyzed and interrogated as to how far it can allow a specific social relation between the arts and the subject, an experience of subjectivity, a field for and of the creating subject.

For this purpose, we first inquire into the term subjectivity. We will then connect it with art and finally relate art and subjectivity with the institutional framework of the museum.

Subjectivity: An Exploration

The definitions of subjectivity are mainly drawn on authors like Foucault (2014), Negri (2017), Deleuze and Guattari (2009) as well as Rolnik (in

Fernández Polanco & Pradel, 2015). They are supplemented by thoughts and works of different artists, mainly Lygia Clark, Hélio Oiticica, Roberto Jacoby.

In alignment with these authors, it should first be stressed that subjectivity is never understood in a reductionist way as the experience of the isolated subject. It is rather the subject in relationship to the other and the political landscape where it is interwoven, including this very entanglement. For good reason, Rolnik refers to Lygia Clark's Moebius strip in her *Caminhando* ("Walking," 1964) artwork, because it visualizes "the relation between subjectivity's two modes for deciphering the world, i.e. the subject and the outside-of-the-subject" (Fernández Polanco & Pradel, 2015).

For Foucault, subjectivity is in the first place the relation to oneself, a "means of relations of mastering of the self by the self or of knowledge of self by self" (Foucault, 2014, p. 299). Yet, for him, this is not a solipsistic condition because the relationship to oneself implies "a relationship of dependence in regard to another" (id.: 4). These ideas stem mainly from his thoughts articulated in *Subjectivity and Truth* (1998), his lectures held at the Collège de France, together with *Truth Telling, Wrong Doing* (2014), the lectures imparted at Louvain University. Both connect the history of subjectivity and the analysis of forms of governmentality. So, the process of becoming a subject implies navigating existing power mechanisms and dominance (political) as well as assuming the responsibility for one's actions including one's form of self-care (ethical; Sajnani, Marxen, & Zarate, 2017; Foucault, 1998, 1983).

Foucault (1998, 1994, 1978, 1975) examined the "modes of objectification of the subject in realms of knowledge such as those dealing with language, labor, and life." Furthermore, he focused on "the divisions operating in society in the name of madness, disease, delinquency, and their efforts on the formation of a reasonable and normal subject." At the same time, the related institutions hold apart and discipline undesired subjects with the aim to normalize their supposed deviance. In this sense, the process of "government of the self by oneself in its articulations with relations with others" finds its articulation in disciplines like pedagogy or "counsels regarding conduct, spiritual direction, prescriptions for models of living, etc." The latter is certainly the subject and aim of education, counseling, psychology, psychiatry, and any kind of therapy, including the creative arts therapies (Brion & Harcourt, 2014, p. 299).

In fact, "interaction between those two types of techniques—techniques of domination and techniques of the self" was crucial for Foucault due to his interest in "the points where the technologies of domination of individuals over one another have recourse to processes by which the individual acts upon himself [themselves]." In other words, he analyzed "the points where the techniques of the self are integrated into structures of coercion or domination" (Brion & Harcourt, 2014, p. 300).

In his Foucault reading, Toni Negri (2017) focuses on labor and its relation to power and subjectivity. For him and Hardt and Negri (2009), the economic process "is also an ontological process through which … subjectivity [is] transformed and constituted" (Negri, 2017, p. 173). Power and labor are closely related to each other. Living labor is always connected to capital. Yet, in this relationship, there is always an imbalance of power. "Labor power not only produces capital but also composes and organizes a society" and the self (Negri, 2017, pp. 184–186). Yet, this labor power is dominated by the hegemonic discourse of society, the "machine of power." It organizes any sphere of life, from the factory to society. "This machine of command progressively extends itself, dominates every space, permeates populations and is, for this reason, subjected to a constant movement and tendency to rupture." There is certainly an "overlap between organisation of economic exploitation and the organisation of political command… Exploitation is transformed and consolidated into a *habitus*: discipline in the form of life… At this point the essence of being human is directly exploited by capital" (Negri, 2017, pp. 184–186). Hardt & Negri (2009) have termed these phenomena as "biopolitical" because "biopolitical production is aimed constantly at producing forms of life" (p. 175).

In this context, Lazzarato (2014) distinguishes between different semiotics in capitalism to control and produce subjectivities according to the capitalist creed. Stressing capitalism's extra linguistic forces, Lazzarato describes on the one hand asignifying semiotics such as monetary signs, exchange rates, and stock market values. They are produced in asignifying apparatuses, i.e. the stock market and rating agencies, that "depoliticize and depersonalize power relations" (Lazzarato, 2014, pp. 41–42). On the other hand, there are signifying semiologies: language, discourses, etc. They "are used and exploited as techniques for control…, undermining established communities." They formulate the subjectivation process and hence subjectivity. Lazzarato highlights the importance of moving beyond language, the signifying, to first understand and then to be able to "untool" power.

In *Discipline and Punish*, Foucault (1975) examines how "exploitation subsumes the whole of society in its effectuality, and, if the whole of society is exploited, little space remains for the genealogy of subjectivity" (Negri, 2017, p. 185). Although capitalist exploitation has invaded everything, being really good in its finesse and precision, it is still not impermeable enough to exclude any form of resistance.

Confronted with this apparently total control of the power machine, Foucault explored the possibilities of spaces for subjectivity and initiated the process of relativization, reconsidering the supposed "absoluteness with which the concepts of norm, of discipline, and so forth, had been constructed up until that point." He opens possibilities of resistance, by pointing out "the double nature of power relations": On the one hand, subjectivity seems to have been annulled, but on the other it re-enters play by practices of resistance: "the concepts of rule and discipline collide with practices of resistance, with logical revolts built on ontological ruptures" (Negri, 2017, p. 186). For Lazzarato (2014), these ruptures are a "'break with causality,' the turn from the expected course of things, the impossible that becomes real, the organization and metamorphosis of subjectivity" (p. 20).

The codifications of capitalist and neoliberal macropolitics can be derailed by a resistance performed on a micropolitical, regional, temporary level. Overcodifications give place to uncertainties and ways of searching instead of expecting easy answers (de la Loza, Molinari, & Rios, 2020; Negri, 2017; Deleuze & Guattari, 2009). In Negri's words:

> There is always a production of subjectivity, because that power relation is not symmetrical, indeed it is always an intransitive relation, and it creates asymmetry now here, now there—sometimes on the side of the capital, at other times on the side of living labour. And when it is on the side of living labour, when the asymmetry is overdetermined on that side, production becomes a production of subjectivity and is revolutionary—without forgetting that the path to the liberation of living labour is from the bottom to the top.
>
> (2017, p. 187)

In order to make the latter happen, Guattari and Negri (2010, 1996) have pointed out the importance of a "productive renewal," of "new ways of imagining and of studying production." They highlight the radical untying of any form of production from capitalism and its penetrations into everyday life. Any development of "new" subjectivities "will be illusory if it does not attack frontally the network of command put in place by IWC [International World Capitalism]." They must separate "from the very model of the capitalist state and all its successors, replacements, derived forms, and assorted functions in all the wheels of the socius, at all levels of subjectivity" (Guattari & Negri, 2010, pp. 95–96).

Concretely, it is a question of opposing any kind "of conservative, degrading, oppressive reterritorialization imposed by the capitalist and/or socialist state, with its administrative functions, institutional organs, its collective means of normalization and blockage, its media, etc." This means "an ungluing of the dominant realities and significations, by creating conditions which permit people to make their territory, to conquer their individual and collective destiny within the most deterritorialized flows" (id.: p. 97).

Negri (2017) also stresses the importance of Deleuze and Guattari's work *The Anti-Oedipus* (1972/2009) within the discussion of subjectivity. These two authors pushed the discussion about subjectivity an important step forward through their analysis of capital, shifting the focus to immaterial capital. Without their work from 1972, contemporary comprehension of the structure of work would be impossible. Other authors have later called the predominance of immaterial labor "cognitive capitalism" (Holmes, 2006, referring to previous works published in the French journal *Multitudes*; Hardt & Negri, 2009 as in Chapter 3).

"The so-called 'precariat' has displaced the traditional 'proletariat.'" In the Global North, the alienated work in factories has been substituted by unstable, free-lance, part-time work, very often without regular labor contracts (Harvey, 2012, p. xiv).

Bifo (2003, p. 4) has described this phenomenon as the "formation of a social consciousness of the cognitariat," a synthesis of "cognitive capitalism," and "proletariat." The latter indicates the precariousness of immaterial labor. It involves "new forms of self-employment in the cultural industries and the emergence of a new self-employed working class that was [is] highly qualified but also over-exploited and impoverished in precarious conditions: the cognitariat" (Ribalta, 2010, p. 243).

Ribalta (2010, p. 242) offers the following:

> [The] global phenomenon of the transformation of Western urban economies to the tertiary sector... began in the late seventies with the first industrial crisis, when tourism became one of the principal economic objectives. In this process of capitalist restructuring, the new urban economies in the post-industrial or post-Fordist age have granted culture a major new role as a production sector.

In this sense, he refers to relevant previous works by various authors such as Jameson (1991), Harvey (1990), Hardt and Negri (2004, 2002).

> The concept of 'cognitive capitalism' has emerged to denote this process of coming together of new information and communication technologies with immaterial, creative, relational and affective labour, which is acquiring new centrality in the cultural industries and breaking the traditional opposition between leisure and work. Capitalism 'sets subjectivity to work', as Paolo Virno [2004, 1996] says in his paradigmatic analysis.
>
> (Ribalta, 2010, p. 242)

Wu Ming describe the worker of the post-Fordism the following way:

> They are the protagonist, sometimes active or passive, deriving from the dissolution of the old social contract and of the precarization of life. Active in the sense that they promote their own instability, opting for the liberation of the Fordism which bound work to the unity of time, space, and action. Passive because they suffer the need to work in any filed, at any moment of life. They watch how capital becomes the parasite of their own creativity, capacity of innovation and to develop projects...
>
> (Fernández-Savater, 2003, as quoted in Laddaga, 2006, pp. 214–215, translated from Spanish by myself)

Regarding workers' struggles, the interesting point is how to shift from the proletariat struggles of the 19th century to the 21st or "to post-industrial economy and post-Fordist production and sociability, to the new protests of self-employed, cognitariat workers" (Negri, 2017; Ribalta, 2010, p. 248; Bifo, 2003). The "precariat" is highly dispersed in time and space, asking the urgent question, "(h)ow such disparate groups may become self-organized into a revolutionary force" (Harvey, 2012, p. xiv; Hardt & Negri, 2009, 2004, 2002).

For Negri (2017), the practice of work, in general, should be an expression of desire and not of exploitation. Exploitation is the control of desire. This exploitation takes equally place in material and immaterial labor. It determines desire production according to its patterns, or in Suely Rolnik's words formulated in her *Another Relationality* seminar held at MACBA, "it drains people's creative desire, makes it go against the grain, by either fossilizing and commodifying originally unruly, critical creative practices or by sponsoring them and making thus, in one way or another, the sponsored obeying capitalism's rules" (Marxen, 2018, p. 45; Ribalta, 2010). As a result, "subjectivity acts positively in favour of the regime's interests from its own desire. The stable and obedient subjectivity of disciplinary power is thus replaced by a fluid and flexible subjectivity" (Rolnik in Fernández Polanco & Pradel, 2015).

This co-option and commodification are possible because capitalism "*can assimilate an astonishing number of revolutionary themes, and can even propagate them without seriously placing its own existence or the existence of the class that possesses them into question*" (Raunig, 2014, p. 9, italics in the original; Borja-Villel, 2010; Deleuze & Guattari, 2009; see Gramsci's ideas in Chapter 3). Finally,

> its function is to aestheticize and spectacularize the misery of the world and make it digestible and then offer it to the audience for enjoyment. And at the cynical end of the chain of appropriation, it turns not only the depiction of misery itself, but *even the struggle against misery into a consumer good.*
>
> (Raunig, 2014, p. 10)

By mechanic reproduction, revolutionary themes can even be converted, or perverted, into spectacles (Escobar, 2008; Debord, 2002).

"Capitalism has turned pimp on us." Whatever we do with our creativity, "we are inevitably brought face to face with this question. What are we being pimped for? In other words, are we breaking with the logic of neoliberal capitalism and the culture industries, or are we reproducing and extending it?" (Marxen, 2018; Ribalta, 2010, p. 263).

Simultaneously with the rise of immaterial labor, Preciado (2013) has stressed the shaping of subjectivities by contemporary methods of control induced by the pharmoco-pornographic industries. He further develops Foucault's ideas about social control and how it is exercised through institutional pillars of society in form of health and penalty and education. However, nowadays a shift has taken place within discipline towards a much subtler form of biopolitical control, one which shifts the panopticon from a purely externalized mode of control to an internalized mode whereby subjects ingest power. This new regime is one that "refers to the process of a biomolecular (pharmaco) and semiotic-technical (pornographic) government of sexual subjectivity" (p. 34). Preciado's focus on sexual subjectivity is of importance since, in his estimation, critical theory of the 20th and 21st century "stopped biopolitically at the belt" (p. 37), preferring to focus on cognition, language, and the symbolic.

> Absent from such theory is the material—the work of material substances, in particular—on how subjects came to be. Providing a rather extensive history of the invention of synthetic hormones and other biomolecular substances, Preciado mapped out the ways in which subjectivity had always already, for much of the 20th century, been invented through the ingestion of molecules developed through pharmaceutical and medical research.
>
> (Marxen & Greteman, 2019: p. 877)

Nowadays, "we are being confronted with a new kind of hot, psychotropic, punk capitalism" (id.: p. 33). He continues explaining:

> The real stake of capitalism today is the pharmacopornographic control of subjectivity, whose products are serotonin, techno-blood and blood products, testosterone, antacids, cortisone, techno-sperm, antibiotics, estradiol, techno-milk, alcohol and tobacco, morphine, insulin, cocaine, living human eggs, citrate of sildenafil (Viagra), and the entire material and virtual complex participating in the production of mental and psychosomatic states of excitation, relaxation, and discharge, as well as those of omnipotence and total control.
>
> (id.: p. 39)

In this way, "pharmacopornographic capitalism" manages biomediatically subjectivities. It subjectifies and modifies the human body and makes it confirm and reify a "preexisting visual and biopolitical order" (id.: pp. 51, 100).

Negri, Hardt and Negri, Deleuze, Guattari, and Foucault had all focused "on the social mechanisms of production of subjectivity in institutional architectures, psychoanalytic discourse, state apparatus." Preciado (2013) updates these mechanisms by those of biomolecular and multimedia technical protocols. Yet, the mentioned authors do not meet "the recognition that subjectivity is produced through apparatuses of power with either celebration or despair. They regard the production of subjectivity rather as the primary terrain on which political struggle takes place" (Hardt & Negri, 2009, p. 172). The quoted two authors (id.) go on pointing out the necessity of intervening "in the circuits of the production of subjectivity," by fleeing "from the apparatuses of control, and construct the bases for an autonomous production" (see also for feminist theory: Rey Chow, 2006). As "apparatuses of control" and "corrupt derivations of the common," Hardt and Negri (id.: p. 177) mention in the first place the family, the corporation, and the nation-state.

As an important example when a massive work of subjectivity took place, Deleuze and Guattari (2009) as well as Guattari and Negri (2010, 1996) have stressed several times the importance of the '68 students' revolts in different countries for the invention, creation, and formulation of new desires and new subjectivities (see also Rolnik in Fernández Polanco & Pradel, 2015). Negri (2017, p. 171) considers the *Anti-Oedipus* (Deleuze & Guattari, 1972/2009) "the first 'new' philosophy, born of the conditions of May 1968," at the time not ending but opening up a period which has been and still is to be continued by movements like feminism (see, for example, most recently the Chilean feminist May in 2018: Zerán, 2018), queer theories (see Preciado, 2013, above), anti-psychiatric circles, deinstitutionalization groups (see for the latter two Chapter 6), etc. They have all been able to activate "the outside-of-the subject experience" (Rolnik in Fernández Polanco & Pradel, 2015). Referring back to Foucault (2014; Negri, 2017, p. 186), these past and present movements are practices of resistance and they are built on or lead to "ontological ruptures." Furthermore, they are marked by their temporality and regionality. In spite of their supposed limitation in time and space, they are able to spread, to germinate beyond their time moment and territory.

Starting from the '68 experience, "the production of subjectivity" is characterized by Deleuze & Guattari as "the capacity to oppose itself to the overcodification of territories by the despotic machine" (Negri, 2017, pp. 171, 173) Concretely, they propose as summarized by Foucault in his foreword of the Anti-Oedipus (2009, pp. xiii–xiv): Freeing "political action from all unitary and totalizing paranoia;" developing "action, thought, and desires by proliferation, juxtaposition, and disjunction." This means preferring the multiple, "difference over uniformity, flows over unities, mobile arrangements over systems," believing in the productive force of nomadism instead of the sedentary. Furthermore, it is a question of opposing sadness and favoring "the connection of desire to reality" and its resulting revolutionary force, instead of retreating "into the forms of representation." Simultaneously, political practice should be used "as an intensifier of thought" and not "thought to ground a political practice in Truth." Finally, "the individual is the product of power," hence the call to "'de-individualize' by means of multiplication and displacement" in order to resist power and avoid becoming enamored by it.

In relation to displacement, Deleuze & Guattari add in *A Thousand Plateaus: Capitalism and Schizophrenia* (1980/1987) the deterritorialization of institutions like the nation-state and any other manifestation of the imperial perspective by deterritorializing practices.

One of Marx' key thoughts was that the self and history are constitutively interconnected "as both production and products of subjective assemblages." So, if resistance by nomadism, desire machine, displacement, and deterrialization is achieved, then "'exploitation'… finds itself emptied of all [its centralized] substance." It can then be pertinently reformulated "within the relationship between subjectivities and signs of potentiality [puissance]" (Negri, 2017, p. 174). Self and subjectivities enter into play and change through spaces of resistances and thus modify history.

Estrategia de la alegría, Strategy of Joy

As just mentioned, Foucault (2009) had already stressed the importance of opposing sadness within the endeavor of subjectivity. In the same vein, Guattari (2006) underlined the importance of rich and unforeseen pleasures. They help to reconstitute the social fabric.

Similarly, Negri (2017, p. 173) refers to Deleuze and Guattari's (1980/1987) "laughter detachment," that helps or is a condition for resistance against capitalism's penetration of suffering that takes the form of the invention or exaggeration of multiple unforeseen dangers and conditions of fear or anxieties. It is a "knowing laugh which accompanies our realistic critique of the dominant powers." Furthermore, it is "a laugh of creation and joy," as "a liberation from the subordination of identities…, autonomous control of the circuits of the production of social subjectivity, and … construction of common practices." Finally, it is destruction, in the sense of an extirpation of attachments to identity, of combating "the institutions that corrupt the common." Although there is a realistic estimation of the sufferings caused by "capitalist exploitation, the rule of property, and the destroyers of the common through public and private control," these opponents will at the end "be buried by laughter" (Hardt & Negri, 2009, p. 383).

In a similar vein, Bifo (in Gago, 2008) understands happiness in collective terms and as a collective process to be subversive (also Hardt & Negri, 2009). It opposes the capitalist machine by the creation of spaces of pleasure, relaxation, and friendship. They are spaces exempted of the premise of accumulation and exchange rate. These ways of being together and to enjoy each other go beyond the disciplinary and commodification regime.

In the arts and during the eighties in Argentina, Roberto Jacoby developed the "Strategy of Joy" (Red Conceptualismos Sur, 2012; Jacoby, 2011). This ongoing artwork meant to oppose the most difficult situations of loss and suffering during the Argentine military dictatorship by organizing punk or rock music and dance events. People would gather in spaces, forbidden by the military rules, to live collectivity, the experience of their bodies moving together with pleasure, challenging thus the military's perverse discipline, moralist impositions, and total fragmentation of social life. In contrast, participants celebrated "the exultation of being alive, of enjoying our bodies, and of transforming them by disobeying disciplinary norms" (Longoni, 2017a).

The contestation of "superabundance of fear" and sadness is a form of resistance against capitalism, since fear and sadness instrumentalize people's lives in a direction of unfree subjectivities (Laddaga, 2013).

The Argentinian artists, activists, musicians of the *Strategy of Joy* as well as Toni Negri (2017) all referred to Spinoza, who had already explained that joy (alegría) is a "fundamental passion-nucleus for the formation of a new political community beyond fear, sadness and inaction" (Red Conceptualismos Sur, 2012, p. 114). Joy is a continuous process of opening "new possibilities, to expand our field of imagination, our abilities to feel and be affected, our capacities for action and passion" (Hardt & Negri, 2009, p. 379). In Negri's words (Ramos, 2011, translated by myself from Spanish):

> Positive passions build community, they liberate relations, they create joy. And this totally determined by the capacity of catching the moment of time and to translate it into an ethic process, ... a process of constructing personal joy, community joy and the free enjoyment of divine love.

In Brazil, Oiticica has expressed very similar thoughts in his work *Creleisure*, a neologism which combined creativity, leisure, and pleasure: "Creleisure is the non-repressive leisure, opposed to diverted oppressive leisure thinking: a new unconditioned way to battle oppressive systematic ways of life" (Oiticica, 1969, as in Skrebowski, 2012, p. 76).

It was meant to happen in a non-specific space and time, a dedication of non-oppressive, unprogrammed free flow of thought where creativity, pleasure, and leisure would meet, together also with a strong sense of community and collectivity. "The idea of community cells or of experimental communities came to me side by side with that of wide-spread collectivities, such as the building of collective sites or abiding places" (Skrebowski, 2012, p. 76; Oiticica, 1969). *Creleisure* aimed at the revolutionary in a political sense. Oiticica called for an "aesthetic revolution at a proliferating cellular level, bypassing the requirement for aesthetic (re-)education as its preliminary condition" (Skrebowski, 2012, p. 77).

There have been many artists, especially in Latin America, who have developed artworks and interventions with bodies who know, think, "and can produce discourse and knowledge. Coming into contact with the other, *being together*, thus produces another kind of knowledge that holds the potential for liberation" from disciplinary and developmentalist politics and regimes towards free subjectivities (González, 2018, p. 56).

Subjectivity and Art

Two artists have already been mentioned who have opposed oppression and dominant subjectification in their thinking and artwork: Roberto Jacoby and Hélio Oiticica.

Guattari (2006, p. 82, 79) had stressed the importance of various disciplines, among them different art forms, to achieve spaces for liberating subjectivities: "Psychoanalysis, institutional analysis, film, literature, poetry, innovative pedagogies, town planning and architecture." He highlights the art's "process of 'becoming'," its capacity of working "against disciplinary boundaries," at the same time being integrated "in the social field." The arts are ideal spaces for subjectivity because they are able to "unframe" dominant discourses, to "rupture senses, forms, and significations" both in the personal and social field, being the two permanently entangled. Through decoding and deterritorializing, the arts can work as desiring machines (Deleuze & Guattari, 2009).

The unframing capacity of the arts leads "to a recreation and a reinvention of the subject itself," so that the "subjectivity of the artist and the 'consumer' is reshaped" (Guattari, 2006, p. 79; also Rolnik in Fernández Polanco & Pradel, 2015). The arts offer individual and collective reappropriation of the production of subjectivity. Their existential impact reconstitutes the social fabric of society. Constantly overthrowing their own current forms, the arts "untool" current forms of social life, of definitions of being together too. Both new subjects and social positions are created, substantiating "a critical cultural analysis, a reason for one's existence" (Larsen, 2006, p. 172). Subjectivity is brought directly in connection with structure—structure of society, structure of artistic institutions and production (Raunig, 2014 with referral to Benjamin's "The Author as Producer"). The spaces between subjectivity and structure are "affective and affecting, on the look-out and primed to change the world, based on embodied experience and testing the relationships." Facilities should be set up to help in this process, to lead to "embodied stances and social machines" in the sense of new social structures. By "experimenting with forms of organization," we experiment with new "forms of social recomposition" (Raunig, 2014, pp. 8, 15; also Deleuze & Guattari, 2009). After all, creating new forms of social composition means finding new forms for the self and vice versa (Negri, 2017; as well as Gramsci's thoughts explained in Chapter 3).

The spaces, however, must not just occupy "the free time of the unemployed and 'marginalized' in community centres," infantilizing them with directed and directive activities which exclude any creative uncertainty (Guattari, 2006, p. 80). Spaces of subjectivity are neither in the service of "self-withdrawal" nor do they distort "the common in 'creative' processes, as it appears individualistically alienated in capitalism," in favor of the "narcissism of the 'creative personality'" (Raunig, 2014, pp. 5–6). They also do not serve the so-called "scientific objectivity" which are reigning universities, submitted under a quantitative paradigm (Guattari, 2006, p. 81).

Coming back to Oiticica and his artwork, and aligning it with that of his close friend Lygia Clark, we can observe their focus on poetic "vivencias, or *lived experience*" (Bishop, 2006, p. 110). Through the sensory, they intended authentic and immediate experiences for and with the spectator-participant which would resist "ideological capture." In their art events, they aimed at external relations (both Oiticica and Clark) as well as psychological states (Clark, especially in her art work *Structuring of a Self*, Marxen, 2011, 2009b). In connection with others (physically or imagined), the spectators-participants subjectivity was addressed, defining the latter as always in relationship with the world and never as a solipsist practice (see Foucault, 2014, above).

In a similar vein, Guy Debord and the Situationists would call the spectator-participant "liver" (Bishop, 2006, p. 99), paralleling what in Brazil, Oiticica,

Clark, and Wanderley have developed as an art that would equate life as a work of art (also Rolnik in Fernández Polanco & Pradel, 2015).

The arts are especially suitable to facilitate spaces where subjectivity can unfold. Regarding different artistic practices, the "artistic dispositif" has been developed and proposed as an articulation of collective speech which refrain from overcoding realities and is able "to produce new figures, forms, constellations—in short, original material and cultural configurations that are inseparable from collective statements" (Marxen, 2018; Holmes, 2006, p. 421).

Among the different art practices and as already described in Chapter 2, art therapy can become an artistic dispositif, if it is freed from the dominant discourse of hegemony and its penetration, in Gramsci's sense; manifesting, for example, critical consideration or non-acceptance of the dominant medical discourse and its diagnosis.

In congruence with Deleuze and Guattari's ideas (1986) on minor language located at the edge of the dominating discourse, in the art therapy space, the participants' narratives can activate their hidden potential beyond the majority thinking and its mechanisms of marginalization and labeling. New horizons and alternatives are thus opened. A new way of being together is experienced, both with adults and peers on a micro level and with society at large on a macro level.

Referring once more to the art-life experience of the Brazilian artists Lygia Clark and Hélio Oiticica, art can function "as a vehicle for the liberation of the subject, in which they could, through the creative experience, reconstitute their own subjectivity and reconnect art and reality" (Carvajal, 1999, p. 51). In the art therapy space as described above, participants can give subjective meaning to their life experience through subjective verbal and artistic expressions of meaning; "these expressions being windows into the inner life of the person" (Denzin, 2014, p. 2).[2]

Facilitating a potential space for alternative narratives should be the common goal of critical art practices prone to be artistic dispositifs, whether in art therapy, ethnographic research, or critical contemporary art (Marxen, 2018). Overcoding and labeling are replaced by an open process that facilitates the free flow of desire expressed in images. Their meanings can challenge representational limits, frontiers, and ideological referencing (Marxen, 2018; Whitaker, 2012, 2005).

Or, in Suely Rolnik's words, through destabilization

> The process of creation might break free, carried off by its own desire, which will produce a different form. In those processes, different becomings of oneself and one's relational field come into being. The compass which guides desire in this case is an ethical compass. Its needle points to life itself, towards that which is asking to be let through so that life can keep breathing, pulsating. A compass which does not guide desire by means of form or content, this being exactly what will have to be created

> so that the new way of seeing and feeling finds a place. …What happens with desire … guided by the colonial-capitalistic unconscious, is completely different. In short, this consists of anaesthetising the affects and percepts, the body's ability to decipher the world from its condition as a living being, that is, from the effects of the world's forces on the forces, which make up the body.
>
> (Fernández Polanco & Pradel, 2015)

The experience of destabilization and uncertainty, however, can have horrible, isolating effects for the subject. According to Rolnik:

> Considering that it is a fundamental experience of subjectivity insomuch that it is the alarm indicating that life has taken us to an unknown state, already present in the body but still with no image, no word, no gesture. It is a state which imposes on desire a demand for thinking/acting, …to invent a new way of existing, other alliances, new feelings, etc.
>
> (Fernández Polanco & Pradel, 2015)

In short, subjectivity is called to participate in the process of creation and transformation of social and subjective existence (Rolnik, 2001).

The artistic dispositif facilitates precisely this searching, mostly in a visual way, favoring heterogeneous expression. At the same time, it gives room for uncertainties, thus opposing over-codification and automatic answers, and also the conditions for the articulation and symbolization of these inquiries. Simultaneously, it connects the subject with its subjectivity in the sense of bridging it with similarly inquiring minds and bodies in transits. Consequently, the feelings of existential isolation and exclusion are cushioned and fueled into new ways of being or becoming together. Then, society can rethink its ways of making and doing, interrupting "the common course of actions in the world" (García Canclini 2014; Laddaga, 2006, pp. 29–30).

We have already mentioned Deleuze and Guattari's concept of minor language. Here, this idea can help deconstruct institutionalized lives and situations of domination through the creation of alternative narratives.

In social science, "narrative is a methodological locus for understanding subjective experience and transformation of self in a cultural context" (Jenkins, 2015, p. 44, referring to Mattingly, 1998; Good, 1994; Peacock & Holland, 1993; Bruner, 1990; Kleinman, 1988; Sacks, 1990).

The contributions of the so-called "cognitive poetic," among others developed by Iser, Schaeffer, and Garrido (see Garrido, 2011; Warning, 1994), explain the prospects of narratives: People can "project in a relational space the possibilities of being" (González Gutiérrez, 2019, p. 97, translated by myself from Spanish). "Human expressions are mediated in the fictional, as a way of expression which complements the real and the possible," making the coexistence of the two possible (González Gutiérrez, 2019, p. 97). Fictionality allows the human being to overcome the narrow limits of the contingent and to be everything one wants to be, at the same time without giving up to be what one is (Garrido, 2011).

A potential relationship has been observed "between the construction of fictional dispositives and the construction of knowledge [in social science research] and the subjective experience" (González Gutiérrez, 2019, p. 98). The narrative is highly important for one's existence, especially since it is based on many social activities and communicative exchanges around the past, simultaneously relating the past to the present with an essential outlook towards the future (González Gutiérrez, 2019, referring to Garrido, 2011, p. 165).

This relates the fictional with the capacity of the arts to condense different time levels in one artwork (as described in Chapter 3) and to link alleged opposites in a poetic way. The same opposites are bridged that for logical, binary thinking are incompatible (Fiorini, 2010). The socially established and the dominant order can thus be overcome, in spaces that can furthermore combine knowledge with pleasure. In an artistic dispositif, subjectivities can be transformed, redeeming their capacities to resist the hegemonic order. The artistic dispositif is an assemblage in the sense of Deleuze and Guattari (1987, 1986), facilitating creative and poetic bridges between the fictional and the real, the personal and the collective, between past, present, and future. The assemblage becomes an "agencement," or what Holmes (2006) called "a 'device' for the articulation of collective speech" (p. 412).

Subjectivity and the Museum

The question now regards how the museum can provide spaces for the unfolding of subjectivity with or through the arts.

An example has already been outlined in form of the MACBA policies between 1999 and 2009. They provided the institutional frame for the art therapy groups to become artistic dispositifs.

But how can a more generalized formulation be found for museums to become artistic dispositifs or to facilitate them?

Claire Bishop (2013) animates "a rethinking of the museum, the category of art that it enshrines, and the modalities of spectatorship it produces" (p. 9). The "rethought" museum should represent an alternative "to the privatized contemporary museum creatively and intellectually crippled by its reliance upon blockbuster exhibitions designed to attract corporate investors, philanthropists, and mass audiences" (id.: p. 55; Chapter 5). In particular, museums of contemporary art should create and maintain space for "new political imaginary" (id.: p. 23, see Mouffe in Chapter 3).

In her book *Radical Museology*, Bishop (2013) describes three museum examples able to fulfil the above-mentioned requirements and characteristics: The Van Abbemuseum in Eindhoven, Netherlands; the Museum of Contemporary Art Metelkova or MSUM in Ljubljana, Slovenia; and the Museo Nacional Reina Sofia in Madrid. Interestingly and regarding the latter, she refers to the leadership of Manuel Borja-Villel, initiated in 2008 until present. Not coincidentally, Borja Villel was precisely the director of the MACBA during the extensively described time period (1999–2008).

In both museums, the rethinking of the usual Education Department has been crucial, both intellectually and economically, in terms of sustaining activities with an "emancipatory social potential" (Bishop, 2013, p. 49, although literally referring to the MSUM). To achieve this, in the first place, involved efforts to redefine the typical "art-appreciation classes," for example, with workshops like "Viewing the Viewers," wherein teenagers "are made aware of the museum as a discursive apparatus" (id.: p. 44). In this way, the typical museum mediation, located between image and viewer, should be replaced by activities that deal with the relation between knowledge and power. Instead of focusing on the represented, representation itself should be discussed and eventually contested (Laseca, 2015).

Manuel Borja-Villel (2010, p. 36 and in Molina, 2005) has opted for a "pedagogy of emancipation," a "potential element of liberation." To achieve this, the museum has to be considered a space for negotiation and dialogue as opposed to an evangelical space of transmission of knowledge about art. The public has to be given agency, from becoming participant to a self-organizing public (see Mouffe's and Borja's thoughts related to Gramsci in Chapter 3). Only in this way can the museum become a political project. In this sense, MACBA served as a platform for political movements and offered spaces to discuss the political movement itself, aspiring towards a new relationship between the artistic and political sphere (see above, Ribalta, 2010, 2006, 2004).

It is also a question of going beyond short-term activities, in the vein of the Program for Advanced Studies in Critical Practices in Madrid, "a free, six-month seminar for young artists, researchers, and activists who, due to the recession and high unemployment, constitute one of the most disaffected groups in the city" (Bishop, 2013, p. 45). The program was set up in strong contrast to the local universities and the profit-oriented courses offered by corporate art schools in the US or the UK.[3]

De/coloniality

Another focus of the Reina Sofia Museum has been the collaboration with the Network Conceptualisms South (Red Conceptualismos del Sur), a research network about critical art projects in Latin America, moving in the thresholds between art and politics, and focusing on art experiences able to oppose political, economic, and social oppression. This collaboration goes along with Borja's effort of the "Museum South," promoting art experiences, thoughts, politics, and practices from the Global South, namely Latin America. Dealing with Spain's colonial past is an important part of it, especially since the museum carries the last queen's name. The prominent role of documentations, archives, and archivists is taken into account by bringing all of the three to public use, i.e. in the museum's library and online, in combination with Public Program's activities. Since 2018, Ana Longoni, a very well-known Argentinean writer, curator, scholar, is its director. She has been publishing and curating Latin American critical/political art uninterruptedly since the beginning of the millennium until today. She is also one of the founding members of Conceptualismos del Sur and promotes "archivos en uso." According to the website, its purpose is to disseminate:

> Digital archives resulting from the collective research the Red Conceptualismos del Sur and Museo Reina Sofía have promoted with regard to the archives of the CADA (Colectivo de Acciones de Arte, Collective of Art Activities) group, from Chile, the creative practices of the Human Rights Movement in Argentina and the work of the Argentinian sociologist and artist Roberto Jacoby. The project addresses the public dimension, not the patronage, of the document, putting forward an alternative way of considering and articulating a museum's collection. … The digitalisation of archives facilitates the dissemination of valuable documentary heritage by means of low-resolution copies that guarantee their circulation and access to the public.
>
> (http://www.museoreinasofia.es/en/fundacion-comunes/archivos-uso-archives-use; see also http://www.archivosenuso.org)

The circulation of these archives is accessible for everybody and for free. The same accessibility applies to *Perder la forma humana* [Losing the Human Form, 2012], an itinerary show and archive of political art in Latin America in the eighties by Red Conceptualismos del Sur: https://jpgenrgb.files.wordpress.com/2017/05/perder_la_forma_humana_una_imagen_sismica_de_los_anos_ochenta.pdf.

In the same sense, the Reina Sofia museum now facilitates some catalogues of current temporary art shows for free, like Spanish feminist artist Ester Ferrer (2017): https://www.museoreinasofia.es/sites/default/files/Catalogos/esther_ferrer_eng.pdf.

The final goal of the museum here is to "increase accessibility to works of art," to concert the institution into an "archive of commons," (Bishop, 2013, p. 44), fostering the permanent exchange between the typical museum activities of collecting and producing exhibition with those of Public Programs. Also in this effort, the MACBA experience was a forerunner with its Study and Documentary Center, a first-class library of contemporary art and related disciplines, for absolute free use (https://www.MACBA.cat/en/ced).

In order to achieve this goal, the collection must be mobile and easy to distribute around the world, rather than being composed of "stones," unique pieces as immobile as the dominant discourse of history (Borja-Villel in Molina, 2005, see also Wodiczko, 1999, and Delgado, 2005, about monuments and the need to re-inscribe them in Marxen, 2009b). The role of museums is crucial in this context, especially since they have contributed or even produced "these stones" with their supposed originality, authenticity, and uniqueness (Crimp, 1993, p. 16).

At the Reina Sofia Museum, the point is to deauratize and defetishize the classical, typical, monumental museum collection by the archive, which itself can be considered a collage or juxtaposition of the official and unofficial, tangible art objects and discourses in the form of magazines, revues, newspaper articles, photos, including oral discourses, etc. The correspondence and exchange between the artistic artefact and the archive lead to "displacements, derivates, alternative narratives and countermodels" (Borja-Villel, 2008, p. 5). These seesaws constitute a new knowledge and aesthetic experience. The collection-archive has not one single root anymore but many different ones, and is rhizomatic in the sense of Deleuze and Guattari (1987; Borja-Villel, 2008).

Benjamin's thoughts of *The Work of Art in the Age of Mechanical Reproduction* (1968) and *The Author as Producer* (1998) are once again relevant. The possibilities of the *mechanical* reproduction of his time are now supplemented by digital means. They help to displace the aura of the supposedly unique collection by collective accessibility, the collection is converted into common goods (Borja-Villel, 2008). Technical possibilities of today can help to make the archive understood as alternative narratives without—in alignment with Benjamin—believing blindly in new technologies' progressiveness: Benjamin's ideas were "by no means marked by a technodeterminism, as he seeks to undermine every kind of determinism…" (Raunig, 2014, p. 8).

The archive is at the same time *topos* and *nomos* of narratives: a place and space to store and support them and a way of organizing accessibility and generating discourse about the archived (Borja-Villel, 2012, 2010, 2008, referring to Red Conceptualismos Sur, 2012; Derrida, 1996).

As a "discourse apparatus," the museum is working on rewriting art history and should give "space to practices that have been historically overlooked" (Bishop, 2013, p. 50). The Reina Sofia museum carries out practices, regarding both arts and political activism, with a special focus on Latin America.[4] This is especially necessary when considering that in South and Central America, artists have often been predecessors of what later in North America or Europe has been marketed, for example, as relational aesthetics. Bourriaud (1998) had claimed to have introduced this concept in Paris, although artists like Lygia Clark had already worked in the eighties in a much more intense way, establishing relational spaces of subjectivity (Butler & Pérez-Oramas, 2014; Marxen, 2011, 2009b; Rolnik, 2005; Borja-Villel & Enguita, 1998).[5] Regarding the dematerialization of the arts, in Argentina, Oscar Masotta (1968; Longoni & Mestman, 2004) had written about it in the same year like Lucy Lippard did, the latter having declared to have been the first (Longoni, 2017b; Longoni & Mestman, 2004; Lippard & Chandler, 1968). Many artists and thinkers of the South have hardly ever been given any credit for their highly relevant previous works. Other schools and currents of thoughts, like Critical Pedagogy, have sometimes been simplified, omitting its long history, the richness of thoughts and authors as well as its geographical variety within Latin America (González, 2018; Chapter 3).

Likewise, both community-based and socially engaged art have rapidly spread throughout North American art practice and academia over the past few decades. Yet, the intellectual, methodological, cultural, and political roots of these practices are to be revived in Latin America, the objective being to "redirect the legacies of the past" by "alternate mapping" (Kelley, 2017, p. 7). Different forms of epistemological imperialism are embedded in the global political economy of knowledge, capitalist subjectification as well as co-option of knowledge and alternative practices. This can be seen in the work of thinkers such as Silvia Rivera Cusicanqui (i.e. 2018a, 2018b, 2010), or Boaventura de Sousa Santos's work about the "epistemicide" (2014), which investigates how to oppose the "cognitive empire" (2018). They aim at detotalizing and decolonizing practices (see also the conference cycle *Learning art and Resistance from the South* organized by Marxen at SAIC, 2018: https://sites.saic.edu/talkingtoaction/events/learning-art-and-resistance-from-the-south-vol-1-brian-holmes-in-conversation-with-iconoclasistas/ and the eponymous issue of the journal FIELD: http://field-journal.com/editorial/field-issue-15-editorial).[6]

Additionally, conceptions of modernity and modern art have been developed parallelly and alternatively in Latin America, in permanent cosmopolitan contact with other parts of the world. They have led to new, plural, and sophisticated ways of understanding modernity. Particularly, they have questioned

> the validity of the modern project in the context of a colonial past and a neo-colonial present. Their reinstatement of the people as a producer of knowledge … stemmed from a conviction that other epistemologies were necessary in order to bring about social change.
>
> (González, 2018, p. 57)

This is especially prominent in the works of the Brazilian artists Tarsila do Amaral (D'Alessandr & Pérez-Oramas, 2017), Lygia Clark (Marxen, 2009b; Rolnik, 2005; Borja-Villel & Enguita, 1998), Hélio Oiticica (Small, 2016), Mira Schendel (Pérez-Oramas, 2009) as well as Gego (Bois et al., 2006), the latter in Venezuela (Borja-Villel, 2010, 2008; for more artists of the continent: González, 2018; Martin & Ruiz, 1999).

Artists have been able to express and denounce forms of epistemological imperialism embedded in an oppressive global political economy of knowledge, initiated at least half a century ago and among others by the University of Chicago in the form of grants for the so-called "Chicago Boys," economy students of Milton Friedman who would study neoliberalism firsthand in order to implement it in their home countries—with the most atrocious violations of human rights (especially interesting are the following films about the Chicago Boys: *The Battle of Chile* I-III by Patricio Guzman, 1976/1998; *The Conspiracy* (original title: *Héros fragiles. Chili 1973. Affaire non classée*) by Emilio Pacull, 2006; *Chicago Boys* by Carola Fuentes and Rafael Valdeavellano, 2015, as is Juan Downey's eponymous video from 1983).

Mignolo has written extensively about the relationship between museums and colonization (2014, 2011, 2010). Until today, museums contribute to the colonialization of knowledge. Regarding the accumulation of money and wealth through colonial exploitation, "Europe also accumulated meaning" (Mignolo, 2011, p. 71) through the crucial institutions of museum and universities. The emergence of the museum as an institution during Renaissance was linked to "the logic of coloniality," meaning "the need to convert and civilize the inhabitants of the planet that were still outside history, the barbarians and primitives" (p. 73). That is why two types of museums were mainly articulated in Europe: That which would document the richness and superiority of European history and another, the ethnographic or natural museum, that would document "the Other," otherness, and the "other cultures." As opposed to the archive of Western civilization, "the archives of the rest of the world" (Mignolo, 2014, p. 7) were not given the same life, because they only consisted of "representative artifacts of 'other memories.'" They never intended to activate these cultural memories, "contained in those ripped off gadgets, displaced from their context" (Mignolo, 2014, p. 7; see also Clifford, 1988).

In this sense, Mignolo (2014) offers three main museums which have embodied the Western colonial museum project: The Ethnological Museum of Berlin, the British Museum in London and the Louvre in Paris. All these museums are based on their nation-state project, including their colonial narrative. After having succeeded (in the case of France) or tried more or less successfully to expel the aristocrat class, the museums also responded to the needs inside the countries to construct and showcase a new national narrative and destiny (Laseca, 2015). Let us not forget that these museums (and others) remained tourist attractions, having even increased their volume. This is neo-colonialism and the present fate of plundered artworks and legacies from former empires (Borja-Villel, 2010).

Mignolo (2011) further proposes what a museum can do in terms of decolonization. For him, it is not enough to change the museum's contents but rather urges for an "epistemic and aesthetic disobedience that opens up and put on the table the decolonial option" (p. 83).

Together with Mignolo, more Latin American authors and artists have been at the forefront of the concept of "coloniality," articulated by Peruvian sociologist Anibal Quijano (2000), and defined by Mignolo (2007) as the concept that "has opened up the reconstruction and the restitution of histories, subjectivities, knowledges, and languages silenced, repressed, and subalternized by the Totality depicted under the names of modernity and rationality" (p. 451).

In return, the Coloniality/Decoloniality framework offers theoretical and cultural "strategies of resistance to a modernity that perpetuates the colonial condition." This "decolonial option of delinking, [has] mostly [appeared] in the form of what has been described as epistemic disobedience and border thinking, … strategies of resistance to a modernity that perpetuates the colonial condition" (González, 2018, p. 267).

In her article "Memories of Underdevelopment: Art and the Decolonial Turn in Latin America, 1960–1985," belonging to the eponymous show and catalogue, curator Julieta González (2018) correctly points out that "this kind of reflection in the cultural field is not the exclusive province of the Modernity/Coloniality/Decoloniality group" (p. 27). Whether Paulo Freire and Ivan Illich's ideas on conscientization and deschooling in the 60s and 70s, Enrique Dussel's *Philosophy of Liberation* (2003) or Néstor García Canclini's *Hybrid Cultures* (2005a), all are proposing "strategies to enter and exit modernity; more recently, many theorists have argued in favor of the epistemologies of the South, as ones that 'adequately account for the realities of the Global South'" (see above and Chapter 3).

Still before or simultaneously to the mentioned authors, many of their thoughts "had been anticipated in the fields of visual arts, architecture, and film, across Latin America, beginning in the early 1960s." The objective of the *Memories of Underdevelopment* show, produced at the Museum of Contemporary Art in San Diego, has precisely been the effort "to identify and map these early instances of a decolonial turn in art and culture as an important part of this history" (González, 2018, p. 27; Chapter 3).

Coming back to the museum, Mignolo has mainly detected two ways to achieve the decolonial museistic turn through aesthetic disobedience: One consists in decolonial interventions in already existing museums. He illustrates this option with Fred Wilson's work, especially his *Mining the Museum* (1992). It consisted of a multiple installation at the Maryland Historical Society, co-organized with the Museum of Contemporary Art. Wilson rearranged different artifacts, thus revealing their colonialist origins, especially in the context of slave trade and racism.

In a vein similar to showing the relationship of racism and museum publics, the Museum of Impact (MOI) denounces the "Western, patriarchal voice of representation" and "ivory tower curation" in museums together with their exclusion of publics of color (Montgomery & Heller, 2017 pp. 156, 163). The MOI intends to put this discrimination into evidence and to change it by proposing a "counter discursive space" of "critical public pedagogy" (Montgomery & Heller, 2017, p. 157; also Sandell, 2016, with further inquiries of museum representations and narratives concerning the LGTBQ collectives; Janes, 2009, for disability representation).[7]

Within this option of decolonial interventions in already existing museum I would also add as another example like the *Decolonizing the Museum* seminar, curated by Preciado at the MACBA (2014: https://www.MACBA.cat/en/decolonising-museum). One of its presenters, Daniela Ortiz together with Xose Quiroga, had elaborated the *Nation State Project* (2013). By means of their photography series, they "read the slave-based colonial past of Barcelona [and Catalonia] through its statues, commemorative plaques and buildings" (https://www.MACBA.cat/en/estat-nacio-part-1-exercici-1-historia-general-joan-prim-i-prats-5100; for more information about Ortiz' work: http://daniela-ortiz.com).

Preciado's seminar is already an example for the second way a museum can work in the decolonization vein: the integration of decolonializing museum practices into other areas of "the socioeconomic spectrum and in the decoloniality of being and *subjectivity*" (Mignolo, 2011, p. 85; italicization added). Education and public programs of museums are considered prone areas. Yet, the decolonializing museum practices are not bound to the museum in its architectural limits. Rather, they should spread to other sectors of the city. In this context, Ribalta had already proposed a "demusealization" ("desmusealización"), a liberation of the museum from its most rigid and authoritarian historical legacies, that is no other than the heritage of the enlightenment project of a popular education (Ribalta, 2010, pp. 240, 225).

The museum should not follow the cultural industry in perpetuating a cult or fetichization of difference. It should rather foster a back and forth movement and feedback with equal rights. It should follow "an inversion of the systems of power/knowledge towards a proactive strategy of relocation" and finally aim at new epistemologies (Laseca, 2015, pp. 46, 76; translated by myself from Spanish).

Gender

Regarding gender, Pollock has developed the Virtual Feminist Museum (2007). It is meant to be an "open laboratory," a "counter-museum," yet not a cybernetic museum space in the internet (Pollock, 2007, p. 11). Here, virtual instead refers to a museum that has never been realized due to gender power mechanism inherent to (art) history. It does not inquire into "what art is *about*," but instead questions "*what artistic practice is doing* and *where* as well as *when* that doing occurs." It aims at changing the canon and is virtual in "the philosophical sense of always becoming and as yet incompletely harvested" (Pollock, 2013, p. xxvii, italics in the original; Pollock, 2007, 1999). She also draws on Foucault and Derrida in order to deconstruct the museum archive. For her, the archive is:

> Pre-selected in ways that reflect what each culture considered worth storing and remembering, skewing the historical record … towards the privileged, the powerful, the political, the military and religious. Vast areas of social life and huge members of people hardly exist, according to the archive. The archive is overdetermined by facts on class, race, gender, sexuality and above all power.
>
> (Pollock, 2007, p. 12)

The Virtual Feminist Museum opposes the chronicle absence of women's histories in archives and aims at refiguring the representation of women. It focuses on

> feminist appropriation of the concept of museum's speciality: the exhibition as *encounter* that opens up new critical relations among artworks, and between viewers and artworks, that points to repressed narratives in the histories of art, and continues … the feminist project of *differencing the canon*.
>
> (Pollock, 2007, p. 13)

She understands the latter as a process of "gendering, engendering and differentiating in relation to an axis of meaning, power and sociality: sex-gender" (Pollock, 2007, p. 14).

Discourse Apparatus

As a discourse apparatus, "the museum…is a figure of the system; at the same time it is shown to provide its cover: it installs the creating subject in its place" (Crimp, 1993, p. 13).

While Foucault had analyzed "modern institutions of confinement –the asylum, the clinic, and the prison—and their respective discursive formations – madness, illness, and criminality," Crimp (1993, p. 48) has added

> another such institution of confinement awaiting archeological analysis – the museum—and another discipline—art history. They are the preconditions for the discourse that we know as modern art. And Foucault himself suggested the way to begin thinking about this analysis.

From its very beginning, the museum has been operated as a disciplinary institution of social control. It has been conceived to regulate, police, and discipline its visitors, who, from the end of the 19th and beginning of the 20th centuries, were mainly the working class. "New display techniques seemed to respond to this anxiety by organizing the walking of visitors, and exhibitions became disciplinary technologies" (Henning, 2007, pp. 42–43). Nowadays, these displays have reached a maximum of technological sophistication and can—besides democratizing the exhibition and the archive (above)—also perfect social control.

In alignment with Foucault, Crimp (1993) has proposed an

> archeology versus art history… a postmodernism of resistance versus a postmodernism of accommodation. An epistemological rupture is necessary to experience the transformations that Foucault describes. But it is not, of course, only the organization of knowledge that is unrecognizably transformed at certain moments in history. New institutions of power as well as new discourses arise.
>
> (p. 14)

Together they form new dispositifs. These two phenomena, the transformation of knowledge and experience as well as the arousal of new institutions, are interdependent.

On an institutional level, this means an experimentation with new kinds of institutions, practices, and rules, through a radical institutional critique (Ribalta, 2010). The idea is to offer a counterproposal to mausoleum museums, "apart from the usual flows in daily life." Museums must be resocialized, once again emphasizing the "commitment that the museum has to the social"

(Bennett, 2009, p. 179, translated from Spanish by myself), without entering into a dynamic of behavioral transformation or control over the population as a panoptic museum in Foucault's sense. Regarding the connection between "museum and mausoleum," Bennett (2009) refers to Adorno (1967) and his text about the "Valéry Proust Museum." There, Adorno contrasts two positions, those of Valéry and Proust, in terms of the life of the artwork: For the latter, the life of the artwork begins where it ends for the first—with the *afterlife* of the work of art. Contrasting Valéry's opinion, the essence is not located in the work itself but is due to the subject who observes it and relates it to their internal life. Yet, according to Adorno, it is not a matter of locating the truth either in one position or in the other, but in "a 'force field' between the subjective and the objective" (ibid, p. 183). The museums have to undertake an effort so that this encounter between the subjective and objective takes place, at the same time as it requires work and an openness of the spectator.

So, museums and other art institutions should open themselves up for interactions and consider the public as

> a project, like the potential for constructing something that does not yet exist… It is precisely this non pre-existence of the public (what we might term its fantasmatic dimension) that suggests the possibility of reconstructing a critical cultural public sphere.
>
> (Ribalta, 2010, p. 231)

Fraser has elaborated on her concept of "subaltern counterpublics" that refers "to the 'parallel discursive arenas where members of subordinated social groups invent and circulate counterdiscourses to formulate oppositional interpretations of their identities, interests and needs'" (Fraser, 1997. pp. 115–117; as in Ribalta, 2010, p. 231).

For this to exist, a free or affordable entrance is paramount but not enough to overcome symbolic barriers, very often due to social class segregations (Rosler, 2013; Bourdieu, 1996a, 1996b, 1984, 1968).

As a "discourse apparatus," the museum should invite collective discussion of what people "consider important in culture" (Bishop, 2013, p. 61) and the meaning of culture itself. It should offer spaces of sociability, participation rather than of consumerism. It should foster relationships, the relational without indoctrination, a space of reflection, of questions rather than answers, a knowledge to explore, critical discussions, and a better understanding of the world which surrounds us (Sesé 2013a, 2013b). These spaces are the necessary first step towards social change (Borja-Villel; 2008).[8]

The artist Hélio Oiticia had articulated similar thought regarding the museum:

> My route through and around the inauguration of the Parangoles thus rearticulates the epistemic shift, …, of an alternate model of a museum: one that does not stand polemically between art and anti-art (or more

> crudely, art and life) but functions as a space for the investigation of living things. …The museum is the world.
>
> (Small, 2016, pp. 226–227)

In alignment with Oiticica's, Foucault's, and Crimp's ideas of discontinuity, epistemological rupture, deterritorialization, and transformation, Bishop (2013) refers for good reason to Walter Benjamin's idea of constellations. They imply "a Marxist project of bringing events together in new ways, disrupting established taxonomies, disciplines, mediums, and properties" (p. 56). An essential element for this is Benjamin's dialectical images. The shock provoked by the dialectical image helps us to understand present conditions in order to change them. The museum should provide the space for this task. Then, art "becomes a primary means for visualizing alternatives; rather than thinking of the museum collection as a storehouse of treasures, it can be reimagined as an archive of commons" (Bishop, 2013, p. 56). These ideas seem directly linked to archivosenuso, MACBA's former and Museo Reina Sofia's current ideas of redefining the relationship between the museum and citizenship, both being "an active, historical agent that speaks in the name not of … hegemony but of creative questioning and dissent" (id., p. 59).

Bishop (2013, p. 59) draws on Benjamin's *Arcades Project* (2002) and his "poetic constellations" which represent a "present-minded approach to history," thus producing an understanding of todays' issues. The "poetic constellations" also mirror the poetic capacities of the narrative space or the artistic dispositif as mentioned before: Different tenses are brought into context, making possible what the pure rational thinking might prohibit but without losing contact to reality. It is a question of tertiary processes, beyond the mere logic, on the one hand ("secondary processes" according to Freud) and the "id" and compulsion-driven primary processes, on the other. Héctor Fiorini (2010) describes the tertiary process as a disorganization of constituted forms, being at the same time a reorganization of new forms or new senses. In addition, they link oppositions and thus establish new networks of meaning, coexisting in different temporary forms. Fiorini compares this tertiary mechanism with an architecture that establishes multiple connections between these different levels of thoughts and between elements of each level (2010). In this way, tertiary mechanisms can link and mediate between opposites, which for secondary thought would be contrasts: center/exterior, life/death, white/black, victory/defeat, etc. In short, they invite for a creative ambiguity.

Agreeing with Borja-Villel (2010, p. 31; 2008), there are three main ways that a museum can disrupt the hegemonic discourse, the neoliberalization of culture, humanities and art, and the culture of spectacle:

- The permanent search for alternative narratives of modern history (also in alignment with Crimp, 1993, see above).
- New forms of intermediation.
- Considering the spectator as an agent, a political subject as opposed to passive subject, a mere contemplator and neoliberalized consumer.

All these tasks would make the museum an artistic dispositif with spaces where participants can develop their own alternative narratives, always in interconnection with the social and the political, changing at the same time themselves and the surrounding world, including re-writing their own and the world's history. In these spaces, personal and collective desire can flow and be articulated.

Re-writing one's own and institutional or institutionalized histories leads us inevitably to the practice of institutional critique. It is based on "a democratic radicalization" and leads to "the dissemination of spaces of criticism, freedom, play and experimentation in other institutional areas (schools or hospitals, for example), thereby extending the symbolic privilege of the artistic to other fields." In summary, it is "a deterritorialized conception of the museum" (Ribalta, 2010, p. 232). The deterritorialized conception of the museum can also be considered as nomadic. In this context, nomadism is a key aspect of our reflections around museums and subjectivity.

Nomadism and the Nomadic Museum

Before, we had already mentioned the "productive force of nomadism" and its importance within the production of subjectivity (Foucault, 2009). In *A Thousand Plateaus,* Deleuze and Guattari (1980/1987) have described how power can be dismantled by "deterritorializing gestures" (Glissant, 2006). Subjectivities should be "nomadic—that is, free and dynamic… moving in the nomadic rhythm of their appearance, against every machine that is fixed, centralisng and castrating" (Glissant, 2006, p. 71). Previously, in the *Anti-Oedipus* (2009), Deleuze and Guattari described the "'deterritorialized' flows of desire, …, the *desiring-machines* that escape … codes as *lines of escape* leading elsewhere" (Seem, 2009, p. xvii). In this vein, they had mentioned art's revolutionary capacity to decodify and deterritorialize, thus opening spaces for desire.

Being without fixed habits or territories, the nomadic produces new "assemblages of enunciation that open onto new rhizomatic arborescences." As "a terrain of subjectivity," they "allow desire to deploy." They travel and are "to be travelled, indefinitely;" they are "never at rest" (Negri, 2017, pp. 175–176). They utmostly challenge the hegemonic, dominant, in the words of Deleuze and Guattari "molar" order, which does not avoid any effort "to absorb the force of desire and to reshape the *dispositifs* with the sole purpose of blocking the pragmatic flux of the molecular." The "molecular flux" with its force of utmost resistance, however, "is ungraspable, it constantly seeks to overturn the *dispositifs* of blockage and to open the way to historicity" (Negri, 2017, p. 176, italics in the original). Referring again to Deleuze & Guattari's *A Thousand Plateaus* (1980/1987), it is a question of "the molecular *dispositif* of desires to resist the molar order, to avoid it, to get around it, to flee it" (p. 176). And that is precisely the revolution: "A line of flight, organised by the creativity of desire, by the infinite molecular movement of subjects, by a pragmatics that is reinvented at every moment" (Negri, 2017, p. 176; also Ribalta, 2010). This infinite process must be turned into event, or *Kairos*, as described by Negri (2000). *Kairos* is "the opportune moment that ruptures the monotony and repetitiveness of chronological time" [*chronos*]. *Kairos* is an event, not measurable in quantitative terms but describes a decisive moment of great importance, a breakthrough that "has to be grasped by a political subject" (Hardt & Negri, 2009, p. 165). Then, political resistance becomes possible through political organization (Krauss, 2017; Hardt & Negri, 2009). *Kairos* is the "restless creator of the future" that actively takes "the world in one's hand to transform it and to innovate it, radically in the common" (Negri, 2000, p. 54; translated from Italian by myself). This "common" has been called "multitude," considering it "a radical plurality, … a multiplicity of irreducible singularities" (Hardt & Negri, 2009, p. 166; 2004, 2000). The opening of *Kairos* towards the future is an imagination in form of a "linguistic gesture." It is "the creative prospecting of the future" (Negri, 2000, p. 30). At the same time, it is the extension of the self towards others, of one *Kairos* to multiple *Kairos*. Together, we are a chain of events, which are created by the process of denominations. "These events of denominating constitute common names" (p. 29). They can confront each other, dialogue with each other, or eventually clash against each other. It is within the rapport with the other that the name extends itself towards the common. The being reveals itself as *Mit-sein*, as "being with" (Negri, 2000, p. 29). Thus, *Kairos* produces subjectivity, the latter understood as the connections of the different monads of *Kairos*. Subjectivity happens after and not before *Kairos*.

Negri's works had been in constant triangular impregnation with Deleuze and Guattari's. That is why it is not surprising that some aspects of Negri's *Kairos* are reflected also in Deleuze and Guattari's concept of minor literature (1980/1987) and vice versa. Deleuze and Guattari summarized minor literature by the three following characteristics: "The deterritorialization of language, the connection of the individual to a political immediacy, and the collective assemblage of enunciation" (Mazzei, 2017, p. 3; Deleuze & Guatarri, 1980/1987, p. 18). Furthermore, "(i)n an assemblage, there are no singulars, only connectives" (Mazzei, 2017, p. 4). Another crucial aspect for the two French authors is the "creation of a new language… as a way to interrupt and rupture our ways of thinking" (Mazzei, 2017, p. 5).

The collective assemblage of enunciation with its minor language as outlined by Deleuze & Guattari (1987) as well as Negri's *Kairos* (2000) bring us back, once again, to the definition of the artistic dispositif, a space of articulation of collective speech and desire (see above; Marxen, 2018; Holmes, 2006).

In his *Poetics of Relation*, Edouard Glissant (1997) starts from Deleuze and Guattri's (1987) critique of the root and being rooted. In return, they propose:

> The rhizome, an enmeshed root system, a network spreading either in the ground or in the air, with no predatory rootstock taking over permanently. The notion of the rhizome maintains, therefore, the idea of rootedness but challenges that of a totalitarian root. Rhizomatic thought

> is the principle behind what I call the Poetics of Relation, in which each and every identity is extended through a relationship with the Other.
> (Glissant, 2006, p. 71)

Nomadism can liberate beings and being, "in contrast, …, to a settled way of life, with its law based upon the intolerant root" and its immobility and restrictiveness. Thus, nomadism leads to anti-conformism, anti-conventionalism, to skepticism as well as anarchy as a life attitude. Yet, according to Glissant, Deleuze & Guattari extol nomadism. Equating its essence with subversiveness would mean to revert it "to ideological claims presumably challenged by this thought." It would submit nomadism under a determinism that the very nomadism opposes (Glissant, 2006, p. 71).[9]

In this sense, Glissant (2006, p. 72) opposes an invading, arrowlike nomadism in favor of a circular one. He defines the latter as "a not-intolerant form of an impossible settlement." The first, however, is characterized by the "devastating desire for settlement," manifest by conquerors and colonializers.

"Exile can be seen as beneficial, when … experienced as a search for the Other (through circular nomadism) rather than as an expansion of territory (an arrowlike nomadism)" (Glissant, 2006, p. 75). It should lead to relations with the Other, and not to their submission. The Other is necessary to find oneself, as a pre-condition and defining for the self.

Also, Merleau-Ponty (1960, 1945; López Sáez, 1996) reasoned about the relation of self-other as a common insertion in a historical and social world. For him, alterity is constitutional, and so is intercorporeality. Simultaneously there is, however, a differentiation of bodies. It is at the same time a relation and tension with the other, like a hinge that is the constitution of intersubjectivity (Marxen, 2012).

Glissand (2006) speaks of "the tale of errantry" which "is the tale of Relation": "…errantry gives-on-and-with the negation of every pole and very metropolis, whether connected or not to a conqueror's voyaging act" (p. 76). The resulting relation of errantry "opposes the totalitarianism of any monolingual intent." The root is monolingual but relationality gives space for identities which do not refer monolinguistically to a sole "creation of the world but to the conscious and contradictory experience of contacts among cultures" (Glissant, 2006, p. 78). These identities stem from a "chaotic network of Relation," instead of "the hidden violence of filiation" (ibid).

At the same time, Glissant (1997) as well as García Canclini (2005b), Gielen (2015), Spivak and Butler (2007) point out the difference in social class, between those who have been forcefully uprooted and those who enjoy a luxurious form of their errantry, which in its "caricatural form" would be tourism (Glissant, 2006, p. 76). For Boltanski and Chiapello (2005), mobility has even become one of the most discriminatory factors, leading to new social class inequalities (see also Larsen, 2006). Especially Gielen (2015) has warned against "the aestheticization of the nomadic existence" in contemporary art institutions, serving with it "the prevailing neoliberal hegemony, including post-Fordist working conditions" (p. 107). The nomad operates in an individual or even individualist structure, institutionally untied and exempted from collective support. This makes them prone to any labor exploitation. Yet, and together with Deleuze and Guattari (2010, 1980/1987), Gielen still assumes a nomadic position of an alternative outsiderness that makes a counter-hegemony possible. It is a question of positioning oneself "in opposition of the organs of State Power" (Deleuze & Guattari, 2010, p. 15). As an artistic strategy, this can only happen if nomadism becomes communist. Together with Gielen, Hardt and Negri (2004, 2002), Guattari and Negri (2010, 1996), Gramsci and de Martino (Chapter 3) do not refer here to a Soviet communist model. The desirable communism, however, is stateless, opposing the one and only authority, in the form of a nation-state, "precisely because it is nomadic … Communism then amounts to a universal call to radical equality in an endless variety of forms" (Gielen, 2015, p. 113; see also Badiou, 2009). For the artists, that means to reveal inequalities, to choose sides to become part "of collective emancipatory subjectivities" (Gielen, 2015, p. 113). Then, this nomadism becomes alive politically (Gielen, 2015; see also Didi-Huberman about Brecht, 2018). If they refuse nomadic communism, they rather use fashionable art travelling. This is done in order to:

> soak up the Other and make it their own, in order to build up … artistic identity. … When artists are tempted to do this, their activities go no further than age-old colonial practice. However ambulatory, engaged or politically radical their work may appear to be, ultimately it remains caught up in the neoliberal war machine. Then … the nomadic rhetoric is no more than a handy marketing strategy.
>
> (Gielen, 2015, p. 113)

Returning to Borja's reasoning of the museum (2010, 2008), he argues in alignment with Glissand (1997), that many cultures tend to base their history of art and literature on some foundational texts that have usually achieved some secret, absolute, divine, and exclusive value for their community. These have often been great narratives constitutive for the ideologies of the 19th and 20th centuries and eventually abused for the claim of power over the rest of the world. These works include, for example, the Old and New Testaments, the Iliad and the Odyssey, and the Germanic and Islandic Sagas (Glissand, 2006). Following Glissant, "these writings are intimately linked to the closed object," to immobility, and linear thinking. Nowadays, however, this form of formal unity has become obsolete, in a world which requires and implies "multiple forms of relation that challenge our mental structures" (Borja-Villel, 2010, p. 31). These complex forms of relationality should lead to the process of a rhizomatic identity, as opposed to archaic and unique. The roots are multiple (rhizomatic) and open the way to other cultures and other ways of doing in our minds and practices (Borja-Villel, 2010, 2008). History is not to be conceived of as composed by great continents but as an archipelago. Instead of one sole origin or myth of origin, there are multiple ones (Borja-Villel, 2005).

> We do not narrate anymore from the privileged palestra of the unique voice but immersed in a multiplicity of micro-narrations whose consequence is a new cartography of art. Now, one cannot say anymore that New York has stolen from Paris the idea of Modern Art [*How New York Stole the Idea of Modern Art* by Serge Guilbaut, 1985], because it shows up in multiple sites and because there is nothing left to steal. There are only relationships to establish and to visualize. … The narratives have to question the notion of *the author* and to renounce the idea of the romantic genius. We cannot conceive anymore history as a succession of great personalities … but as a crowd of secondaries, the multitude … of events, destinies, movements, and vicissitudes.
>
> (Borja-Villel, 2008, p. 4; italics by myself)

Instead of aura, we desauratize and develop the "multitude," as outlined by Negri as the most powerful bodies invested by nomadism, hybridization, and mutation (Negri, 2017, p. 173). This multitude is a new model of resistance against global systems of power and oppression (Hardt & Negri, 2009, 2004, 2002). It is not a static subject or concept "but a project of political organization," shifting from being to making multitude (Hardt & Negri, 2009, p. 169). Art and politics can converge in the production of a common imaginary, at the same time, leading to an agonistic public sphere, one that is not collapsed by an imposed common sense (Mouffe, 2017, 2012, 2007, in Chapter 3; Ribalta, 2010).

Far away from being—or letting itself be—protected by its walls, the nomadic museum should be considered a "heart valve," facilitating a constant flow of inner and outer forces in from of continuous conflicts and debates (Laseca, 2015, p. 18). The walls' porosity is the starting point for "a collaborative, transparent, and self-conscious intelligence." They work like membranes that receive vibrations, amplifying them towards the social territory. "These membranes, furthermore, do not hide their schizoid dimensions in their articulation between the internal and external side of the place. … between centripetal and centrifuge images" (Laseca, 2015, p. 45, the latter opposition stems from Lévi-Strauss, 2004; also Camnitzer, 2018).

Concluding this chapter, Ribalta (2010) relates Deleuze and Guattari's (1980/1987) molecular spaces to the museum in the context of institutional critique and deterritorialization:

> To use the terms of Deleuze and Guattari, we could say that the idea is to introduce molecular spaces into molar structures. The experimental hypothesis is the possibility of constructing a new institutionality that is more in keeping with the conditions of forms of subjectivisation and the social experiences of our times and open to the future.
>
> (p. 232)

Notes

1 In December 2007, he was unanimously elected director of the Reina Sofia Art Center, Madrid. He directs it until today.
2 See for the possibilities of contemporary art to become an artistic dispositif Chapter 5.
3 Previously, at the MACBA, the Program of Independent Studies (PEI, see Chapter 2) had been established, with similar objectives like in Madrid, in the beginning still affordable, yet not for free, and after Borja's leave with a significant increase of tuition fee.
4 The MSUM in Ljubljana operates in a similar vein like the Reina Sofia Museum focusing on East European practices, combating the exclusive "disavowal of the communist past in official discourse" (Bishop, 2013, en. 20).
5 Foster (2006) also mentions Oiticica and Clark as processors and adds Arte Povera, Marcel Broodthaers, and Hans Haacke.
6 See for the same unequal relation between West Europe and North America on the one side and East Europe on the other Cufer (2006).
7 See for the relationship of museum, art, and publics Bourdieu (1996a, 1996b, 1984, 1968) as well as for counter-publics Warner, 2005; Fraser, 1997; Mouffe, 1993; Ribalta, 2010, above.
8 See for the architectural translation of uncertainty Basu (2007). He refers to labyrinthine aesthetics in museums, most notably to Libeskind's Felix Nussbaum Haus (1998) as well as the Jewish Museum (2001). His museum architecture unsettles by distorting "one's habitual perspective" (Basu, 2007, pp. 56–57). It fragments and disorientates, making us questioning what is representable.
9 See also the relevant ideas of movement and non-determinism in anarchism Ibáñez (2014).

References

Adorno, T.W. (1967). Valéry-Proust museum. In T.W. Adorno, *Prism* (pp. 173–185). Cambridge, MA: MIT Press.

Badiou, A. (2009). *L'hypothèse communiste* [The communist hypothesis]. Paris, France: Nouvelles Edtitions Lignes.

Basu, P. (2007). The labyrinthine aesthetic in contemporary museum design. In P. Basu, & S. Macdonald (Eds.), *Exhibition experiments* (pp. 47–70). Oxford, UK: Blackwell Publishing.

Benjamin, W. (2002). *The Arcades Project.* New York, NY: Belknap Press.

Benjamin, W. (1998). *Understanding Brecht.* London, UK: Verso.

Benjamin, W. (1968). The work of art in the age of mechanical reproduction. In H. Arendt (Ed.), *Illuminations: Essays and reflections* (pp. 217–251). New York, NY: Schocken Books.

Bennett, T. (2009). Museo [Museum]. In M.J. Borja-Villel, & J. Ribalta (Eds.), *Ideas concebidas* [Conceived ideas], (pp. 179–195). Barcelona, Spain: MACBA.

Bifo, Berardi, F. (2003). What is the meaning of autonomy today? Subjectivation, social composition, refusal of work. *Transversal – eipcp multilingual webjournal.* Retrieved from: http://eipcp.net/transversal/1203/bifo/en [Accessed 28 January 2019; no longer available].

Bishop, C. (2013). *Radical museology. Or what's 'contemporary' in museums of contemporary art.* London, UK: Koenig Books.

Bishop, C. (2006). *Participation.* London, UK: Whitechapel Gallery and Cambridge, MA: MIT Press.

Bois, Y.A., Amor, M., Brett, G., & Peruga, I. (2006). *Gego. Defying structures* (exh. cat.) Barcelona, Spain: MACBA.
Boltanski, L., & Chiapello, E. (2005). *The new spirit of capitalism.* London, UK: Verso.
Borja-Villel, M.J. (2010). The museum questioned. In M.J. Borja-Villel, K. Cabañas, & J. Ribalta (Eds.), *Relational objects. MACBA collection 2002–2007* (pp. 19–39). Barcelona, Spain: MACBA.
Borja-Villel, M.J. (2008). Museos del Sur. *El País*, 20 December 2008.
Borja-Villel, M.J., & Enguita, N. (1998). (Eds.). *Lygia Clark* (exh. cat.). Barcelona, Spain: Fundació Antoni Tàpies.
Bourdieu, P. (1996a). *The rules of art: Genesis and structure of the literary field.* Stanford, CA: Stanford University Press.
Bourdieu, P. (1996b). *Photography: A middle-brow art.* Stanford, CA: Stanford University Press.
Bourdieu, P. (1984). *Distinction.* London, UK and New York, NY: Routledge.
Bourdieu, P. (1968). Elementos de una teoría sociológica de la percepción artística [Elements of a sociological theory of artistic perception]. Revue Internationale de Sciences Sociales [International Journal of Social Science], XX(4), 640–664.
Bourriaud, N. (1998). *Relational aesthetic.* Dijon, France: Les presses du réel.
Brecht, B. (2014). *Brecht on theatre.* London, UK: Bloomsbury Academic.
Brion, F., & Harcourt, B.E. (2014). The Louvain lectures in context. In M. Foucault, *Truth telling, wrong doing* (pp. 271–321). Chicago, IL: University of Chicago Press.
Bruner, J. (1990). *Acts of meaning.* Cambridge, MA: Harvard University Press.
Buck-Morss, S. (2005). *Walter Benjamin, escritor revolucionario* [Walter Benjamin. Revolutionary author]. Buenos Aires, Argentina: Interzona Editora.
Butler, C., & Pérez-Oramas, L. (Eds.). (2014). *Lygia Clark. The abandonment of art, 1948–1988* (exh. cat.). New York, NY: The Museum of Modern Art.
Butler, J., & Spivak, G.C. (2007). *Who sings the nation? Language, politics, belonging.* Oxford, UK and New York, NY: Seagull Books.
Camnitzer, L. (2018). The museum is a school. In MNCARS (Eds.), *Hospice of failed utopias* (exh. cat.) (pp. 245–254). Madrid, Spain: MNCARS.
Carvajal, R. (1999). The experimental exercise of freedom. In S. Martin, & A. Ruiz (Eds.), *The experimental exercise of freedom: Lygia Clark, Gego, Mathias Goeritz, Hélio Oiticica, and Mira Schendel* (exh. cat.) (pp. 33–54). Los Angeles, CA: Museum of Contemporary Art.
Chow, R. (2006). *The age of the world target.* Durham, NC: Duke University Press.
Clifford, J. (1988). *The predicament of culture: Twentieth-century ethnography, literature, and art.* Boston, MA: Harvard University Press.
Crimp. D. (1993). *On the museum's ruins.* Cambridge, MA: MIT Press.
Cufer, E. (2006). Transnacionala. A journey from East to West. In C. Bishop (Ed.), *Participation* (pp. 138–143). London, UK: Whitechapel Gallery and Cambridge, MA: MIT Press.
D'Alessandr, S., & Pérez Orama, L. (2017). *Tarsila do Amaral. Inventing modern art in Brazil* (exh. cat.). New Haven, CT: Yale University Press.
De la Loza, S., Molinari, E., & Rios, J. (2020). Archivistic encounters, transnational imaginaries and spatial justice: A trialogue. *Field. A Journal of Socially Engaged Art Criticism*, 15. Retrieved from: http://field-journal.com/editorial/archivistic-encounters-transnational-imaginaries-and-spatial-justice-a-trialogue [Accessed 3 March 2020].

De Sousa, B. (2018). *The end of the cognitive empire. The coming of age of epistemologies of the South*. Durham, NC: Duke University Press.
De Sousa, B. (2014). *Epistemologies of the South. Justice against epistemicide*. New York, NY: Routledge.
Debord, G. (2002). *Society of the spectacle*. Detroit, MI: Black & Red Books.
Deleuze. G., & Guattari, F. (2010). *Nomadology: The war machine*. Los Angeles, CA: Semiotext(e).
Deleuze, G., & Guattari, F. (2009). *Anti-Oedipus. Capitalism and schizophrenia*. London, UK: Penguin Books. (Original work published 1972)
Deleuze, G., & Guattari, F. (1987). *A thousand plateaus: Capitalism and schizophrenia*. Minneapolis, MN: University of Minnesota Press. (Original work published 1980)
Deleuze, G., & Guattari, F. (1986). *Kafka: Toward a minor literature (Theory and history of literature)*. Minneapolis, MN: The University of Minnesota Press. (Original work published 1974)
Delgado, M. (2005). *Elogi al vianant. Del 'model Barcelona' a la Barcelona real* [Praise the pedestrian. From the 'Barcelona model' to the real Barcelona]. Barcelona, Spain: Edicions de 1984.
Delgado, M. (2002). *Disoluciones urbanas* [Urban dissolutions]. Medellín, Colombia: Editorial University of Antioquia.
Denzin, N. (2014). *Interpretive autoethnography*. Thousand Oaks, CA: Sage.
Derrida, J. (1996). *Archive fever*. Chicago, IL: University of Chicago Press.
Didi Huberman, G. (2018). *The eye of history. When images take position*. Providence, RI: RIC Books.
Dussel, E. (2003). *Philosophy of liberation*. Portland, OR: Wipf & Stock Publisher.
Escobar, T. (2008). *El mito del arte y el mito del pueblo. Cuestiones sobre arte popular* [The myth of art and the myth of people. Questions about popular art]. Santiago de Chile: Ediciones Metales Pesados.
Fernández González, M. (2014). *Matar al chino: entre la revolución urbanística y el asedio urbano en el barrio del Raval de Barcelona* [Kill the Chino: between urban revolution and the urban siege in the Raval neighborhood of Barcelona]. Barcelona, Spain: La Llevir-Virus.
Fernández Polanco, A., & Pradel, A. (2015). A conversation with Suely Rolnik. *Re-visiones, #5*. Retrieved from: http://www.re-visiones.net/index.php/RE-VISIONES/article/view/50 [Accessed 19 September 2019].
Fernández-Savater, A. (2003). Entrevista con Wu Ming 4: Mitopoiesis y acción política [Interview with Wu Ming 4: Mitopoiesis and political action]. *El Viejo Topo* [The old mole], 180, July 2003. Retrieved from: https://www.wumingfoundation.com/italiano/outtakes/viejotopo_es.html [Accessed 24 March 2020].
Ferrer, E. (2017). *All variations are valid, including this one*. Madrid, Spain: MNCARS.
Fiorini, H.J. (2010). *The creating psyche: Theory and practice of tertiary processes*. Vitoria-Gasteiz, Spain: Agruparte.
Foster, H. (2006). Chatrooms. In C. Bishop (Ed.), *Participation* (pp. 190–195). London, UK: Whitechapel Gallery and Cambridge, MA: MIT Press.
Foucault, M. (2014). *Truth telling, wrong doing*. Chicago, IL: University of Chicago Press.
Foucault, M. (2009). Preface. In G. Deleuze, & F. Guattari, *Anti-Oedipus. Capitalism and schizophrenia* (pp. xi–xiv). London, UK: Penguin Books.
Foucault, M. (1998). Subjectivity and truth: Course summary. In M. Foucault, *The essential works of Michel Foucault, 1954–1984, volume 1: Ethics: Subjectivity and truth* (pp. 87–92). New York, NY: The New Press.
Foucault, M. (1994). *The birth of the clinic*. New York, NY: Vintage Books.

Foucault, M. (1983). The subject and power. In H. Dreyfus, & P. Rabinov (Eds.), Michel Foucault: *Beyond structuralism and hermeneutics* (pp. 208–226). Chicago, IL: The University of Chicago Press.
Foucault, M. (1978). *The history of sexuality. Volume I: An introduction*. New York, NY: Random House.
Foucault, M. (1975). *Discipline and punish: The birth of the prison*. New York, NY: Random House.
Fraser, N. (1997). *Justice interruptus: Critical reflections on the postsocialist' condition*. London, UK and New York, NY: Routledge.
Gago, V. (2008). ¿Quién es y cómo piensa Bifo? Capitalismo y subjetividades [Who is and how does Bifo think? Capitalism and subjectivities]. *La Vaca*. Retrieved from: https://www.lavaca.org/notas/quien-es-y-como-piensa-bifo [Accessed 18 October 2019].
García Canclini, N. (2014). *Art beyond Itself. Anthropology for a society without a story line*. Durham, NC: Duke University Press.
García Canclini, N. (2005a). *Hybrid cultures*. Minneapolis, MN: University of Minnesota Press.
García Canclini, N. (2005b). *Diferentes, desiguales y desconectados. Mapas de la interculturalidad* [Different, unequal, and disconnected. Maps of interculturality]. Barcelona, Spain: Gedisa.
Garrido, A. (2011). *Narración y ficción. Literatura e invención de mundos* [Narration and fiction. Literature and invention of worlds]. Madrid, Spain: Iberoamericana.
Gielen, P. (2015). Nomadeology: The aestheticization of nomadic existence. In P. Gielen (Ed.), *The murmuring of the artistic multitude. Global art, politics and post-Fordism* (pp. 104–114). Amsterdam, Netherlands: Antennae Valiz.
Glissant, E. (2006). Poetics of relation. In C. Bishop (Ed.), *Participation* (pp. 71–8). London, UK: Whitechapel Gallery and Cambridge, MA: MIT Press.
Glissant, E. (1997). *Poetics of relation*. Ann Arbor, MI: University of Michigan Press.
González, J. (2018). Memories of underdevelopment: Art and the decolonial turn in Latin America, 1960–1985. In P. Coleman (Ed.), *Memories of underdevelopment: Art and the decolonial turn in Latin America, 1960–1985* (exh. cat.) (pp. 25–57). San Diego, CA: Museum of Contemporary Art San Diego.
González Gutierrez, L.F. (2019). Metodologias cualitativas en la era de la cibercultura. Aproximaciones y retos para Latinoamérica [Qualitative methodologies in the era of cyberculture. Approaches and challenges for Latin America]. In E. Aguirre-Armendariz, & D. Johnson Mardones (Eds.), *Investigación cualitativa en América Latina (I)* [Qualitative research in Latin America (I)] (pp. 73–118). Santiago de Chile: Escaparate Ediciones.
González Virós, I. (2005). Lecciones aprendidas desde el urbanismo [Lessons learnt from urbanism]. In I. Banal, & J. Canudas (Eds.), *Hospital 106, 4a 1a. El lugar y el tiempo* [Hospital 106, 4a 1a. The place and the time]. Barcelona, Spain: Actar.
Good, B. (1994). *Medicine, rationality, and experience: An anthropological perspective*. Cambridge, UK: Cambridge University Press.
Group Material. (2006). On democracy. In C. Bishop (Ed.), *Participation* (pp. 135–7). London, UK: Whitechapel Gallery and Cambridge, MA: MIT Press.
Guattari, F. (2006). Chaosmosis: An ethico-aesthetic paradigm. In C. Bishop (Ed.), *Participation* (pp. 79–82). London, UK: Whitechapel Gallery and Cambridge, MA: MIT Press.
Guattari, F., & Negri, T. (2010). *New lines of alliance, new spaces of liberty*. Brooklyn, NY: Autonomedia.

Guattari, F., & Negri, T. (1996). *Las verdades nómadas* [Nomadic truths]. Irun, Spain: Iralka.

Guilbaut, S. (1985). *How New York stole the idea of modern art*. Chicago, IL: University of Chicago Press.

Hardt, O., & Negri, T. (2009). *Commonwealth*. Cambridge, MA: Belknap Press.

Hardt, O., & Negri, A. (2004). *Multitude: War and democracy in the age of empire*. London, UK: Penguin Books.

Hardt, O., & Negri, A. (2002). *Empire*. Cambridge, MA: Harvard University Press.

Harvey, D. (2012). *Rebel cities*. London, UK: Verso.

Harvey, D. (1990). *The condition of postmodernity*. Cambridge, MA: Blackwell.

Henning, M.H. (2007). Legibility and affect: Museums as new media. In P. Basu, & S. Macdonald (Eds.), *Exhibition experiments* (pp. 25–46). Oxford, UK: Blackwell Publishing.

Holmes, B. (2006). The artistic device, or, the articulation of collective speech. *Ephemera* 6(4): 411–432.

Ibáñez, T. (2014). *Anarquismo es movimiento. Anarquismo, neoanarquismo y postanarquismo* [Anarchism is movement. Anarchism, neo-anarchism, and post-anarchism]. Barcelona, Spain: Virus Editorial.

Jacoby, R. (2011). *El deseo nace del derrumbe. Acciones, conceptos, escritos* [Desire arises from collapse. Actions, concepts, writings]. Barcelona, Spain: La Central.

Jameson, F. (1991). *Postmodernism or, the cultural logic of late capitalism*. Durham, NC: Duke University Press.

Janes, R.R. (2009). *Museums in a troubled world: Renewal, irrelevance, or collapse*. New York, NY: Routledge.

Jenkins, J.H. (2015). *Extraordinary conditions. Culture and experience in mental illness*. Oakland, CA: The University of California Press.

Kelley, B. Jr. (Ed.). (2017). *Talking to action. Art, pedagogy, and activism in the Americas*. Chicago, IL: School of the Art Institute of Chicago.

Kleinman, A. (1988). *The illness narratives: Suffering, healing, and the human condition*. New York, NY: Basic Books.

Krauss, N. (2017). *Forest dark*. New York, NY: HarperCollins.

Laddaga, R. (2013). Interview with Roberto Jacoby. *The BAR. Buenos Aires Review*. Retrieved from: http://www.buenosairesreview.org/2013/11/interview-with-roberto-jacoby/ [Accessed 21 October 2019].

Laddaga, R. (2006). *Estética de la emergencia* [Aesthetics of emergence]. Buenos Aires, Argentina: Adriana Hidalgo Editora.

Larsen, L.B. (2006). Social aesthetics. In C. Bishop (Ed.), *Participation* (pp. 172–183). London, UK: Whitechapel Gallery and Cambridge, MA: MIT Press.

Laseca, R. (2015). *El museo imparable. Sobre institucionalidad genuina y blanda* [The unstoppable museum. On genuine and soft institutionality]. Santiago de Chile: LOM.

Lazzarato, M. (2014). *Signs and machines. Capitalism and the production of subjectivity*. Los Angeles, CA: Semiotext(e).

Lévi- Strauss, C. (2004). *Raza y cultura* [Race and culture]. Madrid, Spain: Catedra Edicione

Lippard, L., & Chandler, J. (1968). The dematerialization of art. *Art International*, 12(2), 31–36.

Longoni, A. (2017a). *34 Exercises of freedom: #9 Between terror and revelry. Collective strategies of resistance during dictatorships in Argentina and Brazil*. Retrieved from: https://

www.documenta14.de/en/calendar/969/-9-between-terror-and-revelry-collective-strategies-of-resistance-during-dictatorships-in-argentina-and-brazil [Accessed 21 October 2019].

Longoni, A. (Ed.). (2017b). *Oscar Masotta. Revolucion en el arte* [Oscar Masotta. Revolution in the art]. Buenos Aires, Argentina: Mansalva.

Longoni, A., & Mestman, M. (2010). *Del Di Tella a Tucumán Arde - Vanguardia artística y política en el 68 argentino* [From Di Tella to Tucumán Arde – Artistic avant-garde and politics of the Argentinean '68]. Buenos Aires, Argentina: Eudeba.

Longoni, A., & Mestman, M. (2004). After Pop, we dematerialize: Oscar Masotta, happenings, and media art at the beginnings of conceptualism. In I. Katzenstein (Ed.), *Listen here now! Argentine art of the 1960s: Writings of the avant-garde* (exh. cat.) (pp. 156–172). New York, NY: The Museum of Modern Art.

López Sáez, C. (1996). La fenomenología existencial de M. Merleau Ponty y la sociología [The existential phenomenology of M. Merleau Ponty and sociology]. *Papers: Revista de Sociologia* [Papers: Journal of Sociology], 50, 209–231.

Mahony, E. (2016). The uneasy relationship of self-critique in the public art institution. *Curator The Museum Journal*, 59(3), 219–238.

Marginyà, F., & Maza, G. (2001). Inmigración y huecos en el centro histórico de Barcelona (1986–2000) [Immigration and holes in the historical center of Barcelona (1986–2000)]. In Migración y cambio social [Migration and social change]. Número extraordinario dedicado al III Coloquio Internacional de Geocrítica (Minutes of the colloquium). *Scripta Nova. Revista electrónica de Geografía y Ciencias Sociales* [Scripta Nova. Electronic Journal of Geography and Social Sciences], 94(62).

Martin, S., & Ruiz, A. (Eds.). (1999). *The experimental exercise of freedom: Lygia Clark, Gego, Mathias Goeritz, Hélio Oiticica, and Mira Schendel* (exh. cat.). Los Angeles, CA: Museum of Contemporary Art.

Marxen, E. (2019). Transforming traditions: Walter Benjamin, art, and art therapy. In R. Hougham, S. Pitruzzella, & H. Wengrower (Eds.), *Traditions in transition: New articulations in the arts therapies* (pp. 251–271). London, UK: Ecarte (European Consortium of the Arts Therapies).

Marxen, E. (2018). Artistic practices and the artistic dispositif – A critical review. *Antipoda. Journal of Anthropology and Archeology*, 33, 37–60.

Marxen, E. (2012). 'La comunidad silenciosa'. Migraciones filipinas y capital social en el Raval (Barcelona) ['The silent community'. Filipino migrations and social capital at Raval (Barcelona)]. PhD thesis. On-line publication: Tarragona, Spain: University Rovira i Virgili. http://www.tdx.cat/bitstream/handle/10803/96667/TESIS.pdf?sequence=1 [Accessed 20 October 2019].

Marxen, E. (2011). *Diálogos entre arte y terapia. Del 'arte psicótico' al desarrollo de la arteterapia y sus aplicaciones* [Dialogues between art and therapy. From 'psychotic art' to the development of art therapy and its applications]. Barcelona, Spain: Gedisa.

Marxen, E. (2009a). La etnografía desde el arte. Definiciones, bases teóricas y nuevos escenarios [Ethnography from art. Definitions, theoretical bases and new sceneries]. *Alteridades* [Alterities], 19(37), 7–22.

Marxen, E. (2009b). Therapeutic thinking in contemporary art. Psychotherapy in the arts. *The Arts in Psychotherapy*, 36, 140–147. doi: 10.1016/j.aip.2008.10.004.

Marxen, E., & Greteman, A. (2019). Ingesting power. *RECIE. Electronic Cientific Review of Educational Research*, 4(2), 875–886.

Masotta, O. (1968). Después del pop: Nosotros desmaterializamos [After Pop: We dematerialize]. In O. Masotta (Ed.), *Consciencia y estructura* [Consciousness and structure] (pp. 218–244). Buenos Aires, Argentina: Editorial Jorge Álvarez.
Mattingly, C. (1998). *Healing dramas and clinical plots: The narrative structures of experience*. New York, NY: Cambridge University Press.
Maza, G., McDonogh, G., & Pujadas, J.J. (2002). Barcelona, ciutat oberta: transformacions urbanes, participació ciudadana i cultures de control al barri del Raval [Barcelona, open city: Urban transformations, citizen participation and cultures of control in the Raval district]. *Revista d'Etnologia de Catalunya* [Journal of Catalan Ethnology], 21, 114–131.
Mazzei, L. (2017). Following the contour of concepts toward a minor inquiry. *Qualitative Inquiry*, 23(9), 675–685. doi: 10.1177/1077800417725356.
McDonough, G. (2005). Discourses of the city: Policy and response in post-transitional Barcelona. In S.M. Low (Ed.), *Theorizing the city. The new urban anthropology reader* (pp. 342–376). New Brunswick, NJ: Rutgers University Press.
Merleau-Ponty, M. (1960). *Le visible et l'invisible* [The visible and the invisible]. Paris, France: Gallimard.
Merleau-Ponty, M. (1945). *Phénoménologie de la perception* [Phenomenology of perception]. Paris, France: Gallimard.
Mignolo, W. (2014). *Activar los archivos, descentralizar a las musas* [Activate the archives, decentralize the muses]. Barcelona, Spain: MACBA.
Mignolo, W. (2011). Museums in the colonial horizon of modernity. Fred Wilson's *Mining the Museum* (1992). In J. Harris (Ed.), *Globalization and contemporary art* (pp. 71–85). Hoboken, NJ: Blackwell Publishing.
Mignolo, W. (2010). *Desobediencia epistémica. Retórica de la modernidad, lógica de la colonialidad y gramática de la descolonialidad* [Epistemic disobedience. Rhetoric of modernity, logic of coloniality and grammar of decoloniality]. Buenos Aires, Argentina: Ediciones del Signo.
Mignolo, W. (2007). Delinking: The rhetoric of modernity, the logic of coloniality and the grammar of de-coloniality. *Cultural Studies*, 21(2), 449–514.
Molina, A. (2005). Entrevista con Manuel Borja-Villel. Debemos desarrollar en el museo una pedagogía de la emancipación [Interview with Manuel Borja-Villel. We must develop a pedagogy of emancipation in the museum]. *El País*, 19 November 2005. Retrieved from: http://elpais.com/diario/2005/11/19/babelia/1132358767_850215.html [Accessed 18 October 2019].
Montgomery, M.O., & Heller, H. (2017). Visitor as activist. A mobile social justice museum's call for critical visitor engagement. In P. Villeneuve, & A. Rowson Love (Eds.), *Visitor-centered exhibitions and edu-curation in art museums* (pp. 153–165). Lanham, MD: Rowman & Littlefield.
Mouffe, C. (2017). An agonistic conception of the museum. In Fictilis (Ed.), *Museum of capitalism* (pp. 78–79). New York, NY: Inventory Press.
Mouffe, C. (2012). Alfredo Jaar: The artist as organic intellectual. In A. Jaar (Ed.), *The way it is. An aesthetics of resistance* (pp. 264–281). Berlin, Germany: Realismus-Studio of NGBK, New Society for Visual Arts.
Mouffe, C. (2007). *Prácticas artísticas y democracia agonística* [Artistic practices and agonistic democracy]. Barcelona/Bellaterra, Spain: MACBA/Universidad Autónoma de Barcelona.
Mouffe, C. (1993). *The return of the political*. London, UK: Verso.

Negri, T. (2017). *Marx and Foucault*. Malden, MA: Polity Press.
Negri, T. (2000). *Kairos, Alma Venus, Multitudo. Nove lezioni impartite a me stesso* [Kairos, Alma Venus, Multitude. Nine lessons taught to myself]. Rome, Italy: Manifestolibri.
Oiticica, H. (1969). The senses pointing to a new transformation. Unpublished. Retrieved from: http://www.itaucultural.org.br/aplicExternas/enciclopedia/ho/home/index.cfm [Accessed 18 October 2019].
Peacock, J.L., & Holland, D.C. (1993). The narrated self: Life stories in process. *Ethos*, 21(4), 367–383.
Pérez-Oramas, L., (Ed.). (2009). *León Ferrari and Mira Schendel: Tangled alphabets* (exh. cat.). New York, NY: The Museum of Modern Art.
Pollock, G. (2013). *After-affects. After-images. Trauma and aesthetic transformation in the virtual feminist museum*. Manchester, UK: Manchester University Press.
Pollock, G. (2007). *Encounters in the virtual feminist museum: Time, space and the archive*. New York, NY: Routledge.
Pollock, G. (1999). *Differencing the canon: Feminist desire and the writing of art's histories*. London, UK: Routledge.
Preciado, P. (2013). *Testo junkie: Sex, drugs and biopolitics in the pharmacopornographic era*. New York, NY: The Feminist Press.
Quijano, A. (2000). Coloniality of power, eurocentrism, and Latin America. *Nepentla: Views from the South*, 1(3), 533–580.
Ramos, S. (2011). Roberto Jacoby y la estrategia de la alegría [Roberto Jacoby and the Strategy of Joy]. *La Nación*, 25 November 2011. Retrieved from: https://www.lanacion.com.ar/espectaculos/musica/roberto-jacoby-y-la-estrategia-de-la-alegria-nid1426125 [Accessed 18 October 2019].
Raunig, G. (2014). *The machinics of political art. Another twelve theses on the actualization of Walter Benjamin's 'The author as producer'*. Bilbao, Spain: Consonni.
Red Conceptualismos Sur. (2012). *Perder la forma humana. Una imagen sísmica de los años ochenta en América Latina* [Losing the human form—a seismic image of the eighties in Latin America]. Madrid, Spain: MNCARS.
Rendueles, C., & Useros, A. (2015). *Atlas Walter Benjamin. Constelaciones* [Walter Benjamin Atlas. Constellations]. Madrid, Spain: Círculo de Bellas Artes and Sociedad Estatal de Conmemoraciones Culturales.
Ribalta, J. (2010). Experiments in a new institutionality. In M.J. Borja-Villel, K. Cabañas, & J. Ribalta (Eds.), *Relational objects. MACBA collection 2002–2007* (pp. 225–265). Barcelona, Spain: MACBA.
Ribalta, J. (2006). Patrimoni comú, modernitat perifèrica, educació política, crítica institucional. Notes sobre la pràctica del MACBA [Common cultural heritage, peripheral modernity, political education, institutional critique. Notes on the MACBA practices]. *Papers d'Art* [Art Papers], 90, 28–31.
Ribalta, J. (2004). Mediation and construction of publics. The MACBA experience. Retrieved from: http://republicart.net/disc/institution/ribalta01 en.htm [Accessed 29 September 2019].
Ribalta, J. (2003). On public service in the age of cultural consumption. *Parachute*, 111, 144–155.
Rivera Cusicanqui, S. (2018a). *Un mundo ch'ixi es possible. Ensayos desde un presente en crisis* [A *ch'ixi* world is possible. Essays from a present in crisis]. Buenos Aires, Argentina: Tinta Limón.

Rivera Cusicanqui, S. (2018b). *Sociología de la imagen. Miradas ch'ixi desde la historia actual* [Sociology of the image. *Ch'ixi* views from present history]. Buenos Aires, Argentina: Tinta Limón.
Rivera Cusicanqui, S. (2010). *Una reflexión sobre prácticas y discursos descolonizadores* [A reflection on decolonizing practices and discourses]. Buenos Aires, Argentina: Tinta Limón.
Rolnik, S. (2005). *Lygia Clark. De l'œuvre à l'événement* [Lygia Clark. From the artwork to the event] (exh. cat.). Nantes, France: Musée des Beaux-Arts.
Rolnik, S. (2001). *¿El arte cura?* [Does the art cure?]. Barcelona, Spain: MACBA.
Rosler, M. (2013). *Culture class*. Berlin, Germany: Sternberg Press.
Sacks, O. (1990). *Seeing voices*. New York, NY: Vinatge Books.
Sajnani, N., Marxen, E., & Zarate, R. (2017). Critical perspectives in the arts therapies: Response/ability across a continuum of practice. *The Arts in Psychotherapy*, 54, 28–37. doi: 10.1016/j.aip.2017.01.007.
Sandell, R. (2016). *Museums, moralities and human rights*. New York, NY: Routledge.
Seem (2009). Introduction. In G. Deleuze, & F. Guattari, *Anti-Oedipus. Capitalism and schizophrenia* (pp. xv–xxiv). London, UK: Penguin Books.
Sesé, T. (2013a). Siempre nos quedará el museo [We will always have the museum]. *La Vangaurdia*, 20 January 2013.
Sesé, T. (2013b). Museos: Cómo ganar recursos sin ser populistas [Museums: How to earn resources without being populist]. *La Vangaurdia*, 21 January 2013.
Small, I. (2016). *Hélio Oiticica. Folding the frame*. Chicago, IL: University of Chicago Press.
Smith, N. (2000). Del Lower East Side al Raval [From the Lower East Side to Raval]. *La Vanguardia*, 8 December 2000.
Skrebowski, L. (2012). Revolution in the aesthetic revolution. Hélio Oiticica and the concept of Creleisure. *Third Text*, 26(1), 65–78.
Spence, J. (2005). *Más allá de la imagen perfecta. Fotografía, subjetividad, antagonismo* [Beyond the perfect image. Photography, subjectivity, antagonism] (exh. cat.). Barcelona, Spain: MACBA.
Subirats, J., & Rius, J. (Eds.). (2006). *Del Chino al Raval. Cultura y transformación en la Barcelona central* [From Chino to Raval. Culture and transformation in central Barcelona]. Barcelona, Spain: Centre de Cultura Contemporànea de Barcelona.
Vattimo, G. (2005). Art beyond aesthetics: Alfredo Jaar. The commitment rediscovered. In A. Jaar (Ed.), *The aesthetics of resistance*. Barcelona, Spain: Actar.
Virno, P. (2004). *A grammar of the multitude: For an analysis of contemporary forms of life*. New York, NY: Semiotext(e).
Virno, P. (1996). *Virtuosity and revolution: The political theory of exodus*. Minneapolis, MN: University of Minnesota Press.
Warner, M. (2005). *Publics and counterpublics*. New York, NY: Zone Books.
Warning, R. (Ed.). (1994). *Rezeptionsästhetik. Theorie und Praxis* [Aesthetics of reception. Theory and practice]. Stuttgart, Germany: UTB.
Whitaker, P. (2012). The art therapy assemblage. In H. Burt (Ed.), *Art therapy and postmodernism. Creative healing through a prism* (pp. 344–366). London, UK and Philadelphia, PA: Jessica Kingsley Publishers.
Whitaker, P. (2005). Going through the motions: Improvisation and cooperative learning as ways of exploring contemporary subjectivity and social activism within art therapy practice. In L. Kossolapow, S. Scoble, & D. Waller (Eds.),

European arts therapy. Different approaches to a unique discipline. Opening regional portals (pp. 62–68). Münster, Germany: LIT.

Witte, B. (1976). Krise und Kritik. Zur Zusammenarbeit Benjamins mit Brecht in den Jahren 1929–1933 [Crisis and critique. About the collaboration of Benjamin with Brecht between 1929–1933]. In P. Gebhardt, M. Grzimek, D. Harth, M. Rumpf, U. Schodlbauer, & B. Witte (Eds.), *Walter Benjamin - Zeitgenosse der Moderne* [Walter Benjamin - contemporary of modernity] (pp. 9–36). Kronberg, Germany: Scriptor Verlag.

Wodiczko, K. (1999). *Critical vehicles. Writings, projects, interviews.* Cambridge, MA: MIT Press.

Zerán, F. (2018). *Mayo feminista. La rebelión contra el patriarcado.* Santiago de Chile: Lom.

5 Critical Art, Co-options, Resistance, and the Museum

This chapter starts with the description and potentialities of "critical art," defining it mainly as able to challenge the hegemonic discourses of society. Different ways of critical and relational art practices are outlined with a special attention in favor of those practices that offer a space for alternative narratives.

Regarding narratives, a link is drawn to contemporary elaborations about the thresholds and intersections of anthropology and contemporary art, particularly regarding shared inquiries about detotalizing proposals in opposition to dominant narratives.

Afterwards, the limitations of spaces of alternative narratives in form of cooperate co-options, neutralizations, and instrumentalizations are conveyed with a special focus on the art museum. Finally, thoughts and strategy of resistance are explored.

Ways of "Critical Art"

As outlined in Chapter 3 and in accordance with Mouffe (2012, 2007), the term "critical art" is preferred over "political art," because the latter is considered redundant and inevitably leads to an incorrect topology: All art embraces a political dimension, since it reflects a given symbolical order. At the same time, politics always embrace an aesthetic dimension, in the symbolic order of social relationships.

The arts can either reify or challenge society's mechanisms of control and oppression. What is of interest is which art forms can defy the hegemonic societal discourse, facilitating spaces for resistance, alternatives, and eventually, a potential for change (Marxen, 2018, 2016, 2013; Sajnani, Marxen, & Zarate, 2017). In the words of Rancière (2006, p. 83): "Critical art intends to raise consciousness of the mechanisms of domination in order to turn the spectator into conscious agent in the transformation of the world."

Agreeing with Mouffe (2007), as well as Longoni (2011), who discusses a "politicity" ("*politicidad*" in the Spanish original) in the arts, and adding to the theories of Marxen (2019, 2018, 2016, 2013), different critical art practices have been identified:[1]

First, and most obviously, there is *activist art*, when artists work with activists, such as campaigning for human rights.

For example, in Argentina, in the 80s, within the *Siluetazo* ("big silhouette movement"), artists worked hand-in-hand with human rights groups against the disappearances of human beings during the military dictatorship in Argentina (Longoni & Bruzzone, 2008). The silhouettes symbolized the disappeared and the artists' job was to design and supply technique as well as materials which were accessible for everybody and functional in public space. In central squares, people would lie on the ground while others contoured their silhouettes on big paper or cardboard. The Siluetazo aspired to reintegrate the previously fragmented collective memory. The military dictatorship, with its history of tortures, censorships, and disappearances, had fractured the social body of the country. People were horribly afraid to protest in public or even to show their grief. Consequently, they locked themselves in their homes where their losses fueled anxiety and terror. Movements of conjunction between human rights initiatives and artists in public space combat exactly this paralyzing fragmentation (for more details: Marxen, 2019; Figure 5.1a–c).[2]

Subsequently in Argentina, the Grupo de Arte Callejero (Street Art Group, GAC) and the more performance-oriented artist group Etcétera fought alongside human rights groups like HIJOS (the children of the disappeared)[3] against the impunity of the military dictators via their famous *escraches*, a public humiliation and calling protest intervention. In their design similar to street signs, they were "indicating the location of clandestine detention centres, city maps showing the addresses of the perpetrators of repression" as well as one of their most symbolically effective *escrache* denouncing the "flights of death" carried out by the Argentinian dictatorship between 1976 and 1983 and also by their Chilean counterparts between 1973 and 1989 (Longoni, 2017; Martí & Etcétera, 2017; Wright, 2008, p. 9 with images of various *escraches*, so the "flights of death"; GAC 2009; Longoni & Bruzzone, 2008). This particular *escrache* symbolizes the flight of death through a sign of a plane with a person inside: the plane is colored (stenciled positive) and the person inside is without color (stenciled negative), the latter symbolizing the absence and disappearance of the killed person (for more details: Marxen, 2019; Longoni, 2017).

The GAC group, composed mainly of female artists and graphic designers, creates the *escrache* by itself and in turn facilitates their use by others for free. The success of these actions has to be stressed, fostering public awareness and protest. Due to public protests, various of the "escrached" and former military officials who had never been punished were fired from their jobs, investigated, and brought to trial. The interventions and artefacts of GAC and Etcétera showed an incredibly high symbolic efficiency and efficacy which has entered contemporary art theory (among others, di Filippo, 2015; Whitener, 2010; Wright, 2008).[4]

For good reason, Bishop (2012) has articulated skepticism about activist art, because it is not sufficient for social change and needs to be aided by other institutions. This conjunction was exactly the case in the aforementioned examples in form of collective efforts and protests by artists, human right groups, and a significant part of the population. For other authors, social change could only happen if bourgeois society were eliminated entirely. It would be the task of the artist to contribute to the very abolishment of the bourgeoisie, as explained by Benjamin (1998, 1968) and Brecht (2014; see Chapter 4).

Figure 5.1 (a) María Zurita. El Siluetazo. Buenos Aires, September 21/22 of 1983. Photography by Eduardo Gil. (b) Bettina Tarnopolsky. El Siluetazo. Buenos Aires, September 21/22 of 1983. Photography by Eduardo Gil. (c) Siluetas y canas [Silhouettes and policemen]. El Siluetazo. Buenos Aires, September 21/22 of 1983. Photography by Eduardo Gil.

Yet, critical art can also be performed in other ways, for example, by criticizing a political reality through *art as denouncement*. In this vein, Leon Ferrari (*Western Christian Civilization*, 1965) and Nancy Spero (*Bomb Shitting*, 1966) protested against the Vietnam War and Ferrari also against the Catholic Church's collaboration in the violation of human rights (Estévez, Díez Fischer, & López, 2017), Barbara Kruger (2010) and once again Nancy Spero (2009 and the film *Golub/Spero* by Blumentahl & Quinn, 2004) produced critical art focused on gender. For Hans Haacke (2012, 1995, 1975), this form has crossed every aspect of his life.

Another form is *institutional critique*, when art critiques the political condition of the production, distribution, and reception of art by official artistic institutions. Roberto Jacoby has articulated this critique on both literal and metaphorical levels (2011, most notably his project *Bolas de nieve* [Snowballs] for institution-free circulation of art, 1999 in its first edition and then from 2005 to 2006 ongoing as an online database and permanent visual exhibition of mainly Argentinian artists: http://www.boladenieve.org.ar/en/acerca_de). The Guerilla Girls (i.e. 2003, 1998) directly denounced gender imbalance in the art world. Again, Hans Haacke, together with the sociologist Pierre Bourdieu (1995), exposed in dialogue form the abuse of the arts for the accumulation of symbolic capital by multinational companies.

Artists like Dora García and Krzysztof Wodiczko explore and display positions and identities opposed to the mainstream—alterities, marginalization, and oppression. Of course, ethical issues may arise when the "other" is abused as "rough material" for a widespread fashion trend in the art world with an indiscriminate urge to include "the other" into representation.[5] Still, this "*alterity-form*" can offer a space for alternative narratives, "minor language," in the same sense proposed by Deleuze and Guatarri (1986): refracting majority thinking and activating hidden potentials from a minority position (Marxen, 2016, 2013, 2018; Sajnani et al., 2017; Chapter 4; Figure 5.2).

Other artists have created spaces of experimentation, in opposition to capitalism, facilitating an *experimentation of utopia and subjectivity* as an alternative to normalization. New ways of inhabiting the world are evidenced, deconstructing institutionalized models and points of view (Longoni, 2011). The possibility of change through agency is transmitted mainly through images (Marxen, 2011a). At the same time, a critical analysis is undertaken by questioning hegemony, in the sense of Gramsci (Sajnani et al., 2017; Chapter 3; Marxen, 2016). Some very heterogeneous representatives of this art form are Lygia Clark, with her ongoing *Structuring of a Self* (1976–1988; Rolnik, 2005; Marxen, 2013, 2011a, 2009b; Borja-Villel & Enguita, 1998); on a more abstract level, in form of geometrical and architectural sculptures, Gego (Bois et al., 2006); addressing gender, Jo Spence and Nancy Spero (Marxen, 2011; Figure 5.3); and, again, Roberto Jacoby (2011), in this case, his technologies of friendship, his experimental communities/societies and micro-societies, such as *Proyecto Venus* (2001–2006).

Figure 5.2 The artists without works: A guided tour around nothing, 2009. Performer: Michelangelo Miccolis, Spanish Pavilion 54th Venice Biennale, Private Collection. © Dora García.

Figure 5.3 Nancy Spero, "The Hunt," 1999. © 2020 The Nancy Spero and Leon Golub Foundation for the Arts/Licensed by VAGA at Artists Rights Society (ARS), NY.

Art has been further circulated *in popular spheres* by accessible production techniques. Juan Carlos Romero explored this modality with serigraphies and printmaking as political denouncement, partly working in public space with passers-by (Romero, Davis, & Longoni, 2010); Jo Spence developed photography workshops about gender and social class (Marxen, 2011a; Spence, 2005). They both used techniques that are easily accessible to amateurs.

Also, the Buenos Aires-based artist duo Iconoclasistas (Pablo Ares and Julia Risler) work in public spheres. Their work consists of critical collaborative mapping and strategies of critical cartography. They organize free, graphic *dispositifs* for collective, collaborative, participatory research. Their materials and methodologies are also disseminated for free on the internet through Creative Commons licensing, such as the *Manual of Collective Mapping: Critical Cartographic Resources for Territorial Collaborative-Creation Processes* (2016). In workshops with these two artists, participants are encouraged to take a bird's-eye view of the territory and conflict to be mapped. They aim at a change of consciousness, a simultaneous transformation of the self and the territory, as well as bi-directional feedback between artists and participants. Instead of making an artwork and sharing it afterwards with the public, Iconoclasistas share a space and a methodology in order to develop an artwork with others. Their work very often protests against the pillage, plundering, and exploitation of the environment, which leads to the pollution of entire communities. They frequently engage with activist groups, developing works denouncing environmental and political oppression and also maps as well as cartographies of alternatives to the capitalist creed. Thus, they combine at the same time different ways of critical art (Figures 5.4–5.6).

Figure 5.4 Tour *Rebellious Cosmovision*, 2008–2010. Iconoclasistas.

Figure 5.5 *Manual of Collective Mapping. Critical Cartographic Resources for Territorial Processes of Collaborative Creation*. Extending the Practice, 2013 (2016 English version). Iconoclasistas.

Figure 5.6 *Mapamundi. Who owns the land?* Exhibition Centre Pompidou, 2016. Iconoclasistas.

Finally, other professionals can organize subjective work to maintain the capacity for symbolization, using artistic techniques (like art therapy) or verbal association about art, the consistency of its production and underlying social ties (a form of applied psychoanalysis). Spaces are then created which offer alternative narratives for institutionalized lives and hegemonic discourse (see, for example, Marxen & Rodríguez, 2012; Chapter 2). Adequate professional training and continuity, which allow the participants' processes to unfold, are essential for this work of *art and subjectivity* (Marxen, 2016, 2013, 2011b).

The different ways which have been outlined for critical art are mainly carried out or organized by professional artists and experts in the arts.[6] The institutional frames are various: reaching from anti-institutional and street work (i.e. Siluetazo), institutional critique (such as Haacke), public art (for example Wodiczko, Gego), community-based practices (like Romero and Spence) and in its form conventional but altering art pieces fitting into museums and galleries (Ferrari, Spero).

Other critical art practices are possible with participants not necessarily initiated in the arts. The MACBA art therapy and analytical dispositifs are some examples and belonged to the MACBA politics and its efforts to oppose capitalist co-opting of the arts.

Relationality and Its Limits

Claire Bishop (2006, p. 10) has observed

> artistic practices since the 1960s that appropriate *social* forms as a way to bring art closer to everyday life: intangible experiences such as dancing samba (Hélio Oiticica) or funk (Adrian Piper); drinking beer (Tom Marioni); discussing philosophy (Ian Wilson) or politics (Joseph Beuys); organizing a garage sale (Martha Rosler); running a café (Allen Ruppersberg; Daniel Spoeri; Gordon Matta-Clark), a hotel (Alighiero Boetti; Ruppersberg) or a travel agency (Christo and Jeanne-Claude).

Focusing on participatory art, Bishop (2012, p. 66) explores artists' motivations regarding social participation and the involvement of the audience, ideally, converting it from passive to active. This should represent "its mythic counterpart, passive spectatorial consumption" and "emancipate it from a state of alienation induced by the dominant ideological order—be this consumer capitalism, totalitarian socialism, or military dictatorship."

From the audience perspective, Bishop has noted:

> … A shift from an audience that demands a role (expressed as hostility toward avant-garde artists, who keep control of the proscenium), to an audience that enjoys its subordination to strange experiences devised for them by an artist, to an audience that is encouraged to be a co-producer of the work (and who, occasionally, can get even paid for this involvement).
>
> (2012, p. 72)

Earlier, Kaprow had already concentrated on participation as the main focus of his art. "It engages both our minds and bodies in actions that transform art into experience and aesthetics into meaning. Our experience as participants is one of meaningful transformation" (Kelley, 2003, p. xviii). Participating in actions differs from participating in contemplating, the latter has been equated by Kaprow as mere good manners or, eventually, expected "good aesthetic taste." He aimed at a participation that led to experience, particularly the experience of everyday life. For this, the difference between audience and artists must be completely abolished, in favor of a fusion of viewers, artists, and the "space-time of the performance." Finally, the audience as such together with "the last shred of theatrical convention" should be eliminated entirely (Kaprow, 2006, p. 103). In this sense, he coincided with his Brazilian contemporaries Lygia Clark and Hélio Oiticia.[7] The first stressed the "poetic lived experience and the subjective charge" (Clark & Oiticica, 2006, p. 110). The latter "also felt this necessity of killing the spectator or participator." He was strictly against unbearable "dull experiences" or "facile participation." Together with Lygia Clark, they aspired to annul the subject-object relationship, in favor of "an interpersonal practice that leads towards a truly open communication: a me-you relation…; no corrupted benefit … should be expected" (Oiticica, 2006, P. 111, 115).

Some participatory art projects reflect the "commodification of the human body in a service economy (since voluntary participatory art is also unpaid labor)." Paradoxically, participatory art contributes to, and has been co-opted by, populist agendas. In some of the worst-case scenarios, it serves as a platform for "banal egos," and instead of opposing the "society of spectacle," as coined by Debord (2002), it has merged with it (Bishop 2012, pp. 72–73).

This critique is confirmed by Bourriuad's (1998) theory of "relational aesthetics." Ribalta (2010) examined participation and relationality in the context of the contemporary art museum, precisely the MACBA. For good reason, he criticizes Bourriaud's conception of relational aesthetics (1998) as "immobilist and regressive in that it 'aestheticises' the immaterial communicative paradigm and its implicit social and creative processes, imposing an expository regime that interrupts their mobility, and freezes and makes fetishes of practices." The result is "a perverse objectification of both political activism and the new forms of immaterial, affective, communicative and relational production of post-Fordism" (Ribalta, 2010, p. 252; Chapter 4). In other words, it seems "to aestheticize … our service economy ('invitations, casting sessions, meetings, convivial and user-friendly areas, appointments')" (Foster, 2006, p. 195).

Foster (2006, p. 193) has criticized the illusion of "an inclusive society," "a democratic community," "non-hierarchical" practices, and "an egalitarian world." This is credulous in a process dominated by art institutions. The anthropologist Delgado (1999) had warned of "false democratizations." Although his warning refers to the audio-visual research process, it should be extended to the images that pass through almost any art-related institutions. They can hardly ever be "innocent" or non-hierarchical. Any conception of the artwork is decided beforehand by the artist. During its production and display, the artist or curator will inevitably take some major decision about the use of the images in favor of their career or the institution (Camnitzer, 2018; Marxen, 2018).

Other authors, almost equally critical with relational aesthetics, have considered its boom as a symptom of the "loss of 'social bond'" in society as well as a "deficit of politics" or "social reproduction in dire straits" (Larsen, 2006, p. 177; Rancière, 2006, P. 90, 92). It has been delegated to artists to repair these deficits. In the relevant artworks, people can find "the illusion of an interactive democracy in more or less truncated channels of communication" (Foster, 2006, p. 195). In this vein, problematizing this loss would be more interesting. So, "the shrinking of public space and the effacement of political inventiveness in a time of consensus gave a substitutive political function to the mini-demonstrations of artists" (Rancière, 2006, p. 92). Art as a social construct is considered to be able to construct the social body (Weibel & Latour, 2007).

Some artists, however, have chosen collaborative and participatory practices "as a good in itself," and "simply getting together sometimes seems enough" (Foster, 2006, p. 194). Or, it is the option following a fashion, a marketing trend (García Canclini, 2014) and "new orthodoxy" without questioning "the purpose to which it is deployed and how unsettling it is allowed to be" (Basu & Macdonald, 2007, p. 20). Altogether, "'relational aesthetics' might be sucked up in the general movement for a 'post-critical' culture – an art and architecture, cinema and literature 'after theory'" (Foster, 2006, p. 195).

This trend is embedded in an "industry of consensus," an illusion of an imaginary of consensual multiplicity. Art has become "a cosmetic and instrumental condition" (Laseca, 2015, pp. 12–13; translated by myself from Spanish).

As shown with the previous art examples, critical art has creatively opposed dominant thinking in very different ways but only succeeds in doing so if there is an ongoing questioning if capitalist logic and its mechanisms are broken or at least revealed, or rather reproduced and extended (Ribalta, 2010). This question should be at least taken into account both by the artists (micro-political level) and the institutions (meso or macro level), whether the latter are of private or public constitution. Only then can they work as an artistic dispositif, "escaping from overcoding realities" and producing new constellations opposed to hegemony, facilitating flows of desire beyond established norms, opening up new ways of inhabiting the world (Holmes 2006; see above).

Encounters between Contemporary Art and Anthropology

Opposing "overcoding realities" has been a significant subject in the abundant recent literature on encounters between art, ethnography, and anthropology. Artists and anthropologists have shared research pursuits and tend to oppose dominant narratives, aiming at detotalizing proposals, including ambiguity and uncertainty, while simultaneously rejecting universalizable answers (Marxen, 2018; García Canclini, 2014, see also the special issues of the journals *Antípoda*: "The Anthropology of Images: Mutual Intrusions Between Art, Philosophy, and Anthropology," 2018, and *Field. A Journal of Socially Engaged Art Criticism*: "The Art of Research Practices Between Art and Anthropology," 2018, dedicated to the confluences of contemporary art and anthropology). Both have particularly questioned issues of representation and its crisis (Basu & Macdonald, 2007; Marcus & Fischer, 1986). But also subjects such as research and methods, participation, fieldwork, polyphony, alterity, rapport, complicity, transnationalism, Nation State, institutions, institutional critique, and archivism have been inquired in both disciplines. For many artists and anthropologists, it is a question of pushing these ideas to their very limits to open up new horizons for their use or, rather, their deconstruction.

Focusing on the encounters between contemporary art and anthropology, García Canclini (2014) described the "ethnographic turn" (artists leaning on ethnographic research practices; before mentioned by Foster, 1995, p. 305) and "transdisciplinary turn" in contemporary art (bridging art, anthropology, and sociology). Moreover, new enactments in the arts in form of (combining) "sculpture, images, texts, and music" with speech, drama, and digital means have led to a "performative turn": "The artwork is no longer the dream of autonomy, of the absolute, and of sovereignty, but a practice of service." Instead of exhibiting objects, the exhibition of these practices become experiments (Weibel & Latour, 2007, p. 107).

More and more artists have drawn on ethnographic methods and thoughts, especially leaning on subjects of representation and engagement (Basu & Macdonald, 2007). On the other hand, artists have inspired anthropologists in questions such as the open process and the multi-site in form of deterritorialization and decentralization (Marcus, 2010) as well as conceptualism (Ssorin Chaikov, 2013; see for both more below). Most notably, artists have pushed ethnography and anthropology to move beyond logocentrism in representational concerns without yet resolving the authoritarianism of representation (Marxen, 2012, 2009a; Basu & Macdonald, 2007).

The mentioned above is demonstrated in the works and writings of artists such as Dora García (2011a, 2011b), Roberto Jacoby (2011), Antoni Muntadas (2011), Jo Spence (2005), Ester Ferrer (2017), Martha Rosler (2013), and Krzysztof Wodiczko (1999).

One of the main ideas of ethnography is to provide spaces in the field where participants can develop alternative narratives, in the sense of Deleuze and Guattari's "minor language" (1986). It refers to the activation of hidden potentials in a minority or subaltern groups (Marxen, 2012; Fortun, 2010; Tyler, 2010; Marcus, 1998; see Chapters 3 and 4). This used to happen on a verbal and written level in ethnography but does also on an artistic one if art forms are included in this research process (Marxen, 2012). Then, ethnography's intention of showing heterogeneous narratives and experiences is reinforced by artistic expression, thus combating overcoding and labeling. This can happen because artistic expression is a suitable possibility for overcoming the verbally established beyond one simple and determining signifier by opening up new meanings (Marxen, 2020, 2012, 2009a). It should be stressed that narrative throughout the entire book is not understood as a literal verbal explanation or translation of a state of desire (Camnitzer, 2018). Rather, it is considered a space where the subjective desire can unfold, establishing relations and connections to others.

These spaces of resistance are exactly the point in common between ethnography, critical contemporary art, and art therapy as explained in Chapter 2. They merge *in the artistic dispositif, challenging disciplinary overcoding and preconditioning as well as institutional frontiers (Marxen, 2018). Dominant identities can be modified and agency can be strengthened as a way of self-determination. A "minor language" (Deleuze & Guattari, 1986) can be achieved, stemming from minority position and located at the margins of majority thinking that they can refract, unframe and, eventually, overthrow.*

Moreover, Marcus (2010) has stressed that the multi-sited approach holds another common ground between ethnography and art. Both develop projects that are multi-sited, multi-disciplined, and multi-temporal as they engage and trace the circulation of theories and practices as they transverse various contexts and times, connecting seemingly distant locations and histories through an analysis of the circulation of neoliberal capitalism. They engage with transnationalism and transculturalism, understood as a process that forges and sustains "multi-stranded social relations." Social fields are built "that cross geographic, cultural, and political borders" (Basch, Glick Schiller, & Szanton Blanc, 1994, p. 7).

In these spaces, people, goods, affections, capital, services, information, images, and desires flow constantly; at the same time, the ideas and representations of origin and destination oscillate. These dynamics occur thanks to the present technological context, which allows immediate and simultaneous access to different mass media and facilitates a variety of transport possibilities (Appadurai, 1996). In short, these transnational realities have impacts on artistic practice and vice versa (Marxen, 2020).

Besides the multi-site, art and anthropology employ experimental, collaborative, "open lab," participatory, and social conceptualization and dissemination. Furthermore, both tend to aesthetics of projects and practices of uncertain closure which inevitably introduce the concept of open (meaning creative) process (Marxen, 2018; Marcus, 2010, 1998). This is another point in common with non-directive art therapy.

Ssorin-Chaikov (2013) proposes an ethnographic conceptualism, an encounter between conceptualist art and ethnography. It explicitly constructs the reality it studies, instead of claiming to represent an existing reality.

Ethnographic conceptualism takes a performative and transformative approach. Regarding the construction, rather than representation, of reality, Bishop's critique against hastily equating social and artistic practices seems essential. Social and artistic judgments and critiques do not easily merge; they are not directly compatible and should, rather, "exist in continual tension with each other" (Bishop 2012, p. 71, referring to Boltanski & Chiapello, 2005).

"Models of democracy in art do not have an intrinsic relationship to models of democracy in society. The equation is misleading and does not recognize art's ability to generate other, more paradoxical criteria," relations, and realities (Bishop, 2012, p. 76).

Bishop's thoughts (2012, p. 82) related to participatory art, as already quoted in Chapter 3, are important for the artistic dispositif and its "double ontological status," being "both an event in the world and at one remove from it." This process is exemplified by intangible experiences within the artistic dispositif. They shift between the subjective and collective, in the permanent interaction of "creative singularity and potential social mutations" (Marxen, 2018; Guattari, 2006, p. 80).

Limits of the Museum

The museum encounters different obstacles in its efforts to oppose capitalist co-opting of the arts, whether it is related to participatory, ethnographic or any form of the mentioned critical art, doing exhibition or other artistic activities with professional artists or other participants.

In this sense, Bishop's question (2013, p. 56) is: "Can a museum be anti-hegemonic?"

In the very first place, many museums that have been (previously) funded by public money have "come under pressure from neoliberal governments and city councils playing the mood music of austerity." This has been *the* occasion for private funders to step in, all too willingly "because museums are not only economic generators, but can enhance social status" (Bishop, 2013, p. 56). Private funders can live out their "philanthropic narcissism" (id) and multi-national companies can accumulate symbolic capital in form of "good press" and publicity (Haacke & Bourdieu, 1995; Chapter 2). Neither the presence nor the source of funds can be considered neutral. Their influence "is both economic and ideological" (Rosler, 1998, p. 94).[8] The consequences are a neoliberalist imposition of economic values and "language of accounting." Its "systems of assessment increasingly have to justify themselves according to metrics (grant-income revenue, economic impact, citation as a measure of influence)" (Bishop, 2013, pp. 61–62). In the museum world, it is translated into the already mentioned discourse of accessibility understood merely in quantitative terms (Chapters 2 and 3) and of money as measure of worth to a market. Thus, museum politics are collapsed into capitalist values (Janes, 2009). Additionally, the corporate museum operates with global imaginaries of consumption as opposed to local experiences that are just annulled in the measurement of global accountancy (Laseca, 2015).

In the MACBA example, we have seen how the general and public program directors were held responsible by the museum board, funders, and politicians for the *Las Agencias* project (The Agencies, 2001). They were accused to have transgressed their institutional limits. This had served the authorities to tame the museum's anti-capitalist engagement (Mahony, 2016).

The museum has become "a reflection of neoliberal capitalist society" (Camnitzer, 2018, p. 248). It has been seized by the "insatiable overfall" of the corporate world (Laseca, 2015, pp. 12–13; Alberro, 2009). The latter concentrates art in a disciplinary space, ideally an emblematic museum, to control, neutralize, and simplify its possible tensions and uncertainties. Thus, the "global corporate museum" becomes a "normalizing archive" and normalizing dispositif, placed in midst "an engineering of global consensus …" (Laseca, 2015, p. 19). This leads to "limited subjectivations," to calculated, calculable, and administrable encounters with spectators, rather than participants. Finally, the museum ends up being a disciplinary dispositif, "subrogated to the global governability" (Laseca, 2015, P. 28, 30).

As already outlined in Chapter 3, the neoliberalist co-option of art, art practices, and art institutions happens frequently through the conversion of the artistic experience into consumption. As shown above, in criticizing Bourriaud's "relational aesthetics," another conversion takes place through spectacle, fossilization, and anesthetization of supposed creative and unruly processes.

In the same commodification vein, museums are nowadays permanently exposed to the tourist industry, real estate speculation, and gentrification processes. On numerous occasions, they are built to regenerate a previously degraded neighborhood, like the MACBA museum in Barcelona (see Smith, 2009, 2000, and Chapter 2).

"For good or bad, museums today form part of the collective imaginary of a city" (Borja-Villel in Sesé, 2013; translated by myself from Spanish). This imaginary makes sponsors conceive agendas very often oriented on tourists' rather than the local visitors' budgets, interests, and inquiries. The first are characterized by fast viewing and consumption, "images *prêt-a-porter*" (Laseca, 2015, p. 44). Exhibitions are adapted to their short visit in the city, as opposed to the participation in long- or middle-term activities (Laseca, 2015). As a result, the museum becomes tamed by the tourist industry.

Another trend is the "Blockbusterities" (Conn, 2006, in Basu & Macdonald, 2007, p. 18), the favoring of exhibitions of well-known artists, at the sacrifice of providing spaces of agonistic artistic practices. These exhibitions circulate globally and achieve a spectacle status. Blockbuster events are supposed to attract thousands of visitors who very often need to line, queue, and push themselves through crowds. Thus, reflection and contemplation are converted into a stress. Yet, they fulfil the sponsors' expectation of quantitatively monitored access that will lead in the next future to more patronage, sponsors, and funds. The quantitative measurement of access has "to do with consumption, not [at all] with the transformation brought about in the consumer," or their experience (Camnitzer, 2018, p. 246). Both would be absolutely unmeasurable in quantitative terms. So, the concept of "access" itself should be analyzed, including who is accessing what and how and by whom this access is assessed (Camnitzer, id).

In this circuit, donors place their favorite artists in exhibitions in order to raise their values for the sake of the donor-owners. Meanwhile, many artists, curators, art educators, and art therapists adopt "the language of accountants, and their thinking becomes more like accountants' (or salespersons') thinking" (Rosler, 1998, pp. 99–100). Art educators and art therapists finally end up doing "public relations work to increase circulation numbers … and justify increased funding" (Camnitzer, 2018, p. 246). "'Arts management seminars' teach ways … 'how to identify and solicit the most receptive customers—through marketing surveys, direct mail, or whatever means has [sic] proven best'" (Rosler, 1998, pp. 99–100; referring to Putney, 1982).

Furthermore, the neoliberalist and tourist agendas promote and sponsor buildings of elite architecture that fulfill an iconographic function for the city, a public visibility, and inscription in the global circuit of modernity and entertainment. This circuit imposes a city that is equally conceived in global terms with supposed equal needs like mobility and modernity. Thus, urbanism is reduced to surface interventions, far away from a social urban planning (Laseca, 2015). The Tate Modern in London, Palais du Tokyo in Paris, the franchising of Guggenheim Museums such as in Bilbao and other cities are good examples. In this vein, the Guggenheim museum business has been compared to Disneyland leisure (Krauss, 1990). Interestingly, in the museums of London and Paris, Nicholas Bourriaud had prominent directive roles and conceived his relational aesthetics (1998). The museum architecture goes frequently hand in hand with the commodification of culture, the spectacle industry as well as the quantification of access and shop revenues. This leads inevitably to a clash of values between the local communities the museum serves and the funding they receive (Janes, 2009).

The museum is at the same time a building and a concept. The latter is a flexible and abstract idea, whereas the building itself is immobile and solid. Frequently it is difficult to distinguish between the politics of the container and those of the content. The concept must not stop with the building inauguration; rather it should take off then in order to include or be even based on the territory where it resides (Laseca, 2015).

Relevant Artworks

Regarding relevant artworks that express the limitations of the museum, the critical art form of institutional critique is certainly the most relevant. As summarized before, institutional critique expresses through art the political condition of the production, distribution, and reception of art by official artistic institutions.

The Group Material (2006, pp. 135–136) explains this methodology as "to question every aspect of our cultural situation from a political point of view." They ask "What politics inform accepted understandings of art and culture? Whose interests are served by such cultural conventions? How is culture made, and for whom is it made?". Transferred to art and the museum, Oiticica raised similar questions: A museum should not ask "what is art?" but "'when is art? and, most importantly, 'what can it do?'" (in Small, 2016, p. 227; Chapter 4).

Originating in the sixties, institutional critique had focused on the circulation, reception, and distribution of art in relation to the power dynamics of art institutions. It was also embedded in a time when there was a general protest against rules, norms, and institutions that were considered obsolete or reactionary. This was manifest in the '68 revolutions around the world. As we will see in Chapter 6, they protested against many institutions such as the asylum, the prison, the university, the school, the court, the factory, and the family. So, art was no exception and was institutionally critiqued.

With the shift from Fordism labor to cognitive capitalism, the absorption and co-option of art by the latter should be analyzed within this critique (Borja-Villel, 2010). This is the case in *Capital* (2001) by Cummings and Lewandowska. They show the analogue role the Tate Modern museum and the Bank of England play in the global circuits of capital. They considered the Tate with its high ambition to occupy an important role in the country's and world's art industry "a central bank in …a *symbolic economy*" (Cummings & Lewandowska, 2007, p. 135). "The dematerialization of financial value [from gold in former times to debt related, abstract financial products nowadays] has accelerated the penetration of the 'economic' into all spheres of contemporary life." This includes areas that used to be protected or at least kind of separated "from the vagaries of the 'market'," such as education, health, art, and culture, etc. (id, p. 136; Krauss, 1990). The Tate with its symbolic and immaterial economy is like the bank connected "with the vast network of other exhibitionary institutions and agencies, from museums, galleries, curators, collectors, and dealers, to various funding and sponsoring bodies both nationally and internationally that make up the global economy of art" (Cummings & Lewandowska, 2007, p. 137).

Moreover, they put into evidence the "visibility of some kinds of art patronage versus the invisibility of the financial contribution of ordinary taxpayers" (Basu & Macdonald, 2007, p. 5). The symbolic economy of the Tate is highly "indebted to private, public, and corporate gifting," in forms of funds and sponsoring. As a consequence, the museum is bound to "economics networks of obligation and indebtedness obscured from public scrutiny." With the constant decrease of public funding and increase of corporate sponsoring, exchanges and symbolic repayments are required, such as "my logo on your publicity – but others, as with the true gift, are left unspecified" (Cummings & Lewandowska, 2007, p. 139).

The logo and other publicity forms are actually a very common corporate sponsoring practice to be illustrated by a concrete example: When the art-therapeutic and analytical MACBA practices were halted, the most important local bank manifested its intention to step in with its funding. As an "exchange," they did ask for publicity in form of their logo. Additionally, they already had posted other of their "social art" sponsoring on YouTube with highly criticizable ethical implications. Upon Marxen's and Rodríguez's refusal to participate in this circuit, they lost any interest in funding. Once again, Bourdieu and Haacke's work about symbolic capital and art should be stressed (1995). It takes form of "good press" and publicity that lead to an accumulation of symbolic capital. Simultaneously, other unpopular corporate practices are hidden and made forgotten. The company projects its image "as a good corporate citizen," at the same time advertising its products. These dynamics have been called by corporate public relation agents themselves (from Exxon) a "social lubricant" (Haacke, 2009, p. 286). In the example of the local bank in Catalonia, the massive evictions of people affected by Southern Europe's economic crisis would have stepped at least into the background of their public image. Hans Haacke had dedicated an entire show and catalogue to this particular "social" bank practice (1995). Afterwards, he carried out another exhibition about real estate speculation in Spain (2012). Both took place in museums directed by Manuel Borja-Villel, the Tàpies Foundation in the first case and the Reina Sofia Museum in the second. Previously (1975), Haacke had already alleged the link between gentrification and the Guggenheim museum in his artwork *Shapolski et al. Manhatten Real Estate Holdings, a Real-Time Social System as of May 1, 1971.* As a result of his research, the implication of board members in the New Yorker speculations was revealed. As a consequence of Haacke's negative to remove this piece, his retrospective show was censured by the Guggenheim; the curator was fired. The official reason of the director by then, Thomas Messer, was the negative to allow documents (the list of real-estate holdings) in a space "reserved exclusively for ideas." Haacke questioned the museum's autonomy and neutrality. Finally, "[t]he separation between the space of the street and the museum ideal was completely reformulated (Borja-Villel, 2010, p. 25; Burnham, 1975; Haacke, 1975).

In his work *Must de Rembrandt* (1986), Haacke alludes to the instrumentalization of the arts by multinational companies, juxtaposing their philanthropic endeavors in form of the Cartier Art Foundation with their exploitation of workers and mines in collaboration with the apartheid-government in South Africa. They reportedly repressed brutally and violently workers' labor and human rights (Cauwet, 2017). In the same corporate context, the artist Martha Rosler explains in her text "Theses on Defunding" (1998, pp. 94–95): "By lending an air of philanthropy and generosity, corporate benevolence can be used to defuse charges of wholesale theft, as in the case of Mobil or Exxon." Simultaneously, "large and influential corporate funders are quite willing to congratulate themselves (before business audience) for the public relations value of their contributions to culture."

Most recently, art therapy has manifested a significant lack of critical thought in allowing Karen Pence, wife of the current Vice President of the United States, to choose art therapy—specifically, pediatric art therapy—as her philanthropic focus. This common practice of charity by politicians and/or their partners—mainly wives—matches the accumulation of symbolic capital in the form of positive publicity which allows politicians to hide unpopular dynamics behind the philanthropic facade. In spite of protests, the board of the American Art Therapy Association maintains its association with Pence. This is particularly alarming considering the racist, xenophobic, neoliberal, anti-environmental, anti-human rights agenda of the current administration which Karen Pence represents. Moreover, the contrast between her endorsement of pediatric art therapy and the intended abolishment of Deferred

Action for Childhood Arrivals (DACA) by the US government as well as the entire humanitarian drama taking place at the Southern US border is more than striking. The first would dramatically uproot so many young people for whom the US is the only home they have ever known. On its own, the permanent danger of deportation will inevitably cause much psychological trauma, requiring therapeutic treatment that the affected young people will probably not get. The second, however, is causing accumulative traumas because of severe human rights violations on a daily level.

Artists, art activists, educators, and therapists cooperating with politicians and companies very often lack of critical insight in their role "as promoters of acquiescence." Many are really convinced that their collaborations are in best service for the arts. In Haacke's words, "[s]uch a well-intentioned delusion can survive only as long as art is perceived as a mythical entity above mundane interests and ideological conflicts" (2009, p. 287). Instead, art practitioners should be more critical of the consequences of the corporate overfall into their fields and aware of their participation in this circuit of symbolic capital and symbolic economy, including the ethical constraints of the resulting obligation (Alberro, 2009; Haacke & Bourdieu, 1995). In the mentioned MACBA case, it would have meant blurring a good deal of the ethical boundaries of confidentiality in therapy and analysis. The task of the artist should be to reveal these obligations and make them obvious, in line of Haacke (2012, 1995, 1975) and Cummings & Lewandowska (2007), for example.

Other important artists who have worked in the line of institutional critique are Roberto Jacoby (2011), Joseph Kosuth (2002), Andrea Fraser (Fraser & Medina, 2016), Fred Wilson (Mignolo, 2011), Adrian Piper (2003), among many others (see for an overview: Alberro & Stimson, 2009). Artists such as Rogelio López Cuenca (2019) and Luis Camnitzer (2018) have challenged in their artworks the "ideological charge" of language and its supposed consensus. They "examine the contradictions established between language as a site of power and the artist who wants to assume this power" (Camnitzer, 2018, p. 253; also Hall, 2005).

Before, in 1968, the experience of Tucumán Arde, Argentina, also aimed at an institutional critique against the art establishment, although they did not denominate their way of doing as such. Artists and sociologists worked in collaboration with print media unions, showing the disastrous consequences of the neoliberalization in the form of the monopolization of the sugar cane industry in the northern Argentinian region of Tucumán. They chose the print media union's headquarters in Rosario and Buenos Aires as their exhibition spaces in order to reach out to alternative publics, as opposed to or besides the typical art world consumers. They aspired to an "art of making" as opposed to an "art of having," equating the latter to the bourgeois understanding of art, the private possession of the privileged and its circulation in cooperate funded art spaces (Longoni and Mestman, 2010; Benjamin, 1998, 1968).

Of course, any institutional critique can be co-opted by museums and other art institutions. This happened, for example, with the *Tucumán Arde* experience as displayed at the Documenta 12 in 2007. Its political density, value, and tension had been completely neutralized by its aseptic montage. The same has happened to objects of Lygia Clark's *Structuring of a Self* or to the *escraches*: Some objects were torn apart and put into some showcase. From the action of *escrachar*, blaming the torturers in public, eventually only a photo or some poster is exhibited that cannot give account for the action, its surroundings, participants, and context (Longoni, 2007). The art institutions thus neutralize the politicity of the mentioned artworks, institutionalizing and taming them. This is inevitably the danger for art that consists of actions, the experience of the here and now and that moves in the threshold of art and political activism. Yet, this should not suggest the impossibility of transmitting it. It is a question of redefining the exhibitional dimension and the archive (for the latter see Chapter 4). There is also no single solution for general application. Rather, in every case, the challenge has to be taken and worked upon. Instead of dismissing any possibility of transmission because of its ephemeral character, the experience- and action-based artworks should be shown in adequate ways, so that future generation can learn from them. Some highly succeeded examples are the already mentioned archive-catalogue-itinerary show *Perder la forma humana—una imagen sísmica de los años ochenta en América Latina* (Losing the human form—a seismic image of the eighties in Latin America, 2012) by the network Conceptualisms South. Another is the readaptation of *Tucumán Arde* by former member of the *Tucumán Arde* group Graciela Carnevale together with Ana Longoni, Fernando Davis, and Ana Wandzik at the Parque de España in Rosario, Argentina, 2008. It was titled *Inventario. Archivo Graciela Carnevale (1965–1975)* [Inventory. Archive Graciela Carnevale (1965–1975)]. Its indicated time frame (1965–1975) gives justice of all the events and developments before and after the actual *Tucumán Arde* exhibitions in 1968.

These two examples were conjunctions of exhibitions, research material display, archives & archiving, together with other activities like discussions and conferences. They succeeded in becoming counter-dispositifs. They were able "to produce new figures, forms, constellations—in short, original material and cultural configurations that are inseparable from collective statements" (Marxen, 2018; Chapter 4; Holmes, 2006, p. 421). At the same time, they produced "a specific social relation between artwork and spectator," without taming the original density of the works. This encounter "might in some cases lead to changes 'in the way art functions in society,' even when that art appears in museums" or other art institutions (Crimp, 1993, pp. 27, 25).

About the practice of *institutional critique of the museum*[9] as a "self-critical exploration," Ribalta stresses "the shift from a representational to a relational paradigm." Furthermore, it involves

> its socialisation beyond the limits of the museum. If institutional critique remains limited to the museum and the exhibition, it could easily become a new formalism. The vocation of institutional critique is to go beyond its own limits and contribute to the construction of new institutions, new practices and new rules. We at the Museum were able to contribute to this process, which is why we sought to bring down the institutional borders

> that exist between different fields. We realised that the radicalisation of institutional critique involves its de-institutionalisation—it has to be removed from the museum to contribute to a new global institutional framework that takes into account demands for democratic radicalization.
>
> (Ribalta, 2010, p. 256)

This process of de-institutionalization implies inevitably practices of deterritorialization, decentralization, and "nomadization," as explained in Chapter 4.

After deinstitutionalization new institutions have to be invented and built. The clue is

> how to effect a transition from a culture of resistance to a culture of management, how to translate the radical artistic and social experiences of recent years into an effective form of management that does not lose the potential to transform.
>
> (Ribalta, 2010, p. 256)

Negri (2017, p. 127) operates with his concepts of the multitude and the common in this question. "Multitude" is defined at the same time as resistance against the global system of power and oppression and as difference, powerful bodies invested by nomadism, hybridization, and mutation (see Chapter 4). "The common is the product of multiplicity." The common is "a matrix that singularities experience and express." The shift from multitude to the common happens through a "subjective moment," "a moment of subjectification," also understood as decision. "The common is the element that renders the multitude expressive in biopolitical terms." Considering Ribalta's question above, of how to avoid a reinstitutionalization of deinstitutionalizing practices, Negri formulates organization as "the very *dispositif* of our common existence. It is a problem of ontological determination" (id.). In short, "'making multitude' means building one's own institutions," and consequently unbuilding and rebuilding them, in a constant movement (Ibáñez, 2014).[10]

A crucial factor is also the temporary. Within the neoliberal hegemony, critical practices' lifespan is rather limited. They can temporarily liberate an area from the control of the state and the market before it is co-opted, absorbed, or commodified. Yet, this limitation in time should not be seen exclusively negative, even less should the experience itself be seen useless. It will reemerge in other spaces and places, eventually in an improved way if the actors could learn from previous mistakes and challenges. Then, they can resume their critical experience and renovate other institutions (Mahony, 2016).

Finally, it is crucial to maintain the molecular forces of resistance in order to oppose the molar and its capacity of absorbing these resistances (Negri, 2017; Raunig, 2014; Ribalta, 2010; Deleuze & Guattari, 2009, 1987). A new institutionality depends on the constant challenge of molecular spaces and practices in order to maintain its power of resistance, opposition, and originality. There is always the risk "that 'knowledge production'...; and, equally, ... the experimental is co-opted to support that to which it might direct its challenge" (Laseca, 2015; Basu & Macdonald, 2007, pp. 20–21). Also, institutional critique can become institutionalized if it does not go beyond critiquing the existing apparatus: "[E]ven beyond transforming them, it is a question of inventive … and persistent practices of the present becoming of institutions, of instituent practices." The latter is always twofold, of constituting and the endless return of instituting. We need "countless smaller and larger impulses of wish production, …the long breath of a constant and manifold new beginning" (Raunig, 2014, p. 14).

In the words of Lukács (2007):

> So if we are ever going to be able to understand the way in which reactionary ideas infiltrate our minds, and if we are ever going to achieve a critical distance from such prejudices, this can only be accomplished by hard work, by abandoning and transcending the limits of immediacy, by scrutinizing all subjective experiences and measuring them against social reality. In short it can only be achieved by a deeper probing of the real world.
>
> (p. 37)

Or applied to the museum: "A museum cannot act politically without being aware of its own position as a prime nucleus of social reproduction and a revitalising agent of districts and tourist attraction" (Borja-Villel, 2010, p. 27).[11]

Forms of Resistance

For Borja-Villel (2010, p. 30, 2008), there should be alternatives for a museum, opposing cooption, spectacle, touristic and urban neoliberal investment. He sees the museum in a place "between subversion and absorption, contemplative passivity and active breakaway, the state and the masses, creation and the market." Although artistic practices difficultly abolish frontiers, they can at least displace them. For him, some of the essential questions are, how to move events without fetishizing them? How to conceive a museum without monumentalizing what it is explaining or exhibiting? To achieve this, he proposes the constitution of "federations of free communities, a process which starts from below and deals with autonomy rather than a state [or market] takeover" (Borja-Villel, 2008, p. 6; 2010).

"Below" means to give agency to the immediate surroundings of the museum and its people. It is not so much a question of a department of Education but of establishing lose networks in and of new territories for agonistic practices and "the configuration of critical intersubjectvities" (Laseca, 2015, p. 77; see Chapter 3 and 4; Mouffe, 2017, 2012, 2007).

It is crucial to think and develop alternatives that are able to oppose the mindset of quantitative values with its "banalities of a spreadsheet or the statistical mystification of an opinion poll, but enable us to access a rich and diverse history, to question the present, and to realize a different future" (Bishop, 2013, p. 62).[12]

The oppositional museum would derail the foreseeable encounters of quantitative corporate logics in favor of new conditions within the indefinite relations with and in between images, the individual, the collective, and the institution. It would focus on the "complex social processes of … local imaginaries, … beyond the normalizing image" of the global and globalized business domain (Laseca, 2015, p. 30). In short, this museum would be an artistic counter-dispositif. Spaces of sociability and communications should be built and constantly renewed. These spaces take form of a collective sensing of our places in the world, in form of dialects between common and singular. They should "produce in the participants 'a difference which makes a difference'" (Basu & Macdonald, 2007, p. 17). These spaces should be "terrains of productive contradictions" that do not have fixed meaning but facilitate process of the search and inquiry of meanings. The museum should aim at new epistemologies, always considering itself as an object of studies and critique (Laseca, 2015, pp. 76–77, 89). Finally, the objective consists of producing displacements of senses and meanings (Borja-Villel, 2010, 2008).

The permanent question should be: "Is micro-political criticism of the molecular museum a way of interiorising the demands of cognitive capitalism or a form of resistance?" (Ribalta, 2010, p. 263). For any response to this question, the participants of the projects have to be asked about their effects, addressing "the singularity of the experiments—in short, an empirical, non-ideological bottom-up reading is required." In alignment with ethnographic research, the focus should be the experience itself and not its quantification.

In the same vein, Martha Rosler (2013) has pointed out the complexity of the expansion of art beyond its official institutions towards the provision of different services of different communities and towards its inclusion in areas of daily life. The danger, according to her, lies in the simultaneous expansion of government and cooperate control as well as instrumentalization through the expansion of artistic activities. Although Rosler is aware that critical analysis is bound to its historical and cultural context, it still is an escape from these instrumentalizations. Co-options can only be avoided through a critical analysis of the insertions and redefinitions of art so that it can continue to radically question beliefs and orders in opposition to controlling agents and hegemonic discourse.

Luis Camnitzer imagines the museum with an

> osmotic membrane that is both outside and inside at the same time. … A museum in particular should promote the possibility of heresies, the questioning of the canon. … The function of the museum should not be to grow the number of visitors, but to help transform them. The institutional role should … not [be] a training ground for taste.
>
> (in Behar, 2016)

"Rather than to refine visitors' consumption habits," it should open spaces where people can think for themselves (Camnitzer, 2018, p. 245). The visitor is then able to re-create their own aesthetic experience (Borja-Villel, 2010).

Notes

1 The mentioned art practices and artists are, of course, not limited to the quoted examples. They have been chosen according to their very heterogeneous ways of expression and their strong potential of criticality.
2 Consistency, repetition, and insistence were crucial factors within the artistic public protest that led their interventions to be successful. The Red Conceptualismos Sur (Conceptualisms South) network effectively retrieved, disseminated, and exposed similar experiential projects in different Latin American countries during the eighties. In particular, their book-catalogue and exhibition, *Perder la forma humana—una imagen sísmica de los años ochenta en América Latina* (Losing the human form—a seismic image of the Eighties in Latin America, 2012) deserves special mention.
3 See for the implication of Hijos and other civil rights organizations *Genocide in the Neighborhood* edited by Brian Whitener, 2010.
4 The free transmission of the *escrache* interventions led to its reception in Barcelona, Catalonia/Spain, by the art-activist group Enmedio. They developed actions against evictions during the economic crisis in Southern Europe, in collaboration with PAH (Plataforma de los Afectados por la Hipoteca, the activist platform for people affected by evictions; http://www.enmedio.info/tag/escrache). The former leader of PAH, Ada Colau, has been Barcelona's mayor since 2015.
5 Yet, see Bishop's caution (2012, p. 74) not to "reduce art to a question of ethically good or bad examples." Art displays a different way of "reality" and there is no literal translation from the artistic experience to the social world.
6 As a form of distinction between the professional artist and non-professional participant, I suggest the criteria of the capacity to maintain a discourse. A professional artist has to be able to do so, but this is a demand not to be necessarily imposed on the participant. In socially engaged art, it is precisely this supposed hierarchy that is to be blurred. It aims at overcoming "this division by directly thematizing the nature and dynamics of the actual social process of artistic production within specific political, cultural and economic sites" (Aldouri, 2015, pp. 1–2; referring to Kester, 2011).
7 Besides the two Brazilian, there was a vivid exchange between Kaprow and the Argentinian artist, theorist, and psychoanalyst Oscar Masotta (1967; see Chapter 6).
8 This quote refers to Rosler's reasoning about the differences between state, federal, foundation, and corporate funding in the US context.
9 Raunig (2004) has considered the institutional critique of the museum as the third wave of institutional critique. The first stemmed from the position of inferiority of the artist towards the critiqued institution. The second was carried out by the artist as an already institutionalized figure. See also Steyerl (2009, p. 492) for whom the first period of institutional critique aimed at the integration into art institutions (i.e. minority groups), the second struggled for inclusion into representation and the third is dealing with its absorption into precarity.

> [W]hile critical institutions are being dismantled by neoliberal institutional criticism, ...[i]t is on the one side being adapted to the needs of ever more precarious living conditions. On the other, there seems to have hardly ever been more need for organizing the new struggles and desires that this constituency might embrace.

For the institutionalization of institutional critique see (Fraser 2009).

10 Ibáñez (2014) explains anarchism as a constant movement in this sense; Negri (2017), however, rejects anarchist positioning in favor of communisms.
11 This statement has been contextualized with protests against MACBA's employment practices (Mahony, 2016); something I cannot confirm from my own freelance practice with the museum.
12 In this context, I wish to stress again the importance of the non-quantitative and non-exhibitionary MACBA practices and research as carried out by Rodríguez and Marxen (Chapter 2).

References

Alberro, A. (2009). Institutions, critique, and institutional critique. In A. Alberro, & B. Stimson (Eds.), *Institutional critique. An anthology of artists' writings* (pp. 2–19). Cambridge, MA: MIT Press.

Alberro, A., & Stimson, B. (Eds.). (2009). *Institutional critique. An anthology of artists' writings*. Cambridge, MA: MIT Press.

Aldouri, H. (2015). The dialectics of artist and non-artist. Three historical moments. Unpublished paper. Retrieved from: https://www.academia.edu/38021393/The_Dialectics_of_Artist_and_Non-Artist_Three_Historical_Moments [Accessed 19 October 2019].

Appadurai, A. (1996). *Modernity at large: Cultural dimensions of globalization*. Minneapolis, MN: University of Minnesota Press.

Basch, L., Glick Schiller, N., & Szanton Blanc, C. (Eds.). *Transnational projects, postcolonial predicaments, and deterritorialized nation-states*. London, UK: Routledge, 1994.

Basu, P., & Macdonald, S. (Eds.). (2007). *Exhibition experiments*. Oxford, UK: Blackwell Publishing.

Basu, P., & Macdonald, S. (2007). Introduction: Experiments in exhibition, ethnography, art, and science. In P. Basu, & S. Macdonald (Eds.), *Exhibition experiments* (pp. 1–24). Oxford, UK: Blackwell.

Behar, I. (2016). Solution, problem, problem, solution: On the art of Luis Camnitzer. *The Seen*. Retrieved from: http://theseenjournal.org/art-seen-national/solution-problem-problem-solution-art-luis-camnitzer-2/ [Accessed 19 October 2019].

Benjamin, W. (1998). *Understanding Brecht*. London, UK: Verso.

Benjamin, W. (1968). The work of art in the age of mechanical reproduction. In H. Arendt (Ed.), *Illuminations: Essays and reflections* (pp. 217–251). New York, NY: Schocken Books.

Bishop, C. (2013). *Radical museology. Or what's 'contemporary' in museums of contemporary art*. London, UK: Koenig Books.

Bishop, C. (2012). Participation and spectacle: Where are we now? In D. García (Ed.), *Klau mich. Mad Marginal. Cahier # 3*, (pp. 63–83). Cologne, Germany: Verlag der Buchhandlung Walther König and Documenta 13.

Bishop, C. (2006). *Participation*. London, UK: Whitechapel Gallery and Cambridge, MA: MIT Press.

Boltanski, L., & Chiapello, E. (2005). *The new spirit of capitalism*. London, UK: Verso.

Borja-Villel, M.J. (2010). The museum questioned. In: M.J. Borja-Villel, K. Cabañas, & J. Ribalta (Eds.), *Relational objects. MACBA collection 2002–2007* (pp. 19–39). Barcelona, Spain: MACBA.

Borja-Villel, M.J. (2008). Museos del Sur [Museums of the South]. *El País*, 20 December 2008.

Borja-Villel, M.J., & Enguita, N. (1998). (Eds.). *Lygia Clark* (exh. cat.). Barcelona, Spain: Fundació Antoni Tàpies.

Bourdieu, P., & Haacke, H. (1995). *Free exchange.* Cambridge, UK: Polity Press.

Bourriaud, N. (1998). *Relational aesthetic.* Dijon, France: Les presses du réel.

Brecht, B. (2014). *Brecht on theatre.* London, UK: Bloomsbury Academic.

Bois, Y.A., Amor, M., Brett, G., & Peruga, I. (2006). *Gego. Defying structures* (exh. cat.). Barcelona, Spain: MACBA.

Burnham, J. (1975). Steps in the formulation of real-time political art. In H. Haacke (Ed.), *Framing and being framed* (pp. 127–141). Halifax, NS: Press of Nova Scotia College of Art and Design.

Camnitzer, L. (2018). The museum is a school. In MNCARS (Ed.), *Hospice of failed utopias* (exh. cat.) (pp. 245–254). Madrid, Spain: MNCARS.

Cauwet, L. (2017). *La domesticación del arte. Política y mecenazgo* [The domestication of art. Politics and patronage]. Barcelona, Spain: Incorpore.

Clark, L., & Oiticica, H. (2006). Letters. In C. Bishop (Ed.), *Participation* (pp. 110–106). London, UK: Whitechapel Gallery and Cambridge, MA: MIT Press.

Conn, S. (2006). Science museums and the culture wars. In S. Macdonald (Ed.), *Companion to museum studies* (pp. 494–508). Oxford, UK: Blackwell.

Crimp. D. (1993). *On the museum's ruins.* Cambridge, MA: MIT Press.

Cummings, N., & Lewandowska, M. (2007). From *Capital* to enthusiasm: an exhibitionary practice. In P. Basu, & S. Macdonald (Eds.), *Exhibition experiments* (pp. 134–153). Oxford, UK: Blackwell Publishing.

Debord, G. (2002). *Society of the spectacle.* Detroit, MI: Black & Red Books.

Deleuze, G., & Guattari, F. (1986). *Kafka: Toward a minor literature (Theory and history of literature).* Minneapolis, MN: The University of Minnesota Press.

Deleuze, G., & Guattari, F. (1987). *A thousand plateaus: Capitalism and schizophrenia.* Minneapolis, MN: University of Minnesota Press.

Delgado, M. (1999). Cine [Cinema]. In M.J. Buxó, & J.M. de Miguel (Eds.), *De la investigación audiovisual. Fotografía, cine, vídeo, televisión* [From audio-visual research. Photography, cinema, video, television] (pp. 49–77). Barcelona, Spain: Proyecto A Ediciones.

di Filippo, M. (2015). Arte, política y subjetividad. Algunas reflexiones a partir del análisis del Grupo de Arte Callejero [Art, politics, and subjectivity: Some reflections starting from the analysis of the Street Art Group]. *Revista Pilquen. Sección Ciencias Sociales*, 18(2), 12–22. Retrieved from: http://revele.uncoma.edu.ar/htdoc/revele/index.php/Sociales/article/view/1388/html [Accessed 19 October 2019].

Estévez, R., Díez Fischer, A., & López, M.A. (2017). *The words of others: Leon Ferrari and rhetoric in times of war.* Zurich, Switzerland: JRP Ringier and Los Angeles, CA: Redcat.

Ferrer, E. (2017). *All variations are valid, including this one.* Madrid, Spain: MNCARS.

Fortun, K. (2010). Foreword to the 25th anniversary edition. Of Writing Culture, 2020. In J. Clifford, & G. Marcus (Eds.), *Writing culture. The poetics of ethnography.*

25th anniversary edition (pp. vii–xxii). Berkeley and Los Angeles, CA: University of California Press.

Foster, H. (2006). Chat rooms. In C. Bishop (Ed.), *Participation* (pp. 190–195). London, UK: Whitechapel Gallery and Cambridge, MA: MIT Press.

Foster, H. (1995). The artist as ethnographer? In G. Marcus, & F. Myers (Eds.), *The traffic in culture. Refiguring art and anthropology* (pp. 302–309). Berkeley, CA: University of California Press.

Fraser, A. (2009). From the critique of institutions to an institution of critique. In A. Alberro, & B. Stimson (Eds.), *Institutional critique. An anthology of artists' writings* (pp. 408–417). Cambridge, MA: MIT Press.

Fraser, A., & Medina, C. (2016). *De la crítica institucional a la institución de la crítica* [From institutional critique to the institution of critique]. Mexico City, Mexico: Siglo XXI and Barcelona, Spain: MACBA.

GAC (Grupo de Arte Callejera). (2009). *Pensamientos, prácticas, acciones* [Thoughts, practices, actions]. Buenos Aires, Argentina: Tinta Limón.

García, D. (2011a). *The world according to Dora García*. Berlin, Germany: Argobooks.

García, D. (2011b). *Mad Marginal. Cahier 2. L'inadeguato. Lo inadecuado. The inadequate.* Berlin, Germany: Sternberg Press; Trieste, Italy: Fondazione Galleria Civica di Trento and Mousse Publishing.

García Canclini, N. (2014). *Art beyond Itself. Anthropology for a society without a story line*. Durham, NC: Duke.

Guattari, F. (2006). Chaosmosis: An ethico-aesthetic paradigm. In C. Bishop (Ed.), *Participation* (pp. 79–82). London, UK: Whitechapel Gallery and Cambridge, MA: MIT Press.

Guerilla Girls. (2003). *The Guerilla Girls' illustrated guide to female stereotypes*. London, UK: Penguin Books.

Guerilla Girls. (1998). *The Guerilla Girls' bedside companion to the history of Western art*. London, UK: Penguin Books.

Haacke, H. (2012). *Castles in the sky* (exh. cat.). Madrid, Spain: MNCARS.

Haacke, H. (2009). Museums, managers of consciousness. In A. Alberro, & B. Stimson (Eds.), *Institutional critique. An anthology of artists' writings* (pp. 276–288). Cambridge, MA: MIT Press.

Haacke, H. (1995). *Obra social* [Social work] (exh. cat.). Barcelona, Spain: Fundació Antoni Tàpies.

Haacke, H. (1975). *Framing and being framed*. Halifax, NS: Press of Nova Scotia College of Art and Design.

Hall, S. (2005). The rediscovery of ideology: Return of the repressed in media studies. In M. Gurevitch, T. Bennett, J. Curran, & J. Woollacott (Eds.), *Culture, society and the media* (pp. 52–86). New York, NY: Routledge.

Holmes, B. (2006). The artistic device, or, the articulation of collective speech. *Ephemera*, 6(4), 411–432.

Ibáñez, T. (2014). *Anarquismo es movimiento. Anarquismo, neoanarquismo y postanarquismo* [Anarchism is movement. Anarchism, neo-anarchism, and post-anarchism]. Barcelona, Spain: Virus Editorial.

Iconoclasistas. (2016). *Manual of collective mapping: Critical cartographic resources for territorial collaborative-creation processes*. Buenos Aires, Argentina: Iconoclasistas. Retrieved from: https://www.academia.edu/28625755/Manual_of_Collective_Mapping._Critical_cartographic_resources_for_territorial_processes_of_collaborative_creation_2016_ [Accessed 22 October 2019].

Jacoby, R. (2011). *El deseo nace del derrumbe. Acciones, conceptos, escritos* [Desire arises from collapse. Actions, concepts, writings]. Barcelona, Spain: La Central.
Janes, R.R. (2009). *Museums in a troubled world: Renewal, irrelevance, or collapse.* New York, NY: Routledge.
Kaprow, A. (2006). Notes on the elimination of the audience. In C. Bishop (Ed.), *Participation* (pp. 102–104). London, UK: Whitechapel Gallery and Cambridge, MA: MIT Press.
Kelley, J. (2003). Introduction. In J. Kelley (Ed.), *Allan Kaprow. Essays on the blurring of art and life* (pp. xvi–xxix). Berkeley and Los Angeles, CA: University of California Press.
Kester, G. (2011). *The one and the many. Contemporary collaborative art in a global context.* Durham, NC: Duke University Press.
Kosuth, J. (2002). *Art after philosophy and after: Collected writings, 1966–1990.* Cambridge, MA: MIT Press.
Krauss, R. (1990). The cultural logic of the late capitalist museum. *October*, 54, 3–17.
Kruger, B. (2010). *Barbara Kruger.* New York, NY: Rizzoli.
Laseca, R. (2015). *El museo imparable. Sobre institucionalidad genuina y blanda* [The unstoppable museum. On genuine and soft institutionality]. Santiago de Chile: LOM.
Longoni, A. (2017). A long way. Argentine artistic activism of the last decade. In B. Kelley Jr. and G. Kester (Eds.), *Collective situations: Readings in contemporary Latin American Art, 1995–2010* (pp. 98–111). Durham, NC: Duke University Press.
Longoni, A. (2011). Experimentos en las inmediaciones del arte y la política [Experiments in the immediacies of art and politics]. In R. Jacoby (Ed.), *El deseo nace del derrumbe. Acciones, conceptos, escritos* [Desire arises from collapse. Actions, concepts, writings] (pp. 5–29). Barcelona, Spain: La Central.
Longoni, A. (2007). Escraches en el museo [Escraches in the museum]. *La Vanguardia Cultura/s*, 22 August 2007.
Longoni, A., & Bruzzone, G. (Eds.). (2008). *El Siluetazo* [The silhouette movement]. Buenos Aires, Argentina: Adriana Hidalgo Editora.
Longoni, A., & Mestman, M. (2010). *Del Di Tella a Tucumán Arde – Vanguardia artística y política en el 68 argentino* [From Di Tella to Tucumán Arde – Artistic avant-garde and politics of the Argentinean '68]. Buenos Aires, Argentina: Eudeba.
López Cuenca, R. (2019). *Keep reading, giving rise* (exh. cat.). Madrid, Spain: MNCARS.
Lukács, G. (2007). Realism in the balance. In *Aesthetics and politics. Theodor Adorno, Walter Benjamin, Ernst Bloch, Bertolt Brecht, Georg Lukács* (pp. 28–59). London, UK: Verso.
Mahony, E. (2016). The uneasy relationship of self-critique in the public art institution. *Curator The Museum Journal*, 59(3), 219–238.
Marcus, G. (2010). Contemporary fieldwork aesthetics in art and anthropology: Experiments in collaboration and intervention. *Visual Anthropology*, 23, 263–277.
Marcus, G. (1998). *Ethnography through thick and thin.* Princeton, NJ: Princeton University Press.
Marcus, G., & Fischer, M. (1986). *Anthropology as cultural critique. An experimental moment in the human sciences.* Chicago, IL: University of Chicago Press.

Martí, R., & Etcétera. (2017). Etcétera. In B. Kelley Jr. and G. Kester (Eds.), *Collective situations: Readings in contemporary Latin American Art, 1995–2010* (pp. 58–78). Durham, NC: Duke University Press

Marxen, E. (2020). Introduction to Learning art and resistance from the South. *Field. A Journal of Socially Engaged Art Criticism*, 15. Retrieved from: http://field-journal.com/editorial/introduction-to-learning-art-and-resistance-from-the-south [Accessed 3 March 2020].

Marxen, E. (2019). Transforming traditions: Walter Benjamin, art, and art therapy. In R. Hougham, S. Pitruzzella, & H. Wengrower (Eds.), *Traditions in transition: New articulations in the arts therapies* (pp. 251–271). London, UK: Ecarte (European Consortium of the Arts Therapies).

Marxen, E. (2018). Artistic practices and the artistic dispositif – A critical review. *Antipoda. Journal of Anthropology and Archeology*, 33, 37–60.

Marxen, E. (2016). La expresión veraz de los saberes corporeizados [The fearless expression of embodied knowledges]. In I.A. Hernández, F. Grijalva Maza, & A.R. Gómez Rossi (Eds.), *Más allá del texto. Cultura digital y nuevas epistemologías* [Beyond the text. Digital culture and new epistemologies] (pp. 67–78). Mexico City, Mexico: Editorial Itaca.

Marxen, E. (2013). Deshaciendo fronteras: el arte como denuncia [Undoing frontiers. Art as denouncement]. In P. Laverde (Ed.), *No nos cabe tanta muerte* [We do not accept so much death anymore] (exh. cat.). Barcelona/Granollers, Spain: Roca Umbert.

Marxen, E. (2012). 'La comunidad silenciosa'. Migraciones filipinas y capital social en el Raval (Barcelona) ['The silent community'. Filipino migrations and social capital at Raval (Barcelona)]. PhD thesis. On-line publication: Tarragona, Spain: University Rovira i Virgili. http://www.tdx.cat/bitstream/handle/10803/96667/TESIS.pdf?sequence=1 [Accessed 20 October 2019].

Marxen, E. (2011a). Pain and knowledge: Artistic expression and the transformation of pain. *The Arts in Psychotherapy*, 38, 239–246. doi: 10.1016/j.aip.2011.07.003.

Marxen, E. (2011b). *Diálogos entre arte y terapia. Del 'arte psicótico' al desarrollo de la arteterapia y sus aplicaciones* [Dialogues between art and therapy. From 'psychotic art' to the development of art therapy and its applications]. Barcelona, Spain: Gedisa.

Marxen, E. (2009a). La etnografía desde el arte. Definiciones, bases teóricas y nuevos escenarios [Ethnography from art. Definitions, theoretical bases and new sceneries]. *Alteridades* [Alterities], 19(37), 7–22.

Marxen, E. (2009b). Therapeutic thinking in contemporary art. Psychotherapy in the arts. *The Arts in Psychotherapy*, 36, 140–147. doi: 10.1016/j.aip.2008.10.004.

Marxen, E., & Rodríguez, M. (2012). *Alleged opposites: On the public sphere, art and the clinic. Research working group*. Retrieved from: http://www.macba.cat/en/alleged-opposites [Accessed 19 October 2019].

Masotta, O. (Ed.). (1967). *Happenings*. Buenos Aires, Argentina: Jorge Álvarez Ed. (reedited by Corregidor Ed., 1990).

Mignolo, W. (2011). Museums in the colonial horizon of modernity. Fred Wilson's *Mining the Museum* (1992). In J. Harris (Ed.), *Globalization and contemporary art* (pp. 71–85). Hoboken, NJ: Blackwell Publishing.

Mouffe, C. (2017). An agonistic conception of the museum. In Fictilis (Ed.), *Museum of capitalism* (pp. 78–79). New York, NY: Inventory Press.

Mouffe, C. (2012). Alfredo Jaar: The artist as organic intellectual. In A. Jaar (Ed.), *The way it is. An aesthetics of resistance* (pp. 264–281). Berlin, Germany: Realismus-Studio of NGBK, New Society for Visual Arts.
Mouffe, C. (2007). *Prácticas artísticas y democracia agonística* [Artistic practices and agonistic democracy]. Barcelona/Bellaterra, Spain: MACBA/Universidad Autónoma de Barcelona.
Muntadas, A. (2011). *Between the frames: The forum*. Barcelona, Spain: MACBA.
Negri, T. (2017). *Marx and Foucault*. Malden, MA: Polity Press.
Oiticica, H. (2006). Dance in my experience. In C. Bishop (Ed.), *Participation* (pp. 105–109). London, UK: Whitechapel Gallery and Cambridge, MA: MIT Press.
Piper, A. (2003). *Adrian Piper. Desde 1965* [Adrian Piper. Since 1965]. Barcelona, Spain: MACBA.
Putney, V. (1982). More than talent. *Pace*, March/April.
Rancière, J. (2006). Problems and transformations in critical art. In C. Bishop (Ed.), *Participation* (pp. 83–93). London, UK: Whitechapel Gallery and Cambridge, MA: MIT Press.
Raunig, G. (2014). *The machinics of political art. Another twelve theses on the actualization of Walter Benjamin's 'The author as producer'*. Bilbao, Spain: Consonni.
Raunig, G. (2004). The double criticism of parrhesia: Answering the question "What is a progressive (art) Institution"'. *Republicart*, 4. Retrieved from: http://www.republicart.net/disc/institution/raunig04_en.htm [Accessed 19 October 2019].
Red Conceptualismos Sur. (2012). *Perder la forma humana. Una imagen sísmica de los años ochenta en América Latina* [Losing the human form—a seismic image of the eighties in Latin America]. Madrid, Spain: MNCARS.
Ribalta, J. (2010). Experiments in a new institutionality. In M.J. Borja-Villel, K. Cabañas, & J. Ribalta (Eds.), *Relational objects. MACBA collection 2002–2007* (pp. 225–265). Barcelona, Spain: MACBA.
Rolnik, S. (2005). *Lygia Clark. De l'œuvre à l'événement* [Lygia Clark. From the artwork to the event] (exh. cat.). Nantes, France: Musée des Beaux-Arts.
Romero, J.C., Davis, F., & Longoni, A. (2010). *Juan Carlos Romero*. Buenos Aires, Argentina: Fundación Espiga.
Rosler, M. (2013). *Culture class*. Berlin, Germany: Sternberg Press.
Rosler, M. (1998). Thesis on defunding. In G. Kester (Ed.), *Art, activism & oppositionality. Essays from Afterimage* (pp. 94–102). Durham, NC: Duke University Press.
Sajnani, N., Marxen, E., & Zarate, R. (2017). Critical perspectives in the arts therapies: Response/ability across a continuum of practice. *The Arts in Psychotherapy*, 54, 28–37. doi: 10.1016/j.aip.2017.01.007.
Sesé, T. (2013). Museos: cómo ganar recursos sin ser populistas [Museums: How to earn resources without being populist]. *La Vangaurdia*, 21 January 2013.
Small, I. (2016). *Hélio Oiticica. Folding the frame*. Chicago, IL: University of Chicago Press.
Smith, N. (2009). Son los museos tan solo un vehículo al servicio del desarrollo inmobiliario? [Are museums just a vehicle at the service of real estate development?]. In M.J. Borja-Villel, & J. Ribalta (Eds.), *Ideas concebidas* [Conceived ideas], (pp. 130–149). Barcelona, Spain: MACBA.

Smith, N. (2000). Del Lower East Side al Raval [From the Lower East Side to Raval]. *La Vanguardia*, 8 December 2000.

Spence, J. (2005). *Más allá de la imagen perfecta. Fotografía, subjetividad, antagonismo* [Beyond the perfect image. Photography, subjectivity, antagonism](exh. cat.). Barcelona, Spain: MACBA.

Spero, N. (2009). *Nancy Spero. Dissidances* (exh. cat.). Barcelona, Spain: MACBA.

Ssorin-Chaikov, N. (2013). Ethnographic conceptualism: An introduction. *Laboratorium: Russian Review of Social Research*, 2. Retrieved from: http://www.soclabo.org/index.php/laboratorium/article/view/336/864 [Accessed 19 October 2019].

Steyerl, H. (2009). The institution of critique. In A. Alberro, & B. Stimson (Eds.), *Institutional critique. An anthology of artists' writings* (pp. 486–492). Cambridge, MA: MIT Press.

Tyler, S. (2010). Post-modern ethnography: From document of the occult to occult document. In J. Clifford, & G. Marcus (Eds.), *Writing culture. The poetics of ethnography. 25th anniversary edition* (pp. 122–140). Berkeley and Los Angeles, CA: University of California Press.

Weibel, P., & Latour, B. (2007). Experimenting with representation: Iconoclash! and making things public. In P. Basu, & S. Macdonald (Eds.), *Exhibition experiments* (pp. 94–108). Oxford, UK: Blackwell Publishing.

Whitener, B. (Ed.). (2010). *Genocide in the neighborhood.* Oakland, CA: Chainlinks.

Wodiczko, K. (1999). *Critical vehicles. Writings, projects, interviews.* Cambridge, MA: MIT Press.

Wright, S. (2008). Behind police lines: Art visible and invisible. *Art & Research: A Journal of Ideas, Contexts and Methods*, 2(10), Summer 2008. Retrieved from: http://www.artandresearch.org.uk/v2n1/wright.html [Accessed 19 October 2019].

6 Deinstitutionalizing and Rearticulating Art and Psychiatry

Deinstitutionalization has been one of several approaches usually collapsed into the term "anti-psychiatry." The deinstitutionalization movement in psychiatry was coined by the Italian psychiatrist Franco Basaglia (1924–1980) who achieved the legal abolition of psychiatric hospitals in Italy.

"Anti-psychiatry" has been comprised of several currents of thoughts, academic research, and clinical and community practices with significant differences amongst each. To give justice to the variety of thoughts and approaches within anti-psychiatry, it is more appropriate to consider it in plural: Anti-psychiatr*ies* (Hochmann, 2015). Within this variety, important similarities in underlying thinking and convictions were shared. Most notably, they were joined by a common, profound critique and rejection of conventional or traditional psychiatry as carried out until the 1960s.

In this chapter, deinstitutionalizing practices, anti-psychiatry approaches, and institutional therapy achievements will be summarized as they have been developed by psychiatrists, psychoanalysts, and scholars such as Basaglia (Italy); Tosquelles, Oury, Guattari, Fanon, Deligny, Mannoni, Foucault (France); Laing, Cooper (Great Britain); Goffman, Szasz (USA); the Socialist Patients' Collective (Germany); da Silveira (Brazil); and Masotta (Argentina).

Their relevance for the present areas of concern is highlighted, particularly for art, the clinic, and artistic practices.

Psychiatry, Anti-Psychiatries, and Deinstitutionalization

Many of the anti- or deinstitutionalizing psychiatrists were trained psychiatrists themselves. They shared in common a deep dissatisfaction regarding psychiatry itself, its methods, epistemological and ideological bases, academic and clinical training, as well as "the weight of politico-administrative measures and of economic necessity" in treatments (Mannoni, 1973, p. 490). Although they differed significantly in their conceptions of existence, etiology, and methods dealing with mental illness, they rejected any reduction of the debate around it "to a discussion of administrative, therapeutic or technical measures" (Mannoni, 1973, p. 489). They converged in a deep inquiry of reaching to deeper political spheres of the discussion in the form of existential subjects like personal freedom, societal tolerance, stigma, institutional and state violence as well as professional ethics. At the core of these discussions lies, still to this day, the question: What do we mean by the "insane" or mentally ill? "And, what kind of care should be taken of them?" They all, in one extension or another, called "in question a whole ideology, and not merely hospital practice" (id, p. 501).

The anti-psychiatrists intended to encounter psychological episodes labeled as "delirious" in a way different than as pathology. They opposed to varying degrees the way psychiatrists medicated and treated mental troubles. They denounced the attacks against patients' freedom, interning them arbitrarily often in order to eventually please family members and certainly a society that sees its order threatened by uncommon and bizarre behavior (Hochmann, 2015). They were concerned about the violence occurring inside asylums and hospitals in form of isolations, prolonged physical contentions, electroshocks, psychosurgery. These violations of human rights have been abundantly condemned in various art forms such as films that show the violence inside the psychiatric hospital and its arbitrary. Examples include *One Flew over the Cuckoo's Nest* by Milos Forman, 1975, or *Bicho de Sete Cabeças* [Brainstorm] by Laís Bodanzky, 2000, based on the autobiographic book by Carrano Bueno *Canto dos Malditos*, or *Monkeys as Becky* about lobotomy and schizophrenia, 1999, by Joaquim Jordà. Simultaneously, books have given account of the violence in psychiatry, such as *Down Below,* the autobiographic essay about being interned in an asylum by the painter Leonora Carrington (1998/2017), to name one. On an academic level, Goffman's ethnography *Asylums: Essays on the Social Situation of Mental Patients and Other Inmates* details his experiences inside an asylum (1961), and his conceptualization of the Total Institution has been crucial.

1961 turned out to be a challenging year for psychiatry: Besides Goffman's book, two other crucial texts for the anti-psychiatries movements were published (and are mentioned below in this chapter): *History of Madness* by Foucault in France (1961/2006) and *The Myth of Mental Illness* by Thomas Szasz (US). Additionally, one year before Sartre had published in France *The Critique of the Dialectical Reason.* These four books would become the theoretical base for many anti-psychiatrists and their reasoning, most notably for the British (Laing & Cooper).

The "remarkable convergence" of anti-psychiatries on an international level seems

> to suggest that the similarity of these movements merely reflects the universal shortcomings of traditional psychiatry... Instead of a clearly defined doctrine it had a body of ill-assorted empirical knowledge, accumulated over the centuries; its diagnoses were based on descriptions of symptoms....
>
> (Mannoni, 1973, pp. 490–491)

In this sense, psychiatrists in Shanghai undertook similar innovations like anti-psychiatrists Cooper and Laing in England or deinstitutionalizer Basaglia in Italy. In the first case, they leaned on Mao saying:

> 'The leaders can turn for instruction only to those whom they lead.' Thus they adopted traditional Western psychiatry wholesale, but offset their borrowing by contending that only those who were being led-the madmen [and women]-could teach them what should be done with it.
>
> (Mannoni, 1973, p. 494)

It was a "transnational movement, with constant exchanges of ideas and people, collective publications and translations of key texts. Volunteers moved from country to country," within Europe and beyond (Foot, 2015a, p. 2).

The protesting psychiatrists criticized the mechanisms as well as the term diagnosis. As a term it is "borrowed from medicine, somewhat inappropriate. … an administrative solution to the problem is found by assuming them to be 'ill.' The psychiatrist on duty provides the certificate which is required for administrative purposes" (Mannoni, 1973, p. 491). This "certificate" has important medical, administrative, and political consequences for the affected person and is emitted from a position of power of the psychiatrist.

Still today, psychiatric diagnosis lacks the level of precision found in other medical fields. Psychiatric diagnosis:

> is based on a provisional grouping of symptoms without any certain biological substratum … diagnosis in psychiatry is less the acknowledgment of a reproducible dysfunctioning beyond the context where it is pronounced but rather a provisional definition, bond to a certain state of social tolerance, in a given moment and place, and given by a community of specialists submitted themselves to multiple influences.
>
> (Hochmann, 2015, pp. 15–16, translated by myself from French; also Kleinman, 1991a)

Nowadays, these influences are mainly imposed by the pharmaceutical industry, insurance companies (see Taussig, 1992, in Chapter 3), and associations of clients and family, themselves eventually exposed to the first two lobbies.

In psychopathology, the line between the professed normal (or, more accurately, non-pathological) and pathological is extremely thin, both ontologically and culturally. Several studies have been carried out that show that the common psychopathologies are articulated, treated, tolerated, and cured quite differently across different cultures (i.e. Kleinman, 1991b). "One can only be mad by comparison" (Hochmann, 2015, p. 16). The pharmaceutical industry and insurance companies have exercised an important pressure on mathematical ascertainment in diagnosis; ignoring the "fragile and contestable character of the initial information" provided by clients, they try to convert it into a mathematical reality (Hochmann, 2015, p. 16).

In spite of these vague "scientific" basis, psychiatry has been included in medicine, being in charge of "diseases" that would not hold this definition in other medical fields. Because of this vagueness, it has always occupied an inferior status within the larger medical field. Nevertheless, or maybe motivated by this inferiority, psychiatrists are still reifying their identity as physicians.

Simultaneously, and moving to a macro level, society has assigned psychiatrists the role of guardians of social order. They decide via diagnosis who is suffering a mental pathology, eventually interning clients into hospitals and thus fulfilling administrative tasks of social exclusion (Hochmann, 2015). This exclusion is usually based on dichotomized labels like "normative/powerful" against "dissident/oppressed." Within this binary, "'sane' could function as a moral category used to underline the violence and irrationality of existing categories and power structures, but 'insane' could equally function affirmatively, defined as a 'half-compelled, half-chosen' response to and rejection of the prevailing society" (Proctor, 2018, p. 3; referring to Cooper, 2015). The latter designation of insane destroys the opponent's credibility and any attempts to expose the illegitimacy of state violence are discredited. In this way, psychiatric diagnosis becomes a reactionary weapon.

In not too distant history, a heighten version of this task has been seen in moral policing during World War II (WWII) and the totally perverted collaboration of psychiatrists with Nazi Germany, first forcedly sterilizing and then killing the supposed mentally ill (Thys, 2015; and Dora García's video *Extermination*, 2008, with Erik Thys as narrator about the terror: https://vimeo.com/86824747).

Anti-psychiatrists have all opposed this perversion and have put into evidence the role of moral policing. Instead of auxiliating perverted or moralist authorities or intolerant societies, they have opted to give meaning to mental unease and to bring the affected people's subjectivity in the forefront of any kind of treatment.

Particularly, in Germany, the Socialist Patients' Collective (SPK) has taken the most radical position within anti-psychiatries, certainly motivated by the horrible past collaboration of psychiatrists with the Nazis, and aspiring to achieve a revolution that would both abolish psychiatry and capitalism.

After all, "[p]sychiatrists have realized that they are victims of the system just as other people are. … They submit to it. Basically, it is this abstract system that is being attacked by the anti-psychiatrists" (O. Mannoni, 1973, p. 491). For others, they were not only serving power but directly forming part and contributing to it (Foot, 2015a).

The anti-psychiatries came up in a time when "[i]nstitutional power was contested in all its forms – as encapsulated in the protagonists of this power: teachers, doctors, psychiatrists, lecturers, priests and politicians" (Foot, 2015a, p. 3). Mainly with the students' movements and revolutions of May '68, institutions came under fire: "[t]he asylum, the prison, the university, the school, the court, the factory and the family… in turn [they were] often compared to the concentration camp, understood as the violent extreme towards which all oppressive institutions end" (Proctor, 2018, pp. 3–4). Decolonization discourses were partly included as well.

Power issues were discussed all over.

> Those with power often contested themselves, by denying their own authority, by stripping themselves of the symbols of power (white coats, for example, as a first step, but also titles and academic degrees), or by attempting to place themselves on the same level as those they were treating, teaching or giving sermons to.
>
> (Foot, 2015a, p. 3)

There is like a "rope-ladders of the history of ideas" in the so-called anti-psychiatry (Mannoni, 1973, p. 493). In spite of their different theoretical bases, degrees of political radicalism, and ways of focusing the issues of mental health, wellness, and unease, many approaches are complementary rather than exclusionary.

They share their links to the 1968 revolts, revolutions, and searches for new forms of life and subjectivities. "In allowing for the liberation of the self, it converged with the broader philosophy of 1968" (Foot, 2015a, p. 5).

Let us recall from Chapter 4 (p. 98) authors like Negri, Deleuze & Guattari, Foucault, and Rolnik:

Negri (2017, p. 171) considered the conditions of May '68 as "at the time not ending but opening up a period which has been and still is to be continued by movements like feminism…, queer theories…, *anti-psychiatric circles, deinstitutionalization groups…*" "They have all been able to activate 'the outside-of-the subject experience'" (Rolnik in Fernández Polanco & Pradel, 2015). Referring back to Foucault (2014; Negri, 2017), these past and present movements are practices of resistance and they are built on or lead to "ontological ruptures."

Anti-psychiatries formed part of the *Zeitgeist* of the sixties and seventies. The violence of asylums and the labeling of the mentally ill "were clear examples for many of the most oppressive features of the capitalist system" (Foot, 2015a, p. 1). Many of the anti-psychiatrists succeeded in opposing "capitalism and the system with a clear idea of what was to be done, and how…in 1968, at least, the movement was pushing in the same direction. Doors were opening and barriers were broken down, both literally and metaphorically" (Foot, 2015a, p. 7).

The different forms, ways, and foci of anti-psychiatry, deinstitutionalization, and similar movements range between the decisive political militarism in favor of a leftist revolution, converting mental illness into a weapon against the capitalist system (the Socialist Patients' Collective in Germany, SPK) and the equation of mental illness with a personal development and even enrichment (Laing & Cooper in the United Kingdom). Institutionally, there was a spectrum of thought including abolishing psychiatry and its hospitals without any substitutes (SPK), converting them into communes where anti-psychiatrists and formerly called patients would live non-hierarchically together

(Laing & Cooper, Deligny in France), founding alternative communities beyond psychiatry while maintaining certain differences between professionals and clients (Maud Mannoni in France), deinstitutionalizing psychiatric hospitals and replacing them with open community centers and treatments (Basaglia and the deinstitutionalization movement in Italy and Brazil), humanizing and de-totalizing the psychiatric hospital (da Silveira in Brazil, the Institutional Therapy in France as developed mainly by Tosquelles, Oury, Guattari, and Fanon). Different professionals were involved in anti-psychiatries too: physicians or psychiatrists themselves (Basaglia, Cooper, Laing, Tosquelles, Oury, the founder of the SPK Huber, da Silveira, Szasz), nurses (Roll first in SPK and then in deinstitutionalization), anthropologists like Bateson (UK and USA), psychoanalysts (Guattari, Maud Mannoni, Masotta) and (anti) educators like Deligny. There were also academics in the same battle, most notably Goffman (sociologist, USA) and Foucault (philosopher, France).

Distinct stances were also taken within the consideration and comprehension of mental illness. For most of them, "[w]hat was known as mental illness … was in some way created by social forces, inside and/or outside the family unit. This characteristic has been seen, by some writers, as the essence of anti-psychiatry." For some, madness was considered "as socially constructed" (Foot, 2015a, p. 2). Others went so far as to assert that mental illness did not even exist (Szasz, Goffman, Foucault); or it was a reaction of "unbearable stresses in life" (Basaglia, Laing; Foot 2015a, p. 3[1]). For the SPK, it was the normal reaction to a capitalist system, arguing that the wrongly called "normal" were actually the ill ones for not reacting to this system.

They also diverged regarding their adhesion to psychoanalysis and its influence on their work. In spite of a frontal rejection of some of the "anti-psychiatrists" (SPK, Foucault, deinstitutionalization movement in Trieste, Italy), its influence is undeniable, considering a firm rejection nevertheless an influence (Mannoni, 1973). Others were psychoanalysts themselves (Tosquelles, Oury, Guattari, Maud Mannoni, da Silveira, Masotta), with Lacan being the most prominent reference.

Psychoanalysis and psychoanalysts consider themselves until today as crucial in opposing traditional psychiatry (Baldiz, 2017). This belief has value in the sense that they favor the listening to patients above any other psychiatric procedure, allowing for spaces for the unfolding of subjectivity.

Yet, and in opposition to more anti-hierarchical representatives of anti-psychiatries, most psychoanalysts "have not always rejected the persona of the 'doctor', which to some extent emphasizes their difference from the patient, nor have they overcome their fascination with the image of the 'Master'" (Mannoni, 1973, p. 492). This is most evident in the concept of SSS (the subject supposed to know in its initials in French, *sujet supposé savoir*, and Spanish, *sujeto supuesto saber*) as developed by Lacan (1977). In general terms, "in any kind of therapy, even the most liberal, there is an educational dimension, the imposition of conformity of right thinking, right talking, right acting, and right living together" (Hochmann, 2015, p. 22).

Psychoanalysts have usually considered themselves as highly liberal and radical in their practice (Baldiz, 2017). Yet, with many non-psychoanalytical anti-psychiatrists, they have been shown their limits. In 1967, psychoanalyst Winnicott sent Laing and Cooper in his place to a psychoanalytic conference in Paris because he himself could not attend. The latter two "were only tolerated because of the authority of Lacan, who took the opportunity to remind the congress of the problems of the relationship between human liberty and human madness. These problems are obviously central to…question[s] of psychiatry and anti-psychiatry" (Mannoni, 1973, p. 495).

Without a doubt, Freud himself had a problem with psychosis and supposed psychotics. He did not consider them apt for his method (Mannoni, 1973). Psychoanalysts immediately following him, such as Karl Abraham (1953) and Melanie Klein (1961, 1932), adapted the psychoanalytic field to include psychoses with new thoughts and methods (see also Nasio, 2000).

At least in its beginnings, psychiatry borrowed from psychoanalysis, but in a way that degraded it "into just another routine practice." At the same time, psychoanalysis "for its part…suffered from certain compromises with medical psychiatry" (Mannoni, 1973, p. 491, 492). Yet, a psychoanalytic psychiatrist would usually have training and knowledge that allow them to engage in a practice "much subtler than symptomatological descriptions." In alignment with anti-pyschiatries, they have been able to understand "that psychotic states could be benign and very widespread, and that psychosis should not in itself be considered so catastrophic as was often supposed" (Mannoni, 1973, p. 493). Most notably, Winnicott (1958) stressed that psychoses should not always be combatted. In psychoses, situations might be unfrozen "'by the various healing phenomena of ordinary life, namely friendships, nursing during physical illness, poetry'; and he remarked that psychosis cured itself spontaneously in this way, whereas psychoneuroses (neuroses), do not have this advantage" (Mannoni, 1973, p. 493). The latter are often much more persistent and far off a state of wellness. In the estimation of poetry in relation to psychosis, Winnicott coincided with Tosquelles (2003). Interestingly, the artist Lygia Clark similarly regarded the persistence of neurosis and even considered it an obstacle to a state of openness for the "vibratile body" and its possibility of creative energy as expressed in her work *Structuring of a Self* (Marxen, 2011, 2009; Borja-Villel & Enguita, 1998).

In short, "[w]hen anti-psychiatrists like Laing condemn psychoanalysis they condemn it as the psychoanalyst Winnicott did: because it is useless or injurious in the case of psychoses" (Mannoni, 1973, p. 493).

Turning to consider the relationship of the arts to anti-psychiatries, the Surrealists leaned both on Freud's theories and anticipated some kind of anti-psychiatry by evaluating mental alterations as moments of geniality and sources of creativity. They considered them heroic fights against social norms and the triumph of the unconsciousness overcoming the rules of rationality and logic imposed by society. At the same time, they were reluctant of psychiatric treatment because they were prone to destroy and numb people's creativity and talents (Rosenberg, 2004; Mannoni, 1973). This coincided with a period of a significant idealization of madness and of the supposed "psychotic art" as a social construction (Marxen, 2011; Foster, 2000; Klein, 1997; Maclagan, 1997; Rhodes, 1994).

The following parts give a short overview about interesting representatives of the so-called "anti-psychiatries" movements. Without pretending to be exhaustive in neither the quantity of anti-psychiatrists nor the full amount of their thoughts, summaries are given of what is considered essential in their work and surroundings. Additionally, links are drawn to their relevance for art and artistic practices.

The intention here is for the reader to embark with the present vignettes of different forms of opposition to psychiatry onto an effort to sketch their own ideas and thoughts. Just the way Argentinian Oscar Masotta knew how to knot psychoanalysis, social structures of unconsciousness, art, and critique together, the reader can hopefully start their own endeavor on the crossroads of anti-psychiatries, deinstitutionalization, and institutional therapy, as well as deinstitutionalizing art and art practices. Visually Dora García's *Genealogies* can help us to imagine this journey (Figure 6.1).

Usually, anti-psychiatry or anti-psychiatries are attributed to white European or North American men (Proctor, 2018). Of course, this forms part of the epistemological imperialism already outlined in Chapter 4. Certainly, countries of other continents should feature in this history, too. In relation to my professional experience, I have tried to give justice to the extremely sophisticated mental health panorama in Latin America, where the "radical" or "anti" forms of psychiatry and psychology are common. There,

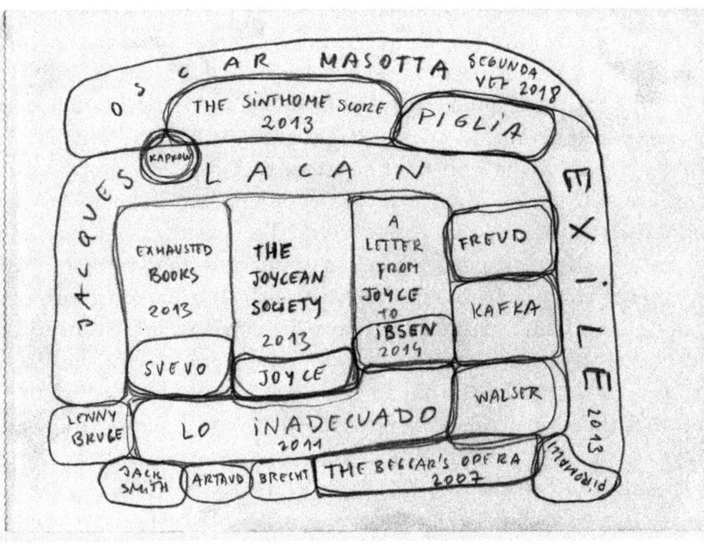

Figure 6.1 Dora García, Genealogías, works 1999–2018. Pencil on paper.

psychoanalytic communities have always engaged in leftist movements and leftists have always been interested in psychoanalysis, as opposed to Europe, aside from France (Proctor, 2018). With this in mind, the Argentinian artist-psychoanalyst Oscar Masotta and the Brazilian psychiatrist-psychoanalyst Nise da Silveira are described in their own subchapters. Moreover, special mention is given to the deinstitutionalization politics in Brazil. Staying with the same country, Suely Rolnik's practice is mentioned in the context of Institutional therapy and her collaborations with Félix Guattari. Her thoughts about subjectivity have already been presented in Chapter 4.

The focus on the decolonization by Caribbean Frantz Fanon is described within Institutional therapy, too. A summary that is certainly too short of the *Radical Therapist* journal and its contributions by and about the Black Panther Party is included in the subchapter of anti-psychiatries in the US.

Regarding gender, the over-presence of men probably reflects the disproportionate percentage of male psychiatrists and professors over female (until today) as well as the hierarchies within the mental health field which favor psychiatrists over other professions such as psychologists, therapists, nurses, social workers, all of which are more prolifically represented by women.

Although many anti-psychiatrists wished or pretended to abolish this very hierarchy, the physicians very often remained in power as decision makers. In this context and in her generation, Nise da Silveira had to face a totally male dominated psychiatry world. She and psychoanalyst Maud Mannoni (as well as psychoanalyst Suely Rolnik and nurse/social worker Carmen Roll) are exceptions in this chapter.

Although research has been undertaken about gender and queer studies in relation to anti-psychiatries, the sixties movements, politics, and their aftermaths (for an excellent overview see Proctor, 2018), studies about anti-psychiatries beyond Europe and North America are still needed. More transmission of Latin American experiences as well as others carried out in former Yugoslavia, Japan, and China—most notably the so-called Shanghai psychiatrists group—deserve special attention (Proctor, 2018; Mannoni, 1973).

Having arrived at the end of this introduction, a few words about terminology are considered important. As Foucault said (later in this chapter, in Hochmann, 2015, pp. 151–152): "Over the centuries, various moralist, taming, and 'purifying' operations were applied to 'mad people,' 'patients,' 'clients,' independently from the label the affected person had received." In this sense, we focus in the first place on labeling itself and its oppressive consequences. I have decided to leave the terminology the quoted authors have used themselves, such as "patient" as opposed to "client." I also disagree that the shift from patient to client would have been progressive. The term client gives evidence of a total commodification of the mental business, something all the quoted authors have assiduously rejected during their entire life. "Patient" might seem submissive but when deriving it from "patience," it might give justice to the need of time and process in the search of well-being.

"Madness" has been used all over the frequented texts and has been left in its context without opting for purifying or converting it into "mental illness."

In many texts, due to their historic context, generic references are exclusively male. This gender sidedness has been corrected.

Deinstitutionalization: Franco Basaglia and Brazil

In Italy, "anti-psychiatry" took the form of deinstitutionalizing practices. It was mainly initiated by psychiatrist Franco Basaglia. We start with this approach since deinstitution forms part of the title of the present book and is one of its main contents.

Franco Basgalia (1924–1980) was born to a wealthy Venetian family. During WWII, he joined the resistance and was imprisoned by the fascists. The end of the war in 1945 meant his release. Before jail, Basgalia had started medical school where he was as an excellent student and eventually graduated in 1949. Afterward, he studied philosophy and psychiatry. He was not of the psychoanalytic orientation but followed phenomenological and Sartrian thoughts as well as the work of Goffman and Foucault later on. His career was more dedicated to ideas and thoughts than to clinical practice. As such, a brilliant academic career seemed assured for him. Yet, probably because of his unruliness, he was excluded from academia and sent to Gorizia at the very border to former Yugoslavia, now Slovenia, to work as an asylum director. Geographically and professionally, this post was meant to be a dead end of his career (Foot, 2015b, 2014). But the opposite happened: From this position, he started to revolutionize psychiatry. In Gorizia, he forbade conventional psychiatric treatments like physical contention, opened the doors and brought staff, doctors, nurses, and patients together in assemblies and meetings in order to humanize and de-hierarchize interpersonal relationships. He did not deny the existence of mental illness but rather fought to free patients from the asylum's oppression, working to restore their freedom and dignity. Simultaneously, he unmasked "psychiatric science" as an ideology aimed at legitimizing exclusion. He published *The Negated Institution* (1968/2013, until today untranslated into English)[2] and engaged in a radical contestation of psychiatric hospitals, mainly from the Northeastern Italian city Trieste (Hochmann, 2015). He started to succeed in closing hospitals, in Trieste and beyond, until the "Basaglia Law" (1978) closed them in the entire country. "Closing hospitals" was meant in a literal and legal but also symbolical sense. Yet, in no way it meant simply releasing people and letting them find their own destiny without any care or support. The deinstitutionalizing movement would substitute hospitals by opening community centers for mental health and wellness. For Basaglia, mental illness was produced by society and for that reason must also be treated *in* and *by* society, as opposed to interning patients in closed wards usually located in the peripheries of cities or beyond (Passos, 2011). For him, the violence of the institution and its social control over poor or lower class people who had less means to defend themselves against oppression was the main focus of his struggle.

While he succeeded in abolishing barriers among professionals and between professionals and clients, he very soon noticed other barriers outside the hospital: Society did not accept the released patients. As a result, the deinstitutionalization movement soon concentrated on stigma and intolerance against mental illness and people affected by it.

> Basaglian thought and practice exposed the brutal workings of the state machine, the repression of deviancy (especially the deviant poor), and extended this analysis to an entire group of institutions, beginning with psychiatric hospitals and expanding to the rest of society.
>
> (Foot, 2015a, p. 6)

The movement immediately found echoes in other '68 advancements. For Basaglia, it was clear that deinstitutionalizing psychiatrists or mental health workers had to spread and create bonds with other groups of society. For Basaglia, the deinstitutionalizers were like organic intellectuals in Gramsci's sense, working for the social, cultural, and political transformation of society (see Chapter 3).

In this sense, first Gorizia and then Trieste were "stepping-stones for the long march through and at the same time against institutions, which would soon take in a whole series of other organizations, from universities and schools to the judiciary and the medical world in general" (Foot, 2015a, p. 6). In this vein, the deinstitutionalizers opened up asylums and facilitated a double flow: Releasing and integrating former patients into the city and opening up the former segregated and fenced asylums for the outside world. They became spaces of discussions, assemblies, art activities, protests, activism. They encouraged people to come in, volunteer, cooperate, share, listen, and participate. Thus, asylums became open forums with special invitation to students' movements. "As the asylums opened up towards the cities ..., these links formed a dual purpose, breaking down stigmas towards the mentally ill and creating connections between social change, urban change and psychiatric reform" (Foot, 2015a, p. 6). The sculpture horse Marco Cavallo became the symbol of both the liberation and double flow between the city and the hospital. Created in 1973 by artists, staff, and patients of the San Giovanni hospital (by then directed by Basaglia), the tall blue horse was displayed for public via parade, joined by about 400 patients. It had received its name honoring a horse that used to transport laundry and garbage between the asylum and the city.

> Some patients had a close relationship to this animal and noted that Marco was one of the few 'residents' allowed to leave the asylum... The horse thus symbolised 'a process of liberation for all those suffering under the living conditions at the asylum'.
>
> (Schwarz, 2015, https://biapsy.de/index.php/en/9-biographien-a-z/151-cavallo-marco-e, quoting Scabia 1976/1979, p. 5)

Obviously, it is also to be associated with the Trojan Horse in Homer's Iliad, wherein Greek soldiers were smuggled in the horse's stomach into the city of Troy.

The exchange between artists and the Trieste movement has been vivid since its very beginning. Dario Fo, Guiliano Scabia, and others offered their theater work. Ornette Coleman similarly contributed his music. Basagalia and his follower Rotelli used the fascination of some artists with the insane to bring them into the hospital and develop their activities. These efforts formed part of the above described double flow. That did not mean that the psychiatrists would share the same passions, thoughts, or ideas of the artists. Their relationship to art and the artists with whom they worked was never romantic. For the Trieste psychiatrists, the arts were a tool within their ongoing struggle for transformation (Roll, 2011).

A vestige of this relationship is the still existing Accademia della Follia [Academy of Madness] of Claudio Misculin, a self-organized theater group for people with experience in psychiatry.[3] Yet, within the deinstitutionalization movement, there is a lot of skepticism or even rejection against the creative art therapies:

> All of these kinds of music therapies, art therapies, design therapies, riding therapies … because when you're mad, you no longer have the right to enjoy things. And everything that normal people enjoy becomes therapy. And, I am really against this. I cannot deal with these questions; I immediately become suspicious of them. Because I think that enjoying music, dancing, singing … is a right, you know? But for people who have been labelled as being mad, all these activities become therapies. And I think the special thing about Trieste is that … [w]e can go singing and sailing and on holidays and to the theatre, and do a painting workshop … but we must not make therapies out of these things.
>
> (Roll, 2011, p. 6)

In short, the creative arts therapies are seen as depriving certain people the opportunity to participate in art activities without said activity being labeled as "therapy." This label refies the role of the patient rather than empowering them.

The Spanish artist Dora García has intensively researched the deinstitutionalization and anti-psychiatries movements. In this context, the video "The Deviant Majority" (2010) is the first of her *Mad Marginal* series (initiated 2009) and is inspired by Franco and Franca Basaglia's eponymous book (1971/2014). García adds "from Basaglia to Brazil" because Basaglia's work was the base for psychiatric reform in this country where at that time the deinstitutionalization movements coincided with protests against the military dictatorship fought by psychiatrists, psychoanalysts, artists, and other activists (Passos, 2011; see also Fusar-Poli, Bruno, Machado-de Sousa, & Crippa, 2009).

García (2010) draws from anti-psychiatry and deinstitutionalization practices as a prism for examining marginality as a potential creative position. She also deepens into "the concepts of the mainstream and counterculture, anti-institutional movements, and the notion of outsider art" (p. 11). Regarding the latter, she reflects that "[a] term such as 'outsider art' deserves some reflection. Outside of what? Obviously the term 'outsider' implies exclusion, exclusion from something" (p. 18).

"The Deviant Majority" video was shown at the São Paulo Bienal in 2010. Then, it formed part of the Spanish Pavilion titled *The Inadequate* at the 2011 Venice Biennale. The pavilion included another, eponymous, video about James Joyce, psychoanalysis, Trieste, and language[4] as well as ongoing performances, debates, monologues, silence, theater, and archive material of creative processes undertaken in total institutions (asylums, jails, etc.) by people's own motivation, without the framework of creative arts therapies or similar activities. The artist offered spectators movements through different continents and art projects, such as the theater group Accademia della Follia in Trieste, the Theater of the Oppressed in Brazil, and the Italian imprisonment publishing cooperative Sensibili alle foglie [Sensitive to pages; a play on words because a similar pronunciation with different spelling is follie: madness]. Simultaneously, Dora García invited the visitors for an open route around references to Basaglia, the SPK, Deligny, Goffman, Joyce, Artaud, and others. The inadequation represented different positions: independent, underground, dissident, unofficial, marginal, and exiled. *The Inadequate* focused on the notion of marginality and its relation to art. It embraced sub-concepts such as "deviation, outsider, exclusion, radicality, censorship, language, Basaglian [practice] and notes on the margin" (García, 2018, p. 99). On purpose, the visitor was deprived of the clarifying limits of the interpretative armor of an exhibition and "had to assimilate by themselves this strange assembly of bodies and voices" (Beard, 2018, p. 87; see Figure 5.2 in Chapter 5).

Later, the series *Mad Marginal* was followed by more works about psychoanalysis, therapy, psychiatry, and potential resistance, such as *The Hearing Voices Café* (2014; http://thehearingvoicescafe.doragarcia.org/), *Jacques Lacan Wallpaper* (2013), The *Sinthome Score* (2013 and 2014–2016), and more.[5] More books, journals, and videos have come out of the long lasting research; Roll's and Passos' quotations are some extract of it (in García, 2011a; https://vimeo.com/20869108).

Dora García participated with this artwork, related research, and her thoughts in the final seminar about the psychoanalytical and art therapeutic practices at MACBA (see Chapter 2). In the seminar's discussion, we drew links between Dora García's work and the importance of a critical vision of psychiatry, psychology, and therapy. Even though not always explicitly referenced, the ideas and concepts of the representatives of the Sociology of Deviance and Labeling Approach, like Becker and Goffman, are present in her work, as are the thoughts of Foucault.

The art therapy program under the auspices of MACBA shared similarities with the principals of deinstitutionalization. With the help of the museum, a service was established beyond psychiatry and medication very much appreciated by its participants, as outlined in Chapter 2.

Basaglia himself had also worked on an international organization to bring the different anti-psychiatries and anti-psychiatrists together, the Psichiatria Democratica. Yet, this organization was paralyzed because of too many conflicts among different representatives (Foot, 2015a).

Nevertheless, the deinstitutionalization movement has spread beyond Trieste. Nowadays and "[a]ccording to the World Health Organization (WHO), the 'Trieste model' of public psychiatry is one of the most progressive in the world" (Portacolone, Segal, Mezzina, Scheper Hughes, & Okin, 2015, p. 1).

As already mentioned, it has been and still is crucial in Brazil. Basglia's followers have been in close contact with mental health organizations of different countries such as Australia and New Zealand. The anthropologist Scheper Hughes and other public health officials of San Francisco and the Bay Area carried out encounters with the directives of Trieste in order to examine a possible implementation of the Trieste model (Portacolone et al., 2015). Due to structural differences of the two areas (a very thoroughly developed plan regarding public health coverage, affordable housing, and living costs in Italy fosters social integration, as opposed to San Francisco and the US), a literal translation of the model seems impossible. Yet, the challenge consists in grasping essential aspects of the Trieste model for its transnational implantation, adapting it to local facilities. In co-authorship, Californian academics and Mezzina, current director in Trieste, describe the details of the model. Among other aspects,

> [p]ersons in crisis or with acute psychiatric conditions sleep in their facilities rather than in the hospital (Mezzina, 2014). As soon as their condition improves, they receive day care at home or in a community center. Started with the aim of reducing psychiatric hospital admissions and promoting rehabilitation and social integration, the community centers constitute the core of mental health services (Mezzina and Vidoni, 1995). The community mental health centers epitomize the philosophy of the Basaglian deinstitutionalization through their design, locations, and services.
>
> (Portacolone et al., 2015, p. 4)

Yet, the deinstitutionalization movement is not safe of neoliberal and reactionary attacks either, whether in Italy or Brazil (Rotelli, 2011). Furthermore, neoliberal and social injustice agendas have weaponized deinstitutionalization in order to cut budgets, closing hospitals without any serious alternatives. Once again, the co-option capacity of hegemony as described by Gramsci (Chapter 3) is at work.

Moreover, it is highly important to consider the methods of already deinstitutionalized centers. It is not enough "just" to close hospitals and convert them into day centers if the same infantilization continues in open wards. A closer look is necessary if these spaces allow the clients' subjectivity to unfold or if they paternalize/maternalize participants and re-label them (see Chapters 2 and 4).

In the words of Brazilian deinstitutionalizing psychologist Eduardo Passos (2011):

> The de-institutionalization process must be continuous. It can never stop. The first step is to de-hospitalize, but this is certainly not the end of it. You need to undertake alternative action, as an alternative to kidnapping [the mentally unstable from society/their entourage]. Psychiatric reform is first and foremost de-localization. It creates a utopia, a nonplace. You have to destroy the place. Certainly, the mentally unstable will receive treatment, but this treatment will not imply displacement to a place of treatment. Treatment will be undertaken on the subject's own territory, which is a territory and not a place: this is de-localization.
>
> (p. 50)

Basaglia had an important influence on the psychiatric reform in Brazil. As already mentioned, protests against asylum psychiatry coincided with the battles for democracy and against the military dictatorship (1964–1985). Mental health workers fought together with artists and activists for the freedom of patients and the freedom of the country. Basaglia's work and book were an important source:

> So, because of this situation, psychiatric reform in Brazil, which was just a subgroup of the bigger health reform, acquired great symbolic value in Brazil and became identified with the fight for democracy. And so much so that, when the time came to draw up the constitutional text of the new republic, those agents who had taken part in Brazil's health reform were called upon to participate. …
>
> And so in the Constitution of '88, of the new republic, there was a very progressive legal enunciate regarding health care: 'health care is a right for every citizen and a duty of the State'. Before that, health care had not been a right; it had been something you paid for. Since the new '88 Constitution, health has ceased to have exchange value, now it only has a use value. And this is guaranteed by the Constitution. And when I say 'every citizen', I mean everyone who is at this moment on Brazilian territory, including you, even if you are a foreigner. And this phrase, 'a right for every citizen, a duty for the State', was expressed in three principles: universality in access to health care; equality in this same access; and integrality-that is, health must be directly related to quality of life.

> … So the psychiatric reform in Brazil, following the path of Basaglia, understood that it was only possible to progress if two important forms of authoritarianism were eliminated: the psychiatric hospital and medical centralism, the power of psychiatric knowledge.
>
> (Passos, 2011, pp. 48–49)

Until today, the Brazilian Association of Mental Health (Abrasme) follows these principles. Their focus is on community treatment and they combat medicalization in psychiatry. In their conferences, professionals and clients merge, relying on the mutual exchange of knowledge and experience.

Nise da Silveira

Earlier and simultaneously, Nise da Silveira (1905–1999), a Brazilian psychiatrist and psychoanalyst, opposed the male-dominated traditional psychiatry world. Imprisoned for Marxist activities during the New State military dictatorship, she was released in 1936 and only readmitted to hospital work in 1944 (Magaldi, 2018). She rejected firmly from the very beginning of her career aggressive treatments like "confinement, electroshock, insulin therapy, lobotomy" believing these methods were just destined to suppress symptoms.[6] Instead, da Silveira was interested in the subjective experience of psychosis. For her, "true therapy consists of … supplying the individual with an atmosphere of emotional support" (da Silveira, 1992, p. 13).

She also intended to avoid the terms "schizophrenia" or "disease" and used "the notion of the state of being," thus opposing psychiatric diagnosis (Magaldi, 2018, p. 9).

Her life was entirely dedicated to the humanization of psychiatry and the respect for patients. In this vein, she very early introduced "expressive activities" and developed her method named "The Images of the Unconsciousness" because for her, "the use of images became the main key to accessing what she called the patients' inner world" (Magaldi, 2018, p. 7). Moreover, she founded the Service of Occupational Therapy, the Museum of the Images of the Unconsciousness, and the Casa de las Palmeras [Palm House] (da Silveira, 2004).

Notoriously unmentioned in the US-dominated (and to some extent UK) history of art therapy, she elaborated very similar methods as those of her North American counter parts, such as Edith Kramer and Margaret Naumburg. Already around 1940, in Rio de Janeiro, she observed that patients would search on their own motivation any accessible material (like toilet paper) to draw and express their images. Similarities to her European psychiatrist counterpart Hans Prinzhorn are obvious (Prinzhorn, 1972). Yet, he focused on the collection and publication of patients' artworks without much interest for their subjectivities or their consent (see Dora García's video *Extermination*, 2008). As opposed to Prinzhorn, da Silveira never searched her patients' art for pathological aspects or psychopathology itself (Mello, 2004).[7]

She founded the workshop of occupational therapy based on the Images of the Unconsciousness in order to facilitate a space where the participants could represent their unconscious images, to give shape to their interior world and phantasms.

She understood art not as a medium but possessing its own value, considering the image itself as crucial (da Silveira, 2004). In the workshop itself, the respect for patients, by then totally deprived of their subjectivity and dignity by the institution, was crucial. They were given freedom in their art without the facilitator inducing or imposing their opinion. Within Anglo-Saxon art therapy, her approach is closer to Kramer's Art as Therapy (1998, 1993, 1958) than to Naumburg's Art Psychotherapy (1980), since for the Brazilian psychiatrist, the images themselves were therapeutic as a "primary route of expression" and not mere starting point for verbal association or translation (Magaldi, 2018, p. 8). Her way of art therapy was certainly non-directive. The activity took place in an open studio method, with a trained mental health worker-artist and other participants. She said: "[R]eality depends, in the first place, on the relationships of trust with others" (da Silveira, 2004, p. 14). Thus, she related art with subjectivity and understood the latter as always in relationship with others.

Additionally, da Silveira had an affinity with Jungian psychoanalysis, linking the symbols of the images to archeology, archetypes, mythology, art history, and religions (da Silveira, 2004).

She herself clearly rejected occupational therapy understood as making copies of images or objects under the direction of a "technician," as this procedure curtails any spontaneous creativity. Although she definitely opposed this kind of method in favor of a subjective implication into the creative process, she still called her workshop Occupational Therapy Service (da Silveira, 2004). This naming has not been the most fortunate because of ongoing misconceptions it might cause.

Da Silveira enjoyed an immense support by art critic Mário Pedrosa. He encouraged her work and curated exhibitions of her artist-patients (Cabañas, 2018; Mello, 2004). As a very prominent art critic, he did a lot to affirm the aesthetic value of the patients' works. He also wanted said work to be in the official art museum. Nevertheless, he supported Nise in the foundation of institutions dedicated to the art of the mentally unstable.

In Chapter 3, Pedrosa's work in the Allende Museum has been mentioned. He was exiled from Brazil after the military coup to Chile, from where he had to flee again after 1973. In that chapter, his work has also been related to the organic intellectual in the sense of Gramsci, a role Basaglia wanted the radical psychiatrists to fulfil (see above).

Da Silveira herself was surprised that her work was so much more appreciated in the art world as compared to psychiatry. Her work and life could finally spread on a more international level thanks to the film *Nise: The Heart of Madness* (2015, by Roberto Berliner).

SPK—Socialist Patients' Collective

The anti-psychiatry movement has probably taken its most radical form in Germany, specifically by the Socialist Patients' Collective (SPK), closely linked to the University of Heidelberg and its founding professor Huber. "[R]ather than contending with the hospital, social or family structures (as occurs in other countries), they found themselves opposing the political authorities and adopting a revolutionary standpoint" (Mannoni, 1973, p. 501).

For the SPK, mental illness was the healthy reaction to a capitalist society. They believe that by abolishing capitalism, mental illness would also disappear.

There was no intention to substitute psychiatry with other, similar institutions. For them, medical institutions and physicians were mercenaries, executors, and guardians of capitalism exercising social control (SPK, 1972/2013; Sartre, 1972/2013, p. viii). In this vein, they performed a radicalization of the orthodox Marxist academics of medical anthropology as described in Chapter 3. They considered disease as a direct result of capitalist production relations. Jean Paul Sartre wrote the foreword to the SPK book *Turn Illness into a Weapon* (1972):[8]

> Illness—you point out—is the only possible form of life in capitalism. … Cure—this is self-evident—can't be understood in our system to mean the elimination of illness: it serves exclusively as the maintenance of the ability to go to work where one stays sick. … those recognized as sick, who are rendered incapable of performing wage work, and whom one sends to the psychiatrist. This 'policeman' begins by placing them outside the purview of the law by denying them the most fundamental rights. He is clearly an accomplice of the atomizing powers: he approaches individual cases as if psycho-neurotic disturbances were the personal flaw and fate of an individual.
>
> (p. viii)

Sartre and the SPK (1972/2013; Roll, 2011) argued disturbances are exclusively conditioned by social forces. For both, disease has to be considered an efficient protest and weapon against capital, derailing its functioning. They wanted patients to take administrative control in public hospitals, make decisions regarding the content of medical trainings, and above all retain the right to make decisions about themselves and their treatments, and to question whether they required treatment at all.

Of course, SPK and Sartre (id.) were overtly against psychoanalysis. They considered it bourgeois and ruled by a power asymmetry that is manifest in the fact that the psychoanalyst turns their back against the patient lying on their couch. By contrast, the SPK aimed at equal rights between the alleged specialists and patients, actually considering the latter the actual specialists.

Most notably, the SPK unveiled the perverse collaboration of psychiatrists with the Nazis that culminated in the killing of psychiatric patients and the disabled, both of whom were considered as not worthy of life. This extermination became a "sinister rehearsal for the Holocaust" (García, 2010, p. 12; Dörner, 1969/1995).

They also put into evidence the perverse Nazi past of many contemporary and prominent psychiatrists, hospital directors, physicians, and university professors (Roll, 2011). "How could subjects formed under these social conditions avoid reproducing them?" (Proctor, 2018, p. 4). The fight against the silencing of these facts by the previous generations coincided with the '68 movement in Germany and Italy. The SPK equated the asylum with a concentration camp. Former SPK and now Trieste member Carmen Roll explains:

> As a member of the SPK, I was tried [trialed] and absolved. They accused me of setting the new forensic ward in the psychiatric hospital of Wiesloch[9] on fire. Someone indeed had gone there with the intention of burning it. Before they left, they wrote on the walls, 'From Auschwitz to Wiesloch, one way.'
>
> (2011, p. 15)

Later, Agamben (1998) would develop his notion of camp, starting with the Nazi concentration camps and applying it to contemporary situations and conditions. He defines camp as a space where people's pure biopolitical existence depends on the non/moral of the person in charge of them, being deprived of any right to defend themselves or to oppose the perversion and cruelty against them (see in this chapter also Goffman's concept of the Total Institution).

The SPK and Basaglia shared their focus on class analysis. For both, psychiatry was, in the first place, a means of controlling the lower class, depriving them of any rights. They also coincided in the social condition and etiology of mental disturbances, the SPK going beyond this consideration by converting illness into a weapon. Furthermore, they shared in the fight against fascism and its vestiges in postwar Italy and Germany (Roll, 2011).

Yet, the SPK was radically anti-institutional, as opposed to Basaglia's deinstitutionalization, with the former rejecting any collaboration with official authorities. According to Roll (2011), this led to an impossibility of change and transformation on a macro level. The SPK opted for the exodus strategy as opposed to Gramsci's war of positions (Chapter 3). This was also due to the fact that in Germany, by that time, institutions were not available for dialogue. Altogether, some SPK members went even further and joined the armed struggle of the seventies. Many of them were imprisoned, whether convicted of armed struggle or not (Roll, 2011). Some SPK members joined the Red Army Fraction (RAF, also known as Baader-Meinhof Group, named after two of their protagonists). They stood in total contrast of the "after career" of Laing, Cooper, and some of their peers, surrendering to a spiritual, "depoliticized 'growth movement'." In this context, Yvonne Rainer's film *Working Title: Journeys from Berlin/1971* includes the "reading of a letter by Ulrike Meinhof to the former SPK member Hanna Krabbe when both women were in prison" (Proctor, 2018, p. 9). The very recent documentary *SPK Komplex* (Kroske, 2018) reflects the overreaction of the state against the supposed revolutionary tendencies of the SPK with the result of silencing their real struggle against the oppression and violence in psychiatry and its perverse Nazi collaboration.

Institutional Therapy: François/Francesc Tosquelles, Jean Oury, Félix Guattari, Frantz Fanon...

In France, long before the boom of anti-psychiatries in the sixties and seventies, a way of doing psychiatry was developed that was denominated by "institutional therapy" (Daumézon & Koechlin, 1952).[10] Representatives of this approach accepted the psychiatric hospital as an institution but intended to humanize it, to make it less total, by decongesting and subverting it from within. An institution pretending to provide therapy "must first have a critique of itself as an institution" (Faramelli, 2017, p. 4). Theoretically, institutional therapy was dually sourced in Marxism and psychoanalysis. With the first, they opposed social alienation as well as working conditions and relations of production. The second helped to focus on psychopathological alienation and to reframe the institution for care. In this vein, they aimed at erasing the oppressive character of the asylum. They opened its doors and windows, in a literal and metaphorical sense. The goal was to de-hierarchize the relationships between patients and professionals, as well as among the different types, "classes," of professionals: psychiatrists, nurses, therapists, staff. Common meetings, assemblies, and organizations were created with the main objective to reassess everybody's subjectivity through mutual attention to each other. Additionally, daily life activities were reframed and considered as therapy. Patients were active in organizing them. By giving them a very active role, their agency was retrieved. In this sense, an institutional journal was published, day trips were organized, as were an ongoing cinema, arts and crafts, and discussion groups. Additionally, an annex institution in form of a club was created and co-directed by patients and professionals. In summary, the institution itself should have therapeutic effects, by offering an appeasing encounter with reality. Thus, the patients' delirium and anxiety decreased. By this relative democratization, the institution became a "huge couch" where psychoanalytic transference could happen in an extended way, not only towards the psychoanalyst in a private setting with its couch but towards the entire institution and its staff.[11]

After WWII, community therapy (*psychiatrie du secteur*) was publicly launched. It was a kind of institutional therapy expanded beyond the walls. Under the mission of social rehabilitation, clients were left in their usual environment and used open treatments centers assisted by mobile professionals.

Hospital stays were significantly reduced, although not abolished entirely like in Italy. The time and freedom clients have at their disposal was equally considered as therapeutic and so was their active participation in their treatment (Hochmann, 2015).

In this context of French institutional and community therapy, the word "institution" has acquired a different meaning: Differentiating it from establishment, institution was understood as a dispositif of thoughts, a "metabolization of daily life events" in a certain frame, determined in place and time. It should facilitate the symbolization of experience that allows the patient to detach from the concreteness of the real. The latter is meant in Lacanian terms, implying the impossibility of symbolization. It is not to be equated with reality but the enigmatic, the incomprehensible, the unimaginable that lies beyond any order or logic. It provokes a great deal of anxiety, especially when language is not available to enclose this void. Meaning is then absolutely vanished (Dorenbaum, 2018; Marxen, 2011; Evans, 1996, pp. 163–164; Lacan, 1974–1975, 1975–1976). The relational network of institutional or community therapy, however, institutes a collaboration, a "micro-team," dedicated to the patient's care. Through dialogues with different interlocutors, and in steady connection amongst themselves, the patient can find a model to coordinate the fragments of their psychological life, an organization of their thoughts in search of organization and symbolization (Hochmann, 2015).

Although *Francesc/François Tosquelles* (1912–1994) had not coined the term "institutional therapy" himself, he was certainly one of its intellectual and practical-clinical founders.

After going to medical school in Barcelona, Tosquelles became a psychiatrist in his Catalan hometown of Reus at the Pere Mata Institute. He benefited immensely from the Catalan political and cultural innovations during the time before the Spanish Civil War (1936–1939). In this sense, the Pere Mata Institute was built between 1897 and 1912 by Domènech i Muntaner, one of the key architects of Catalan Modernism. The building is one of the architectural icons of *Modernisme* even today. During the thirties, the hospital already counted on services of ergotherapy, hydrotherapy, theater, and dance activities in its efforts. The employees brought food to the patients formally dressed up as waiters (Tosquelles in Angosto, 1993).

Tosquelles' mentor, the psychiatrist Emili Mira i López, introduced Tosquelles into psychoanalysis and phenomenology. In order to deepen into psychoanalysis, Tosquelles started his own psychoanalysis with Sandor Eiminder, a Hungarian Jewish refugee in Barcelona that was considered little Vienna because of all the East Europeans who had settled there, fleeing from the Nazis in the early thirties (Robcis, 2016; Periáñez, 1997). In Vienna, Eiminder had formed part of the group around Aichhorn who had applied psychoanalysis to social education and who inspired the work with the adolescents at the MACBA described in Chapter 2. Eiminder focused on the challenges of psychoanalyzing in a foreign language. Thus, he discovered the importance of the tone of the client's discourse and their breaks rather than their words (Periáñez, 1997). Tosquelles would adapt that experience and extend it to the human body and how it moves in space.

Together with Mira, Tosquelles had always insisted on applying psychoanalysis beyond an exclusive individual setting. Although his practice was definitely rooted in psychoanalysis, he never considered himself a psychoanalyst (Tosquelles, 2014; Tosquelles in Angosto, 1993).

During the same time period, Tosquelles became politically active and joined the POUM, the Workers Party of Marxist Unification (Partido Obrero de Unificación Marxista). Based on Catalonia's anarchist heritage, the POUM rejected Stalinism, dogmatism, and the centralization of power, becoming thus the target of Soviet reprisals. The focus on decentralization together with Catalan "psychiatric nationalism," a structural decentralization of "psychiatric care through the implementation of district divisions known as *comarcas*" had a significant influence on Tosquelle's understanding of psychiatry (Comelles, 2010, p. 407; Robcis, 2016, p. 214; Tosquelles, 2014). He considered "decentralization, self-management, and solidarity within the confines of the psychiatric hospital, as mechanisms to prevent authoritarianism and reification" (Robcis, 2016, p. 214).

Although his work has always been based on both Marx and Freud, he used to be more than skeptical of Marxists and Freudians. He identified himself rather as a critical Marxist and critical Freudian. The same happened with his Lacanian influence and approach. He learned a lot from all three but above all he had learned to criticize them. Finally, he considered his patients his main teachers (Tosquelles, 2014; Angosto, 1993).

In 1936, Franco's fascist troupes initiated their coup d'état and started the Civil War. Emilio Mira became director of Psychiatric Services of the Republican Army fighting against the Franco fascists. He assigned Tosquelles to direct psychiatric services along the southern red line. Tosquelles excelled in this role with his capacity for improvisations and innovations, setting up psychiatric dispositifs in the most ferocious war situation. Together with Mira, he insisted on the necessity of treating civilians, combatants, and the doctors. Regarding the latter, he assisted bourgeois physicians and their broken illusion of a bourgeois and quiet life. For him, doing good (anti) psychiatry work excluded being a "good citizen" because psychiatry implies an "anti-culture" (Periáñez, 1997, p. 4; Tosquelles in the film *Francesc Tosquelles: Une politique de la folie* [Francesc Tosquelles: A politics of madness] by Pain, Polack, & Sivadon, 1989).

Tosquelles followed a practice of "geopsychiatry," going into homes, villages, and institutions in order to socialize with the locals. For this purpose, he recruited local volunteers who, among many others, included priests and prostitutes. This holistic approach, developed first during the atrocities of war, "remained consistent in all of Tosquelles' work, especially in relation to the hospital which, he argued, was an institution that also needed to be treated and cured" (Robcis, 2016, p. 216).

During the Civil War, the POUM was finally persecuted by both fascist and Stalinist communists. Ken Loach's film *Land and Freedom* (1995) and

George Orwell's book *Homage to Catalonia* (1938) about his own activism in POUM give justice to this civil war within the Civil War.

The fascists took over the country in 1939, and as a result, many of the Republican army, composed of socialists, communists, Trotskyists, and anarchists, were killed. Those who could fled abroad, mainly climbing over the Pyrenees to France. So did Tosquelles, escaping his secured death. In 1939, he was confined with so many other fellow citizens in one of the refugee camps in France (Sept-Fons). The conditions there were unbearable as the confined became sick dying of hunger, diseases, and despair. Even in this tragic situation, Tosquelles set up kinds of psychiatric dispositifs to resist the aforementioned conditions. There, he "recruited various political activists, artists, and musicians who were imprisoned within the camp to help him organize activities—concert, theater production, publications, but also group therapies—that would temper some of the psychological effects of the 'camp psychosis'" (Robcis, 2016, p. 217).

Because of his striking capacities in total war conditions, he was recruited to work in the psychiatric hospital Saint Alban in Southern France in 1940. He stayed in France where he became known as and published under the name François Tosquelles. However, he was initially denied medical licensure based on his Spanish degree. So, he had to step down and start off as a nurse.

Also in Saint Alban, his approach was hands on, literally tearing down asylum walls and in the first years, during German occupation in France, fighting for the survival of patients and helping the French resistance movement by hiding them from the Nazis inside the hospital. Similarly to their perverted killing of mentally ill and disabled people in Germany, the Nazis continued organized starvation of patients in their plundered territories (Robcis, 2016; von Bueltzingsloewen, 2007; Lafont, 1987).

As a result, during WWII, the small town of Saint Alban became a crossroads and refuge for many people escaping the Nazis from the East and Franco from the West.

His several tragic experiences with occupations (by the fascist Franco troupes in the Civil War, Stalinist persecution within communist parties, refugee camp, Nazis in Vichy France) "had convinced Tosquelles that occupation was not only a social and political reality but also a psychic structure. Thus, the search for a true freedom needed to go through a form of psychic 'disoccupation'" (Meyers, 2014, pp. 2–3). He developed disoccupation strategies in the civil war, in the refugee camp, and finally in the Saint Alban hospital.

Other communist and decolonialist psychiatrists or psychoanalysts were attracted by Saint Alban, including Lucien Bonnafé, Frantz Fanon, and Félix Guattari. So were intellectuals like Georges Canguilhem as well as surrealist artists and poets, for example, Paul Éluard and Tristan Tzara. The first expressed his impressions *in Souvenirs de la maison des fous* (1946/2012, Memories of the madhouse). They all "were seeking refuge from fascism. … Saint-Alban offered the possibility of reconciling Marx and Freud. It provided a model to rethink the relationship between psychoanalysis and politics, and more specifically between political and psychic disoccupation" (Meyers, 2014, p. 3). In this sense, Marx and Freud were complementary for social change, "the two sides of one same struggle towards what [Tosquelles] called a 'politics of madness'," against both social alienation and psychic disaffection (Robcis, 2016, p. 212; Tosquelles, 2014, 2001). From the very beginning, theory was always linked to practice, the way Gramsci described it for the organic intellectual (Chapter 3). In this vein, the politics of madness or institutional therapy can be thought of as:

> both an intellectual project and a very concrete practical endeavor that involved demolishing the walls and gates of the hospital, getting rid of uniforms and doctor blouses, setting up workshops, clubs, and other activities adapted to psychotic patients and designed to promote a different understanding of the social.
>
> (Meyers, 2014. p. 3)

For Tosquelles, psychotherapy should never mean focusing only on the individual but always their historical and concrete context. He was skeptical about the part of anti-psychiatry movements that considered mental illness as a myth or social construct. He did start from the position of accepting mental illness as a fact but insisted on its social aspects in etiology and care.

He considered psychiatry to be social work in the sense that any work is social because the human being is social. The task of psychiatry is to return the subject to society, as the process of interning somebody means excluding them from society. Yet, he would maintain the psychiatric hospital as an institution for those who need it, always considering it with its architecture, its activities, and its staff as a "healing collective" (Robcis, 2016, p. 218; Angosto, 1993). By expanding and reconceptualizing the Freudian concept of transference towards the institution, Tosquelles succeeded in developing a psychoanalytic method for psychosis, something Freud had considered impossible (Robcis, 2016). At the same time, Tosquelles would strictly reject the biologistic and neurologic approach to psychiatry and its reduction to pharmaceuticals. After all:

> Institutional psychotherapy was not a rigid and all-encompassing model but rather, an ethics, a way of thinking and living. Constantly evolving, adapting, and always revisable, institutional psychotherapy was a form of permanent revolution of politics, society, and psychic life, all at once.
>
> (Robcis, 2016, p. 220)

Tosquelles also believed in the critical importance of psychiatrist leaving the hospital in order to get to know the environment and social context. They have to go into the field and relate to people, to real life, in the streets, schools, popular fairs. The geopsychiatry initiated during the Civil War in the form of interactions of therapeutic groups with external communities and networks between multiple different spaces was a leitmotiv throughout his work and life.

In this sense, he always stressed the importance of *la penya*, which in Catalan has a meaning of discussion circles in cafes and bars. Opposing Stalin, who claimed "All the power to the soviets!", intending to impose Spanish on Catalan communists, Tosquelles answered "All the power to the penyes!" (Tosquelles in the film by Pain et al., 1989). "All the power to the taverns!" (Periáñez, 1997, p. 4).

La penya was a model for the hospital clubs for patients, staff, and neighbors, a pillar in institutional therapy. There, lively discussions took place and collectivity was practiced.

Regarding art and artistic practices, Tosquelles did actively employ theater activities, including psychodrama. He frequently mentioned "ergotherapy stations" such as pottery, book printing and binding, and wood workshop. He was following the model of earlier German psychiatrist Hermann Simon (1867–1947), in spite of Simon's Nazi affinity. He had changed patients' forced inactivity due to confinement into an "active therapy" in the form of workshops. At the same time, he fostered patients' freedom and independence by opening doors and an important change in the attitude of the carer-cared relationships. For Tosquelles, in ergotherapy, the produced objects do "not have a therapeutic value in itself, but it is invested with affective, economic, and social values that we must help the patient discover. This form of consciousness-raising or of discovery of the other is the goal of ergotherapy" (Tosquelles as quoted in Johnes, 2010, p. 43; in Robcis, 2016, p. 219).

Yet, Tosquelles (1972) also offered interesting reflection on using art with severely mentally disabled children. As typical for the institutional therapy, he considered the art space as an extension of the body towards the social and the painting as an exteriorization of the body. The setting must allow the free expression of conscious or unconscious desire of the participants. The presence of the group members as well as the facilitator allowed for a certain socialization of desire. He called the facilitator "educator." Their job was to deprive themselves from aesthetic judgments, from impatience expecting tangible and "good" results, from mistaken interpretation according to their own desires and fantasies. They must know to wait for the adequate moment to intervene, to propose, to help. Tosquelles knew already about the adults' difficulties in taming their eagerness.

Besides painting, he suggested the three-dimensional work with *papier mâché*. By making figures and persons as well as playing with them, children's hands become social and constructive as opposed to destructive or expulsive (see similar thoughts in art therapy in Chapter 2). Although Tosquelles did not use the words therapy or therapist in this context, this making and playing towards the social arena are reminiscent of puppet therapy, where art therapy (making) and drama therapy (playing) come together.[12] The discovery of the other and the social world has also been conceptualized in art therapy. Working with people diagnosed as psychotic a "phenomenological isolation" has been observed, in the sense that the affected person does not share the same signifiers with the social world around them. This is mainly due to the collapse of the symbolical order and leads to a feeling of isolation and abandonment (Wadeson, 1980). The artwork in an art therapy setting can help to re-bridge this gap. Particularly, some might like to write the name of the drawn or painted object in the same sheet as an attempt to rejoin the social world by re-organizing the signifiers (Marxen, 2014; Schaverien, 1997).

Rodríguez (2015 and her letter for Dora García's artwork *Exile*, 2013) had already related the MACBA devices (Lacanian psychoanalysis applied to the museum and psychoanalytic art therapy with an anthropological understanding) to Tosquelles' work, precisely considering said devices as its clinical extension. The legacy of Tosquelles should not be confined to the intra-hospitalarian context but be pushed to its margins. Referring to Pierre Délion, it is neither intra nor extra-hospitalarian but a practice of unlocking the alienated subjects, at the same time providing the possibility of a rearticulation with the cultural historical context.

For good reason, Rodríguez asks in her letter why the same few institutions that try to retrieve the Tosquelles' legacy in Catalonia do not take into consideration the practices that have extended this legacy in the form of the MACBA devices? As a possible conclusion the society of control is offered, with its mechanism to include or not a political knowledge.

Although his books, practice, and thoughts are well distributed and followed in France and French, in Catalonia and Spain it is almost impossible to get Tosquelles' books. They are out of stock and barely present in libraries, while his knowledge has been absolutely erased by hegemonic psychiatry, psychology, and psychotherapy.

The sociologist Maurizio Lazzarato together with the artist Angela Melitopoulos conceived the artwork *Déconnage* (2011) based on the previous film (1985) by filmmaker François Pain and psychoanalysts Jean-Claude Polack and Danielle Sivadon about Tosquelles. Lazzarato has already been mentioned in the context of his extensive research about and against cognitive capitalism as well as immaterial labor (Chapter 4). Melitopoulos is known, among others, for her video artwork about Toni Negri, *The Cell* (2008). *Déconnage* consists of a video tryptic where the psychoanalyst/psychiatrist Pollack and the philosopher/artist Elisabeth von Samsonow comment 26 years later on Tosquelles narration about subjects of his life, the wars, confinement, psychiatric dispositifs, and institutional therapy. It is a visual research about psychiatry and its margins as well as its political effects, in the past and present. Thus, it fosters new reflections for its future.

As already mentioned, many psychiatrists, psychoanalysts, artists, poets, and intellectuals visited Saint Alban, seeking refuge against the perversions of totalitarism and fascism. The psychiatrists Frantz Fanon and *Jean Oury* as well as Félix Guattari worked with Tosquelles and applied the experience to their own practice and further developed institutional therapy with their thoughts (see also Oury, Guattari, & Tosquelles, 1985).

After studying medicine, Oury (1924–2014) joined Saint Alban as an intern in 1947. These learning years had an immense impact on him. After his stay in Saint Alban, Oury started his own psychoanalysis with Lacan who would have an important influence on him too. Oury did become a psychoanalyst. Yet and similar to Tosquelles, Oury knew how to keep a critical stance regarding their supposed teachers (Angosto, 1993). Most notably, Oury remained critical "of a certain structuralist rigidity of Lacan's early texts" (Meyers, 2014, p. 4) that would too much foreclose and precondition the subject in their given diagnosis.

After a stay in a conventional psychiatry setting, he decidedly turned apart from it. As a consequence, he bought and founded the psychiatric clinic La Borde in Cour-Cheverny, France, in 1953. There, he carried on the institutional psychotherapy he had learned firsthand in Saint Alban. Inspired by Tosquelles, he further adapted psychoanalysis to psychosis in La Borde (Oury, 2001, 1986; Oury et al., 1985). In this vein, he focused on "dissociated transference," a key concept of institutional therapy: Some people in a severe psychosis state might find themselves fragmented, torn into pieces, and unable to operate therapeutic transference on a single professional. At the same time, the therapeutic relationship can seem threatening when it cannot be distinguished from a real one because of a lack in abstract and symbolical thinking. With dissociated transference, multiple channels of transference in form of multiple relationships within the institution, such as with psychiatrists, psychologists, psychoanalysts, therapists, nurses, and also staff members, maintenance employees, etc. can be experienced, according to patients' preferences and needs (Chiche, 2014). Transference is hence distributed on several people.

The splitting of transference has also been made useful in art therapy with psychotic participant. The artwork and artistic process diminishes intensity from the therapist-client relationship in favor of a heightened focus on the arts dynamics. The art and its related process thus work like a mediator (Schaverien, 1997).

Moreover, Oury developed the concept of "pathoplasty," which described "the way in which disorders were constructed in correlation with the environment." The sickness of the institution, manifest, for example, in rigid hierarchies and routines, produced and aggravated pathologies, both for patients as for the professionals and staff (Caló, 2019, p. 120; see also below the Total Institution by Goffman). The environment further included architecture and design, an aspect that overlaps with the deinstitutionalization of Trieste until today (Portacolone et al., 2015; Oury, 1967).

Oury was outspokenly critical against contemporary psychiatry and its singular focus on the individual and their brain. For him, it was a question of bringing the social, the biological, and the psychic together. Subjectivity was formed, dependent, and interconnected by all three fields. They were all integrated in institutional therapy that additionally included operational access to deal with the real as the void of symbolization (Oury, 2001).

In this sense, he did prescribe psychopharmaceutical drugs when he considered them necessary but only "as a complement to the institutional psychotherapy." For the psychological, every patient had an individual analytic treatment. At the same time, the social was of high importance. Oury devoted "so much effort to thinking through the structure of the hospital," with its different "forms of group therapy through the multiple meetings and workshops that occur during the day" (Robcis in Meyers, 2014, pp. 6–7). He very much focused on the autonomy of patients to combat their "lack of investment in and engagement with their own life" as well as social life (Caló, 2019, p. 121; Oury, 2001).

The clinic La Borde became a prominent place for intellectual and political activity during the sixties and seventies. La Borde attracted those who during and after the events of May '68 were still struggling with the disoccupation of minds. Most concretely, they were driven by the question of why workers and the subaltern would frequently act and vote against their own interests, something Gramsci and de Martino had analyzed by the common sense co-option of the hegemonic classes (Chapter 3). In France, for thinkers like Althusser, Foucault, Deleuze and Guattari, Derrida, and Irigaray, this sabotaging of the oppressed's own potential emancipation

> had to be explained not in social and economic terms but rather at the level of subjectivity. Subjects had been conditioned to think and act a certain way through a particular insidious process. Althusser called this ideology, Deleuze and Guattari Oedipalization, Foucault subjectivation, and Irigaray phallogocentrism.
>
> (Robcis in Meyers, 2014, p. 3)

Whereas Freud and Freudians had "resisted politics in many important ways, Marxism after Marx has also struggled to formulate a theory of subjectivity" (Robcis, 2016, p. 213). Yet, at La Borde, people met to bring Marx and Freud together.[13]

Two more reasons for the attraction of La Borde have been identified (Robcis in Meyers, 2014, p. 4). Its concept was based on a permanent effort (or illusion) of self-management opposing centralization, authoritarianism, conventionalism, and hegemonic discourses of health and the social. "This was a model of politics that many of these intellectuals were also very committed to" (Robcis, 2016, p. 213). La Borde as before Saint Alban was meant to rethink its social and political dimensions as "a way to rethink community at large," as an "attempt to turn psychiatry into a form of systematic critique, into a form of permanent revolution" (p. 213).

Additionally, many of the thinkers above struggled in some way with psychoanalysis and its Lacanian hegemony in France. As already mentioned, Oury criticized the rigid structuralism of the early Lacan. Deleuze & Guattari dedicated their efforts to contest psychoanalytic normativity, mainly the repressive traditional family constellation, in their *Anti-Oedipus* (1972/2009; Robcis in Meyers, 2014).

Félix Guattari (1930–1992), psychotherapist, philosopher, yet not a psychiatrist, was hired by Jean Oury to work at La Borde. There, he worked as an active developer of institutional therapy. His experience at La Borde served as the base for his prolific publishing activities, combining psychoanalysis, institutional psychotherapy, and philosophy. Many of his books were co-authored with Gilles Deleuze, most notably the *Anti-Oedipus* (1972/2009), and others with Toni Negri (2010, 1996). He has already been quoted in the context of subjectivity (Chapter 4), a subject he had developed assiduously throughout his life, especially in the context of institutional therapy.

He saw in the latter a way out of the totalitarian disciplining hospital/asylum on the one hand and the (neo) liberal, commodified psychoanalysis in private settings on the other. In this vein, the very opposition to neo/liberalism and world capitalism was another leitmotiv of his life and work.

Following Tosquelles and Oury as well as Foucault, he critiqued the disciplining role of asylums where patients' subjectivities were conditioned through "the lens of guilt and reason" and labeled as inferior "to both their keepers and to the general public." He called this a "subjected-group," disciplined and controlled by hegemonic forces (Faramelli, 2017, p. 5; Guattari, 2015).

Institutional psychotherapy and geopsychiatry "resist hegemonic psychiatric practices and the asylum's ordering of space. This focus on the reordering and opening up of space constitutes institutional psychotherapy's creative practice, the creation of therapeutic heterotopias" (Caló, 2011, p. 82). The hierarchical division between doctors, nurses, and patients has been flexibilized, although not fully abolished.

For Guattari, it was imperative to link the unconsciousness to the social. His therapeutic approach in the clinic consisted in "the assumption that its organizational principles were not independent from the therapeutic process" (Caló, 2011, p. 82).

Inside and beyond the clinic, Guattari realized that as opposed to Lacan, it was impossible to reduce the field of the unconsciousness to language or "to structure it on signifying horizons." Instead, it has "to be related to the whole social, economic and political field. The objects of desire are determined as a reality that is coextensive with the social field (and consequently with the field defined by political economy)" (Negri, 2017, p. 168).

In this context, Guattari (2015) conceptualized transversality as a dimension between verticality and horizontality. Relations flow through different levels and directions, towards an "extended ecology." New arrangements would create new subjectivities and avoid fixations (Caló, 2011, p. 83).

By his concept of transversality, Guattari opposed the traditional transference of psychoanalysis. For him,

> the idea of transference was too caught up in language and in the dual relationship between patient and psychoanalyst, making it necessary to conceptualise the hypothesis of an open relation to the multiplicity of spaces … beyond the sphere of language only.
>
> (Caló, 2011, p. 83)

Going beyond language and the dual relationality meant opening up to the world as crucial for the production of subjectivities. A "diversity of places of existences" was fostered through heterogeneity of people and spaces. Clients and employees were seen active agents in the daily organization of the institution and the collective, the latter understood "in the sense of a multiplicity" (Caló, 2019, p. 125). The collective is never a given, it has to be (re)constructed on a daily basis and by common effort. In the case of La Borde, it was the clinic as the third object facilitating this widening for "multi-investments" (Caló, 2019, p. 125, 2011; Negri, 2017; Guattari, 2015;). Yet, "[t]he institutional space should be understood not merely as a simple container of social relationships, but as an active element in the process of producing singular subjectivities" (Caló, 2011, pp. 84–85). In summary, Guattari elaborated a "polyphonic and transversal conception of subjectivity [that] breaks with the absolute position of the subject in the ordering of the world, as well as [their] function of constituent of the object" (Caló, 2011, pp. 84–85). Guattari's conception of treatment was multidimensional, including the social, the psychological, the biological, and the environmental (Caló, 2019).

The already mentioned Brazilian psychotherapist and art critic *Suely Rolnik* had worked intensively with Guattari both clinically at La Borde and as co-writers (Guattari & Rolnik, 2007).

She refers to Guattari's term "cartography" as:

> a mode of thought production which redraws the map of a new territory of existence, at the same time and inseparable from the process of creation of that territory, answering life's demand. Cartography is the name of that politics of desire's thinking action. ... this concept was that of acting micropolitically to undo the dominant mode of subjectivation that naturalises maps, i.e. the drawing out of prevailing existing territories, which are also naturalized.
>
> (Fernández Polanco & Pradel, 2015)

Rolnik started her own psychoanalysis with Guattari after a significant existentialist crisis, including a suicide attempt. Yet, he wanted to get her out of the dual analytical relationship, towards the collective. So, after some effort, he succeeded in engaging her for a long planned artistic dispositif, specifically the clinic's carnival party with sophisticated costumes. For this, she brought together the artist and clinic community, though some had already overlapped. Workshops were organized that involved

> everybody in the clinic, both the 'cared for', as they called the patients there, and the 'carers', as they called those who worked there: not just the psychiatrists, the psychoanalysts, the nurses, but all members of staff, such as the cooks, because it was the daily life of that community that which was deemed to have the therapeutic power...It was all a dispositive with which I tried to summon up an utterance for each person to express

> what was trying to break through in their body but had not yet found the form, or rather, they didn't have enough strength to do so.
> (Fernández Polanco & Pradel, 2015)

With this "soft," joyful reminiscence to her home country, from which she had exiled because of the atrocities of the military dictatorship, she could reconnect with what she later described as vibratile body, "an 'existential focal point,' an 'existential source' for my subjectivity which had become non-existent" (Fernández Polanco & Pradel, 2015; Rolnik, 1998; Chapter 4).

She concludes beautifully in her own words:

> Clinical practice should be an act of creative experimentation, and not a medical act from the perspective of the Western tradition. Guattari gave me the strength to create an existential source for my life, and the dispositive I created in that process, in turn, brought about the conditions for other existential focal points to the inhabitants of the clinic.

And she describes desire as something

> where life finds a possibility to exist again. That idea of creating an existential focal point is beautiful, and I think that this is exactly the aim of a clinical work, as practiced from this perspective. It consists of: listening to the storm behind the symptoms of each person, looking for specific forces which have been crushed by what produced their storm, and, once these forces have been identified, imagining along with him or her where their desire can be connected so as to create an existential source from where a process of existentialisation could be triggered. In that sense, we have to create specific conditions in tune with the specifics of each case, to make this possible.
> (Fernández Polanco & Pradel, 2015)

Another example of the process of existentialization through the arts has been realized through a wonderful Butoh performance by Tanaka Min in the park of La Borde. Min was invited by Félix Guattari and the film was made by Josephine Guattari and François Pain (1987; https://www.youtube.com/watch?v=VgErye7jXbI). Additionally, a lively discussion took place with the artist and all the public, composed of patients and workers of the clinic, about their impression on the performance (https://www.youtube.com/watch?v=VgErye7jXbI). It was animated by Félix Guattari and invited for free verbal association, reminiscent to the Lacanian psychoanalysis applied to the MACBA museum where also participants (diagnosed with psychosis) engaged in a free verbal association about art, the museum exhibitions, and related processes (Rodríguez, 2015).

A couple of decades later, Rolnik showed the first video performance in one of her seminars at the MACBA museum. That is how this existentialization experience circled through time and space.

The thoughts, practices, and writings developed in and around institutional therapy have revolutionized psychiatry without a doubt. Particularly, the various authors have contributed to the elaboration on the crossroads between Marxism and psychoanalysis, contributing thus to new possibilities of subjectivities. In my opinion, their special merit lies in the democratization and decommodification of psychoanalysis, as well as its widening beyond the private cabinet. Within their approach, however, the asylum system in itself remains (Foot, 2015a, p. 4). They thought to avoid totalitarianism in the psychiatric hospital. Yet, wherever there are two main groups living under the same roof, one with a significant loss of autonomy and having been labeled to one degree or another by the other group that, in one way or another, is in charge of objectifying the others' behavior according to certain explanatory theories, there, almost inevitably, the conditions of a total institution are recreated (Hochmann, 2015).

Additionally, critiques have been raised of gender and class issues. In this sense, there were splits between "glamorous Parisian intellectuals enamoured with Jacques Lacan and working class nurses … [that] accused the former group of romanticising psychosis and rejecting practical grassroots organizing" (Proctor, 2018, p. 5). As opposed to Rolnik's (above) and Robcis (2016) positive accounts on the success of combining the clinical, theoretical, and political, there are reports about Oury and Guattari avoiding "discussing a recent scandal that had seen a group of radical student nurses fired from their hospital" (Proctor, 2018, p. 5, referring to Sherry Turkle, 1992).

Also Carmen Roll (2011) had stated Guattari's contradictions:

> Guattari wrote books about ethics and aesthetics, but he did not have the praxis. … He was practising electroshock treatment in '77. … we followed him with a fake electroshock bed; we followed him all around Trieste. Written on the bed was, 'Guattari, come to have your electroshock chez nous'. Only Basaglia carried out the praxis.
>
> (p. 15)

Although *Frantz Fanon* (1925–1961) has always been more related to anti-colonial, black liberation (Gordon, 2015), and postcolonial theory (Bhabha, 1994), his work as a psychotherapist or "anti"-psychiatrist is highly important too and should be read together with his political writings (Faramelli, 2017).

Frantz Fanon had worked in Saint Alban under Tosquelles' supervision starting in 1952. According to Tosquelles (in Angosto, 1993), he was a crucial collaborator and force in the community. His concentration on peasantry as a motor for political change during his time in Algeria as well as his militarism for the National Liberation Front (FLN, the principal nationalist movement during the Algerian War and ruling political party of the Algerian state) stemmed probably from both his experience in his home island Martinique and his work at Saint Alban.

Fanon's critique of psychiatry also coincided a great deal with Foucault's. Yet, the first expanded it to colonialism and its domination of space, one of Fanon's main inquiries. In this sense, he focused on how subjects occupy or are made to occupy the space of a clinic.

His first experience with colonial psychiatry dated from his work in France, Lyon, with North African, mainly Algerian patients. By that time, he conceptualized the "'North African Syndrome', a psychosomatic disorder affecting the North African population in France fostered by the lived experience of racism in poor slums" (Faramelli, 2017, p. 3).

In 1953, he started to work as a psychiatrist in colonial Algeria at the Blida-Joinville Psychiatric Hospital. Similarly to Foucault, he observed psychiatry as a confinement system of social control to discipline the deviant who would threaten the public order. Whereas Foucault applied this to a minority, Fanon widened the system towards colonialism itself that targeted the entire colonized population, infantilizing and diagnosing them of a "primitive psyche" (Fanon, 2008). In this sense, the Blida-Joinville Hospital "with its racial and ethnic segregation, inequalities and indifference to the Muslim patients, represented a microcosm of Algerian society at the time" (Faramelli, 2017, p. 7). Fanon applied institutional therapy, first very successfully in the ward of European women. With cultural and craft activities he managed to convert "the space into a communal French society, fully inverting the sterile, cold, and isolating space of the hospital" (Faramelli, 2017, p. 8). Yet, he failed considerably in the same attempt within the Arabic male ward. Not speaking Arabic and thus not being able to fully engage with the local population, the endeavor of institutional therapy turned into a colonialist imposition and a space of cultural alienation. The latter became two-folded: Clients were infantilized as psychiatric patients and deprived of their cultural spaces. Fanon, like before Tosquelles, concluded that for any clinical work and planning, it is paramount to engage with the world around the clinic, its culture and traditions (Faramelli, 2017).

Then, Fanon converted the hospital into a refuge for the FLN combatants during the Algerian Independence War. Again, similar to Saint Alban in WWII, the Blida became a space of disoccupation and liberation, "a heterotopic space in its resistance to the confinement of colonialism" (Faramelli, 2017, p. 9). Simultaneously to his dedication to the resisting, he also had to treat the French during the Algeria war. His case studies of both are an important contribution to decolonialist psychiatry (Fanon, 1991).

Finally, in 1959, Fanon took his post at the Hospital Charles-Nicolle in Tunis, which he in turn transformed into Africa's first day clinic, undoing first the building itself.

After all and thanks to his focus on space, Fanon developed an anti-colonial manner of psychotherapy, resisting "French colonialism's enclosure of space" and opening up "heterotopic sites of creativity and liberation" in the broader society (Faramelli, 2017, p. 2). His approach has been called a "geo-social therapy, a therapeutic practice that encompasses social, cultural and physical spaces..., as institutional psychotherapy's de-colonisation and its liberation from confined clinics and hospitals" (Faramelli, 2017, p. 10).

Maud Mannoni

Belgian born psychoanalyst Maud Mannoni (1923–1998) lived most of her life in France where she worked with a special emphasis on children and psychosis (1987). She was a trained Lacanian psychoanalyst. Especially the work of Lacanian Françoise Dolto had influenced her significantly, particularly Dolto's work with psychotic children. But Mannoni also drew many conclusions from Winnicott's work, mainly from his subject of holding (see its explanation in Chapter 2). Additionally, she learnt from Argentinean psychoanalysis, precisely from Enrique Pichon-Rivière and José Bleger.

Another important influence on her was British anti-psychiatry, most notably the work of Laing. His ideas and critiques against psychiatry were substantiated during her work in psychiatric institutions which she contested decisively as places where the person as a subject was annulled (Mannoni, 1979). As a psychoanalyst, by contrast, she offered a listening space for the subject in their search for meaning.[14] She shared with Laing an emphasis on the role of the family in the etiology of psychosis. For Maud Mannoni, psychosis was never a fact of the individual alone but always tied into a net of relations. With Foucault she had in common the contestation of any pretension of psychiatry to "heal." This would mean nothing else than "returning mad people into the clan of the 'well' thinkers." In this sense, she insisted to the institutional therapist that they would not go far enough by reorganizing, thus reifying psychiatry and its closed (or semi-open) hospitals. Community psychiatry was for her an "adaptation police" moved beyond the hospital (Hochmann, 2015, p. 197).

During her life, Maud Mannoni was on the threshold regarding whether she believed madness was still to be treatable in a humanist and humanizing way or a "triumphant rebellion against reason" (Hochmann, 2015, p. 199). Her first book *The Backward Child in His Mother: A Psychoanalytic Study* (1964/1972) has been considered the first anti-psychiatry book in France (Mannoni, 1973).

In 1969, her studies of Freud, Dolto, Lacan, Winnicott, and Laing made her found the experimental school or "anti-institution" Bonneuil-sur-Marne, nowadays in the suburbs of Paris, by then rather in its surrounding countryside. She drew from the English experimental Kingsley Hall commune (Laing and Cooper below) and rearticulated it psychoanalytically. In the first place, this meant to oppose the idealization of having found the perfect place to live in. The claim "that there is a contrast between these communities and the family fail to notice that they are similar in so far as these [anti-psychiatry] communities claim to be ideal and aspire to permanence" (Mannoni, 1973, p. 500). The articulation of tensions and conflicts are thus repressed and this reproduction of the family situation produces new pathologies as well as reactivates old ones.

In Maud Mannoni's "anti-psychiatric village," allowance was given for these difficulties. It included children on the autism spectrum or suffering from mutism, psychotic disorders, and those who were labeled as "uneducable." The crucial point of the anti-institution was the non-treatment, non-reeducation; in short, the absence of impositions. Far away from transmitting the idea of an ideal, the children were given time and space "of wanting something for themselves" (Mannoni, 1973, p. 500). Activities were open for free and voluntary enrolment. A special emphasis was given on crafts, spending time with artisans and farmers. Many stayed in farmers' households. This change of company compared to their original homes and families together with the familiarization of daily life activities was highly beneficial for the children.

The method of Bonneuil did not consist of a list of "good practices" neither "assumptions about what should be done, but on analytical criticism of what should not be done. The training given at the school is based upon such experience of criticism, and includes no technical training"[15] (Mannoni, 1976, 1986; Mannoni, 1973, p. 501).

The school attracted many volunteers, among them students of La Sorbonne university. It matched with the *Zeitgeist* and search for new or anti-institutionalities.

As a matter of fact, many children did improve and change in Bonneuil. Yet,

> the successes achieved, even if spectacular, would not of themselves prove the effectiveness of the attitudes adopted. The proof is rather to be found in the fact that no child has remained in his [their] original condition or become a chronic case.
>
> (Mannoni, 1973, p. 500)

Finally, Maud (1999) drew her attention to trauma and creativity and how the infantile trauma can lead to artistic creation. In this vein, she dedicated an entire book to the writer Virginia Woolf and how writing her book *To the Lighthouse* helped her to control her hallucinations (Marxen, 2011; Mannoni, 1998). Upon finishing it, Woolf did not hear the voices of her dead mother anymore.

> The consequence was a kind of 'birth,' a relief of not continuing in her adult life in company of the invisible presence of that mother of childhood who reached to turn off with her voice the sound of Virginia's. Getting rid of the dead is an intent to recover as a subject.
>
> (Mannoni, 1998, p. 35, translated by myself from Spanish)

The last part of the book about Woolf shifts to subjects of feminism and psychoanalysis. The bridging part is Woolf's awareness of male dominance of the written word and publishing activities. In this context, her book *Orlando* (1928/2005) on gender performativity is highly relevant too.

During her entire life, Maud Mannoni's publishing activity was prolific as she gave birth to over 20 books.

Fernand Deligny

Fernand Deligny (1913–1996) was considered an educator; however, he himself preferred anti-educator as well as poet or ethnologist. After abandoning his university studies of philosophy and psychology, he started off working as a substitute teacher for the wrongly called "inadapted children" in Paris and its periphery between 1937 and 1938. During WWII, he worked in a psychiatric hospital in the North of France. There, he used the chaos of war in order to turn around hierarchies, to suppress sanctions and to organize activities outside the asylum. Then, he founded the "prevention houses of delinquency" in Lille where he occupied abandoned and destroyed buildings to accommodate a network of mutual help between delinquents, workers, and members of the Resistance. Meanwhile, he achieved a diploma for education of "deranged" children. After the war, he founded La Grande Cordée [The big rope] together with members of the communist party. Their mission was free treatment to accommodate adolescents sent by social services and psychiatry. The Big Rope was a processor of community intervention. Deligny's ongoing struggle through different settings was directed against labeling, stigma, pathologizing, and institutionalization. In this sense, he considered the adolescents "so alive that no social worker can stand them," stressing the healthy parts of them (Planella, 2015, p. 24, translated by myself from Spanish).[16] In 1968, he shifted from his fight against the institutional and institutionalized management of delinquency to an experimental commune for children on the autism spectrum in the Cervennes mountains (Monoblet), beyond any institutional frame. This move coincided with the rebellions of the '68 movements in favor of a deinstitutionalization of education. The Monoblet community was a refuge for young people who had been considered as "incurable," on the upper end of the autism spectrum and unavailable for verbal language. In this phase of his life, Deligny dived into an anthropological inquiry of language and against the supremacy of verbal language. For him, autism did not mean "a 'rejection' of language, but a way (and a world) of perception where the absent language is not missing" (Álvarez de Toledo, 2009, p. 12, translated by myself from Spanish). He wanted to search beyond language for other forms of existence (Planella, 2015). Similarly to the way Laing and Cooper had focused with a certain idealization on schizophrenia, Deligny did so with the autism spectrum. In alignment with Cooper's idea, Deligny combatted the absurdity of logics (Hochmann, 2015).

In the community, the children stayed in peasants' houses and settings, for short or long terms, including for "stays of rupture" from their institutions such as psychiatric hospitals or foster homes (Hochmann, 2015, p. 200). They were not given any order nor any form of therapy. Deligny wanted to offer an existence beyond psychiatry and psychotherapy, "in a vacation of language" (Planella, 2015, p. 36).

Similar to Maud Mannoni, there was an apparent "no-method." The children could walk freely around and join the countryside activities if their chose to do so. The objective was in no way the reconnection with or through language. Deligny strived to find "a language equivalent to artistic forms." He aimed at creating a dispositif of an alternative life beyond any institution that he defined "with the metaphor of a raft" (Álvarez de Toledo, 2009, p. 8). Any form of psychiatric diagnosis was rejected.

He shared with Maud Mannoni the preference for rural settings with a certain idealization of the "authentic" and simple peasant life. In spite of his reluctance towards psychoanalysis, the first children sent to him came from Lacanian psychoanalysts: Maud Mannoni, Françoise Dolto, and Jacques Nassif.

As a matter of fact, the children changed during their stay and returned appeased to their families and institutions, as all families have confirmed (Álvarez de Toledo, 2009).

Deligny had been invited to intern with Guattari and Oury in their hospital La Borde. He also shared ideas with Tosquelles, especially the fact of recruiting "non specialized," common people for their therapeutic (Tosquelles) or anti-therapeutic (Deligny) communities.

His inquiry about and against language made Deligny invent a "system of transcription." The adults traced and sketched the gestures and movements of the children all over the terrain on large pieces of cardboard. Their moves were supposed to be free and "non-operative" (Planella, 2015, p. 36). This graphic work should "stimulate the invention of a vocabulary," the one of localizing, of trimmers, of "lines of wandering" [*lignes d'erre* in French]. The latter is a kind of graphic transcriptions of the children's trajectories. He considered *tracer* [tracing] as one of his main achievements, insisting "in the original and common character of gestures and strokes" (Deligny, 2009, p. 135). It is opposed to drawing and exempted of any intention of representation (Álvarez de Toledo, 2009).

Film as an experimental practice was an important part of Deligny's work too. He considered film as a means against exclusion and normalization[17] long before "militant cinema." He developed both films with his participants of the Grande Cordée and Monoblet commune as well as documentaries about these places. In this context, special attention deserves *Ce gamin, là* (1975) directed by Renaud Victor and produced by François Truffaut. The film is of an extraordinary poetic language, extremely slow, refractory of verbal language. Yet, in its slow-motion pace and apparent non-communication, important reactions, trajectories, and interactions happen with water and the other elements or through mundane activities like bread baking. It includes the lines of wandering. Additionally and because of Truffaut's insistence, Deligny appears as well. He opted for a poetic text that intentionally does not help at all to "'understand' something that he did not want to be understood nor taken as a dogma or an assignment." The film became successful and an important document of anti-psychiatry. Besides Truffaut, Deligny was also in contact with Chris Marker (Álvarez de Toledo, 2009, p. 9).

Furthermore, he organized "drawing workshops" that were actually "workshops of invention," very much appreciated and important for the participants.

They "functioned" in a completely non-directive way, in an open studio mode (Planella, 2015, p. 32).

The eighties led to an exhaustion of anti-institutional experiments and their utopia. Deligny's work became less required although he continued to fight against the invasion of technocracy and bureaucratic language and norms in mental health and education (Álvarez de Toledo, 2009).

His abundant writings, however, have remained. For him, writing was an essential and ongoing activity, even a necessity. In 2009, the MACBA museum published a selection of Deligny's writings in Spanish, titled *To allow, to trace, to see* [Fernand Deligny: Permitir, trazar, ver]. The book was presented in the eponymous seminar.

Permitting was a leitmotiv in Deligny's life work together with freedom. He opted for a "slight presence" of the (non) educator. People must not be enclosed neither dominated. "It is a question of 'freeing' the subjects so that they can have free lives" (Planella, 2015, p. 21). Or, in other words, their subjectivities can unfold.

Deligny's work was nomadic, shifting through different places, geographies, populations, and deinstitutionalizing various settings. He wanted education to be nomadic, in the sense of "mobilization against static positions of societies ... and established order." He invited for a "labyrinth topography" as opposed to the "powers of identities" (Planella, 2015, pp. 16–17).

Asking for only a "light presence" from the (non) educator, Deligny considered educating permitting and not submitting. Education

> is not the model but the reference. It is not a lecture but an encounter... [It is] giving to the other the real possibility of being, existing, and making it by oneself (and not the adults or professionals deciding for the other).
> (Planella, 2015, p. 9, 25, 29)

It is an anti/pedagogy of transgression, both nomadic and poetic. It is based on Marxism and affine to ethnology and anthropology, inviting to be self-critical with the excess of activities and to permit the transitions to "no places" (Planella, 2015, p. 38).

Michel Foucault

As a philosopher and academic Michel Foucault fought against oppressions in their various forms (1961/2006, 1975, 1978, 1983). As already outlined in Chapter (p. 92), a special part of his dedication belonged to subjectivity, its developments, unfolding, as well as its constraints and repression by power. Let us recall from Chapter 4 that he focused on

> 'the divisions operating in society in the name of madness, disease, delinquency, and their efforts on the formation of a reasonable and normal subject.' ... the related institutions hold apart and discipline undesired subjects with the aim to normalize their supposed deviance.

Furthermore, "he analysed 'the points where the techniques of the self are integrated into structures of coercion or domination" (Brion & Harcourt, 2014, pp. 299–300).

Psychiatry had required his special attention, leading to his effort to dismantle *any* of its pretentions to heal or to cure (Hochmann, 2015). In this sense, *History of madness* (1961/2006) is an archeology of psychiatry in the Western world through a deep historical study about madness and its in/tolerance in societies. Foucault "shows how the values of unreason have finally, as a result of political measures and the activity of the police, been crushed under the erroneous concept of 'mental illness'" (Mannoni, 1973, p. 493).

While Middle Age and Renaissance society more or less accepted people considered "mad," classical age, the Age of Reason, marked an end to this supposed (and historically questioned) acceptance. The distinction of reason and unreason dichotomized people into two groups of sane and insane, shutting away the latter to the "Great Confinement." Later, in the 19th century, the asylum replaced confinement where a new relationship between the doctor and the patients developed (Foucault, 1994, 1961/2006). Over the centuries, various moralist, taming, and "purifying" operations were applied to "mad people," "patients," and "clients," independently from the label the affected person had received. It is precisely the moral/ist aspect of the treatment of the insane to which Foucault paid very special attention. Whether religiously and morally motivated or driven by the "pedagogy of good spirit," from the very beginning of the discipline of psychiatry (end of the 18th century), the psychiatrist has been the "guardian of reason" and the social agent of exclusion (Hochmann, 2015, pp. 151–152). For Foucault, psychiatry formed "a network of spaces of internment, judicial spaces, disciplining conditions and procedures of social exclusion." Together with the norms of industrial labor and bourgeois morality, psychiatry has become a "whole network between discursive spaces" (Faramelli, 2017, p. 1). There is absolutely no way to liberate psychiatry from its controlling, moralizing, and converting-into-reason aspects. Any humanist revolution in psychiatry only masks "its function as the ultimate guardian about the frontier between reason and unreason." "Healing" in psychiatric terms is nothing else than "abusive normalization." His discourse is a "psychiatricide" (Hochmann, 2015, pp. 154–155). Psychiatry presses people into a pattern of being imposed and controlled by power mechanisms of society. Psychoanalysis and psychoanalysts are only the bourgeois version of the same dynamics, having been the bourgeoisie in charge of giving themselves their own moralizing institution according to their own norms and values.

Finally, madness is the "absence of the work of art. It is the ultimate point where the artwork is annihilated."[18] This void is not only negative, on the contrary: It marks the artwork's limits. It is the epiphany of the artwork. As opposed to other anti-psychiatrists (Laing & Cooper), Foucault does acknowledge the suffering related to psychosis. Explaining the trajectory and art of Artaud, Foucault reminds us that the void means suffering and even terror. Yet, it is inherent to creation and not a question of erasing, compensating, or

Figure 6.2 Dora García, Genealogías, works 1999–2018. Pencil on paper.

"healing" it (Hochmann, 2015, p. 154; Foucault, 1961/2006). This very much resonates with the ideas of Brazilian Lygia Clark who had introduced the "empty-full" to describe the void. Also for her, it was necessary for the creative process. One should allow it. Then, step by step, it fills itself up again and creation can be resumed (Rolnik, 1999). For Foucault, the true artwork is the ascension over the abyss of the absence of artwork (1961/2006; Figure 6.2).

Ronald Laing and David Cooper

So-called British anti-psychiatry brought together, in various constellations, phenomenology, psychoanalysis, Marxism, Hinduism, and the use of psychedelic drugs. It was connected to the local counter-culture, beatnik, and hippie movements around the '68 events (Hochmann, 2015).

Ronald Laing (1927–1989) has often been credited as the original founder of anti-psychiatry despite rejecting this label. Originally from Glasgow, Scotland, he started off as a psychiatrist in the most conventional setting, in a psychiatric hospital where electroshocks, insulinshocks, and even lobotomy were daily business. Still in Scotland, he engaged in philosophy and read Feud, Nietzsche, Sartre, Genet, Dostoevsky, phenomenologists such as Kierkegaard, Heidegger as well as philosopher-psychiatrist Jaspers.[19] His intellectual heritage was thus from continental Europe but he was additionally informed by Scottish skepticism, most notably David Hume and John Macmurray (Gordon, 2009).

Moving to London, England, he studied psychoanalysis at the famous psychoanalytic Tavistock Clinic. His studies included the required personal psychoanalysis as an analysand. Donald Winnicott was his supervisor. Laing adopted from the former his partly positive view on psychosis, considering it in some cases a release and relief from too tight defense mechanisms and a path towards personal growth.

By then, Laing challenged his psychotherapy colleagues by blurring lines of self-disclosure, therapeutic boundaries, and the use of psychedelic drugs, particularly Lysergic Acid Diethylamide (LSD). His special focus laid on "an existential-phenomenological foundation for a science of persons and a description of the experience of those labeled schizophrenic" (Gordon, 2009, p. 11). In this context, he developed his concept of "ontological insecurity" (Laing, 1969/1990, 1959/1990). It mainly dealt with the sensation "of not being able to trust myself as the subject of my own experience, of not being able to take for granted that I have a place in the world." The result is an extreme insecurity that renders the subject less able to hold oneself over against the Other (MacCallum Sullivan, 2009, p. 8). For Laing (1967), mental disturbance and its related behaviors were a "special strategy that a person invents in order to live in an unlivable situation" instead of evidence for clinical diagnosis. These strategies are then manifest in "false self systems" that "fend off psychological and emotional catastrophes" (p. 95). Laing's intention was to "to make madness and the process of going mad comprehensible" to a bigger audience, including the affected people, and he was successful in doing so (Gordon, 2009, p. 11). For this, he focused on people's experience, as always related to the experience and existence of others.[20] He shifted from the client being "an object-to-be-changed" to "a person-to-be-accepted" (Laing, 1967, p. 45, as quoted in MacCallum Sullivan, 2009, p. 8).

For this purpose, he co-founded the Philadelphia Association[21] in 1965, together with David Cooper and others. He would chair it until 1981. The Association works until today in the UK, pursuing a "community and psychotherapy" approach with therapy activities, housing, and study programs. Its philosophy has always been "a creative approach to therapy," questioning "the social norms that often contribute to someone's unhappiness." The intention is to engage with philosophy, anthropology, spirituality, and arts (https://www.philadelphia-association.com).

Laing shared with all the anti-psychiatrists the critique of approaches that explain mental disturbances exclusively in the individual (whether behavioral or bio-chemical wise). He particularly critiqued the family as a reason for madness. His research looked into the families of schizophrenics as much as it did into the schizophrenics themselves (Esterson & Laing, 1964). Family was seen as a repressive system or social structure, as in alignment with the movements around '68 that put bourgeois and traditional ways of living under way, in the first place the traditional family. Esterson and Laing concentrated on contradictory messages within families where a facade of harmony is maintained at costs of the repression of any disagreements.

> By escaping from the family unit, or creating alternatives to the traditional nuclear family (through leaving home, going 'on the road', gay relationships and/or communes) people felt they could free themselves from the possibly toxic effects of their own families. For many young people in the 1960s and 1970s, this became a necessity. They had to get away, somehow.
>
> (Foot, 2015a, pp. 4–5)

In this vein, in 1965, a "'household' for 'patients'" was set up by (anti)psychiatrists Laing, Cooper, and Esterson, together with psychiatric nurse Joan Cunnold and social worker Sidney Briskin, named after the building they settled in London: Kingsley Hall. At that moment, the building was squatted in by students. Before, it had housed or sheltered a lot of protest and resistance movements. Notably, Mahatma Gandhi had stayed in it in 1920 (Hochmann, 2015).

Kingsley soon became *the* famous anti-psychiatry commune. Whereas Laing, as well as Cooper, had worked before in some kind of clinical setting and research, they would now shift their views on psychosis from a struggle against disintegration and its consequent experiences towards a "breakthrough," a voyage into a new and much richer world. The commune would be a totally "demedicalized" space wherein psychiatrists, psychologists, and other mental health workers would live together with patients on this voyage, blurring also any kind of hierarchy among them. In no way would psychotic crisis be repressed but rather encouraged; psychedelic drugs were applied for this purpose too. Psychosis, particularly schizophrenia, constituted "a position crisis in the formation of the personality; normally such a crisis can be expected to lead automatically to a solution which is a step forward—not a cure, but a new state of the personality..." Laing called this a solution, a *metanoia.* He borrowed this term from "evangelism, in which it has the etymological meaning of 'change of mind', 'conversion'" (Mannoni, 1973, p. 495). So, the question was not at all to cure this crisis because this would mean to step back to a previous, supposedly preferable state. Yet, thanks to *metanoia* people would achieve a higher level of mind (Mannoni, 1973).

Additionally, Kingsley Hall organized groups and activities for residents and which were open to neighbors including "painting, weaving, yoga, poetry readings, Indian temple dancing, exhibitions, films and lectures on anthropology, psychiatry, the theatre, etc." (Mannoni, 1973, pp. 496–497).

Other anti-psychiatrists stayed there like Maud Mannoni and Maxwell Jones, as did counter culture celebrities and other "people curious about communal living, as well as those seeking an alternative to the mainstream mental health system" (Proctor, 2018, p. 5; Hochmann, 2015).

The most famous member was probably Mary Barnes who spent a significant amount of time at Kingsley, after having shown a history of mental disturbances. Encouraged and invited by Laing, she came to the commune to experience her crisis. Among other features, she urinated in her bed and "painted" the walls with her feces. Her mates tried to make her abandon this activity because it became olfactorily unbearable, not because of social conformity. Laing's reaction became one of the most known sentences of anti-psychiatry, remarking that this was nice but some color was missing. This comment apparently embarked her into her painting career. After the closure of Kingsley Hall in 1970, Mary Barnes rented an apartment where she painted and wrote. She also held conferences on a national and international level. She finally passed away at the age of 78, after having become almost a national celebrity (Hochmann, 2015). Together with her anti-psychiatrist Joe Berke, she co-authored a book about their common voyage titled *Mary Barnes: Two Accounts of a Journey Through Madness* (1972).

With the distance of time, some critical voices have emerged about this exceptional trajectory of Barnes. For one, it seemed staged the way she "postponed" her crisis until her entrance into Kingsley. For some authors (i.e. Hochmann, 2015), she and her family confirmed almost too exactly to previous theories of Laing. Moreover, her capacity is striking when she managed to hold on her crisis while referred temporarily to a general hospital for physical health issues.

Basaglia and others have critiqued the false illusion of a space without hierarchies, without an apparent method. The very anti-psychiatrists or ex-psychiatrists were the ones setting up the rules of the supposed abolition of hierarchies. The paradox is the therapist who declares themselves no-therapist to the no-patient, who, thanks to the former, can live their own experience. Basaglia (1971/2014) called this "an impossible strategy."

Furthermore, the supposed "absence" of methods is a method in itself and should be recognized and declared as such in order to avoid false democratizations.

There was a cleavage between theory and practice: "[D]ismantling routines, reorganizing spaces, redefining roles and redistributing activities did not automatically entail the destruction of structural inequalities between people" or the final "abolition of hierarchies" (Proctor, 2018, p. 5).

Finally, the ex-/anti-psychiatrists personality, not to say charisma, was crucial:

> [A]lthough Laing and his colleagues wished to divest themselves of all social and professional functions, their presence and their personalities inevitably had certain effects: when other places on the same lines were set up, the absence of the same mediators produced less good results.
>
> (Mannoni, 1973, p. 499)

Simultaneously, Kingsley Hall and other communes were set up as a utopia, claiming "to be ideal places to live in" (Mannoni, 1973, p. 500). It was an institution that denied its own institutionality (Battersby in Basaglia & Basaglia, 1971/2014). Thus, they repressed possible conflicts from the very beginning, as opposed to Maud Mannoni and her approach which did allow these conflicts around living together to manifest.

After his peak of recognition and fame in the sixties and seventies, when he was "a pillar of the zeitgeist," the professional and common interest into Laing's work decreased. His activities then circled around Buddhist meditation and techniques of collective rebirthing. He was disbarred from medical practices because of his alcohol consumption and the Philadelphia Association "parted company with him." Particularly, a public mass rebirthing session led by him tired his association colleagues, as stated by a later chair of the Philadelphia Association, Paul Gordon (2009, p. 10). Yet, his legacy is important, in the sense of his ongoing struggle to change the way people think about "madness." He insisted upon spaces of acceptance, tolerance, and especially listening.[22] This gave people the sensation of relief, of not being alone. "Madness was not unreason, a total unintelligibility, a total difference between the sane and the insane" (MacCallum Sullivan, 2009, pp. 7–8). Laing strived throughout his life to make the meaning of madness understandable: "[T]he discourse of the disturbed might well make sense if listened to" (Gordon, 2009, p. 12).

Also credited with influence on the anti-psychiatry movement is *David Cooper* (1931–1986), most notably for having coined the term "anti-psychiatry" by his book *Psychiatry and Anti-Psychiatry* (1967/2013). Some of his beliefs coincided with Laing's, just with more political emphasis. As a follower of Sartre, he had engaged into New Left movements that contested completely the values of bourgeois society, among others the family (Cooper, 1970). In Cape Town, his hometown, he fought in the underground anti-apartheid resistance. He also spent time in China for political education and in Cuba to witness the revolution (Chapman, 2016).

He went to London to specialize in psychiatry after having studied medicine in South Africa. Very early he saw that the politicization of psychiatry was indispensable. He argued that psychiatry was a pseudo-science that paralleled capitalism as a system or structure of repression in society. The main aim of psychiatry was to teach citizens how to conform to society through medicalizing defiance and persecute the non-obedient. He considered "the treatment imposed in psychiatric hospitals and by society as a pointless and unjustified act of violence." For him, diagnosis of psychosis was unscientific and paradox: "[W]hen one locks up a 'madman' [or woman], one cannot be sure that it is the 'right one'; the real madman [-woman] may be another person connected with him [them], who stands to gain from the situation" (Mannoni, 1973, p. 495, referring to Cooper).

Similar to Laing, he believed that madness/psychosis developed from a conflict between one's self identity and one's social identity, in relation to society and its expectations. After co-founding the Philadelphia Association, he was pivotal in coordinating the *Dialectics of Liberation* conference in 1967. Presentations were centered on the nature of violence and the possibility of liberation. Protagonists were the German Marxist philosopher Herbert Marcuse from the Frankfurt School,[23] the anthropologist Gregory Bateson, member of the Palo Alto group (see below), as well as the Pan-Africanist and member of the US Civil Rights Movements Stokely Carmichael (Carmichael, Cooper, Laing, & Marcuse, 2015).

Before Kingsley Hall, Cooper was known for his Vila 21 experience and research wherein a psychiatric hospital in London gave him the infrastructure to lead service of only 19 in-bed patients between 1962 and 1966. Cooper tried to de-hierarchize the relationships between professionals and clients, so that eventually the cared became caregiver and vice versa. The illusion behind this agenda was to re-find a lost unity, something equally criticizable in Kingsley Hall as the ideal commune to live in (above). Interestingly, he shifted from a more conventional mode of occupational therapy with structured activities towards a non-directive approach. His team quickly realized "the defensive role of this time filling." Fostering the "'capacity of being-alone' (once again a concept taken from Winnicott)," they gave up to organize clients' time, giving the latter their freedom in this regard (Mannoni, 1973, p. 496). The staff would only take the role of interlocutors, answering to eventual demands and questions. This method coincided with Maud Mannoni's.

Like Laing, Cooper also shifted from this still clinical setting to a more radical rejection of any kind of clinical frame which meant "going beyond this field" (Mannoni, 1973, p. 496). He laudably fought for integrating madness into society and to help people find a way to live with madness. Yet, with his shift to Kingsley Hall, Cooper joined the appraisal and eventual idealization of psychosis and its crises. He wanted to set up a place where people could become "mad" in a safe way, without psychiatric interferences (Cooper in Basaglia & Basaglia, 1971/2014).

Still after Kingsley Hall, he abandoned any anti/psychiatric activity and delved into mysticism together with an extreme idealization of libertarian love and "free" (allowed) crime (Hochmann, 2015).

Similarly, although apart from Laing, Cooper and other peers, "turned inwards … to explore the ineffable mysteries of the cosmos – away from the mundane world with its inconvenient and intractable-seeming social ills" (Proctor, 2018, p. 9). This attitude was completely opposed from the extreme political activism of the German SPK.

Anti-Psychiatries in the US

In the US, the anti-psychiatry movement was rather heterodox and is therefore difficult to summarize. There were academics, most notably Goffman, who opposed psychiatry by ethnographic research. Then, Gregory Bateson (1972) and the Palo Alto group with Don Jackson, Paul Watzlawick, Jay Haley, and John Weakland focused on the theory of "modes of communication" in relation to schizophrenia. Their ideas of the "double bind" resembled those of Laing regarding the repressed conflicts in families and their role in the etiology of madness.

The psychiatrist Maxwell Jones started therapeutic communities where professionals and clients would live together to co-create new forms of therapy.

At Belmont Hospital, he set up a community for people with a record of labels of "inadaptation" with the goal of democratizing the relationship between clients and professionals as much as possible and to reconcile the patients with an exterior world they had up to that point experienced as persecutor (Jones, 1952). In Baltimore, during the twenties, Harry Stack Sullivan had already preceded in stressing interpersonal relationships with the person's environment in the form of family and clinical teams in the treatment of schizophrenia. He was followed by the private establishment of Chestnut Lodge, most notably influenced by the psychoanalysts Frieda Fromm Reichmann and Harold Searles (Hochmann, 2015).

Moreover, there were various clinics and communities with their own approaches, ideologies, and politics. Psychiatry went along with other social and political protests around the '68 movements (Mannoni, 1973).

In this sense, the US journal *Radical Therapist* (1970–1972) gave justice of mutual connection between political and mental oppression. "The journal included articles on Fanon and anti-imperialism, the Vietnam War, Chicano activism, and prison revolts" (Protector, 2018, p. 11). Some contributors worked as physicians for Black Panther Party free clinics. Some argued that revolutionary praxis would be therapeutic itself. The journal very much insisted on not only including articles about "black, brown and Third World people's struggle" but on also having authors from all the mentioned collectives. Stokely Carmichael's participation in the *Dialectics of Liberation* event has already been mentioned. He very much focused on "the pathologisation and incarceration of politicised black men in American asylums" (Protector, 2018, p. 4). There was clearly a link between political struggle and pathologization (see also Metzl's *Protest Psychosis. How Schizophrenia Became a Black Disease*, 2009).

A prominent figure in US anti-psychiatry was *Thomas Szasz* (1920–2012), psychiatrist, psychoanalyst, university professor (University of New York at Syracuse), and chairman of the Board of Directors of the American Association for the Abolition of Involuntary Mental Hospitalization. As a prolific writer, he is especially known for his books *The Myth of Mental Illness* (1961), *The Ethics of Psychoanalysis* (1965), and *The Manufacture of Madness* (1970). As two of the titles indicate, he had argued against mental illness and psychiatry during his entire life, particularly against involuntary mental hospitalization that he considered "a crime against humanity" (Hochmann, 2015, p. 164; Szasz, 1991). He insisted on the difference between physical and mental illness, shaping his view of mental illness as a metaphorical illness. For him, there was absolutely no objective definition of mental illness. Psychiatry has usurped a medical model and "this medical disguise does not have any scientific nor logic base" (Hochmann, 2015, p. 165). Psychiatry has unsuccessfully strived for its medical identity. In this effort, it has launched a myth into the social space, the myth of mental illness. Psychiatry "has abusively transformed into illness different ways of being, thinking, acting, expressing, … that do not correspond to accepted norms" (Hochmann, 2015, p. 165). Interestingly and accurately, he mentioned as one example the madwoman who would not accept her insignificant identity as a housewife as opposed to her "normal" counterpart (Szasz, 1973).

Szasz believed that a psychiatric diagnosis was an opportunity for abuse of power between the psychiatrist and patient. Naming people diseased or ill is an opportunity to control them through denying them responsibility as moral agents: "The language of psychiatry thus de-ethicizes and depoliticizes human relations and personal conduct… The process feeds on itself, transforming more and more human problems and situations into specialized technical 'problems' to be 'solved' by so-called mental-health professional" from psychiatry and its related disciplines psychoanalysis and psychology (Szasz, 1973, p. 505). Szasz further quotes P. Rome, senior consultant in psychiatry at the Mayo Clinic and former president of the American Psychiatric Association: "'Actually, no less than the entire world is a proper catchment area for present-day psychiatry, and psychiatry need not be appalled by the magnitude of this task'" (Szasz, 1973, p. 506; Rome, 1968).

The ever-growing psychopathologization and medicalization correspond to the bureaucratization of life. The ideology of insanity is "communicated through the scientistic jargon of psychiatric 'diagnoses,' 'prognoses' and 'treatments,' and embodied in the bureaucratic system of institutional psychiatry and its concentration camps called 'mental hospitals'" (Szasz, 1973, p. 507).

Diagnosis categorizes people into groups and those that strayed away from medical norms are controlled and stigmatized through medication and treatment. This control is possible because of the social class and status of psychiatrists and thus the power they have in society. His proximity to Goffman's and Foucault's positions is obvious.

Ideology was another of Szasz, foci, equating psychiatry with a secularized form of Christianism. The favorite task of the ideologist of insanity is manufacturing more madness (Szasz, 1973).

> Instead of being born into sin, man [the person] is born into sickness. Instead of life being a vale of tears, it is a vale of diseases. And, as in his [their] journey from the cradle to the grave man [person] was formerly guided by the priest, so now he is [they are] guided by the physician. In short, whereas in the Age of Faith the ideology was Christian, the technology clerical and the expert priestly; in the Age of Madness the ideology is medical, the technology clinical and the expert psychiatric.
>
> (Szasz, 1973, p. 507)

He raised important questions for anybody working in mental health:

1 Is the scope of psychiatry the study and treatment of medical conditions, or the study and influencing of social performances? In other words, are psychiatry's objects of inquiry diseases or roles, happenings or actions?

2 Is the aim of psychiatry the study of human behavior, or the control of human (mis)behavior? In other words, is the goal of psychiatry the advancement of knowledge, or the regulation of (mis)conduct?
3 Is the method of psychiatry the exchange of communications, or the administration of diagnostic tests and curative treatments? In other words, what does psychiatric practice actually consist of—listening and talking, or prescribing drugs, operating on the brain, and imprisoning persons labeled as 'mentally ill'?
4 Finally, is the guiding value of psychiatry individualism or collectivism? In other words, does psychiatry aspire to be the servant of the individual or of the State? (Szasz, 1973, p. 510)

The last question is closely linked to his insistence on personal responsibility, self-discipline, and freedom. He considered all three as central to the person as moral agent in the Western world.[24] For him, any kind of public psychiatry meant control and restriction or even annulment of freedom. Szasz considered the ostensible "community psychiatry," as introduced by US president John Kennedy in 1963, a "secularized religion," the state pursuing the domination of individuals by a "moral persuasion and political coercion" (Hochmann, 2015, p. 166). Nowadays, he would very likely be in favor of abolishing public health care together with the Republican Party.

This part of his work is certainly to be criticized, especially since the abolition or short cutting of public health would inevitably lead to an injustice regarding who can and cannot afford help if needed (and not imposed). Yet, Szasz was able to raise attention against involuntary hospitalization, dehumanization, arbitrariness, and bureaucratization of and in psychiatry.

Finally, and like Maud Mannoni in France, he also dedicated a book to Virginia Woolf (Szasz, 1987). With her example, he examines the fictitious character of ideas of genius and madness.

Sociologist *Erving Goffman* (1922–1982) from the University of Chicago had studied the subject of psychiatry as an academic, similar to Foucault. Whereas Foucault, as a philosopher, studied archeology of psychiatry, mental illness, and confinement, Goffman, as a sociologist, did so regarding the (by then) present situation of those diagnosed as mentally ill. For his book *Asylums: Essays on the Social Situation of Mental Patients and Other Inmates* (1961), he had undertaken a year-long ethnography in a psychiatric hospital. His assiduous research led him to the conceptualization of the Total Institution: These are institutions where people are staying day and night and where all parts of their life are condensed in one single space. The total absorption is architecturally manifest in walls, control towers, wires as well as other modes of confinement, making free circulation of the individual almost impossible. Goffman distinguished between five different types of Total Institutions. They vary regarding the purpose of confinement and the characteristics of the confined individuals ("Characteristics of Total Institutions," 1957/1961). In the first place, there are institutions for people who are considered "harmless" but "unable" to care for themselves, such as the former orphanages or nursery houses. Then, there are places for people who are involuntarily threatening society like psychiatric hospitals (former asylums) and quarantine wards for contagious illnesses. The third type is the jail set up for persons considered as deliberately "dangerous." Others are adapted to the needs of their work tasks: boarding schools, the military, long-term running boats, and also the "housing" of servants whenever they have to live in the same building of their employers. Finally, there are retreats from the world such as monasteries, convents, etc.

Although there are certainly slight differences among the mentioned types, they share significant characteristics. It starts with a "ritual of entrance" that consists of a dispossession and depersonalization or even dehumanization. Entering (voluntarily or not) the institution means for the affected people to lose their "identity kit" in form of personal objects, clothes, and relationships. They are mostly deprived of their contacts with other social groups beyond the institution. Moreover, they are under surveillance for 24 hours a day. A process of "mortification" begins, devaluating the person as such, restringing their physical and psychological spaces up to annulling people's dignity. This is also the result of the bureaucratic functioning of Total Institutions: They are set up in order to make the institution function, disregarding human needs. The person is set under administration; their "status is reduced to that of mere administration fodder" (Mannoni, 1973, p. 502). Frequently, the institutional dynamics are of punishment (for the "bad," "rebellious" inhabitant) and award (little easements for the "good," adapted one). Perversely, some ways of punishment, such as electroshock or physical confinement, are even applied as professed "therapeutic methods." Another similarity shared by all types of total institutions is the fact that it is impossible or highly difficult to denounce transgressions and aggressions committed by the staff. Inhabitants' integrity, or even their lives, depends on the non/moral of the staff in charge of them (i.e. guards). That is the reason why total institutions can become camps in the sense of Agamben (above).

In order to situate Goffman's reasoning, his theoretical position should be summarized: In spite of his urge for independence from "schools," his work formed part of symbolic interactionism, by then very much promoted at the University of Chicago. This current focused on roles and symbolic representations. The way people "play," or are obliged to play their roles, constitute social interaction and society.[25] Moreover, Goffman is another representative of the labeling approach. As already explained in Chapter 2, this approach examines how labels are constructed in permanent interaction and almost always in opposite pairs ("correct-deviated," "healthy-ill"). Both the labeler and the labeled are analyzed, being the actors in positions of power in society who establish the hierarchies (see especially Becker, 1963/1971, for a summary Bergalli, 1980).

Furthermore, Goffman distinguished different phases of the psychiatric patient: before, during, and after internment ("The Moral Career of the Mental Patient," 1959/1961).

The psychiatric pre-patient, according to Goffman, is usually sent to psychiatry against their will by family members, other physicians, social workers, educators, etc. This "referral" happens because the pre-patient has shown a "deviant" behavior, having transgressed social norms or obligations. In this sense, the internment is a way of social control and not a common medical procedure. Once interned, psychopathological labels are placed on the person. The person's past is analyzed in various ways to find a "scientific" basis for the label. During the internment, the person's behavior does not fall into a normative void but is conditioned by the Total Institution. In this sense, every affected person tries to adapt to the situation in their way, from rebellion to total conversion, obeying the rules and even considering the institutional world as one self's. For Goffman, the so-called "symptoms" are nothing else than adaptation mechanisms and reactions or even reflexes to the totalizing nature of the hospitalization (Hochmann, 2015). For example, a possible physical reaction against the brutality of confinement is labeled as "personality disorder," another way of adapting such as the desperate search for some time of reclusion could be considered as "autistic." For Goffman, the alleged psychopathology was a product of confinement. As opposed to any other form of medicine that relates to physical unease, psychiatry exclusively serves social control (Goffman, 1969).[26] Just as Gramsci did, Goffman "unmasked psychopathology as a social and political construct intended to limit marginalized people's social action and participation" (Sajnani, Marxen, & Zarate, 2017, p. 30). Consequently and sadly, the post-patient, after confinement, has to suffer with a great deal of stigma that restricts their freedom of action too. The mental suffering stems much more from stigma, exclusion, and marginality than from a supposed mental illness. Goffman had an important impact on the other anti-psychiatrists. For them and also the '68 movements

> (t)he total institutions were at the same time a reality and a metaphor of the entire system: they showed the relentless contraposition between oppression and liberation… oppressed and oppressors, victims and butchers, they were all there [in the asylum] in their clearest expression … The excluded, the deviant, the waste products of capitalism, 'the wretched of the earth' were to be found there, living and breathing – inside the asylums, the prisons, the orphanages.
>
> (Foot, 2015a, p. 7)

Nowadays and thanks to the different anti-psychiatry movements, the former asylum has improved in many places. Yet,

> [t]he *staff* is carrier of an ideal of reformation of the *inmates* that remains impregnate by moralizing terms, even it is expressed in psychoanalytical terms or within the new vocabulary of social rehabilitation and cognitive remediation. This ideal transmitted to the inmates through behavioral reinforcements, sanctions and awards cannot be negotiated like in

> an ordinary conversation, by commentaries, questioning, explanations. The exchange between the two classes remains … limited and foremost codified.
>
> (Hochmann, 2015, p. 161, italics of the original)

Furthermore, pharmaceutical treatments are frequently used to confine a person in the sense of sedating and annulling subjectivity. Although medication is certainly necessary in many cases and up to a certain dosage, it very often serves to silence the problem instead of treating it psychologically and socially. So, the logics of the confinement of the past and the treatment of the present have not been completely interrupted. This has become manifest by a "biopolitical cord that connects alienation, control, and profit" (Dorenbaum, 2018, p. 69, referring to Mieli, 2015). With the ever growing number of psychiatric disorders, the state and the corporate world are expanding their biopower, in the sense of Foucault (1997), over every possible sphere of our lives, whether health, education, sexuality, birth, and death (Marxen & Greteman, 2019; see also Preciado in Chapter 4).

Finally, the total institution inevitably contaminates its employees. They might want to empathize with clients but at the same time think to protect themselves against them. The totalizing nature of the institutions leads straight to burn out, if the job load is not organized in digestible shifts.

Goffman's findings have found their confirmation in form of the research undertaken by psychologist David Rosenhahn (1973; Hochmann, 2015) from the University of Stanford. His researchers, apparently exempted from mental disturbances, pretended to have auditory hallucination and were interned all together in eight psychiatric hospitals. Once interned, they declared to be free of these symptoms. Still, they were kept in their hospitals, partly diagnosed as schizophrenic and medicalized as such. Their biographies were manipulated according to their "diagnosis." Additionally, Rosenhahn's study confirmed the dehumanization of patients and the bad quality of relations between patients and professionals.

Goffman had not included art in his research. His work, however, is essential for artistic practices in (total) institutions in order to de-totalize and not re-totalize, to de-label and not re-label people (see Chapter 2).

Oscar Masotta

The inclusion of the Argentinean Oscar Masotta (1930–1979) is not following the same scheme compared to all previous authors and anti-psychiatrists as he had never worked in or about psychiatry. Yet, his work in between and at the crossroads of psychoanalysis and conceptual art has been exceptional and must be retrieved for the present and future.

He started his career with unfinished university studies in philosophy in his hometown Buenos Aires. His activities included literary critique, artistic avant-garde, mass culture (particularly comic), and Lacanian psychoanalysis.

He operated as a writer, artist, critique, producer, and as the facilitator of study groups in all the mentioned fields. Being situated on the antipodes of the contemporary scientific "specialist," his wandering through fields and establishment of unexpected connections has also been related to his origins, belonging to intellectual groups in Buenos Aires in the fifties and sixties that developed "relations between theoretical bodies that in [so called] central countries were seldom read connectedly" (Longoni, 2017a, p. 19, translated by myself from Spanish).

He had an extraordinary capacity of incommoding, moving to and in between unusual places, and foreseeing new intellectual developments. In this sense, he was in constant pursuit of new explication for new occurrences (Longoni, 2017a).

Regarding avant-garde art, one of his first foci was pop art which was related to his interest in mass culture and the blurring of the line between the supposed high and low culture (Masotta, 1967a; Longoni, 2017a). The latter inquiry inspired research into comics and produced related events, most notably the First World Comics Biennial (Masotta, 1970).

He then inquired into happenings, very much in alignment with the thoughts of Allan Kaprow (Masotta, 1967b). In both cases, he was extremely interested in the collective unconsciousness. This inquiry led him to the theory of information/theory of media, following the work of Marshall McLuhan and combining it with structuralism and semiotics. In 1966, he engaged together with Roberto Jacoby, Eduardo Costa, and Raul Escari into Media Art.[27] A Media Art dispositif consisted of spreading announcement of fake happenings in mass media, inviting people to participate in order to belie the action. It could also take the form of an anti-happening: a happening that would only exist in media. The intentions of this way of art making were various: blaming the veracity of media, the artifacts of information construction, and especially showing how the event itself does not matter, but rather its construction in media (Longoni, 2017a, 2017b). In Jacoby's words (1967, p. 128 as quoted in Longoni, 2017a, p. 47): "Media art proposes to 'constitute a work in media', whose materiality is 'susceptible to be elaborated aesthetically.'"

As already explained in Chapter 4, Oscar Masotta (1968; Longoni & Mestman, 2004) wrote about the dematerialization of art in the same year as Lucy Lippard did, the latter having declared to have been the first (Longoni, 2017a; Longoni & Mestman, 2004; Lippard & Chandler, 1968; Lippard, 1973). Oscar Masotta referred to an article by the Russian Constructivist El Lissitzky, originally published in 1926.

Lissitzky proposed

> the integration of artists in the publishing industry through new typography and design. The Russian avant-garde artist was advocating for books as an art form for their expressive possibilities, and their ability to take many forms, noting that 'dematerialization is the characteristic of the age'
> (Longoni & Mestman, 2004, p. 157)

in which the new communication technologies result in the diminishing of physical materiality and the increase of "liberating energy." Masotta was inspired by these thoughts and further developed them "in terms of the contemporary artistic processes and forms of communication" that sought to dissolve art into social life (Longoni, 2017b).

In this vein, Masotta delivered a lecture at the DiTella Institute (center of artistic avant-garde in Buenos Aires) in 1967: "Después del pop, nosotros desmaterializamos" [After pop art, we dematerialize] with extensive referrals to El Lissitzky's ideas.

Masotta's ongoing writing activities should be stressed too. He published books about all the aforementioned subjects. Furthermore, he gave conferences and organized study groups as well as reading cycles. Theory/ies and conceptualization were a *leitmotiv* in his life. "In contradistinction to the strongly anti-intellectual climate of that time, he defended the theoretical as a specific mode of emancipatory political intervention" (MACBA, 2018 exhibition text *Theory as Action*). In this sense, he insisted "in the political condition of the exercise of thinking" (Longoni, 2017a, p. 22).

Yet, Masotta's own happenings *To Induce the Spirit of the Image* (1966), *The Helicopter* (1967), and media art *The Phantom Message* (1967) were important artistic events and crucial for his conceptualizations and seminars.

Masotta had always considered himself a Marxist and he believed Media Art was the ideal way to promote political change in society by acting upon its collective consciousness through popular channels. He strived to equate consciousness and structure: "The philosophy of Marxism must be rediscovered and particularized in the modern doctrines (or 'sciences') of languages, structures and the unconscious. In linguistic models and in the Freudian unconscious" (Masotta, 2017, p. 182).

Yet, in militant leftist circles, he was neither accepted as an organic (in the sense of Gramsci) nor committed (in the sense of Sartre) intellectual (Longoni, 2017a, 2017b). As opposed to

> the anti-intellectualist trend that… insisted on a movement towards direct action as the only means of militant political commitment, he insisted on (for himself and for intellectuals in general) a fundamental theoretical role in the historical process. He emphatically defends thought and theory as the specific labor of intellectuals in the context of the revolutionary feat.
> (Longoni, 2017b, p. 35; Masotta, 1968/1990)

Masotta mentioned Lacan for the first time in his publications in 1965, in an article titled "Jacques Lacan or the Unconsciousness in the Founding Principles of Philosophy." It stemmed from a paper delivered at the Enrique Pichon-Rivière School of Social Psychology (Hernández, 2017). The publication coincided with his most active time in the Argentinian art scene (see above).

His friendship with Enrique Pichon-Rivière, by some considered to be one of the founders of social psychology, was mainly based in art and philosophy.

Pichon-Rivière might have been the first to recommend Lacan's books to Masotta. This is significant as some years later, in 1969, Masotta would shift his principal focus from art to Lacanian psychoanalysis (Hernández, 2017).

Masotta's inquiries bridging existentialism and structuralism, particularly Marxist structuralism in the vein of Althusser, together with his work on happenings and media art led him to the study of mass communication. This research inevitably included the collective unconsciousness and its structures. Finally, he found his interests reflected in Lacan who, in his beginnings, had synthesized unconsciousness and structuralism. Masotta introduced Lacanian psychoanalysis into Spanish language. His activities in the Argentinean psychoanalytic scene have even been considered "an extension of his aesthetic ideas and his artistic practice" (Hernández, 2017, p. 221).

His lifelong demonstrated capacity of capturing in the present "an advanced theoretical offer" (Terán, 1991, quoted in Longoni, 2017a, p. 15) can be treated as equivalent to the psychoanalyst's sensitivity of capturing the signifier, the capacity of detecting potentials worth further elaboration.

In strong contact with the Lacanians in Paris, mainly Lacan's protégé Jacques-Alain Miller, Masotta became a catalyst in the psychoanalytical world. Thanks to his "aesthetic position on psychoanalysis,"[28] he reminded them that "Freud's psychoanalysis had included an indissoluble link to art, which the medicalization of psychoanalysis promoted by North American analysts would come to forget" (Hernández, 2017, p. 224, 225; see also Fiorini, 2010).

His hometown, Buenos Aires, already had a more than vivid psychoanalytical scene and does so until the present. So, the location was extremely fertile for the introduction of Lacanian psychoanalysis. He set up a very successful study group on Lacan. Additionally, he disseminated the outcomes of his group in the *Cuadernos Sigmund Freud* and founded the Escuela Freudiana de Buenos Aires (EFBA, the Buenos Aires School of Freud). Not uncontroversially, he authorized himself with this foundational act and finally introduced himself as a psychoanalyst.[29]

The violent and fascist climate shortly before the military coup in Argentina made Masotta flee to Europe. He finally settled in Barcelona where he died prematurely in 1979. In Catalonia and Spain, he also introduced Lacanian psychoanalysis through his study groups. He is well remembered in the local psychoanalytic scene in both locales.

In 2017, Ana Longoni together with Masotta's daughter Cloe Masotta conceived and curated the exhibition *Oscar Masotta. Theory as Action*. The title gives justice to the importance of thinking as a political act. The exhibition was launched by the MUAC (The University Museum of Contemporary Art) in Mexico City, itinerated then to the MACBA in Barcelona and concluded in Buenos Aires. The show very much reflected the confluences of contemporary art and psychoanalysis, also manifested in activities held together by artists and psychoanalysts, such as the MACBA seminar *Deflagractions. Oscar Masotta. The Avant-garde and Psychoanalysis* (https://www.MACBA.cat/en/deflagractions-oscar-masotta-avant-garde-psychoanalysis).

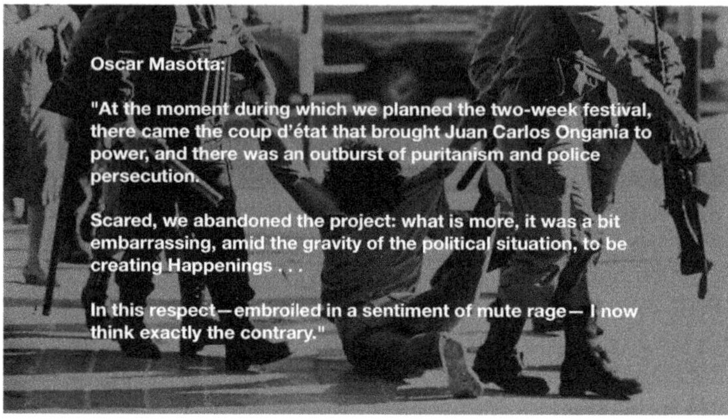

Figure 6.3 Segunda Vez, digital film, 94', 2018. © Dora García.

One of the participating artists was Dora García who had previously inaugurated "her project *Segunda Vez* [*Second time*; 2014–2018] … that uses the figure of Oscar Masotta as the trigger for an investigation on art, politics and psychoanalysis" (Longoni, 2017b, p. 30). García "repeated" Masotta's happenings in different cities and condensed them into a film with an extensive reflection about the im/possibilities of repetition as outlined by authors of different fields such as Freud (in the context of repression in the psychoanalytical sense) or Kaprow (contradicting his advising of the non-repetitiveness of happenings, García, 2018; Figure 6.3).

Relevance for Today

The importance of the thoughts and works of anti- and deinstitutionalizing psychiatrists for the present are both multiple and critical.

Their critiques of psychiatric diagnosis based on mere descriptions of symptoms without regarding people's experience led inevitably to an annulment of subjectivity (see also Jenkins, 2015). This has culminated in the now 5th edition of the Diagnostic and Statistical Manual of Mental Disorders (DSM-5). Different lobbies collaborated on this edition in the form of the pharmaceutical industry, insurance companies, and also journalism occasionally simplifying the public opinion (Hochmann, 2015; Taussig, 1992; Chapter 3). As Szasz had already observed: "The process feeds on itself, transforming more and more human problems and situations into specialized technical 'problems' to be 'solved' by so-called mental-health professional" (Szasz, 1973, p. 505). Nowadays, the commodification of the mental seems to be perfected (Marxen & Greteman, 2019; Dumit, 2012; Horwitz, 2010; Chapter 3).

The present mental health dispositifs are anchored in biologist models and refuse to question their mental disorder categories, accepting them as diseases "and banishing the subjectivity inherent to mental processes" (Montejo Alonso, 2013, p. 1). The affected people are reduced to passive objects of expensive prescription drugs. The human mind and well-being has become "financialized object, constant prey to quantification … and measurement, while diagnostic tools [DSM] and clinical descriptions are increasingly influenced by the pressure to medicalize psychiatry" (Caló, 2019, p. 116).

By contrast, all the aforementioned authors and practitioners of anti-psychiatries did focus on subjectivities. They took mental disease out of the asylum hospital in order to reintegrate it into the community, resignifying it beyond the individualist-biologist discourse.

Unfortunately, some parts of the anti-psychiatries have been co-opted: "Ruminations on 1968 tend to conclude in one of two ways: despairing narratives of recuperation (with a suspicion of spontaneity and emphasis on individualistic life-stylism, libertarian pleasure-seeking and hedonistic soulsearching fully compatible with neoliberalism) or hopeful narratives of prefiguration," the latter giving rise to present and future forms of resistance (Proctor, 2018, p. 13).

In this sense, the collective Stop DSM works from a psychoanalytical perspective and from different countries against the simplification of mental health as manifest by the DSM (https://stop-dsm.com/en/why-should-we-contest-adhd/; see also https://stopdsm.blogspot.com/ with its immense amount of supporting institutions in the Spanish and Portuguese speaking worlds).

While I have been finishing this book, a very welcome surprise caught me one morning, which came by way of email. On September 5, 2019, the Superior Health Council of Belgium had advised against the use of the DSM and urged for a change of paradigm in mental health politics on a governmental level. The authoring working group was composed of "people with backgrounds in psychiatry, lived-experience expertise, psychology, sociology, and philosophy" (Superior Health Council, 2019, p. 5). Most notably, the group critiqued the DSM as it presents

> a number of fundamental problems in terms of epistemology, validity, and reliability. We estimate that the quality of the instrument in its current set-up and form cannot be substantially improved. This inherent problem is often not recognised in institutional and clinical use.
>
> (Superior Health Council, 2019, p. 25)

Of course, this by no way means "a denial of the suffering people experience—only as a refutation of the *system* that's being used to explain that suffering" (Simon, 2019, italics in the original). In this vein, the report (Superior Health Council, 2019) confirms: "Psychological complaints must be dealt with regardless of their seriousness, in a non-medical way, with perspective and meaning at the center" (p. 2). In this vein, they urge "a complete reversal in the way mental health treatment is sought, obtained, and reimbursed. They advise that a mental health diagnosis should not be required for a person to receive help." According to the report, the treatment of mental health issues should include the narrative of the affected person, a contextualization of the person's life experience, a consideration of a "continuum from crisis to recovery" for the specific individual, and a practice of envisioning psychiatric disorders as interactive, in a way that gives justice of the person's struggle with their environment (Simon, 2019; Superior Health Council, 2019).

So, there is an advancement in favor of considering people's experience and subjectivities in relation to the world we live in.

Another lesson we should take from the anti-psychiatrists is their insistence regarding

> the social and psychic conditions that allowed for the rise of the far-right. Unlike in so much contemporary discussion, in the aftermath of 1968 this question was (re)posed not to some vaguely imagined distant demographic but to everyone and was understood as a question that the Left also needed to pose to itself.
>
> (Proctor, 2018, p. 13)

After WWII, Foucault, in his preface to the *Anti-Oedipus* (1972/2009, p. xviii), similarly warned against ongoing fascism:

> In us all, in our heads and in our everyday behavior, the fascism that causes us to love power, to desire the very thing that dominates and exploits us …How does one keep from being fascist, even (especially) when one believes oneself to be a revolutionary militant?

Facing nowadays the raise of fascism we must not forget that subjects are formed by society and its structures but at the same time "society is also formed by subjects whose social formation can obstruct the transformation of society" (Proctor, 2018, p. 13). As already explained in Chapter 3, the arts and artistic practices can re-conduct that obstruction and some artists have done so by leaning on anti-psychiatries, deinstitutionalization, and institutional therapy.

Retrieving the anti-psychiatries should form part of the endeavor to transform society. As a step before, we should reflect on the resistance of society to reclaim this knowledge and detect the agendas behind hegemonic psychiatry and psychology that have either already successfully erased it from the canon or are working profitably to diminish it. Hegemony is threatened by ways of knowing and doing that are linked to different traditions and theories of strongly rooted left-wing thoughts that reinscribed mental trouble within a community practice. At the same time, its followers did not stop to question and to subvert moral habits and the professed established scientific knowledge. In this sense, they unceasingly insisted on the function of the discipline and punish mode of a society that reduces community to an administrative unit or—worse—to competition and struggle for life (Montejo Alonso, 2013).

Following the thoughts of Deleuze and Guattari (1972/2009), it is a question of how the social machine reacts to desiring machines and productions, in how far the macro (molar) positions itself to the molecular (micro) desiring forces. Can the molar withstand the reversal of power by the molecular? Together with Maud Mannoni, they wonder if society can handle the desiring machines coming close to the social, bringing the two into communication? All the mentioned authors in this chapter (and most of the entire book) have in one way or another worked in favor of the desiring machines. Very often, society has reacted with the repression of desire in the form of its bureaucratization, neutralization, commodification or even violence.

The revolutionary force of the desiring machines shocking against the retrogressive nature of the social machine are also possible answers to the question above, regarding why the same few institutions that try to retrieve the Tosquelles' legacy in Catalonia today do not take into consideration the practices that have extended this legacy in the form of the MACBA devices (Figure 6.4).

Within this panorama, it is of special interest that it has been very often the role of contemporary artists to retrieve these powerful, unruly knowledges and desiring machines. Dora García with her series *Mad Marginal*, Ana Longoni and Cloe Masotta curating Oscar Masotta, Maurizio Lazzarato together with Angela Melitopoulos actualizing Tosquelles in their work *Déconnage* (2011) are sophisticated examples. Coming back to the museum of contemporary art, Álvarez de Toledo (2009) stressed its role in this inquiry in the context of MACBA's work on Deligny. The museum as an institution should question itself "about its institutional practices, its political responsibility, its objective of inquiry in an epoch when art is self-indulging in the denial of its history and its anthropological meaning" (p. 5).

Figure 6.4 Dora García, La verità è rivoluzionaria, Trieste, 2009. Photograph, variable dimensions.

Notes

1 With some of my variations of his scheme taken from Double (2006).
2 English translations of Basaglia have been scarce. In the context of the United Kingdom, Foot (2014) contributes this scarcity and the consequent misinterpretation of Basglia and his ideas with a persistent and defensive aversion against anti-psychiatry (collapsing the deinstitutionalization movement indiscriminately into it), as associated with Laing and Cooper. In the United States, Scheper-Hughes, Lovell and Shtob (1987) have edited translated *Selected writings of Franco Basaglia.*
3 Instead of the opposites client-doctor, healthy-ill, sane-insane, they use people with or without experience in psychiatry. The former obviously include psychiatrists, nurses, therapists, staff, and patients.
4 Before fascism, Trieste was a town with prolific intellectual life that also embraced psychoanalysis and psychoanalysts. Many of the latter were Jewish and either killed or destined to flee. Their exile contributed to the extremely sophisticated psychoanalytic scene in Argentina and Brazil (García, 2018).
5 See for more works her website http://www.doragarcia.net/; especially the *Inadequate* section (http://theinadequate.doragarcia.org/) with material to download such as her books *Mad Marginal Cahier #1. From Basaglia to Brazil* (2010) and *Mad Marginal Cahier #2. The Inadequate* (2011b) with highly interesting texts and artworks by different authors about non hegemonic knowledge about psychiatry, the mental, stigma, and creativity (also García, 2018, the book-catalogue of her retrospective show).
6 Although she did not completely reject pharmaceuticals, she had the same opinion of them regarding only diminishing symptoms instead of curing them (da Silveira, 1992).
7 For the difference of the perception of the art of the mentally ill between Europe and Brazil (see Cabañas, 2018).
8 The quotes refer to the English translation of the German original *Turn Illness into a Weapon*, retrieved from https://www.indybay.org/uploads/2013/11/14/turn_illness_into_a_weapon.pdf. The translation is anonymous. I have corroborated the correctness of the translation for the present quotations.
9 The German town Wiesloch was one of the most perverted places of Nazi psychiatry and "medicine."
10 Within this current, some preferred the term "institutional therapeutic" or "institutional psychoanalysis," mainly because of their aversion against "psychotherapy" (Tosquelles in Angosto, 1993, p. 43/205).
11 Among the different sectors of institutional therapy, there was a divergence whether it was really the entire institution or yet only team member with their special qualifications, that is to say their own psychoanalysis and training (Hochmann, 2015).
12 For a highly interesting, political, and social approach of puppet therapy working on political oppression and trauma see the Chilean group Puppets in Transit, Muñecoterapia [Puppet therapy]: http://www.munecoterapia.cl.
13 It also happened elsewhere, like in the Frankfurt School with Marcuse and Fromm (Robcis, 2016).
14 See for spaces of listening in medical anthropology Jenkins (2015).
15 This method coincides significantly with the one developed at the UEC in Barcelona (Chapter 2).
16 Emphasizing the healthy part instead of pathologizing adolescents with challenging behaviors was also Winnicott's objective almost during the same time period. This consideration lay also at the core of the MACBA art therapy practice (Chapter 2).

17 He had the same aversion against the term normalization like Foucault.
18 In Lacanian terms, the void is the real that is impossible to symbolize (see above; Dorenbaum, 2018; Marxen, 2011; Evans, 1996, pp. 163–164; Lacan, 1974–1975; 1975–1976).
19 Worth to mention in this context is Jaspers' book *General Psychopathology* (1913/1997).
20 This phenomenological foundation is crucial for many medical anthropologists as outlined in Chapter 3. It can also be read as a definition of subjectivity as always in interconnection with others, a leitmotiv of this book, especially explained in Chapter 4 (also Jenkins, 2015).
21 The word "Philadelphia" was used in its etymological sense of "fraternity" (Mannoni, 1973, p. 496).
22 See again for the importance of spaces of listening in medical anthropology Jenkins (2015).
23 Together with Wilhelm Reich, Herbert Marcuse focused on sexual repression within the mutual constitution of subject and society. Both claimed for sexual liberation. Yet, they diverged in the way to achieve this: "Marcuse pictures a kind of gentle contentment quietly infused into every moment [allowing for lasting pleasure] whereas Reich imagines something closer to a permanent ecstatic orgasmic delirium" (Proctor, 2018, p. 8; Marcuse, 1968; Reich, 1931/1975).
24 In this sense, his work was ethnocentric.
25 *The Presentation of Self in Everyday Life* (1959) is Goffman's relevant book about roles. It microsociologically analyzes daily life and how people act in it. He exclusively uses theater language for this purpose.
26 In this sense, the application of the medical model on the psychiatric hospital is a "false semblance" in Lacanian terms (*faux-semblant*, Evans, 1996). It is like a fake guise, something that is taken mistakenly as similar. Yet, psychiatry only deals with irregularities instead of regularities. The alleged regularities in diagnosis (as presumed in the DSM) are fictional. "The supposed homogeneity of psychiatric troubles is a fabrication of the hospital" (Hochmann, 2015, p. 162).
27 The other three founded the Media Art Group. Although short in life, the group members continued to work in this vein individually or with other collectives, like Jacoby who was one of the principals in the Tucumán Arde group in 1968 (Longoni & Mestman, 2010).
28 His weekly Lacanian reading and psychoanalytical interventions, including the foundational act of a school that would legitimize him in the psychoanalytical terrain, have even been compared to his way of understanding, carrying out, and conceptualizing happenings (Hernández, 2017).
29 The controversies within the institution of psychoanalysis included the fact that he had not finished his own psychoanalysis with the culminating "Pass" (passing over from analysand to analyst). This had given place to polemics and suspicion by other psychoanalysts, in Argentina and abroad. The lack of institutional credentials in all the fields he moved (philosophy, literary critique, art, psychoanalysis) and the relevant challenges had been a leitmotiv in his life.

References

Abraham, K. (1953). *Selected papers*. New York, NY: Basic Books.

Agamben, G. (1998). The camp as the 'Nomos' of the modern. In G. Agamben, *Homo Sacer. Sovereign power and bare life* (pp. 95–99). Stanford, CA: University Press Stanford California.

Álvarez de Toledo, S. (2009). Introducción [Introduction]. In S. Álvarez de Toledo (Ed.), *Permitir, trazar, ver* [To allow, to trace, to see] (pp. 5–13). Barcelona, Spain: MACBA.

Angosto, T. (1993). Entrevista al Dr. Francisco Tosquelles [Interview with Dr. Tosquelles]. *Revista Asociación Española de Neuropsiquiatría* [Journal of the Spanish Association of Neuropsychiatry], XIII(46), 203–210.

Baldiz, M. (2017). La anti-psiquiatría [Anti-psychiatry]. *Ajoblanco*, 1, 78–80.

Barnes, M., & Berke, J. (1972). *Mary Barnes: Two accounts of a journey through madness*. San Diego, CA: Harcourt Brace Jovanovich.

Basaglia, F., & Basaglia, F. (1971/2014). *La maggioranza deviante* [The deviant majority]. Milan, Italy: Baldini & Castoldi. (Original work published 1971)

Basaglia, F. (1968/2013). *L'instituzione negata* [The negated institution]. Milan, Italy: Baldini & Castoldi. (Original work published 1968)

Basaglia, F., Scheper-Hughes, N., Lovell, A.M., & Shtob, T. (Eds.). (1987). *Psychiatry inside out: Selected writings of Franco Basaglia*. New York, NY: Columbia University Press.

Bateson, G. (1972). *Steps to an ecology of mind: Collected essays in anthropology, psychiatry, evolution, and epistemology*. Chicago, IL: University of Chicago Press.

Becker, H. (1963/1997). *Outsiders: Studies in the sociology of deviance*. New York, NY: The Free Press.

Beard, D. (2018). Entre la institución y la acampada [Between the institution and camping]. In D. García (Ed.), *Segunda vez. Que siempre es la primera* [Second time. That is always the first] (exh. cat.) (pp. 80–93). Madrid, Spain: MNCARS.

Bergalli, R. (1980). Origen de las teorías de la reacción social. Un aporte al análisis y crítica del labelling approach [Origin of the theories of social reaction. A contribution to the analysis and critique of the labelling approach]. *Papers: Revista de Sociologia* [Papers: Journal of Sociology], 13, 49–96.

Bhabha, H. (1994). Remembering Fanon: Self, psyche and the colonial condition. In P. Williams, & L. Chrisman (Eds.), *Colonial discourse and post-colonial theory. A reader* (pp. 112–123). New York, NY: Columbia University Press.

Borja-Villel, M.J., & Enguita, N. (1998). (Eds.). *Lygia Clark* (exh. cat.). Barcelona, Spain: Fundació Antoni Tàpies.

Brion, F., & Harcourt, B.E. (2014). The Louvain lectures in context. In M. Foucault, *Truth telling, wrong doing* (pp. 271–321). Chicago, IL: University of Chicago Press.

Cabañas, K. (2018). *Learning from madness. Brazilian modernism and global contemporary art*. Chicago, IL: University of Chicago Press.

Carmichael, S., Cooper, D., Laing, R.D., & Marcuse, H. (2015). *The dialectics of liberation*. London, UK: Verso.

Carrington, L. (1988/2017). *Down below*. New York, NY: New York Review Books.

Caló, S. (2019). 'Can an institution be militant?' In Prospections (Ed.), *Metabolic rifts. A reader* (pp. 115–131). Lisbon, Portugal and Berlin, Germany: Atlas Projectos.

Caló, S. (2011). Félix Guattari and the collective in La Borde - Notes for a conception of subjectivity beyond the human. In G. Vaz Pinheiro (Ed.), *(Des)locações / (Dis)locations* (pp. 80–88). Porto, Portugal: FBAUP.

Chapman, A. (2016). Re-Coopering anti-psychiatry: David Cooper, revolutionary critic of psychiatry. *Critical and Radical Social Work*, 4(3), 421–432.

Chiche, S. (2014). La psychothérapie institutionnelle de Jean Oury [The institutional psychotherapy of Jean Oury]. *Le Cercle-Psy* [The Psych-Circle]. Retrieved from: https://le-cercle-psy.scienceshumaines.com/impressionarticle/32472 [Accessed 22 October 2019].

Comelles, J.M. (2010). Forgotten paths: Culture and ethnicity in Catalan mental health policies (1900–39). *History of Psychiatry*, 21(4), 1–18.

Cooper, D. (2015). Beyond words. In S. Carmichael, D. Cooper, R.D. Laing, R.D., & H. Marcuse (Eds.), *The dialectics of liberation* (pp. 193–202). London, UK: Verso.

Cooper, D. (1970). *The death of the family*. New York, NY: Pantheon.

Cooper, D. (1967/2013). *Psychiatry and anti-psychiatry*. New York, NY: Routledge. (Original work published 1967)

Da Silveira, N. (2004). El mundo de las imágenes [The world of images]. In N. da Silveira (Ed.), *Imágenes del inconsciente* [Images of the unconsciousness] (pp. 10–20). Buenos Aires, Argentina: Fundación Proa.

Da Silveira, N. (1992). *O mundo das imagens* [The world of images]. São Paulo, Brazil: Ática.

Daumézon, G., & Koechlin, P. (1952). La psychothérapie institutionnelle française contemporaine [French contemporary institutional psychotherapy]. *Anais portugueses de psiquiatria* [Annals of Portuguese psychiatry], 4(4), 271–312.

Deleuze, G., & Guattari, F. (1972/2009). *Anti-Oedipus. Capitalism and schizophrenia*. London, UK: Penguin Books. (Original work published 1972)

Deligny, F. (2009) *Permitir, trazar, ver* [To allow, to trace, to see]. Barcelona, Spain: MACBA.

Dorenbaum, D. (2018). El lugar de la palabra en el trabajo de Dora García [The place of the word in Dora García's work]. In D. García (Ed.), *Segunda vez. Que siempre es la primera* [Second time. That is always the first] (exh. cat.) (pp. 62–73). Madrid, Spain: MNCARS.

Dörner, K. (1969/1995). *Bürger und Irre. Zur Sozialgeschichte und Wissenschaftsgeschichte der Psychiatrie* [Citizens and mad people. About social and scientific history of psychiatry]. Frankfurt, Germany: Europäische Verlagsanstalt.

Double, D.B. (2006). Historical perspectives on anti-psychiatry. In D.B. Double (Ed.), *Critical psychiatry: The limits of madness* (pp. 19–39). London, UK: Palgrave-Macmillan.

Dumit, J. (2012). *Drugs for life. How pharmaceutical companies define our health*. Durham, NC: Duke University Press.

Éluard, P. (1946/2012). *Souvenirs de la maison des fous* [Souvenirs from the madhouse]. Paris, France: Seghers.

Esterson, A., & Laing, R.D. (1964). *Sanity, madness and the family*. London, UK: Tavistock.

Evans, D. (1996). *An introductory dictionary of Lacanian psychoanalysis*. New York, NY: Routledge.

Fanon, F. (2008). *Black skin, white masks*. London, UK: Pluto Press.

Fanon, F. (1991). *The wretched of the earth. The handbook of the black revolution that is changing the shape of the world*. New York, NY: Grove Weidenfeld.

Faramelli, A. (2017). The decolonised clinic: Fanon with Foucault. *London Journal of Critical Thought*, v1(2). Retrieved from: https://www.academia.edu/34099969/The_Decolonised_Clinic_Fanon_with_Foucault [Accessed 22 October 2019].

Fernández Polanco, A., & Pradel, A. (2015). A conversation with Suely Rolnik. *Re-visiones*, #5. Retrieved from: http://www.re-visiones.net/index.php/RE-VISIONES/article/view/50 [Accessed 19 September 2019].
Fiorini, H.J. (2010). *The creating psyche: Theory and practice of tertiary processes*. Vitoria-Gasteiz, Spain: Agruparte.
Foot, J. (2015a). Taking over the asylum: Critical psychiatry, Franco Basaglia and social struggle. *Verso Blog*. Retrieved from: https://www.versobooks.com/blogs/2271-taking-over-the-asylum-critical-psychiatry-franco-basaglia-and-social-struggle-by-john-foot [Accessed 22 October 2019].
Foot, J. (2015b). *The man who closed the asylums. Franco Basaglia and the revolution in mental health care*. London, UK: Verso.
Foot, J. (2014). Franco Basaglia and the radical psychiatry movement in Italy, 1961–78. *Critical and Radical Social Work*, 2(2), 235–249. doi: 10.1332/20498601 4X14002292074708.
Foster, Hal. 2000. No man's land: On the modernist reception of the art of the insane. In C. de Zegher (Ed.), *The Prinzhorn Collection: Traces upon the Wunderblock* (pp. 9–24). New York, NY: The Drawing Center.
Foucault, M. (1997). The birth of biopolitics. In P. Rabinow (Ed.), *Ethics, subjectivity and truth* (pp. 173–179). New York, NY: The New Press.
Foucault, M. (1972/2009). Preface. In G. Deleuze, & F. Guattari, *Anti-Oedipus. Capitalism and schizophrenia* (pp. xi–xiv). London, UK: Penguin Books. (Original work published 1972)
Foucault, M. (1994). *The birth of the clinic*. New York, NY: Vintage Books.
Foucault, M. (1983). The subject and power. In H. Dreyfus, & P. Rabinov (Eds.), *Michel Foucault: Beyond structuralism and hermeneutics* (pp. 208–226). Chicago, IL: University of Chicago Press.
Foucault, M. (1978). *The history of sexuality. Volume I: An introduction*. New York, NY: Random House.
Foucault, M. (1975). *Discipline and punish: The birth of the prison*. New York, NY: Random House.
Foucault, M. (1961/2006). *History of madness*. New York, NY: Routledge.
Fusar-Poli, P., Bruno, D. Machado-de Sousa, J.P., & Crippa, J. (2009). Franco Basaglia (1924–1980): Three decades (1979–2009) as a bridge between the Italian and Brazilian mental health reform. *International Journal of Social Psychiatry*, 57(1), 100–103. doi: 10.1177/0020764009344145.
García, D. (2018). *Segunda vez. Que siempre es la primera* [Second time. That is always the first] (exh. cat.). Madrid, Spain: MNCARS.
García, D. (2011a). *The world according to Dora García*. Berlin, Germany: Argobooks.
García, D. (2011b). *Mad Marginal. Cahier #2. L'inadeguato. Lo inadecuado. The inadequate*. Berlin, Germany: Sternberg Press; Trieste, Italy: Fondazione Galleria Civica di Trento and Mousse Publishing.
García, D. (2010). *Mad Marginal Cahier #1. From Basaglia to Brazil*. Berlin, Germany: Sternberg Press; Trieste, Italy: Fondazione Galleria Civica di Trento and Mousse Publishing.
Goffman, E. (1969). The insanity of place. *Psychiatry*, 32(4), 357–388.
Goffman, E. (1961). *Asylums. Essays on the social situation of mental patients and other inmates*. New York, NY: Anchor Books/Random House.
Goffman, E. (1959). *The Presentation of self in everyday life*. New York, NY: Double Day Publisher.

Gordon, L. (2015). *What Fanon said: A philosophical introduction to his life and thought.* New York, NY: Fordham University Press.

Gordon, P. (2009). RD Laing in context. *The Psychotherapist.* UKCP. 43, 10–12.

Guattari, F. (2015). *Psychoanalysis and transversality.* New York, NY: Semiotext(e).

Guattari, F., & Negri, T. (2010). *New lines of alliance, new spaces of liberty.* Brooklyn, NY: Autonomedia.

Guattari, F., & Negri, T. (1996). *Las verdades nómadas* [Nomadic truths]. Irun, Spain: Iralka.

Guattari, F., & Rolnik, S. (2007). *Molecular revolution in Brazil.* New York, NY: Semiotext(e).

Hernández, M. (2017). Masotta's dilemma. In MUAC (Ed.), *Oscar Masotta. Theory as action* (exh. cat.) (pp. 216–324). Mexico City, Mexico: MUAC, UNAM.

Hochmann, J. (2015). *Les antipsychiatres. Une histoire* [The anti-psychiatrists. A history]. Paris, France: Odile Jacob.

Horwitz, A.V. (2010). Pharmaceuticals and the medicalization of social life. In D.W. Light (Ed.), *The risks of prescription drugs* (pp. 92–115). New York, NY: Columbia University Press.

Jacoby, R. (1967). Contra el happening [Against the happening]. In O. Masotta (Ed.), *Happenings* (pp. 123–133). Buenos Aires, Argentina: Jorge Alvarez Ed. (reedited by Corregidor Ed., 1990).

Jaspers, K. (1913/1997). *General psychopathology.* Baltimore, MD: Johns Hopkins University Press. (Original work published 1913)

Jenkins, J.H. (2015). *Extraordinary conditions. Culture and experience in mental illness.* Oakland, CA: The University of California Press.

Johnes, L. (2010). *Désaliénisme à l'hôpital psychiatrique de Saint-Alban-sur-Limagnole: L'accueil de la folie dans un hôpital public de Lozère de la fin de la deuxième guerre mondiale au début des années 1970* [Dealienism at the psychiatric hospital of Saint-Alban-sur-Limagnole: The reception of madness in a public hospital in Lozère from the end of the Second World War to the early 1970s]. Montpellier, France: Université de Lettres Paul Valéry.

Jones, M. (1952). *Social psychiatry.* London, UK: Tavistock.

Klein, J.P. (1997). *Que sais-je? L'art-thérapie* [What do I know? Art therapy]. Paris, France: PUF.

Klein, M. (1932). The psycho-analysis of children. *The International Psycho-Analytical Library*, 22, 1–379. London, UK: The Hogarth Press.

Klein, M. (1961). Narrative of a child analysis. *The International Psycho-Analytical Library*, 55, 1–536. London, UK: The Hogarth Press.

Kleinman, A. (1991a). What is a psychiatric diagnosis? In A. Kleinman, *Rethinking psychiatry: From cultural category to personal experience* (pp. 5–17). New York, NY: Simon and Schuster.

Kleinman, A. (1991b). Do psychiatric disorders differ in different cultures? The findings. In A. Kleinman, *Rethinking psychiatry: From cultural category to personal experience* (pp. 34–52). New York, NY: Simon and Schuster.

Kramer, E. (1998). *Childhood and art therapy: Notes on theory and application.* Chicago, IL: Magnolia Street Publishers.

Kramer, E. (1993). *Art as therapy with children.* Chicago, IL: Magnolia Street Publishers.

Kramer, E. (1958). *Art therapy in a children's community.* Springfield, IL: Charles C. Thomas Publisher.

Lacan, J.J. (1974–1975). *The Seminar. Book XXII. R:S:I.* Unofficial translation. Retrieved from: http://www.lacaninireland.com/web/wp-content/uploads/2010/06/RSI-Complete-With-Diagrams.pdf [Accessed 22 October 2019].

Lacan, J.J. (1975–1976). *Seminario 23. El sinthome* [Seminar 23. The *Sinthome*]. Buenos Aires, Argentina: Paidós.

Lacan, J.J. (1977). *The Seminar. Book XI. The four fundamental concepts of psychoanalysis.* London, UK: Hogarth Press and Institute of Psycho-Analysis.

Lafont, M. (1987). *L'extermination douce: La mort de 40000 malades mentaux dans les hôpitaux psychiatriques en France, sous le régime de Vichy* [Soft extermination: The death of 40,000 mentally ill people in psychiatric hospitals in France, under the Vichy regime]. Ligné, France: Editions de l'Arefppi.

Laing, R.D. (1969/1990). *Self and others.* London, UK: Penguin.

Laing, R.D. (1967). *The politics of experience.* Harmondsworth, UK: Penguin.

Laing, R.D. (1959/1990). *The divided self.* London, UK: Penguin.

Lippard, L., & Chandler, J. (1968). The dematerialization of art. *Art International,* 12(2), 31–36.

Longoni, A. (Ed.). (2017a). *Oscar Masotta. Revolución en el arte* [Oscar Masotta. Revolution in the art]. Buenos Aires, Argentina: Mansalva.

Lippard, L. (1973). *Six years: The dematerialization of the art object from 1966 to 1972.* New York, NY: Praeger.

Longoni, A. (2017b). Masotta and his specters. In MUAC (Ed.), *Oscar Masotta. Theory as action* (exh. cat.) (pp. 24–36). Mexico City, Mexico: MUAC, UNAM.

Longoni, A., & Mestman, M. (2010). *Del Di Tella a Tucumán Arde - Vanguardia artística y política en el 68 argentino* [From Di Tella to Tucumán Arde – Artistic avant-garde and politics of the Argentinian '68]. Buenos Aires, Argentina: Eudeba.

Longoni, A., & Mestman, M. (2004). After Pop, we dematerialize: Oscar Masotta, happenings, and media art at the beginnings of conceptualism. In I. Katzenstein (Ed.), *Listen here now! Argentine art of the 1960s: Writings of the avant-garde* (exh. cat.) (pp. 156–172). New York, NY: The Museum of Modern Art.

Maclagan, D. (1997). Has 'psychotic art' become extinct? In K. Killick, & J. Schaverien (Eds.), *Art, psychotherapy and psychosis* (pp. 131–143). London, UK: Routledge.

MacCallum Sullivan, M. (2009). RD Laing and his legacy: The wholeness of being human. *The Psychotherapist.* UKCP. 43, 7–9.

Magaldi, F. (2018). Psyche meets matter: Body and personhood in the medical-scientific project of Nise da Silveira. *História, Ciências, Saúde – Manguinhos* [History, science, health – Manguinhos], 25(1), 1–20. Retrieved from: http://www.scielo.br/pdf/hcsm/v25n1/en_0104-5970-hcsm-25-01-0069.pdf [Accessed 22 October 2019].

Mannoni, M. (1999). *Separation and creativity: Refinding the lost language of childhood.* New York, NY: Other Press.

Mannoni, M. (1998). *Ellas no saben lo que dicen* [Women don't know what they are saying]. Madrid, Spain: Alianza.

Mannoni, M. (1987). *The child, his illness and the others.* New York, NY: Routledge.

Mannoni, M. (1986). *Bonneuil, seize ans après* [Bonneuil, sixteen years after]. Paris, France: Denoël.

Mannoni, M. (1979). *Le psychiatre, son fou et la psychanalyse* [The psychiatrist, their mad person, and psychoanalysis]. Paris, France: Seuil.

Mannoni, M. (1976). *Un lieu pour vivre: Les enfants de Bonneuil, leurs parents et l'équipe des 'soignants'* [A place to live: The children of Bonneuil, their parents, and the team of 'caregivers']. Paris, France: Seuil.
Mannoni, M. (1964/1972). *The backward child and his mother: A psychoanalytic study.* New York, NY: Pantheon Books. (Original work published 1964)
Mannoni, O. (1973). The anti-psychiatric movement(s). *International Social Science Journal*, XXV(4), 489–503.
Marcuse, H. (1968). *One-dimensional man.* Boston, MA: Beacon Book.
Marcuse, H. (1955). *Eros and civilization.* Boston, MA: Beacon Books.
Marxen, E. (2014). Art as a bridge for phenomenological isolation. In VV.AA. (Eds.), *Parallel worlds* (pp. 67–74). Cracow, Poland: University of Cracow, Art Faculty; Association of Art and Psychiatry; Ethnographic Museum Seweryn Udziela.
Marxen, E. (2011). *Diálogos entre arte y terapia. Del 'arte psicótico' al desarrollo de la arteterapia y sus aplicaciones* [Dialogues between art and therapy. From 'psychotic art' to the development of art therapy and its applications]. Barcelona, Spain: Gedisa.
Marxen, E. (2009). Therapeutic thinking in contemporary art. Psychotherapy in the arts. *The Arts in Psychotherapy*, 36, 140–147. doi: 10.1016/j.aip.2008.10.004
Marxen, E., & Greteman, A. (2019). Ingesting power. *RECIE. Electronic Cientific Review of Educational Research*, 4(2), 875–886.
Masotta, O. (2017). Robert Arlt, myself. In MUAC (Ed.), *Oscar Masotta. Theory as action* (exh. cat.) (pp. 170–186). Mexico City, Mexico: MUAC, UNAM.
Masotta, O. (1970). *La historieta en el mundo moderno* [Cartoon in the modern world]. Buenos Aires, Argentina: Paidós.
Masotta, O. (Ed.). (1968/1990). *Consciencia y estructura* [Consciousness and structure]. Buenos Aires, Argentina: Jorge Álvarez Ed. (reedited by Corregidor Ed., 1990).
Masotta, O. (1968). Después del pop: Nosotros desmaterializamos [After Pop, we dematerialize]. In O. Masotta (Ed.), *Consciencia y estructura* (pp. 218–244). Buenos Aires, Argentina: Editorial Jorge Álvarez Ed. (reedited by Corregidor Ed., 1990).
Masotta, O. (1967a). *El pop art.* Buenos Aires, Argentina: Columba.
Masotta, O. (Ed.). (1967b). *Happenings.* Buenos Aires, Argentina: Jorge Álvarez Ed. (reedited by Corregidor Ed., 1990).
Mello, L.C. (2004). Flores del abismo [Chasm flowers]. In N. da Silveira, *Imágenes del inconsciente* [Images of the unconsciousness] (pp. 21–38). Buenos Aires, Argentina: Fundación Proa.
Metzl, J.M. (2009). *Protest psychosis. How schizophrenia became a black disease.* Boston, MA: Beacon.
Meyers, T. (2014). Jean Oury and Clinique de la Borde: A conversation with Camille Robcis. *Somatosphere.* Retrieved from: http://somatosphere.net/2014/06/jean-oury-and-clinique-de-la-borde-a-conversation-with-camille-robcis.html [Accessed 22 October 2019].
Mezzina, R. (2014). Community mental health in Trieste and beyond. *The Journal of Nervous and Mental Disease*, 202(6), 440–445.
Mezzina, R., & Vidoni, D. (1995). Beyond the mental hospital: Crisis intervention and continuity of care in Trieste. A four year follow-up study in a community mental health centre. *The International Journal of Social Psychiatry*, 41(1), 1–20.

Mieli, P. (2015). Normality and segregation in Primo Levi's sleeping beauty in the fridge. In P. Gherovici, & M. Steinkoler (Eds.), *Lacan on madness: Yes you can't* (pp. 219–233). New York, NY: Routledge.
Montejo Alonso, F.J. (2013). En un lugar de la Mancha... Francesc Tosquelles y Max Hodnan, creadores de las primeras comunidades terapéuticas durante la guerra civil española [A place in La Mancha ... Francesc Tosquelles and Max Hodnan, creators of the first therapeutic communities during the Spanish Civil War]. *XIV Congreso Virtual de Psiquiatria.com. Interpsiquis 2013* [XIV Virtual Congress of Psiquiatria.com. Interpsiquis 2013]. Retrieved from: https://psiquiatria.com/bibliopsiquis/en-un-lugar-de-la-mancha-francesc-tosquelles-y-max-hodann-creadores-de-las-primeras-comunidades-terapeuticas-durante-la-guerra-civil-espanola [Accessed 21 October 2019].
Nasio, J.D. (2000). *Los más famosos casos de psicosis* [The most famous cases of psychosis]. Barcelona, Spain: Paidós.
Naumburg, M. (1980). Art therapy: Its scope and function. In E.F. Hammer (Ed.), *The clinical application of projective drawings* (pp. 509–517). Springfield, IL: Charles C. Thomas Publisher.
Negri, T. (2017). *Marx and Foucault*. Malden, MA: Polity Press.
Oury, J. (2001). *Psychiatrie et psychothérapie institutionnelle* [Psychiatry and institutional psychotherapy]. Lecques, France: Les éditions du Champ social.
Oury, J. (1986). *Le collectif – Le séminaire de Sainte-Anne* [The collective – The Sainte Anne seminar]. Lecques, France: Les éditions du Champ social.
Oury, J. (1967). Architecture et psychiatrie [Architecture and psychiatry]. *Recherches. Programmation, architecture et psychiatrie* [Research. Programming, architecture, and psychiatry], 6, 271–301.
Oury, J., Guattari, F., & Tosquelles, F. (1985). Pratique de l'Institutionnel et Politique [Practice of the institutional and political]. Vigneux, France: Matrice Editions.
Passos, E. (2011). Eduardo Passos. In D. García (Ed.), *The world according to Dora García* (pp. 45–50). Berlin, Germany: Argobooks.
Periáñez, M. (1997). El origen de las ideas de Francesc Tosquelles [The origin of Francesc Tosquelles' ideas]. Personal blog. Retrieved from: http://mpzga.free.fr/tosqesp.htm [Accessed 22 October 2019].
Planella, J. (2015). Introducción [Introduction]. In J. Planella (Ed.), *Fernand Deligny. Los vagabundos eficaces* [Fernand Deligny. The effective tramps] (pp. 9–41). Barcelona, Spain: UOC.
Portacolone, E., Segal, S.P., Mezzina, R., Scheper-Hughes, N., & Okin, R.L. (2015). A tale of two cities: The exploration of the Trieste public psychiatry model in San Francisco. *Culture, Medicine, and Psychiatry*, 39(4), 680–697.
Prinzhorn, H. (1972). *Artistery of the mentally ill*. New York, NY Springer.
Proctor, H. (2018). Mad world: Radical psychiatry and 1968. *Verso Blog*. Retrieved from: https://www.versobooks.com/blogs/3888-mad-world-radical-psychiatry-and-1968 [Accessed 22 October 2019].
Reich, W. (1931/1975). *The invasion of compulsory sex-morality*. London, UK: Penguin. (Original work published 1931)
Rhodes, C. (1994). *Primitivism and modern art*. London, UK: Thames & Hudson.
Robcis, C. (2016). François Tosquelles and the psychiatric revolution in postwar France. *Constellations*, 23(2), 212–222. doi: 10.1111/1467–8675.12223

Rodríguez, M. (2015). *Esquizofrenias y otros hechos de lenguaje. De la clínica analítica del MACBA (2002–2013)* [Schizophrenia and other facts of language. About the analytical MACBA clinic (2002–2013)]. Madrid, Spain: Brumaria.

Roll. C. (2011). Carmen Roll. In D. García (Ed.), *The world according to Dora García* (pp. 6–15). Berlin, Germany: Argobooks.

Rolnik, S. (1999). Molding a contemporary soul: The empty-full of Lygia Clark. In S. Martin, & A. Ruiz (Eds.), *The experimental exercise of freedom: Lygia Clark, Gego, Mathias Goeritz, Hélio Oiticica, and Mira Schendel* (exh. cat.) (pp. 57–105). Los Angeles, CA: Museum of Contemporary Art.

Rolnik, S. (1998). The hybrid of Lygia Clark. In M.J. Borja-Villel, & N. Enguita (Eds.), *Lygia Clark* (exh. cat.) (pp. 341–348). Barcelona, Spain: Fundació Antoni Tàpies.

Rome, H.P. (1968). Psychiatry and foreign affairs: The expanding competence of psychiatry. *American Journal of Psychiatry*, 125, 725–730.

Rosenberg, A. (2004). Acerca de imágenes del inconsciente [About the images of the unconsciousness]. In N. da Silveira, *Imágenes del inconsciente* [Images of the unconsciousness] (pp. 8–9). Buenos Aires, Argentina: Fundación Proa.

Rosenhahn, D. (1973). On being sane in insane places. *Science*, 179 (70), 250–258.

Rotelli (2011). Rotelli. In D. García (Ed.), *The world according to Dora García* (pp. 17–22). Berlin, Germany: Argobooks.

Sajnani, N., Marxen, E., & Zarate, R. (2017). Critical perspectives in the arts therapies: Response/ability across a continuum of practice. *The Arts in Psychotherapy*, 54, 28–37. doi: 10.1016/j.aip.2017.01.007.

Sartre, J.P. (1960/2004). *The critique of the dialectical reason*. London, UK: Verso.

Sartre, J.P. (1972/2013). Foreword. In SPK (Sozialistisches Patienten Kollektiv), *Aus Krankheit eine Waffe machen*. Munich, Germany: TriKont-Verlag. (Unofficial translation into English: Anonymous [2013]. Turn illness into a weapon (pp. vii–x). Retrieved from: https://www.indybay.org/uploads/2013/11/14/turn_illness_into_a_weapon.pdf [Accessed 22 October 2019].

Scabia, G. (1976/1979). *Marco Cavallo. Un' esperienza di animazione in un ospedale psichiatrico* [Marco Cavallo. An animation experience in a psychiatric hospital]. Turin, Italy: Einaudi [German edition: Das große Theater des Marco Cavallo. Phantasiearbeit in der Psychiatrischen Klinik Triest. Vorwort von Franco Basaglia. Frankfurt on the Main, Germany: Suhrkamp 1979].

Schaverien, J. (1997). Transference and transitional objects in the treatment of psychosis. In K. Killick & J. Schaverien (Eds.), *Art, psychotherapy and psychosis* (pp. 13–37). London, UK: Routledge.

Schwarz, J. (2015). Cavallo, Marco. Sculpture symbolising the psychiatric reform in Italy. In *Biographisches Archiv der Psychiatrie* [Biographic Archive of Psychiatry]. Retrieved from: biapsy.de/index.php/en/9-biographien-a-z/151-cavallo-marco-e [Accessed 22 October 2019].

Simon, P. (2019). Belgian guidelines recommend 'DSM categories not be at the centre of care planning.' *Mad in America. Science, psychiatry and social justice*. Retrieved from: https://www.madinamerica.com/2019/09/belgian-guidelines-recommend-dsm-categories-not-centre-care-planning/ [Accessed 23 October 2019].

SPK (Sozialistisches Patienten Kollektiv). (1972/2013). *Aus Krankheit eine Waffe machen*. Munich, Germany: TriKont-Verlag. (Unofficial translation into English: Anonymous [2013]. Turn illness into a weapon. Retrieved from: https://

www.indybay.org/uploads/2013/11/14/turn_illness_into_a_weapon.pdf [Accessed 22 October 2019].

Superior Health Council. (2019). *DSM (5): The use and status of diagnosis and classification of mental health problems*. Brussels, Belgium: SHC. Report 9360. Retrieved from: https://www.health.belgium.be/sites/default/files/uploads/fields/fpshealth_theme_file/shc_9360_dsm5.pdf [Accessed 23 October 2019].

Szasz, T. (1991). *Ideology and insanity: Essays on the psychiatric dehumanization of man*. Syracuse, NY: Syracuse University Press.

Szasz, T. (1987). *My madness saved me: The madness and marriage of Virginia Woolf*. New York, NY: Routledge.

Szasz, T. (1973). Ideology and insanity. *International Social Science Journal*, XXV(4), 504–511.

Szasz, T. (1970). *The manufacture of madness*. Syracuse, NY: Syracuse University Press.

Szasz, T. (1965). *The ethics of psychoanalysis*. Syracuse, NY: Syracuse University Press.

Szasz, T. (1961). *The myth of mental illness*. New York, NY: Harper.

Taussig, M. (1992). Reification and the consciousness of the patient. In M. Taussig, *The nervous system* (pp. 83–109). New York, NY: Routledge.

Terán, O. (1991). La leyenda [The legend]. *La Mirada*, II(3).

Thys, E. (2015). *Psychogenocide. Psychiatrie, kunst en massamoord onder de nazi's* [Psychogenocide. Psychiatry, art, and mass murder under the Nazis]. Antwerpen, Belgium: EPO.

Tosquelles, F. (2014). *L'enseignement de la folie* [Teaching of madness]. Paris, France: Dunod.

Tosquelles, F. (2003). *Fonction poétique et psychothérapie* [Poetic function and psychotherapy]. Ramonville Saint-Agne, France: Ed. Erès.

Tosquelles, F. (2001). Préface [Preface]. In J. Oury, *Psychiatrie et psychothérapie institutionnelle* [Psychiatry and institutional psychotherapy] (pp. 11–20). Lecques, France: Les éditions du Champ social.

Tosquelles, F. (1972). La pràctica del maternatge terapèutic en els deficients mentals profunds [The practice of therapeutic mothering with profound mentally disabled]. Barcelona, Spain: Nova Terra.

Turkle, S. (1992). *Psychoanalytic politics: Jacques Lacan and Freud's French revolution*. London, UK: Free Association Books.

von Bueltzingsloewen, I. (2007). *L'hécatombe des fous: la famine dans les hôpitaux psychiatriques français sous l'occupation* [The carnage of the mad: Famine in French psychiatric hospitals under occupation]. Paris, France: Aubier.

Wadeson, H. (1980). *Art psychotherapy*. New York, NY: John Wiley & Sons.

Winnicott, D. (1958). *Through paediatrics to psychoanalysis*. London, UK: Tavistock.

Woolf, V. (1928/2005). *Orlando*. New York, NY: Harvest Books. (Original work published 1928)

Index

Note: *Italic* page numbers refer to figures and page numbers followed by "n" denote endnotes.

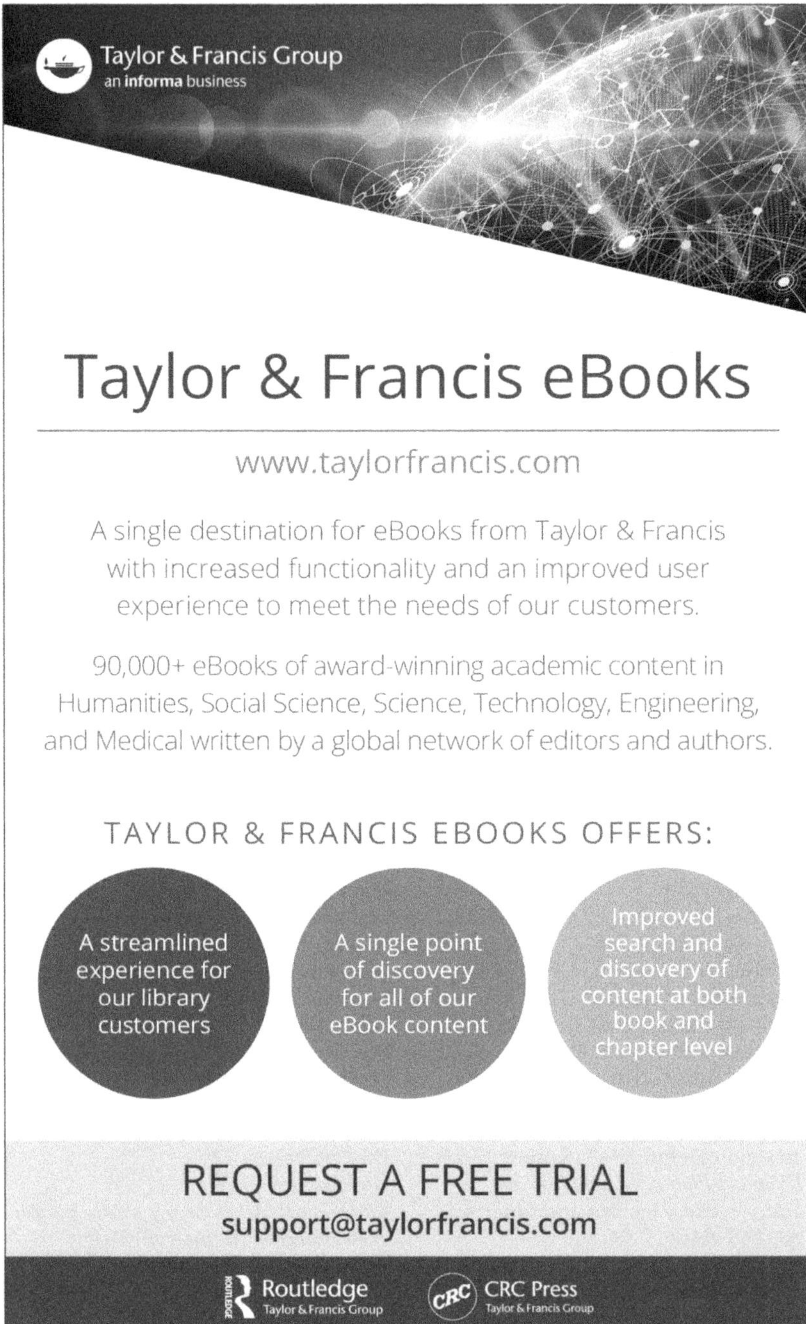
Taylor & Francis Group
an informa business
Taylor & Francis eBooks
www.taylorfrancis.com
A single destination for eBooks from Taylor & Francis with increased functionality and an improved user experience to meet the needs of our customers.
90,000+ eBooks of award-winning academic content in Humanities, Social Science, Science, Technology, Engineering, and Medical written by a global network of editors and authors.
TAYLOR & FRANCIS EBOOKS OFFERS:
A streamlined experience for our library customers
A single point of discovery for all of our eBook content
Improved search and discovery of content at both book and chapter level
REQUEST A FREE TRIAL
support@taylorfrancis.com
Routledge
Taylor & Francis Group
CRC Press
Taylor & Francis Group

For Product Safety Concerns and Information please contact our EU
representative GPSR@taylorandfrancis.com
Taylor & Francis Verlag GmbH, Kaufingerstraße 24, 80331 München, Germany

www.ingramcontent.com/pod-product-compliance
Ingram Content Group UK Ltd.
Pitfield, Milton Keynes, MK11 3LW, UK
UKHW020134200926
475702UK00005B/738

* 9 7 8 0 8 1 5 3 6 1 2 6 8 *